ECONOMIC DEVELOPMENT

ECONOMICS HANDBOOK SERIES

Seymour E. Harris, Editor

THE BOARD OF ADVISORS

Burns, SOCIAL SECURITY AND PUBLIC POLICY
Carlson, ECONOMIC SECURITY IN THE UNITED STATES
Coppock, INTERNATIONAL ECONOMIC INSTABILITY
Duesenberry, BUSINESS CYCLES AND ECONOMIC GROWTH
Hansen, A GUIDE TO KEYNES
Hansen, THE AMERICAN ECONOMY
Hansen, THE DOLLAR AND THE INTERNATIONAL MONETARY SYSTEM
Hansen, ECONOMIC ISSUES OF THE 1960's
Hansen, MONETARY THEORY AND FISCAL POLICY
Harris, INTERNATIONAL AND INTERREGIONAL ECONOMICS
Harrod, THE BRITISH ECONOMY
Henderson and Quandt, MICROECONOMIC THEORY
Hoover, THE LOCATION OF ECONOMIC ACTIVITY
Johnston, STATISTICAL COST ANALYSIS
Kindleberger, ECONOMIC DEVELOPMENT
Lebergott, MANPOWER IN ECONOMIC GROWTH
Lerner, ECONOMICS OF EMPLOYMENT
Taylor, A HISTORY OF ECONOMIC THOUGHT
Tinbergen and Bos, MATHEMATICAL MODELS OF ECONOMIC GROWTH
Valavanis, ECONOMETRICS

ECONOMIC DEVELOPMENT

Second Edition

CHARLES P. KINDLEBERGER

Professor of Economics
Massachusetts Institute of Technology

McGRAW-HILL BOOK COMPANY

New York   St. Louis   San Francisco
Toronto   London   Sydney

ECONOMIC DEVELOPMENT

Library of Congress Catalog Card Number 64-22459
11 12 13 14 15 16 – MAMM – 7 6 5
34579

EDITOR'S INTRODUCTION

It is now six years since Professor Charles Kindleberger published his distinguished volume, *Economic Development,* one of the most successful volumes in the McGraw-Hill Economic Handbook Series. In the new edition, Professor Kindleberger has thoroughly revised his book, brought it up to date, and added several chapters. The resultant volume is an outstanding historical, theoretical, and statistical treatment of economic development. The new volume is probably the best all around study of economic development now available for undergraduate use. Others interested in economic development, a subject in economics that has experienced the greatest rise of interest of any field since the war, will also find this book helpful.

Professor Kindleberger has had a rich experience as a government servant, as a student of economic growth, and as a teacher. His work reflects this experience. He is one of the rare economists who is interested in economic theory primarily for the light that it throws on substantive problems of public policy. I believe the readers of this volume will support this appraisal of Kindleberger's new and thoroughly revised *Economic Development.*

Seymour E. Harris

PREFACE

Originally published in 1958, this book might have been expected to be completely rewritten for the end of the 1960s. Economic theory in the development field has made considerable strides in recent years, and the flow of empirical studies of the development process from the field has reached torrential proportions.

After considerable thought, however, I have decided to limit myself to marginal rather than structural changes. In this course I have been supported by most, if not all, of the advice I have received from friendly critics. The principal consideration, however, was that the original analytical structure seems still to hold good, after some readaptation, for an orderly and systematic attack on the problems of economic development in the less developed countries.

An introductory chapter deals with questions of definition and measurement. Immediately following this is a chapter on noneconomic determinants of economic growth. This book is intended for use in economics courses, and to train would-be economists, but it must be recognized that some aspects of the subject—possibly even causal though hardly strategic—lie outside the normal province of the economist. This material was presented in the previous edition under the rubric of Labor, and some instructors may wish to discuss it at a later stage of the analysis, such as after Chapter 6 on Labor, plunging directly into the economic analysis. Since there is no clearly logical place to put it, and in order not to interrupt the flow of the economic argument, the noneconomic aspects of economic development are treated first. It is hoped that the student will not be persuaded of the noneconomic character of the economic development process and halt his studies after Chapter 2. Those who favor a sociological or sociopsychoanalytical approach to the subject may be comforted by the foreknowledge that we return to the subject in the final chapter on the impact of economic growth on social and political change. In between, the focus is on economics, with occasional reference to points of tangency with noneconomic factors.

Chapter 3 is devoted to a general discussion of the theory of economic growth. The briefest possible historical sketch of the theory is presented, and the main lines of its current development are set forth. This discussion paves the way for Chapters 4 to 10, which, still within the broad topic of analysis, cover the various ingredients of the growth process—Land, Capital, and Labor—in Chapters 4, 5, and 6 and Technology, Organization, Scale, and Transformation in Chapters 7 to 10, inclusive and respectively. These last four topics must be treated, since the record of economic growth cannot be explained by mere increases in the quantity of the inputs of land, capital, and labor, or even by changes in their quality.

Analysis is followed by issues, divided between domestic in Part II and foreign or international in Part III. Domestic issues begin with Chapter 11 and the question whether resources should be allocated directly by authority or left to the guidance of markets and prices. An Appendix by Richard S. Eckaus on the Role of Planning in Economic Development fits in at this point. A special issue of resource allocation or balance is treated separately in Chapter 12 on Industrialization and Agriculture, and repairs a major omission from the first edition. Chapter 13 deals with monetary and fiscal policy and, especially, the issue whether inflation is structural or monetary. Chapter 14 is concerned with the choice of technology by developing countries, whether the techniques employed should be those discarded by developed countries, which are appropriate to their factor proportions, or modern and inappropriate. The familiar Population Issue is covered in Chapter 15 to wind up domestic matters.

On the external front, in Part III, are four chapters, 16 to 19, dealing essentially with Trade, Investment, Aid, and Regional Cooperation, respectively.

As already noted, the book concludes with a return to noneconomic matters, in a sense, asking to what extent economic development brings about or must be accompanied by social and political changes. In particular, it asks whether economic development is possible without political revolution in underdeveloped countries, or to put the burden of proof the other way, whether economic development is a means of averting political revolution.

My gratitude to those who contributed to the first version remains undiminished. In addition, I am beholden for suggestions for revision and points to Martin Bronfenbrenner, Albert Fishlow, Franklyn D. Holzman, Raymond C. Malley, and Raymond Vernon. Don D. Humphrey and I taught a class in economic development together at the Fletcher School of Law and Diplomacy in 1960–1961. This experience was stimulating, partly because of the disagreements between us which we thought would educate, but perhaps only confused, the class. As before, I continue to learn from student papers. Finally, I am grateful to Kenneth D. Frederick who worked as a research assistant during the summer of 1963, to Laura C. Heath who presided with calm and efficiency over the typewriter and the scissors and paste, and once again to Beatrice A. Rogers, departmental editor, proofreader, indexer, and factotum extraordinary.

C. P. Kindleberger

CONTENTS

Chapter 13. Monetary and Fiscal-policy Issues   226

The Inevitability of Inflation with Growth, *227*   Kinds of Inflation, *230*
Monetary versus Structural Inflation, *231*   Deficit Financing without Inflation, *233*   The Limits of Independent Monetary Policy, *238*   The Role
of Fiscal Policy in Development, *240*   The Deficit as a Symptom, *245*
Summary, *247*   Bibliography, *247*

Chapter 14. Labor-intensive versus Capital-intensive Technology   249

Factor Proportions, *249*   Factor Prices and Factor Efficiency, *254*   Dual
Economy, *258*   Objective: Output or Employment, *259*   Community Development and Cottage Industry, *260*   Modern Technology, *263*   Technical Assistance, *266*   Summary, *267*   Bibliography, *267*

Chapter 15. The Population Issue   269

Introduction, *269*   Death Rates, *270*   Birth Rates, *274*   Rates of Population Increase, *281*   Age Distribution, *284*   Migration, *286*   Population
Policy, *288*   Summary, *290*   Bibliography, *291*

PART THREE. INTERNATIONAL ISSUES   293

Chapter 16. Foreign Trade or Autarchy   295

The Case for Comparative Advantage, *295*   The Opposition to Comparative Advantage, *296*   Foreign Trade as a Leading Sector, *304*   Foreign
Trade as a Lagging Sector, *306*   Balance through Foreign Trade, *311*
Which Model?, *313*   Commercial Policy, *316*   Summary, *320*   Bibliography, *321*

Chapter 17. Borrowing Abroad   322

The Need for Foreign Capital, *322*   Capacity to Absorb Capital, *325*
Capacity to Repay, *328*   Forms of Foreign Borrowing—Direct Investment, *332*   Forms of Foreign Borrowing—Government Bonds, *336*   Forms
of Foreign Borrowing—Lending by International Agencies, *337*   Forms

PART ONE | *The Theory of Economic Development*

Economic Growth and Development | 1

WHAT IS ECONOMIC DEVELOPMENT?

Growth and development are often used synonymously in economic discussion, and this usage is entirely acceptable. But where two words exist, there is point in seeking to draw a distinction between them. Implicit in general usage, and explicit in what follows, economic growth means more output, and economic development implies both more output and changes in the technical and institutional arrangements by which it is produced. Growth may well imply not only more output, but also more inputs and more efficiency, i.e., an increase in output per unit of input. Development goes beyond these to imply changes in the structure of outputs and in the allocation of inputs by sectors. By analogy with the human being, to stress growth involves focusing on height or weight, while to emphasize development draws attention to the change in functional capacity—in physical coordination, for example, or learning capacity.

Growth and development go together, of course, at least up to a point where the economy loses its capacity to adapt to changed circumstances. In the early stages, any economy that grows is likely to develop, and vice versa. But the problem of countries that have achieved a considerable measure of development and growth is to keep on growing. This is currently the focus of interest in the United States and Western Europe. In the less developed parts of the world, i.e., in countries that have low incomes or that find difficulty in adapting to the economic opportunities available to them, growth and development go hand in hand. Growth without development—for example, more and more steel in the Soviet Union or more and more coffee in Brazil—leads nowhere. It is virtually impossible to contemplate development without growth because change in function requires a change in size. Until an economy can produce a margin above its food, through growth, it will be unable to allocate a portion of its resources to other types of activity.

Less developed countries and low-income countries are not exactly identical, although the categories overlap to a great extent. Sparsely 3 settled countries, like Australia and Canada at the turn of the twentieth century or the United States in 1850, may be underdeveloped but not poor; another example of a country rich but underdeveloped is Kuwait, with its enormous oil royalties and its high average income per capita, but with the vast majority of the population making no contribution to the high return. On the other hand, it was thought until recently that such countries as Japan and Israel might be developed but poor (because of the sparsity of their natural resources). This book is addressed to the problems of the underdeveloped, low-income countries and how they can achieve growth and development.

THE MEASUREMENT OF DEVELOPMENT

While its emphasis is on development, this book uses a measurement more appropriate to growth, viz., national income. This measure has its drawbacks, which the rest of this chapter will discuss in some detail. Moreover, a distinction must be made between the level of income and its rate of change. When the politicians of a country claim to be interested in economic growth, they are frequently concerned

Figure 1.1 | Countries (A and B) with different rates of growth starting from different levels of income.

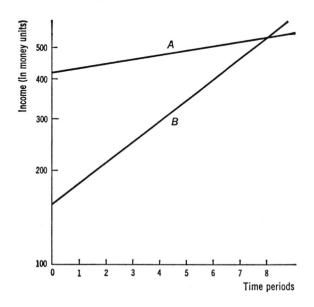

with the level of income, not its rate of change. In the long run, a higher rate of growth implies a higher level of income, as Figure 1.1 shows. In the figure, income is put on a logarithmic scale on the vertical axis, to enable a constant rate of growth to be shown as a straight line, while time on the horizontal axis is set out arithmetically. Country A is richer than country B in time period 1, but with a higher rate of growth in B than in A the latter will ultimately be outstripped. To the politicians and citizens of B, however, it may be more significant that A is richer than B at time periods 1, 2, and 3, especially if the absolute differences are wide and the time periods long. It can occur, of course—a possibility masked by the logarithmic scale—that B will grow at a faster rate geometrically, but that A, for a considerable time, will pull away from B in absolute terms. A 10 per cent increase in an income of $100 a head is only a ½ per cent increase in an income of $2,000 a head.

The level of income and the rate of increase in income are thus only approximate measures of the state of and rate of change in economic development. Statistics on neither are accurate, as we shall indicate. In order to show the characteristics of countries at different stages of development, however, we are more interested in the level of income as a rough approximation of the level of development. Should this be total income, income per person, income per member of the labor force, or income per hour of labor input? Each has merit for particular purposes.

Total income, irrespective of the number of people required to produce it, is an interesting overall measure of the weight of an economy for such a purpose as estimating military potential. A country grows in this sense if its total income grows at 3 per cent a year even though its population expands at the same rate. But if we are interested in development for the sake of human welfare, such growth is desirable only in the country which is underpopulated and needs more people to achieve an increase in income per head (on some basis). A better measure is income per capita, which gives both an idea of the efficiency of production and of success in achieving economic goals. The argument has been made[1] that income per capita is an inadequate measure of welfare because of the hypothetical possibility that it can be increased—without an increase in well-being—by slaughtering low-income receivers. If we exclude genocide as a means of raising average income—though not, as we shall see in Chapter 15, family limitation—average income is a better measure of the state of development than total income.

[1] J. E. Meade, *Trade and Welfare,* Oxford, Fair Lawn, N.J., 1955, chap. VI.

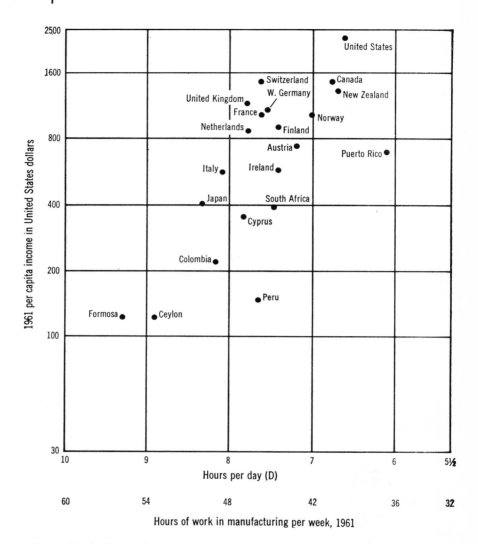

Figure 1.2 | Hours of work in manufacturing compared with income per capita, 1961. SOURCES: Hours of work, *Statistical Yearbook, 1962,* United Nations, New York, 1963, p. 57 (converted, where necessary, from hours per day on the basis of a six-day week); income per capita, table 1.1, Average Income per Capita in Selected Countries, 1949 and 1961.

As already noted, average income can be calculated per member of the population, per member of the labor force, or per hour worked. Assuming for a moment that the statistical estimation of each is equally accurate, which is the best concept? As in so many other connections, it depends upon the end in view. Income per head of population is the appropriate concept if our interest is in consumption; income per member of the labor force, if we are concerned primarily with production; and income per man-hour of input, if we are interested in the efficiency of the economy and want to make allowance for that part of an increase in efficiency which the economy takes out in added leisure.

The fact is that here, as in most other discussions of the subject, we use income per capita of the population to represent the level of economic development. Figures on population are by no means accurate, especially for the less developed countries of high density, such as India and Egypt, but they are more accurate than those of the labor force or of hours worked. Figure 1.2 shows hours of work in manufacturing for only a few countries—to suggest, by the way, that the richer countries take part of their increased income in added leisure—so that the data for income per capita understate, in this respect, the differences in efficiency between the less developed and the more developed countries. But estimates of the labor force, and especially of women employed in agriculture, are subject to wide margins of error,[2] and data on hours of work in agriculture, petty commerce, and domestic service hardly exist at all.

NATIONAL INCOME DATA

So much for the denominator, the population. What about the numerator, national income? Here the estimator faces serious statistical problems of a theoretical and practical nature. In theory, what is national income? If it is defined as all final product, there is the problem of drawing a line between consumption and costs or between final and intermediate product, the latter being used in the production of the former. The heavy meal of the day laborer needed for energy is surely an intermediate product rather than consumption, as it is counted, while the air-conditioned office with modern Danish furniture of the New York advertising man could be regarded as part of his level of living, i.e., consumption, rather than a cost of production. In philosophical terms, the issue can get cloudy indeed. Is work an input or an output: do people (mostly in developed societies, to be sure) fear retirement and enjoy the routine of work with its social life? Do we

[2] Such estimates exist, nonetheless, and are set out by sectors in Figs. 9.2 to 9.4.

work to eat or eat to work? National-income estimators have faced a number of conundrums of this sort and arrived at a long list of decisions as to what is income and what is not.

The difficulties are increased for the Soviet bloc, which, using a rationale derived from Marxism, excludes wide ranges of services, such as government administration, distribution, and transportation, from the concept of national income, concentrating its attention on material output. The exclusions have interesting implications both for planning, which tends to neglect transport and distribution, and for statistical rates of growth, which are exaggerated, compared with those based on more usual concepts of national income, since productivity tends to increase more slowly in the services sector than in manufacturing.

Assume, however, that a clear theoretical line can be drawn between income and nonincome. Statistical problems still present great difficulties. Foremost among these is valuation. Where goods and services are traded in the market, there is an objective test of value, as well as of the fact that they are economic. Housewives' services are excluded from national income, along with exchanges of gifts, which may, in some societies, approach barter. Where some possibility of valuation exists, as in the rental from owner-occupied houses or farm family consumption of food produced on the farm, allowance can be made on an arbitrary basis. But it is evident that in nonmonetary economies, or in economies only partly monetized, the valuation of national income is subject to a wide range of error. Since goods and services produced in the household sector are typically undervalued, and since housewives' services form a larger proportion of total goods and services in the less developed countries than in the more developed countries (where activities such as laundry, baking, and even bread slicing are shifted from the household to the market), there is a strong tendency of measures of money income to overstate the differences in real income between developed and underdeveloped economies.

The bias in estimation is not all in favor of the less developed country, be it noted. In developed countries, national income is understated because of the treatment of durable consumers' goods as consumption instead of investment which produces services through time.

INTERNATIONAL COMPARISONS

There are great difficulties, then, in arriving at useful approximations of national income per capita. In international comparisons the problems multiply. Where full currency convertibility does not exist, there is great difficulty selecting the appropriate exchange rate; second, where an equilibrium exchange rate obtains, conversion of income data between currencies is biased because goods and services traded internationally are not representative of the relationship between total goods and services; third, there is the ever-present index-number problem. A word may be useful on each.

For the Soviet bloc, with its discontinuous changes and generally overvalued rates, conversion of income data into dollars at par rates evidently overstates income per capita by varying amounts. In Table 1.1 (p. 12), conversion rates for countries in the Soviet bloc have seemed so odd that all of them, save the Soviet Union, have been omitted, and the dollar estimate of national income for the U.S.S.R. is arbitrary. Where there is foreign-exchange control and a multiplicity of rates, the par value of the currency is likely to be too high, and the free rate, if the market is thin, to be too low. In these cases, we have converted at an intermediate rate, where such existed. In some instances, it proved necessary to omit an estimate because of the wide dispersion in possible conversion rates and the absence of guidance.

Once local currencies have been converted into dollars, the estimate is completed. We know, however, from the work of Gilbert and Kravis,[3] that when national products are compared, item by item, at the same price level, between countries, a rather different relation emerges than when national product in local currency is converted at the going exchange rate. While the most careful work has been done for the United States and Europe, rough estimates indicate that the discrepancies are still wider in the less developed countries. M. F. Millikan has suggested that the real income of Asian countries in 1950 (excluding the Middle East) amounted to $58 per capita converted at the appropriate rates of exchange; the real level, after elimination for the bias involved in differences in prices of nontraded goods and services, was nearer $195. And for Africa, for the same year, the figures were $48 and $177. The European data and the Asian-African estimates are set out in Figure 1.3.

It makes a difference in the Gilbert-Kravis calculations whether the European national product was valued in United States prices and compared with the U.S. product, or whether the U.S. product was valued at European prices and compared with local estimates. This is the essence of the index-number problem. The values in Figure 1.3 are derived from the geometric mean of the two estimates—an uneasy compromise. One cannot simply compare the United States level of

[3] M. Gilbert and I. Kravis, *An International Comparison of National Products and the Purchasing Power of Currencies,* OEEC, Paris, 1954; and M. Gilbert and Associates, *Comparative National Products and Price Levels: A Study of Western Europe and the United States,* OEEC, Paris, 1958.

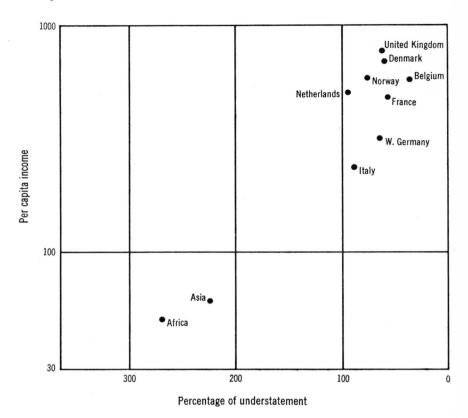

Figure 1.3 | Degree to which money income converted into dollars understates real income, compared with income per capita, about 1950. SOURCES: For degree of understatement, see M. Gilbert and Associates, *Comparative National Products and Price Levels: A Study of Western Europe and the United States,* OEEC, Paris, 1958, tables 5 (p. 30) and 27 (p. 80); for Asia and Africa, statement of M. F. Millikan before the Subcommittee on Foreign Economic Policy of the Joint Economic Committee on the Economic Report, *Hearings,* Foreign Economic Policy, 84th Cong., 1st Sess., pp. 21, 28; income per capita, table 1.1, Average Income per Capita for Selected Countries, 1949 and 1961.

living and, say, the Burmese level directly, because they comprise such different baskets of goods and services. It is possible to value the American basket at American and Burmese prices, which will introduce some bias because American-type goods and services, to the extent that they are available at all, are scarce in Burma and relatively high priced—or Burmese goods and services at Burmese and American prices. The answers are not the same, and an average between them has no clear meaning. Index-number bias can lead to considerable distortion in the estimate of rates of growth within a single country, as Gerschenkron has pointed out for the Soviet Union.[4] The index of industrial production uses early-year weights (a Laspeyres index), which gives heavy representation to those items which were scarce and high priced at the beginning and grew substantially during the period. It thus exaggerates the growth of industrial production. The use of a single set of end-year weights over a long period would impart an opposite bias. In national-income data for a single country over time, with output valued at relative prices which change each year, the index-number problem is not so important. In international comparisons, however, its bias may be serious.

Although money measures exaggerate and distort the differences in income between countries, they are not entirely useless. A study by M. K. Bennett indicates that income-per-capita figures give a fairly accurate picture of the ordinal ranking of countries with respect to real consumption and suggests that differences in income are not much wider than those in consumption.[5]

THE DATA

Table 1.1 presents a United Nations national-income study (calculated in U.S. dollars) for fifty-one countries in 1949, along with a comparable set of estimates for seventy-four countries in 1961 (in a few cases 1960 or even 1959) prepared from United Nations material. Inflation of the United States price level between the selected years— the cost-of-living index rising 15 per cent and the wholesale-price index 35 per cent—explains some of the differences between the two periods for given countries. Growth in real annual income per capita, ranging from 1 per cent in cases of limited growth to as much as 7 or 8 per cent in some of the faster-growing countries, such as Germany, Italy, and France in Western Europe, Japan in Asia, or Mexico and Peru in Latin America, explains more. But the table reflects an inevitable element of random error in the separate years and in year-to-year comparisons for many countries. There is also distortion, for example, in the data for the Soviet Union with its bias in definitions of income, on the one hand, and in exchange rate, on the other. To limit ourselves to the countries outside the Soviet bloc, it is evident, for

[4] See Alexander Gerschenkron, *A Dollar Index of Soviet Machinery Output, 1927–29 to 1937*, RAND Corp., Santa Monica, Calif., 1951.
[5] M. K. Bennett, "Disparities in Consumption Levels," *American Economic Review*, September, 1951, pp. 632–649.

Table 1.1 | *Average Income per Capita in Selected Countries, 1949 and 1961**

Country	1949	1961
United States	1,453	2,308
Switzerland	849	1,463
Canada	870	1,459
Sweden	780	1,445
New Zealand	856	1,313
Australia	679	1,237
Luxembourg	553	1,153
United Kingdom	773	1,149
Denmark	689	1,148
West Germany	320	1,072
Norway	587	1,036
Belgium	582	1,035
France	482	1,034
Iceland	476	925
Finland	348	889
Netherlands	502	864
Soviet Union	308	800
Austria	216	736
Puerto Rico	. . .	685
Venezuela	322	671
Israel	389	627
Ireland	420	570
Italy	235	561
Trinidad and Tobago	. . .	503
Japan	100	402
South Africa	264	396
Malta	. . .	391
Argentina	346	378
Chile	188	377
Jamaica	. . .	373
Panama	183	367
Greece	128	364
Cyprus	. . .	359
Costa Rica	125	291
Mexico	121	279
Spain	. . .	271
Portugal	250	251
Barbados	. . .	245
Yugoslavia	146	223
Colombia	132	222
British Guiana	. . .	218
Syria	100	218
Algeria	. . .	217
Malaya	. . .	215
Dominican Republic	75	205
Mauritius	. . .	203
Philippines	44	200

Table 1.1 | *Average Income per Capita in Selected Countries, 1949 and 1961**
(*Continued*)

Country	1949	1961
Honduras	83	182
Turkey	125	180
Ghana	. . .	179
El Salvador	92	176
Rhodesia and Nyasaland	. . .	156
Guatemala	77	151
Peru	100	145
Ecuador	40	143
Tunisia	. . .	141
Jordan	. . .	139
Brazil	112	129
Ceylon	67	122
Formosa	. . .	122
Morocco	. . .	120
China	27	117
Paraguay	84	113
Sudan	. . .	91
Thailand	36	88
Kenya	. . .	72
India	57	69
Congo (Leopoldville)	. . .	67
Nigeria	. . .	66
Uganda	. . .	57
Pakistan	51	54
Tanganyika	. . .	50
Burma	36	50
Indonesia	25	49

* In U.S. dollars of current purchasing power.
SOURCES: For 1949, *National and Per Capita Income in Seventy Countries*, United Nations, New York, 1949, p. 14. For 1961, average per capita figures were derived from national income in national currency units (pp. 154–155), population (pp. 1–4), and exchange rates (pp. 158–163), *Monthly Bulletin of Statistics*, United Nations, New York, May, 1963.

example, that the United Nations estimate for Indonesia in 1949 is wrong. Indonesian income per capita in that year was higher than Indian, not less than half its level, no matter what the comparison was in 1961 after years of successful Indian growth and Indonesian backsliding. Similar statistical errors intrude throughout, partly because of the crudity of the income estimates, partly through bias in the exchange-rate conversions.

Nonetheless, it may be said that the general impression afforded by the table is accurate. The figures in individual cases must be checked before they can be relied upon for a single year. To estimate rates of real growth with any accuracy it is necessary to go back to the national data and correct them for price-level changes, rather than rely on the roundabout comparison through the dollar exchange rate and the United States price level.

Development, as indicated, has dimensions other than growth. We suggest some of these in the pages that follow by comparing a variety of facets of a variety of national economies with income per capita, as in Figures 1.2 and 1.3. The comparison will normally be with the 1961 income data. As in the earlier figures, the comparisons will be in the form of semilogarithmic charts, with income on the vertical, logarithmic axis and the other variable in arithmetic form along the horizontal. In view of the uncertainty of the income data, to which is joined in many comparisons a degree of uncertainty in the other variable, no relationship is fitted between the variables, nor is a correlation coefficient calculated.

POINT OF VIEW

It goes without saying that the reader should be conscious of the writer's point of view and should apply the appropriate discount. The writer is a native of the developed part of a developed country, and although he attempts to keep a patronizing note out of his style, he may not succeed. There is, so far as he is aware, no regional bias in his thinking. He has not been employed on development planning in any area of the world, has no conscious affinity for any special under-developed country, and is equally objective about (and ignorant of) Latin America, Africa, the Middle East, and Asia. He thinks economic development is a good thing and is disposed on moral and ethical grounds to think that economic and political development in the rest of the world is of concern to his country. In addition, he is persuaded that events abroad have their repercussions on the United States—not all events, to be sure, but certainly cataclysmic ones.

If there is a bias, it is one of skepticism—surely the most appropriate attitude for a social scientist in the mid-1960s. Anyone who claims to understand economic development *in toto,* or to have found the key to the secret of growth, is almost certainly wrong. As a nuclear physicist once told the writer, "Everything is more complicated than most people think."

And yet there is a positive element in what follows. The writer is in favor of the market. He recognizes that the market works badly at the earliest stages of development, and that the market alone cannot overcome all or even most deficiencies. Moreover, he recognizes that the market may sometimes work against desirable social goals or may require such heroic adjustments in the lives of people as to call for a veto of its dictates, or at least of the speed with which they would be put into operation. But development that ignores the market, or provides elaborate substitutes for it, is likely to fail in the grand manner. The market may not be very effective; but in the present stage of economic wisdom, when allowance is made for its evident deficiencies, the result is better than any alternative. The reader who dissents vigorously from this position is put on notice.

SUMMARY

Economic growth is generally thought of as unidimensional and is measured by increases in income. Economic development involves as well structural and functional changes. In the absence of effective measures of the latter, however, states of development are estimated by levels of income, and rates of development by the growth of income. Ordinarily levels of income and rates of increase are given on a per capita basis, to approximate measures of efficiency and welfare.

International comparison of income per capita is beset by difficulties —of differences in concept, difficulties in measuring income which is earned and consumed outside the market, and the fact that the exchange rate fails to represent the real value of money as between countries, even when a convertible exchange rate exists. In direct comparisons, the index-number problem presents difficulties. Despite these possible sources of inaccuracy, income per capita in 1949 and 1961 is calculated in dollars for fifty-one and seventy-four countries, respectively.

BIBLIOGRAPHY

On the theoretical difficulties of measuring national income, see Simon Kuznets, "Some Conceptual Problems of Measurement," *Economic Development and Cultural Change*, October, 1956, reprinted in Okun and Richardson (eds.), selection 20, and Kuznets, "The Meaning and Measurement of Growth" in *Six Lectures on Economic Growth*, Free Press, New York, 1959, pp. 13–19, reprinted in Supple (ed.), selection 1; G. W. Nutter, "On Measuring Economic Growth," *Journal of Political Economy*, February, 1957, reprinted in Morgan, Betz, and Choudhry (eds.), selection 4.

The practical problems encountered in income measurement in

primitive economies are discussed in D. Seers, "The Role of National Income Estimates in the Economic Policy of an Underdeveloped Area," *Review of Economics and Statistics*, 1952–1953, reprinted in Morgan, Betz, and Choudhry (eds.), selection 5. See also Phyllis Deane, *Colonial Social Accounting*, Cambridge, New York, 1953.

An imaginative account of the difference between income as measured by the market and real income is given for a village in southern France by L. Wylie, in "Making Ends Meet," chap. 7 of *Village in the Vaucluse*, Harvard, Cambridge, Mass., 1957.

SUPPLEMENTARY READING

Many of the important articles have been anthologized in four useful collections which will be referred to by the name of their editors only:

A. N. Agarwala and S. P. Singh (eds.), *The Economics of Underdevelopment*, Oxford, Fair Lawn, N.J., 1958.

Γ. Morgan, G. W. Betz, and N. K. Choudhry (eds.), *Readings in Economic Development*, Wadsworth, Belmont, Calif., 1963.

3. Okun and R. W. Richardson (eds.), *Studies in Economic Development*, Holt, New York, 1961.

B. E. Supple (ed.), *The Experience of Economic Growth: Case Studies in Economic History*, Random House, New York, 1963.

For general supplementary reading, W. A. Lewis, *The Theory of Economic Growth*, Irwin, Homewood, Ill., 1955, is a modern classic. One friend of mine in another university claimed good results from requiring an undergraduate class to read a temperate and eclectic text, such as this aspires to be, paralleled on the left by P. A. Baran, *The Political Economy of Backwardness*, Monthly Review Press, New York, 1957, or F. Clairmonte, *Economic Liberalism and Underdevelopment*, Asia Publishing House, New York, 1960, and on the right by P. T. Bauer and B. S. Yamey, *The Economics of Under-developed Countries*, The University of Chicago Press, Chicago, 1957.

It is a virtual impossibility to recommend empirical reading from the outpouring of literature on economic development of particular countries. Perhaps it will suffice to mention the series of studies by the International Bank of Reconstruction and Development dealing with Colombia, Turkey, Guatemala, Cuba, Jamaica, Iraq, Ceylon, Surinam, Syria, British Guiana, Uruguay, Mexico, Nigaragua, Tanganyika, Spain, Uganda, Venezuela, etc.—all published by Johns Hopkins, Baltimore, since 1950—and a list of country studies mainly from my own 1963 course reading list. This list, it should be urged, is only a sample, and not representative.

W. J. Barber, *The Economy of British Central Africa,* Stanford, Stanford, Calif., 1961.

P. T. Bauer, *West African Trade,* Cambridge, New York, 1954.

G. Benviste and W. E. Moran, Jr., *Handbook of African Economic Development,* Frederick A. Praeger, Inc., New York, 1962.

C. Furtado, *The Economic Growth of Brazil,* University of California Press, Berkeley, Calif., 1963.

Government of Pakistan, Planning Commission, *The Second Five-Year Plan (1960–65),* Government of Pakistan Press, Karachi, 1960.

K. Grunwald and J. O. Ronall, *Industrialization in the Middle East,* Council for Middle Eastern Affairs Press, New York, 1960.

W. A. Hance, *African Economic Development,* Harper & Row, New York, 1958.

C. P. Issawi, *Egypt at Mid-Century,* Oxford, Fair Lawn, N.J., 1954.

K. M. Langley, *The Industrialization of Iraq,* Harvard, Cambridge, Mass., 1961.

J. P. Lewis, *Quiet Crisis in India,* Brookings, Washington, D.C., 1962.

W. W. Lockwood, *The Economic Development of Japan,* Princeton, Princeton, N.J., 1954.

W. Malenbaum, *Prospects for India's Development,* Free Press, New York, 1962.

A. J. Meyer, *The Economy of Cyprus,* Harvard, Cambridge, Mass., 1962.

G. A. Petch, *Economic Development and Modern West Africa,* University of London Press, Ltd., London, 1961.

W. B. Reddaway, *The Development of the Indian Economy,* Irwin, Homewood, Ill., 1962.

Y. A. Saugh, *Entrepreneurs of Lebanon,* Harvard, Cambridge, Mass., 1962.

R. Vernon, *The Dilemma of Mexico's Development,* Harvard, Cambridge, Mass., 1963.

L. J. Walinsky, *Economic Development in Burma, 1951–60,* Twentieth Century Fund, New York, 1962.

F. A. Wells and W. A. Warmington, *Studies in Industrialization in Nigeria and the Cameroons,* Oxford, Fair Lawn, N.J., 1962.

M. Zinkin, *Development for Free Asia,* Essential Books, Inc., Fair Lawn, N.J., 1956.

2 | Noneconomic Aspects of Economic Development

There is an important difference of opinion intellectually between those who think that social and cultural conditions shape economic development and those who believe that economic development determines society and culture. The debate takes place in economic history: Was French economic development of the nineteenth century determined by the family firm, a social phenomenon,[1] or was the perpetuation of the family firm a result of such basic economic factors as coal supply?[2] Or the matter can be put in a different context: Is Hispanic feudal culture deadly for economic development, as K. W. Silvert believes, or irrelevant, as Felipe Pazos counters?[3]

It is entirely understandable if the psychologists, psychiatrists, sociologists, and cultural anthropologists proclaim the dominance of

[1] See D. S. Landes, "French Entrepreneurship and Industrial Growth in the Nineteenth Century," *Journal of Economic History*, May, 1949, pp. 45–61 [reprinted in Supple (ed.), selection 16], and "French Business and the Businessmen in Social and Cultural Analysis," in E. M. Earle (ed.), *Modern France*, Princeton, Princeton, N.J., 1951, pp. 334–353; J. E. Sawyer, "Strains in the Social System of Modern France," in *ibid.*, pp. 293–312, and "Social Structure and Economic Progress," *American Economic Review*, May, 1951, pp. 321–329; and D. S. Landes and J. E. Sawyer, "Social Attitudes, Entrepreneurship, and Economic Development: Comments (and Rejoinders)," *Explorations in Entrepreneurial History*, May, 1954, pp. 245–297.

[2] See A. Gerschenkron, "Social Attitudes, Entrepreneurship, and Economic Development," *Explorations in Entrepreneurial History*, October, 1953, p. 11; also H. J. Habakkuk, "The Historical Experience on the Basic Conditions of Economic Progress," in L. H. Dupriez (ed.), *Economic Progress*, Institut de Recherches Economiques et Sociales, Louvain, 1955, pp. 149–169, reprinted in Supple (ed.), selection 4.

[3] In a panel debate at the 1963 meeting of the International Development Association, Columbia University, New York, Apr. 5, 1963. See also Silvert's *Reaction and Revolution in Latin America*, Hauser, New Orleans, La., 1961.

cultural and social aspects over the economic. This attitude is to be expected and conveys no information. What is striking, however, is that E. E. Hagen, a distinguished economist, has been won over to the position that change in cultural personality is the basic explanatory variable in economic development. His *On the Theory of Social Change: How Economic Growth Begins*[4] regards economic variables as mere parameters or conditioning circumstances within which cultural change of a fundamental sort brings about a change from economic stagnation to growth.

The selection of cultural factors as causal by a bona fide economist is significant. This is not to say that cultural factors have been ignored by economists. In *The Process of Economic Growth*,[5] W. W. Rostow suggested that variations in the behavior of people relevant for economic development can be summed up in a number of propensities —propensities to develop science, to apply science to the world about them, to propagate and rear children, and to strive for material advance. Given these propensities, which other disciplines, such as sociology, study and measure, the economist is in a position to investigate economic questions regarding capital formation and foreign trade. Irma Adelman introduces into her production function, which explains economic growth, the variable U_t, standing for the entire social, cultural, and institutional complex of society.[6] Rostow's "propensities" and Adelman's U_t, however, are merely conditioning circumstances, or additional variables, along with land, labor, capital, and scientific and organizational knowledge. This is a reasonable middle position in which social and cultural factors are only two variables among many, including the economic, and in which there is interaction between economic factors, on the one hand, and social and cultural, on the other. For the moment, however, we have to investigate the possibility that while economic factors affect the outcome, social conditions are decisive.

It is impossible for an economist to explore this vast subject in detail in a single chapter and to offer a synthesis of the ways in which people shape and are in turn affected by economic development. The most that can be done is to suggest the aspects of social and cultural conditions which may be significant and something of the variability which inhibits generalization. Although the synthesis is scrappy and overlapping rather than neatly integrated; the subject does not yet lend itself to more systematic and integrated treatment. The various aspects

---

[4] Dorsey Press, Homewood, Ill., 1962.
[5] Norton, New York, 1952, chap. II.
[6] *Theories of Economic Growth and Development*, Stanford, Stanford, Calif., 1961, p. 13.

to be touched upon include the orientation of the individual in his society, family, class, race, and religion, rural-urban differences, national character, size of the social unit, effect of culture on institutions, and interaction of cultural values and economic change.

THE INDIVIDUAL AND HIS ENVIRONMENT

Parsons[7] and Levy[8] have indicated that the relations of an individual to his society will differ in a number of dimensions, of which the most significant involve *cognition, membership,* and *substantive relations.* Cognition, or the way the individual interprets the physical world about him, tends to vary from the irrational to the rational, as societies develop, or from superstition to reason. In terms of membership, development brings with it a change from particularism (or in Parsons' term, ascription) to universalism (or achievement). Under the former, roles in society are chosen on the basis of the individual's family, religion, caste, income; under the latter, the choice is made on the basis of capacity to fulfill such a role. Substantive relationships range from the diffuse, in which the limits of the obligations of people to one another are vague, to the specific, in which they are spelled out in contractual form.

Development along any one of these dimensions is likely to involve a parallel movement along the others, but there may be considerable variation within any one. A society may have progressed beyond belief in magic, the evil eye, or the power of saints' relics to produce cures, but still believe in luck, lotteries, or extrasensory perception. According to an Indian student, the major role played in decisions of Indian families and even business by astrologers is merely equivalent to the role of psychiatrists in America. Particularism, which found one of its highest expressions in the Chinese family, was missing from the Chinese civil service, which was open to competitive examination. The converse is occasionally met in developed countries where the principle is accepted that the best man gets the job, but the best man frequently turns out to be the boss's son. In substantive relations, diffuse obligations can run within the family and neighbors and intimate friends, while contract governs those in a wider circle, or diffuse relations, such as those involved in academic tenure protect the teacher, while the business employee can be fired on short notice.

For economic development to take place, some considerable ration-

[7] T. Parsons and E. A. Shils (eds.), *Toward a General Theory of Action,* Harvard, Cambridge, Mass., 1951, pp. 80–91.
[8] M. J. Levy, *The Structure of Society,* Princeton, Princeton, N.J., 1952.

ality in cognition, universalism in membership, and specificity in relations are needed. Rationality is required not only at the highest levels,
to further the development of science and productive invention, but
throughout the system. It must be understood that identical action by
individuals under identical circumstances leads to identical results
without the whimsical intervention of irrational forces. People must
learn to be goal-oriented, and work to achieve given ends. At some
stage the goal sought and the ends to be achieved must be increased
levels of living: the establishment of what W. A. Lewis calls "the will
to economize," to maximize output for a given input or to minimize
input for a given output, preferably the first. And systems of thought
must be devised, like the invention of accounting by the Italians in the
Middle Ages, which permit a rational view of the world.

Universalism is a less insistent requirement than rationality; but
nepotism, caste, slavery, closed classes, and discrimination against
minority groups waste ability and reduce a society's capacity to
produce. The degree of universalism is perhaps less significant than
its location. The selection of priests, army officers, or social leaders
through class and family ties is less important for these purposes than
the filling of economic and political roles.

In substantive relations, it is important to know not only the nature
of these relations within various groups, but the way they change
toward others. Sharp discontinuities can occur. One may have an
obligation to assist and share one's belongings with members of a
joint or extended family, reaching up and down in terms of generations and out to cousins and second cousins, without being enjoined
even to respect the property of people to whom one is not related. One
may be forbidden to charge interest to a fellow Moslem, but encouraged to gouge and cheat an infidel.

FAMILY STRUCTURE

Intimately connected to these aspects of the individual's relationship to
others is the family structure in a society. Sociologists and anthropologists distinguish many types of family in terms of who lays down the
law and where the newly married couple lives—e.g., the patrilineal,
matrilocal, etc. For present purposes it is enough to observe that the
extended family, under which young adults continue to live with one
set of parents after marriage and contribute earnings to a common
pool, has a distinctly inhibiting effect on many of the factors affecting
economic development: mobility, savings, risk-taking, even willingness
to work more for a higher price. Less rather than more labor may be

forthcoming at higher wage rates because of a limit on economic aspiration or because the personal incentive is dulled by the necessity to contribute all the work while having only a limited share of its fruits. The incentive to take risks in entrepreneurship is blunted in the same way. In the extended family, the necessity to save or acquire assets is reduced, since the family provides insurance for dependents and security for old age out of current production. Mobility is limited, both in space and in occupation. If it is the duty of the son to remain in his father's house, he can shift from agriculture to industry or from farm to farm only when he is freed of his filial obligations by his father's death; he may still be unable to shift if he is encumbered by dependents. The unmarried son may leave for short stretches of city work, but is bound to return.

The family system affects economic development in many other ways. The alleged French entrepreneurial unwillingness to permit enterprises to grow beyond family size has been mentioned. Another factor is the system of inheritance, which may divide land equally among children or among male children or may give it all to the first son. This affects not only the size of the agricultural land input, but also mobility. An extreme form of family relationship to land, mortmain, under which land cannot be alienated outside of the family, restricts efficient use still more.

Closely connected with the family structure is the role of women, which has effects on rate of population increase, proportion of the labor force to total population, demand for household laborsaving devices, and a host of other economic variables. The range runs from some form of purdah, in which women are clearly inferior in status to men and subservient to them, to full equality of rights, decision-making, job opportunities, and equal pay.

How significant family structure is by itself is hard to evaluate, since the more primitive and inhibiting forms of family coexist as a rule in a social matrix loaded with other restrictive aspects. Some caution and skepticism are warranted when it is noted that the Hindu joint family in India is not paralleled in Pakistan, where, by Moslem tradition, the horizontal family system prevails.[9] Indian income in 1961 was substantially higher per capita than that of Pakistan. It may be that advantages in family structure give Pakistan somewhat greater promise in development than India. It is also possible, however, that as economic development proceeds from the force of positive factors, those aspects of family structure which stand in the way—the joint Hindu family, and a residual subjugation of women under Moslem law —will give way and be modified.

[9] I. N. Qureshi, *The Pakistan Way of Life*, Heinemann, London, 1956, chap. 2.

CLASS STRUCTURE

Where social position is governed by a fixed caste system, which limits occupational mobility, or where *awza*, respect for one's betters, is a highly esteemed virtue, as in Burma,[10] it is difficult to develop in the mass of society the will to economize for social advance. Economic development depends upon an open class structure and is particularly helped by the existence of a strong middle class. Where classes are widely separated, as under feudalism or as in Spain today, the gap is too wide to be bridged. The middle class is weak and ineffectual and tends to become dependent on and subservient to the ruling class. The oppressed classes seek relief in revolution; the ruling class defends its position with force. With a strong middle class, however, social mobility in both directions is possible. Agricultural and urban workers can rise to the middle class; dispossessed members of the ruling class can find outlets for their energies short of laboring.

In some societies, social advancement for the vigorous and able is possible only through church or army. Given a middle class widely engaged in commerce, industry, and the other professions such as law, medicine, science, teaching, accounting, engineering—and, one must add, government—these energies and abilities can be harnessed to economic growth.

What makes for an open society with a middle class? At an early stage of development, a middle class is favored by the existence of money (which enables slaves to buy their freedom and permits the accumulation of wealth in other forms than land), by the secularization of education (to free science from the narrowness of church rule), by the existence of a frontier (either to the west, as in the United States, or on the sea, as in Britain and Scandinavia) to preserve mobility, and by the critical start in capital formation and mechanical production necessary to overcome initial inertia. Particular circumstances have important effects in particular cases, such as primogeniture in England, which produced a crop of younger sons originally for the church and army, but later for commerce and the professions; or going further back, the enclosures, which destroyed feudal obligations, created a basis for capital formation in agriculture, and developed a working class to lower the price of labor to entrepreneurs and thus to encourage them to expand; or most recently, the readiness of the aristocracy, first, to open schools and universities to the children of successful entrepreneurs, which would give them the necessary external

---

[10] Louis J. Walinsky, *Economic Development in Burma, 1951–60,* Twentieth Century Fund, New York, 1962, p. 395.

polish for admission to the upper class, and second, to sell them land.

Economic development, of course, has its impact on the class structure. G. D. H. Cole has traced through the distinctive impact on the British class structure of four stages in the Industrial Revolution: the first, in iron manufacturing and coal mining, being highly localized; the second, involving textiles, railways, and the rapid development of banking, emphasizing mobility of human beings, merchandise, and money; the third, mass production, reducing the demand for brawn and calling for higher skills; and, finally, the age of synthetics and automation, which requires highly differentiated, skilled people.[11] Moreover, the growth of the middle class feeds on itself, as the increase in incomes from commerce and industry creates a demand for superior shopkeepers, better attorneys, doctors, teachers.

Of critical importance, frequently, is the value system of the various classes. "In the Middle Ages a gentleman did not engage in economic production. . . . Because we are middle-class minded, America is a society where millionaires go to work as well as everyone else."[12] In many parts of Latin America professional life has traditionally had a prestige well above that of business, and "culture" has been considered more important than wealth.[13] Or the middle class may be intensely competitive, intensely ambitious, but frustrated, by feeling that it is helpless in the face of the politically powerful upper class.[14] Or the society may confuse the shadow with the substance and educate hundreds of thousands of people to middle-class appetites, without providing them middle-class incomes.[15]

RACE RELATIONS

Racial questions are intimately related to class, religion, and economic development. This is not to say that some races are superior to others in economic terms, although the white races have achieved on the

---

[11] G. D. H. Cole, *Studies in Class Structure*, Routledge, London, 1955, chap. II.
[12] H. Grayson, *The Crisis of the Middle Class*, Holt, New York, 1955, pp. 97, 99.
[13] J. Biesanz and M. Biesanz, *Costa Rican Life*, Columbia, New York, 1944, pp. viii, 21.
[14] See J. Biesanz and M. Biesanz, *The People of Panama*, Columbia, New York, 1955, pp. 211ff.
[15] This is a particularly pressing problem in the Middle East and in India. In the latter it was reported that 500,000 out of 5 million persons who have gone through high school are unemployed.

whole a higher material level of living. Figure 2.1 shows some but not a very high correlation between income per capita and percentage of white people. Modern anthropology has exploded the notion of fundamental physiological differences in race. Race relations, however, enter into the question of the aptitude of a people for development. In what follows, the term *race* is used very loosely and is hard to separate completely from culture. Religion and social and cultural attitudes have in the past erected taboos against certain types of essential occupations. On occasion this has led to the subjugation of other races as slaves, as in the Southern United States, the West Indies, and Brazil, to provide cheap labor.[16] At other times taboos against commerce and moneylending led to the importation of other races to carry out these functions. The Christian injunction against usury could be ignored by Jewish moneylenders; the Moslem taboo on the same subject brought Hindus into parts of Pakistan and into Burma, and Jews, Armenians, and Greeks into Turkey; lack of interest in trade brought Chinese merchants to Malaya, Indonesia, and the Philippines.

Races need not remain separate. The major sociological fact about Brazil is the intermingling of the white and Negro races,[17] and everywhere in Latin America, except Argentina and Uruguay (white), and the West Indies (Negro), the majority of the population is mestizo or of Indian origin.[18] Moreover, race and other bases of social stratification cannot be kept completely separate. "Money whitens" is one slogan in Jamaica which exemplifies this, and there are others.[19]

---

[16] It may be argued that the Negro was needed physiologically to be able to withstand the heat involved in cultivating cotton, sugar, coffee. This view, however, runs contrary to that expressed in Chap. 4 below that the barrier to manual labor of white men in the tropics is cultural rather than physical.

[17] G. Freyre, *Masters and Slaves*, Knopf, New York, 1946, p. 83 *et passim*.

[18] See D. B. Brand, "The Present Indian Population of Latin America," in *Some Educational and Anthropological Aspects of Latin America*, Latin-American Studies, V, University of Texas Institute of Latin-American Studies, University of Texas Press, Austin, Tex., 1948, p. 51 (quoted by W. E. Moore, *Industrialization and Labor*, Cornell, Ithaca, N.Y., 1951, p. 81). The definition of white is 76 to 100 per cent Caucasian; mestizo is Indian and white breeds with no more than 75 per cent white blood; Indian is 76 per cent or more Indian. Negroid is all persons with perceptible Negro blood. It may be observed that the racial purity of Argentina and Uruguay is due to the fact that the earliest settlers had no need for labor in their land-intensive agriculture, and therefore imported no Negroes and killed off the Indians or drove them into the mountains.

[19] T. S. Simey, *Welfare and Planning in the West Indies*, Clarendon Press, Oxford, 1946, p. 19. See also J. Biesanz and M. Biesanz, *The People of Panama, op. cit.*, p. 202, where *campesinos* and peons refer to prosperous townspeople as whites, regardless of color.

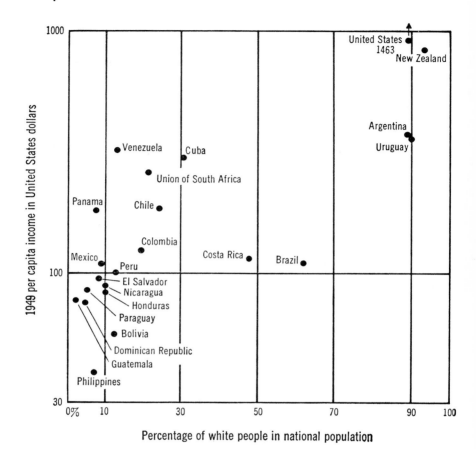

Percentage of white people in national population

Figure 2.1 | Percentage of white people in national population, compared with income per capita, about 1949. SOURCES: Percentage of white people, D. B. Brand, "The Present Indian Population of Latin America," in *Some Educational and Anthropological Aspects of Latin America,* Latin-American Studies, V, University of Texas Institute of Latin-American Studies, University of Texas Press, Austin, Tex., 1948, p. 51 (quoted by W. E. Moore, *Industrialization and Labor,* Cornell, Ithaca, N.Y., 1951, p. 81) except for Brazil, New Zealand, the Union of South Africa, and the United States from *Demographic Yearbook, 1956,* United Nations, New York, 1956, table 7, pp. 256–265; income per capita, table 1.1, Average Income per Capita in Selected Countries, 1949 and 1961.

In some societies rigid taboos hold;[20] in others, economic power given over to an alien race in certain occupations can be gained back with great difficulty. In the Philippines, Malaya, and Indonesia, native populations are using political power to force entry into trade and commerce where the Chinese merchant has economic control, backed by family ties. In these plural societies, apart from the political tension, there is loss of energy and capacity through the racial particularism. At least two solutions are possible, neither very easy. One is the melting pot, in which cultural values and racial attributes are fused through intermingling. This is the solution applied among all races in Latin America and among white races and nationalities in the United States, though thus far not to the Negro on any scale. This solution requires an initial degree of tolerance and a weakening of racial and national characteristics, which is frequently impossible. The other solution is separation or expulsion, applied by the Turks to the Jews, Armenians, and Greeks in 1921, by the Hindus and Pakistani to each other in 1947, by Israel to the Palestinian Arabs, and echoed recently by the Black Muslims in their demand for separation from white Americans. This method is cruel, but where it is used against a privileged minority, rather than against an underprivileged group such as the Cherokee Indians of Andrew Jackson's day or the Negroes in modern South Africa, it has the advantage of requiring the country expelling its moneylenders, merchants, experts, or other economically useful groups to do its own work. It is likely that in the very long run the capacity of the society to develop is thereby enhanced. But the cost in suffering is very great.

RELIGION

Another social factor considered important in economic development is religion. Max Weber[21] and R. H. Tawney[22] emphasized the connection between the Protestant Reformation and economic growth, run-

---

[20] It is interesting to observe that the taboo against employment of people of Jewish extraction in the 1930s, now largely broken down, differed between Europe and the United States. Many Jewish refugees coming to the United States from Germany found the United States much more liberal because they could get employment in government, an occupation closed in Germany. On the other hand, German-Jewish engineers were shocked to learn that United States corporations, equivalent to those for which they had worked in Germany, were not then open to them.

[21] Max Weber, *The Protestant Ethic and the Spirit of Capitalism,* (German original, 1904), English translation, Scribner, New York, 1956.

[22] R. H. Tawney, *Religion and the Rise of Capitalism,* Harcourt, Brace & World, New York, 1952.

ning through the Puritan injunctions to work, save, and achieve spiritual satisfaction through work. Erich Fromm[23] divides religions into masculine and feminine, the former typified by the Protestant and Jewish faiths, emphasizing paternal love which demands performance from the child, and the latter represented by Catholicism, especially before the Reformation, which offered the child love for its own sake. Masculine religions preach salvation through work, which includes money-making; feminine religions preach salvation hereafter, which makes for satisfaction with one's lot.

There is great difficulty in leaning too heavily on the Weberian Protestant ethic or the generalized view that religion shapes economic development. Northern Italy, the Low Countries, and the Rhineland, largely Catholic, participated as fully in the commercial and industrial revolutions as many parts of Protestant Europe. A recent book by a Swedish economic historian[24] has suggested that economic development is to be associated less with religion than with religious minority groups, and that Weber mistook religious toleration of economic activity for positive inspiration of it.

Moreover, there is little evidence that religions impose a uniform personality on a people or that religious ideas toward secular life are incapable of changing. It is well known that Irish, Spanish, and Italian Catholicism are different from one another and from French and Belgian Catholicism where the state successfully wrested control of education from the Church. It is said that the Moslem south of the Sahara—stable, equable, balanced—is an entirely different social being from his North African coreligionist of Morocco, Algiers, or Tunis, who is described as continuously either "one up" in a manic state or "one down" in bitter frustration. A strong revival of Buddhism is under way in Burma, a religion which in its earlier form emphasized asceticism, abstinence, cultivation of the spirit, and almsgiving to the unproductive but numerous priesthood. In its present vein, however, closely associated with a revival of Burmese nationalism and Asian political independence, Buddhism is in process of subtle conversion to a banner of economic advance. Since World War I, and especially since World War II, the Roman Catholic Church in Europe has been increasingly identified with the advance of science, the modernization of industry, and the need for improvement, not acceptance, in the life of the workingman.

---

[23] Or so I have been informed. I can find ideas which come close to this in *Psychoanalysis and Religion*, Yale, New Haven, Conn., 1950, and in *Escape from Freedom*, Holt, New York, 1941, chap. III, but no explicit statement.

[24] Kurt Samuelsson, *Religion and Economic Action*, (Swedish original, 1957), English translation, Heinemann, London, 1961.

CITY–COUNTRY DIFFERENCES

Robert Redfield,[25] the anthropologist, is responsible for the thesis that there is a gradual change in every society between city and country. The isolation of the country, communion with the elements, the inexorable demands of nature tend to stabilize and make rigid social life and values. In the city, on the other hand, the majority of contacts are with man and man-made objects. This increases the need for rationality, universalism, and specificity in the relations of man to his environment; breaks down family, class, racial and religious habits, barriers and taboos; gives plasticity and mobility to social life. Specialization requires the use of money; opportunities for communication build literacy; face-to-face contacts alter the status of women and tend to lower the birth rate. On this showing, the differences between town and country are more significant for development than the differences among towns or among rural societies.

This generalization overlooks plantation society, with its rural proletariat living close together in intimate contact.[26] It further neglects an essentially middle-class agriculture, like that of the Danes, where the Folk High Schools maintained the basis of communication and interchange, or like that of the Middle Western United States, Australia, and New Zealand, where radio, television, the automobile, and rural free delivery of mail, including cheap rates for newspapers and magazines, have kept the farm population in intimate contact with national life.[27] But there may be something to this generalization, especially in the Asian village, isolated and remote, in the Middle East, and in Latin America.

The literature abounds in contradictions, even among field investigators in the same situation. For example, R. R. Jay, writing on rural

[25] See, for example, his *The Primitive World and Its Transformations*, Cornell, Ithaca, N.Y., 1953. Other anthropologists have qualified Redfield's conclusions considerably. See Oscar Lewis, "Urbanization without Breakdown," *Scientific Monthly*, July, 1952, pp. 31–41, on cities; Lewis's *Life in a Mexican Village*, The University of Illinois Press, Urbana, Ill., 1951, on peasant life; and Sidney Wimintz, "Canamelar. The Contemporary Culture of a Rural Proletariat," in Julian Steward, *The People of Puerto Rico*, The University of Illinois Press, Urbana, Ill., 1956, on the plantation.
[26] It should be noted also that different types of crops produce different social patterns.
[27] There are equally considerable differences among aristocratic farmers, e.g., the Junkers who were vigorous, close to the soil, hardworking, and at the same time soldiers and government administrators, on the one hand, and the Russian aristocrats who were not really farmers, and exploited the peasant rather than the land.

Central Java,[28] asserts that, while the villagers and townspeople regard themselves as different, the existence of distinctions based on city and country is largely mythical, and the real problem in city and village alike is the intensifying bitterness between Moslem and non-Moslem political groups. A Dutch missionary, on the other hand, emphasizes the social, religious, moral, and economic differences between village and town in the same area.[29] The outsider, in terms of discipline, culture, and nationality, is unable to judge between such opposing views. Yet there can be little doubt that the agglomeration of cities has an impact on the speed and character of economic development. We shall touch upon this later in Chapter 10 and again in the discussion of community development.

SIZE OF THE SOCIAL UNIT

With economic development, the size of the social unit grows. In the Indonesian village "interest in the affairs of other families, except close kin, for most people extended no further than a radius of 100 to 150 yards."[30] In Greece, Spain, and Italy, regional ties, at least until recently, have been far stronger than national ties. In more developed countries the primary social group is the nation; some expect a further move in Europe to the continent.

The extension of the social unit is of course a necessity in cultivating the characteristics needed for economic development. Nepotism makes excellent sense in a society where honesty is limited to the family circle and intimate friends.[31] To hire a stranger into the firm would be to run the risk of losing its assets the moment one's back was turned.

These generalizations must be modified for particular circumstances, which affect the capacity of a social group to have intercourse with others. Topography, cultural heritage, the communication system, level of education, and a host of other factors play a part. Of these,

---

[28] R. R. Jay, "Local Government in Rural Central Java," memorandum, Center for International Studies, Massachusetts Institute of Technology, Cambridge, Mass., 1955.

[29] H. Bass, "Village and Town in Indonesia," reprinted from *Panjadar,* a theological monthly from Central Java, in *Background Information for Church and Society,* March, 1956.

[30] Jay, *op. cit.*

[31] See M. Mead, *Cultural Patterns and Technical Change,* UNESCO, Paris, 1953, pp. 87–88: "Greek parents are agreed that the principal thing to teach their children is to be honest and tell the truth; but this of course means to be honest in their dealings with their parents and other relatives, all friends of these, and with people who value them and trust them as people."

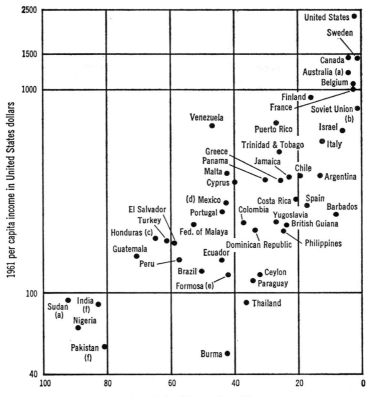

(a) For five years of age and older
(b) For ages nine–forty nine
(c) For ten years and older
(d) For six years and older
(e) For twelve years of age and older
(f) Data for population of all ages

Figure 2.2 | Illiterate population as a percentage of total population above fifteen years of age, various dates between 1945 and 1960, compared with income per capita in 1961. SOURCES: Illiteracy, *Demographic Yearbook, 1960,* United Nations, New York, 1960, pp. 434–439; income per capita, table 1.1, Average Income per Capita for Selected Countries, 1949 and 1961.

the aspects which change with development are primarily education and the system of communication. It has long been observed that there is a strong correlation between literacy and the state of development, despite the possibility of overeducation or maleducation mentioned earlier. Figure 2.2 offers some evidence on the point. The relationship

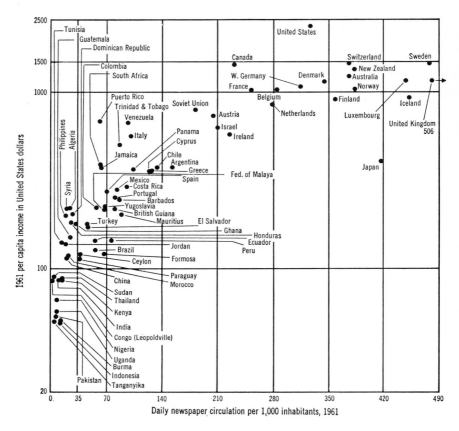

Figure 2.3 | Daily newspaper circulation per 1,000 population, 1961, compared with income per capita, 1961. SOURCES: Newspaper circulation (with slight differences in definitions and dates), *Statistical Yearbook, 1962,* United Nations, 1963, pp. 649–650; Income per capita, table 1.1, Average Income per Capita for Selected Countries, 1949 and 1961.

was particularly strong up to 5 per cent illiteracy and $400 of per capita income in 1961. H. A. Innis,[32] the distinguished Canadian economic historian, has emphasized the role of the communication system in shaping the character and affecting the rate of development. He regards as great stimuli to British economic growth in the nineteenth century the introduction of the penny post and the penny press. Figure 2.3 conveys less than an exact idea of the amount of communication through the printed word because it is limited to news-

[32] *Empire and Communications,* Clarendon Press, Oxford, 1950.

papers appearing six times or more per week and ignores differences in size among newspapers. There seems to be little relation between communication and level of income at the lower end of the scale.

An important aspect of capacity to communicate is language, and a language may or may not lend itself to ready written use. One of the disadvantages of the British withdrawal from India has been the loss of a common language. Urdu in Pakistan and Hindi in India are not the mother tongues of a majority of the two populations. To substitute them for English as the lingua franca involves a high short-run cost. An important reform in Turkey to stimulate communication and interchange was the Latinization of spelling, just as the adoption of the Arabic system of numbers after the Crusades liberated European calculation. The extent to which the Chinese secure acceptance of spelling by characters in such a way as to make communication cheap and efficient will affect the size of the social unit, its cohesion, and in turn the rate of economic development.

In Chapter 9 we shall pay considerable attention to the linkage of markets. The social parallel is a widening of the social unit. In a healthy society the size of the primary unit increases without altogether destroying ties to the lesser ones—the village, metropolitan area, region. But there are other and complex social situations. French nationalism has been characterized as unhealthy since it brooks no loyalties higher or lower than itself and has found no place in the social contract for big industry or the working class.[33] The 100 per cent American or the British jingo is unable to reconcile his patriotism with wider responsibility. What in the total situation permits a healthy system of social relations with a large primary group in one situation, and not in another, lies well outside the scope of this study. Such differences exist, however, and have importance for the effective functioning of the economy. The creation of a large market, which may be necessary for economic development, presupposes some degree of social cohesion, as well as affects it.

CULTURAL PERSONALITY

Up to this stage, emphasis has been on the changes in people needed to enable them to cope with economic growth. Interpersonal attitudes, family and class structure, racial and religious views, and the size of the social unit must alter if economic growth takes place, and in adjusting readily and without convulsion, they assist the process of

[33] H. Luethy, *France against Herself,* Frederick A. Praeger, Inc., New York, 1955, esp. p. 431.

development. If in any aspect these changes are blocked, economic development is impeded or halted.

But the differences in peoples may go deeper than merely their standing on the Parsons-Levy scale or their evolution in societal change. A variety of possible group or national cultures is ingrained in the society from generation to generation. This national character, according to social psychology, is communicated in the process of child raising, is largely unconscious, and alters slowly.[34] It may be that the rate of change picks up with development, particularly as fads in child training develop. But to the extent that national characters differ, that some lend themselves in critical fashion to economic advance while others do not, and small differences in cultural practices can produce large differences in character of significance for the economy, the economist is helpless before this development problem.

Spengler[35] divided peoples into the Apollonian and Dionysian types, the even-tempered and those whose tempers exploded. Ruth Benedict, in *Patterns of Culture*,[36] traced similar attitudes, particularly in the Zuni and Kwakiutl Indians, to permissive and authoritarian upbringing, and emphasized the capacity of the Zuni to work together cooperatively and the competitive hostility of the Kwakiutl Indians, which led to conspicuous and wasteful consumption. Modern anthropology has penetrated into these matters to produce a much wider range of differentiation in matters affecting economic behavior—cooperation and competition, the nature of individualism, attitude toward work, etc.[37] Thus far the social psychologist has been unable to establish the relative importance of various characteristics of a culture for development, to indicate rates of substitution among them, or to suggest to what extent they are independent or linked. The capacity of the Danes to cooperate[38] (and that of Uruguayans and New Zealanders) is a tremendous national asset for development, as is the compulsive urge to

[34] See Abram Kardiner, *The Psychological Frontiers of Society*, Columbia, New York, 1945, for a discussion of how cultural personality is instilled in children in early rearing, and how difficult it is to alter. The theories which emphasize childhood training as a former of personality, and personality as the determinant of social and economic development, are deeply pessimistic about the prospects for accelerating development.

[35] O. Spengler, *The Decline of the West*, Knopf, New York, 1939.

[36] Houghton Mifflin, Boston, 1934; paperback, New American Library, New York, 1950.

[37] See especially M. Mead (ed.), *Cultural Patterns and Technical Change*, where the cultures of Burma, Greece, the Tiv tribe in Nigeria, the Palau in New Guinea, and Spanish Americans in New Mexico are studied.

[38] See C. P. Kindleberger, "Group Behavior and International Trade," *Journal of Political Economy*, February, 1951, and the references on Danish character there.

work of the Germans.[39] But is Uruguayan character important if the country's level of living is no different from that of the temperamentally explosive people of Argentina? How significant is the attitude toward work as it varies from avoidance, philosophic resignation, acceptance, idealization, and compulsive devotion, or the attitude toward time, or toward friends?[40] Even individualism may take different forms. In Britain individualism focused on the sanctity of property, which permitted enclosures, and two centuries later the pauperization of more than half a million agricultural workers through wheat imports. In France, individualism concentrated on the inviolability of personal action, which protected the French peasant in similar circumstances.[41]

There is a possibility that differences in national character are waning as world culture becomes homogenized—some people would think Americanized. David Riesman has identified three stages of social development—the traditional, the inner-directed, and the other-directed.[42] Culture is clearly idiosyncratic in the first of these and tends to perpetuate itself in the steady state. Differences in national character also play a major role in the inner-directed period, as people act out the roles laid down for them in their upbringing, impervious to the effect they are creating in the world about them. The nineteenth-century entrepreneur in Victorian Britain is the classic example of the inner-directed man whose counterpart in the United States was prepared to let the public be damned. Today, the world over, however, people have become much more responsive to their peers, aware of the efficacy of the public relations man and advertising, and in consequence readier to suppress and alter the characteristics acquired in their childhood. Fashions extend to child rearing, changes in which rupture the continuity of national character. Consumption changes from conspicuous to self-conscious. The demonstration effect, which

[39] See H. C. Wallich, *Mainsprings of the German Revival,* Yale, New Haven, Conn., 1955, chap. 12, "Economic Consequences of German Mentality," and esp. pp. 332ff.

[40] Of great interest in this connection is the study of Oscar Lewis, *Life in a Mexican Village,* The University of Illinois Press, Urbana, Ill., 1951, which suggests the difficulties of generalization. Work, industry, and thrift for the purpose of accumulating property (in land and animals) are the highest and most enduring values—in a Catholic country (p. 296) relations are impersonal and reserved —though life is rural and not urban (p. 287). There is much hostility in interpersonal relations, although there are no sharp social differences since the revolution and no conspicuous consumption or boasting (pp. 54, 177, 292, 297).

[41] See Francis Miller and Helen Hill, *The Giant of the Western World,* Morrow, New York, 1930, p. 188. See also K. Polanyi, *The Great Transformation,* Beacon Press, Boston, 1957, which expresses surprise that British society would permit so complete a domination of social by economic considerations.

[42] *The Lonely Crowd,* Yale, New Haven, Conn., 1950.

we shall discuss later, leads people to strive to forsake their traditions in favor of the consumption standards of others, studied through international communication by press, radio, magazines, books, motion pictures, and tourists, including military forces. The desire to conform in consumption standards may be so strong that, given the minimum of resources and capital, impediments in the national culture will be overcome.

THE NEED FOR ACHIEVEMENT

The most specific of the theories which ascribe the beginnings of economic growth to cultural personality is that of E. E. Hagen in *On the Theory of Social Change*. Hagen's theory is that traditional society is perpetuated by the authoritarian personality inculcated in a people by strict bringing up, hedged about by restraints and punishments, which each generation then communicates to the next. To break out of this mold, it is necessary for a substantial group to develop a need for achievement. This need, like all others, is developed in childhood, typically after one or more generations of males have retreated into passivity because their group has lost its role in society and its prestige; i.e., respect of the society has been withdrawn from it. Reacting against this passivity, a generation of mothers applauds activity on the part of infants, rather than seeking to protect or restrain them. In this way, "respect withdrawal" leads after time—frequently a very long time—to "need achievement," which develops a class of entrepreneurs who ultimately achieve economic growth. The groups which play a major role in economic development—the non-Conformists in Britain, the Jews and Huguenots in France, Parsis in India, samurai in Japan, Antioqueños in Colombia, etc.—have in common less the nature of their beliefs than the fact that they have been "outgroups" who have sublimated their social insecurity in economic achievement.[43]

It is important for policy to know how to weigh the achievement motive or need achievement in economic development against the economic variables to be discussed later. But even before this question arises, two issues must be dealt with. Why does the need for achievement take economic form rather than another?[44] And granted that

[43] On the need to achieve, see also David C. McClelland, *The Achieving Society*, Van Nostrand, Princeton, N.J., 1961.
[44] See Bert F. Hoselitz, "Noneconomic Factors in Economic Development," *American Economic Review*, May, 1957, p. 35 [Okun and Richardson (eds.), selection 28, p. 343]. "High-achievement motivation has also been found among military leaders and may be found among scholars, priests, and bureaucrats."

"respect withdrawal" may lead to economic development through sublimation, does this exclude the possibility that economic development can be achieved by conscious choice? It is hard to see how the answers to these questions would support the view that respect withdrawal leading to need achievement is either sufficient or necessary for economic development.

Nor does the sublimation of loss of prestige have to be achieved only over a long period of time. Hagen's linking of the Industrial Revolution of 1780 to the Anglo-Saxon loss of prestige at Hastings in 1066 seems farfetched. The German expansion after 1870 as a response to the loss of the battle of Jena to Napoleon in 1806 fits his timing better. But it is possible to link the Japanese expansion after 1868 to Perry's visit of 1849 instead of to the Tokugawa revolution of 1600, as Hagen does, the Danish transformation of agriculture in the 1880s to the loss of Schlesvig-Holstein in 1864, and the German, French, and Italian expansion after 1950 to their loss of prestige in World War II. In the latter cases, there is no need for the effect of sublimation to work through a profound change in cultural personality. It is impossible to deny the connection between loss of social approval and economic development, but difficult to believe that it operates in a particular way or is central to the entire process.

INSTITUTIONS AND CULTURE

Adam Smith believed that economic development would follow if government provided "law, honesty, peace, and easy taxes." John Stuart Mill added to this list "improvement in public intelligence and the introduction of foreign arts." It may be granted that institutions are an expression of culture, in the usual case, that they are critical for economic development, but that the list extends beyond that of Smith and Mill.

Cultural lag, a familiar social expression, is important here. Many institutions have outlived their usefulness, but have strong holds on a culture and are difficult to change or modify. This applies not only to such matters as corruption or squeeze, systems of land tenure or village family organization, religious or educational practice, but to much imbedded in the habitual patterns of economic production, distribution, and consumption.

Another incongruity, less often noticed, is cultural lead, which occurs when economic institutions are borrowed from a more developed country and grafted onto a society which they do not fit. This is a well-known phenomenon in the political sphere, where constitutions, parliaments, cabinets, and elections abound in countries which are far from democracies. But it is not missing in economics. In the interwar period, money doctors from Britain and the United States traveled to a number of underdeveloped countries and established central banks. Perhaps not too curiously, in countries visited by British experts little Banks of England were established; in those favoring United States experts, little Reserve Systems. One of the basic and devastatingly expensive examples of cultural lead today is the application of Keynesian economic analysis needed for developed countries in periods of unemployment to underdeveloped countries to which the quantity-theory analysis of full employment more truly applies.

To be effective, economic institutions must be adapted to the needs and the culture of a country. This adaptation may be undertaken consciously. In the optimal case, however, institutions evolve to fit a country's economic requirements and its national character in a subtle and unconscious way. In Denmark, when the world price of wheat fell, the marketing cooperative was devised to meet the need for large-scale marketing of the products of labor-intensive and hence necessarily small-scale agriculture. The institutions used in a given country at a given stage of its development for production, distribution, allocation of credit, and for associating producers, consumers, and the public in the process are most effective when they fit both the economic needs and the cultural conditions of the country. Borrowed institutions, like hand-me-down clothes, may fit without alteration, but it is not likely that they will.

THE IMPLAUSIBILITY OF ONE-WAY CAUSATION

Economists are in no position to render final judgments on the importance of noneconomic factors in initiating economic development in stagnant traditional society and in shaping its course thereafter. Much less can we separate causal from dependent noneconomic factors and measure the importance of causal factors either absolutely or relatively. On a priori grounds, however, it seems reasonable to remain skeptical in the face of claims for the primacy of noneconomic factors. Economic development changes attitudes, as well as being the result of changed attitudes. Commerce helps develop a middle class, with rationality, universalism in selection for roles, and achievement as the basis of social approval. Sociocultural and economic factors interact in an ongoing process in which it is unlikely that the one always dominates the other. Sociocultural determinism is no more likely an explanation of the course of economic development than is economic determinism of social history. There is enough in economic development for sociologists and economists to study in their own disciplines without the need to argue the primacy of one subject over the other.

The operational question for policy is whether religious taboos, cultural institutions, and social attitudes make economic development impossible and assistance for economic development a waste of resources,[45] or whether attention to the noneconomic factors along with the economic can get development moving. This tough nut we leave to the final chapter, after we have been through the economic analysis and the economic policy issues.

SUMMARY

Economic development is associated with social changes which pervade the relationship of man to his environment and to his fellows. The individual's interpretation of the world about him, his relationship to his and to other families, classes, races, the size of the social unit, etc., all change. Economic development is also associated with certain religions, city rather than rural life, and cultural attitudes which emphasize competition rather than contemplation.

Whether the social attitudes lead or follow economic change is impossible to say in general. Instances of each can probably be found; in the usual normal pattern, interaction is likely, with some cultural and social habits which fail to give way under economic pressure serving to block further advance.

BIBLIOGRAPHY

Most of the important literature has been mentioned in the footnotes. Perhaps the single most interesting study is E. E. Hagen, *On the Theory of Social Change: How Economic Growth Begins* (footnote 4). However, see also B. F. Hoselitz, *Sociological Aspects of Economic Growth,* Free Press, New York, 1960, and R. Braibanti and J. Spengler (eds.), *Tradition, Values and Socio-economic Development,* Duke, Durham, N.C., 1961. Among the most striking cases of a "strong will to economize," i.e., to improve the standard of living, is that of Israel, discussed in part in S. N. Eisenstadt, *Essays on the Sociological Aspects of Political and Economic Development,* Mouton, The Hague, 1961. See also Daniel Lerner, *The Passing of Traditional Society: Modernizing the Middle East,* Free Press, New York, 1958.

[45] See, for example, the pessimistic views of P. T. Bauer in *United States Aid and Indian Economic Development,* American Enterprise Association, November, 1959, chap. 1.

3 | *Theories of Economic Growth*

ECONOMIC MODELS

An economic model is a statement of relationships among economic variables. Its purpose is to illustrate causal relations among critical variables in the real world, stripped of irrelevant complexity, for the sake of obtaining a clearer understanding of how the economy operates, and in some formulations, in order to manipulate it. The statements may be set out in prose, in geometric form, or in mathematics. However expressed, the variables in a model must be defined and separated into independent and dependent, with the relationship between them indicated. In models which claim scientific validity, moreover, the variables must lend themselves to statistical measurement so that the model can be tested empirically.

The problem in social science is that reality is enormously complex. A simple model which can be readily comprehended runs grave risk of omitting significant factors in the real world. A model which even begins to approach reality in complexity can be understood only with the higher branches of mathematics. The present discussion is limited to prose and simple diagrams and is necessarily restricted to the simpler models, involving generally no more than one output (national income) and two inputs (say, capital and labor), as set forth in the production function in Figure 3.1. A production function expresses the relationship between outputs and inputs and is a key relationship in economic growth. In Figure 3.1, Y, or output, is measured on lines of equal output, or isoquants 1, 2, and 3, where 2 represents more output than 1, and 3 more than 2. Every point on 1 represents the same amount of output which can be produced with varying quantities of labor L and capital K. In this particular production function, land and capital can be substituted for each other in the production of Y at every combination, as the isoquants become asymptotic to the axes. With three factors it is still possible to use geometry, provided one is a master of three-dimensional perspective, but it is more convenient to aggregate factors above two into the second, and reduce the **40** diagram to two dimensions.

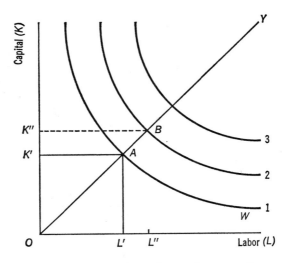

Figure 3.1 | A simple production function: One output (Y) and two inputs (K and L).

In Figure 3.1 economic growth is represented by an expansion path, such as $O\text{-}Y$, which is drawn from one isoquant to the next through points of similar tangency. If $O\text{-}Y$ is a straight line, which means that factor proportions are constant, and if similar distances between isoquants represent similar increases in output, the production function is said to be homogeneous of the first degree. In this sort of production function, the relationship between capital and output, or the capital/output ratio, can be expressed as an average ratio, ($O\text{-}K'/O\text{-}A$ with production at A), or as an incremental ratio ($K'\text{-}K''/A\text{-}B$) if production changes from A to B. Similar ratios can be worked out for labor, but here the term *labor productivity* is used. Output divided by the labor supply is labor productivity, whereas output divided by the capital stock is the inverse of the capital/output ratio, sometimes called the capital coefficient.

THE RICARDIAN GROWTH MODEL

The Ricardian growth model emphasized the limits to growth imposed by land. Unlike Smith, who was interested in "the wealth of nations," which modern economists would call "the income of nations," Ricardo was concerned less for growth than for income distribution and foreign trade. He took pains to show that unless more land could be dis-

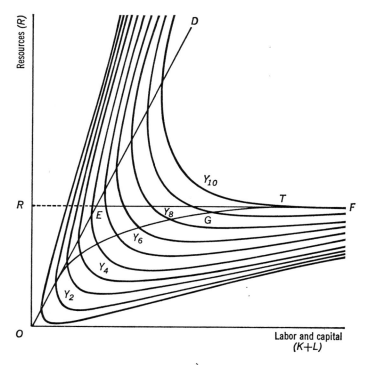

Figure 3.2 | The Ricardian expansion path with growth reaching a limit set by resource availability.

covered, or, more probable, unless food could be imported cheaply from abroad, the limits to growth would quickly be reached.

Like Smith, Ricardo believed that growth resulted from "accumulation," or capital formation.[1] But accumulation in turn was a function of profits, which depended on wages, which depended on the price of food, which depended on the availability of land or of food imports. Barnett and Morse[2] make a distinction between the utopian view

[1] Adam Smith's theory of growth was interesting in a number of other respects beyond his attention to accumulation: the importance of "internal economies of scale" as illustrated by increasing returns in pin making in his famous illustration of the division of labor; the extent of the market, which limited the division of labor; and the invisible hand, which guided resources into the most efficient lines under *laissez faire*. We recur to these themes in later chapters.

[2] See Harold J. Barnett and Chandler Morse, *Scarcity and Growth: The Economics of Natural Resource Availability*, Johns Hopkins, Baltimore, 1963, esp. chaps. 3 and 5.

that there is no limit to output from the side of land, the Malthusian view that all land is of the same quality up to the limits of land, and the Ricardian hypothesis that land diminishes in quality up to the point where it does not pay to work it at the margin. These three positions are illustrated in Figure 3.2 which shows a production function in terms of land R on the vertical axis, and capital and labor $(K + L)$ on the horizontal. (The early isoquants slope away from the axes to indicate that land and capital-cum-labor become redundant complements rather than substitutes outside very narrow limits.) O-D, the straight-line expansion path, is based on the utopian assumption of no limits on resources. The Malthusian expansion path O-E-F follows the utopian until the upper limit of resources is reached at R, and then can grow only through adding capital and labor until the marginal product of land and labor is zero (at point T). With the Ricardian hypothesis of diminishing productivity of land, T is approached more gradually with the expansion path O-G.

Note that the ratio of land to capital-cum-labor, measured by a ray to the expansion path from the origin, declines steadily with growth along the Ricardian path until, after T, it approaches zero. What stops growth at T is the fact that rent, the return to land, has risen to a very high level, and profits have fallen to zero. Wages could not rise in the Ricardian and Malthusian system because population would increase to expand the labor supply if wages exceeded the subsistence level; nor could they fall because labor had to be maintained or starve. The big change was from profits, which were saved, to rents, which were not. This change in income distribution is illustrated in Figures 3.3a and b, which show the growth in national income, overall

Figure 3.3 | Income and distributive shares in the Ricardian system.

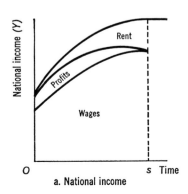

a. National income

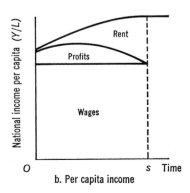

b. Per capita income

and per capita, by income shares.[3] After point S, the economy has reached the stationary state linked to T in Figure 3.2, where growth is impossible.

It was this Malthusian and Ricardian model of growth which gave economics its characterization as the dismal science. Growth was possible up to a point but would then be halted because of diminishing returns to labor and capital. Land at the margin could not yield enough to pay the subsistence costs of labor, even after the profit had fallen to zero. The result was that expansion ceased. No provision was made in the system for technological progress or for substitution of capital-cum-labor for land. The Ricardian view of rent, despite the labor theory of value, made land the limiting factor on growth.[4]

DIGRESSION ON DEMAND AND SUPPLY

An early concern of growth theories, which remains a live issue today, is whether growth is halted by insufficient demand or insufficient supply. Adam Smith and Ricardo opted for supply; they ignored demand (apart from Smith's famous remark about the division of labor being limited by the extent of the market) and focused on accumulation or capital formation. More saving was needed, despite its impact on demand, to expand supply.

These views were developed to counter a contrary position which had existed as early as the seventeenth century. In Mandeville's *Fable of the Bees,* private vices were said to be public benefits; and luxury specifically was a vehicle of economic progress because it expanded people's desires and served the employment of the poor. If forced to choose between two vices, luxury and sloth, David Hume would have preferred luxury, because to banish it without curing sloth would only diminish industry.[5]

The concern of Malthus for sustained demand has been emphasized by Keynes in *The General Theory of Employment, Interest and Money,*

[3] This diagram has been privately communicated by M. Bronfenbrenner.
[4] Karl Marx's theory of the inevitability of the decline of capitalism was based on the labor theory of value and the decline of profits, but paid no attention to rent. In his system, capital piles up as surplus value is reinvested, until the rate of profit falls. This leads to competitive struggles among capitalists, with increasing monopoly, and to overproduction of capital goods and insufficient production for consumption; to periodic crises, the prospect of which leads to hoarding of surplus value and insufficient demand *in toto;* and to increased misery of the workers.
[5] See H. W. Spiegel, "Theories of Economic Development," *Journal of the History of Ideas,* October, 1955, pp. 524, 527.

and Marx's later views on underconsumption have been mentioned. But the Earl of Lauderdale stressed the importance of demand, which depends on income distribution: "A proper distribution of wealth insures the increase of opulence, by sustaining a regular progressive demand in the home market."[6] These people not only oppose Say's law, that supply creates its own demand; they come close to maintaining the opposite, that demand creates its own supply. To a very considerable extent, of course, each rule is valid in particular circumstances: demand can fall behind supply because of hoarding, or supply behind demand because of bottlenecks. A small discrepancy on one or the other side of the "balanced growth" path where supply and demand are equal can interrupt growth. Much of the development literature and many of the development models are concerned with this path.

THE HARROD–DOMAR MODEL

The jump from Ricardo-Malthus-Marx to Harrod and Domar is a long one. For a period economics was largely concerned with other problems than growth—foreign trade, natural resources, the transfer problem, full employment. Part of the reason for the neglect of growth was that it proceeded so effectively in Western Europe and North America, despite the bogey of Ricardian diminishing returns. This was the result of changes in technology introduced by entrepreneurs, which served as the focus of Schumpeter's development theory (see Chapter 7), and of external economies of scale which cheapened output as volume increased—first discussed thoroughly by Alfred Marshall (touched upon later in Chapter 9). Growth was rapid and fairly regular and could therefore be ignored. It was not until after World War II that the question of economic growth arose again, initially as a by-product of the Keynesian revolution in income theory, and later as economists lifted their attention from Europe and America to the less developed countries.

Keynes pointed out that income would be stabilized—possibly at less than full employment—where new expenditure for capital investment coming into the system exactly offset savings being taken out. This model of income determination was concerned with the very short run. But Harrod[7] observed that the full-employment income in period t would not be sufficient in period $t + 1$ because of the additional capacity created by investment in period t. How much more spending would be needed in $t + 1$ could be determined by the

[6] Quoted by Spiegel, *ibid.*, p. 530.
[7] R. F. Harrod, *Towards a Dynamic Economics*, St Martin's, New York, 1948.

relationship between capital and output, i.e., the capital/output ratio. Since investment in period t is determined at the equilibrium level of national income by the marginal propensity to save, economic growth becomes a function of the marginal propensity to save and the capital/output ratio. In algebraic terms where Y is national income, K is capital, I is investment, S is savings, and changes are represented by d, the growth rate $G = \dfrac{dY}{Y_t}$

$$\text{the savings ratio } s = \frac{S_t}{Y_t} \text{ and (since } I_t = S_t) = \frac{I_t}{Y_t}$$

$$dK_{t+1} = I_t$$

$$\text{the incremental capital/output ratio } k = \frac{dK_{t+1}}{dY} = \frac{I_t}{dY}$$

since $\qquad \dfrac{dY}{Y_t} = \dfrac{I_t/Y_t}{I_t/dY} \quad \therefore \; G = \dfrac{s}{k}$

or the rate of growth is equal to the savings ratio divided by the capital/output ratio. If this holds true, growth can be increased by expanding the savings ratio or by lowering the capital/output relation.

As a rough approximation of the rate of growth per capita, one can subtract the increase in population (dP) from the rate of growth of income.[8]

$$\frac{G}{P} = \frac{s}{k} - dP$$

Thus with a rate of saving of 12 per cent, a capital/output ratio of 3, and an increase in population of 2 per cent a year, the economy can increase at a rate of 2 per cent per capita per annum. To spell out what is involved, savings lead to an increase in investment, which leads to an increase in income (through the incremental capital/output ratio), which leads to more savings, more investment, more income, etc. This is a process of growth which Rostow likens to compound interest.[9] It can be represented, as in Figure 3.4, by an exponential

[8] The approximation is only rough because one should divide the increase in real income by the increase in population, rather than subtract it. With small numbers, the differences are not great, e.g., $104/102 \times 100 - 100$ more or less equals $4 - 2$. If longer periods of time, such as decades, are taken, however, the calculation must be made the long way, since $140/120 \times 100 - 100$ is not $40 - 20$.

[9] W. W. Rostow, *The Stages of Economic Growth*, Cambridge, New York, 1960.

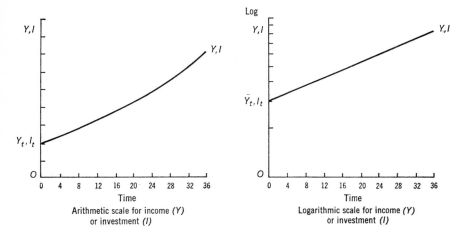

Figure 3.4 | Growth of income (or investment) under the Harrod-Domar model.

curve showing income against time, or on semilogarithmic scale, a straight line representing a constant rate of growth. A different scale applies depending upon whether one is portraying income or investment. The relation between them, of course, is the average capital/output ratio. The figures therefore imply, which is not necessarily the case, that the average and the marginal capital/output ratios are identical. In fact, if there are decreasing returns to capital, as are likely, the marginal and the average capital/output ratios are different. In Figure 3.5, the curve $Y(K)$ representing the relationship between income and capital shows that the rate of increase of income slows down with additional capital investment, whereas if $O\text{-}T$ were the relationship, there would be a constant capital/output ratio at every level of income or capital. At S, where the two curves intersect, the average capital/output ratio of $Y(K)$ is the same as $O\text{-}T$, but the marginal ratio is very different, being represented by the slope of the tangent to $Y(K)$ at S. Where the marginal and the average capital/output ratios differ, separate curves for Y and I will be needed in such a diagram as Figure 3.4.

Harrod's initial concern was with the time path of equilibrium level of income. Savings depended on income, but investment, he thought, was determined by an accelerator, which in a boom would lead to an expansion of income above the equilibrium path, to run the economy up against output ceilings, or in depression, to contraction, which

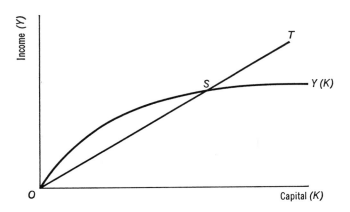

Figure 3.5 | The relationship between capital and output.

would halt growth by keeping realized growth below the warranted potential. Domar's independent working out of the same formula also laid stress on the delicate nature of balance along the equilibrium path, but focused on the enlarged capacity made available for growth in $t + 1$ by investment in period t.[10]

We deal with the capital/output ratio in more detail in Chapter 5. Here our task is mainly to point out the weakness of the Harrod-Domar theory of growth. For one thing, it relies largely on a capital theory of value, in contrast to the Ricardo-Marx labor theory of value. Labor can be introduced into the system, but only at a constant capital/labor ratio. Such a ratio is likely in reality only if labor accidentally grows at the same rates as capital, or if labor is redundant at any and all rates of capital expansion, so that as much labor as needed can be found at very low wages. If labor and capital grow at different rates, under the Harrod-Domar model, either labor or capital must be less than fully utilized. In the second place, the Harrod-Domar model ignores all possibility of change in technology.

Thirdly, the Harrod-Domar model fails on empirical grounds. Growth as observed in concrete situations proceeds faster than can be accounted for by the rate of inputs of capital with a constant capital/output ratio. The theory can be saved by allowing the capital/output ratio to change, but then it ceases to be a theory and becomes a mere

[10] E. D. Domar, "Capital Expansion, Rate of Growth and Employment," *Econometrica*, April, 1946, pp. 137–147, reprinted in *Essays in the Theory of Economic Growth*, Oxford, Fair Lawn, N.J., 1957 [also reprinted in Okun and Richardson (eds.), selection 10]; and his "Expansion and Employment," *American Economic Review*, March, 1947, pp. 34–55.

tautology. (This weakness of the Harrod-Domar model is shared by other growth models, and is discussed after a treatment of the neoclassical model of growth.)

THE NEOCLASSICAL MODEL OF GROWTH

The weaknesses of the Harrod-Domar model of growth led economists to explore more complex theories which allowed for changes in labor, as well as in capital, and substitutions of labor and capital for each other. Robert Solow was one of the first to work along these lines.[11] With variable factor proportions and flexible factor prices, he showed that the growth path was not inherently unstable. If the labor force outgrew the supply of capital, the price of labor would fall relative to the rate of interest, or if capital outgrew labor, the price of labor would rise. Changes in factor prices and factor substitution could mitigate the terrors of the likely departure from the Harrod-Domar growth path.

One production function explored by Solow which permitted capital and labor to grow at different rates was the Cobb-Douglas.[12] In equation form this is

$$Y = \gamma K^\alpha L^\beta$$

where Y, K, and L are output, capital, and labor, γ is a constant, different for different economies, and α and β are exponents which indicate the marginal efficiencies of capital and labor. In the Cobb-Douglas function α and β add to 1, which means that increases in income are fully equal to the marginal physical productivity of the factors times their respective increases. This implies constant returns to scale (a departure from classical diminishing returns).

The neoclassical approach has been taken further and generalized by Meade.[13] There is still one output which can be used for either capital formation or consumption—Meade suggests cows might serve as an example—and three factors. Meade's production function is

$$Y = F(K,L,R,t)$$

[11] Robert Solow, "A Contribution to the Theory of Economic Growth," *Quarterly Journal of Economics*, February, 1956, pp. 65–94.
[12] Paul Douglas, *The Theory of Wages*, Macmillan, New York, 1934, pp. 131ff.
[13] J. E. Meade, *A Neo-classical Theory of Economic Growth*, 2d ed., Oxford, Fair Lawn, N.J., 1963.

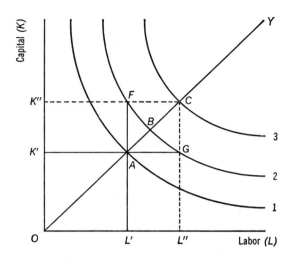

Figure 3.6 | The marginal efficiencies of capital and labor compared with the capital/output ratio and labor productivity.

where K, L, and R are capital, labor, and land, and t stands for time, representing a trend factor for constant technological improvement. If land is regarded as unchanging

$$dY = V \cdot dK + W \cdot dL + dY'$$

where V stands for the marginal efficiency of capital, W for the marginal efficiency of labor, and Y' for the improvement in income due to technology. The marginal efficiency of capital (and of labor) differs from the capital/output ratio (labor productivity) because it measures the increase in output due to an added unit of capital (labor) holding all other inputs constant. In Figure 3.6, which is identical with 3.1, the marginal efficiency of capital is represented by the increase in output derived from increasing capital from OK' to OK'' without changing the amount of labor L'. This is evidently lower than the capital/output ratio. The marginal efficiency of capital is $AB/K'K''$ (B being on the same isoquant as F) as compared with the capital/output ratio $AC/K'K''$.

The Meade formula can be put in terms of rates of growth

$$\frac{dY}{Y} = \frac{VK}{Y} \cdot \frac{dK}{K} + \frac{WL}{Y} \cdot \frac{dL}{L} + \frac{dY'}{Y}$$

where dY/Y, dK/K, dL/L, and dY'/Y are proportionate rates of growth in annual terms of income, capital, labor, and technical progress. Economic growth is thus the marginal product of capital times the proportionate increase in capital, plus the marginal product of labor times the proportionate increase in labor, plus the proportionate increase in output owing to technological change. If technical change is nil, and the proportionate marginal products of labor and land add to the increase in income (as in Figure 3.6) we are back at the Cobb-Douglas production function. But the coefficients can amount to more than 1, with economies of scale, or less than 1, with diminishing returns to a factor (such as land). With diminishing returns, distances between regularly increasing isoquants become further apart; with increasing returns, closer together. Technical progress through time cannot be shown in such a diagram as that in Figure 3.6, because it requires, as we shall see later, a shift of the isoquants toward the origin.

THE KALDOR MODEL

Nicholas Kaldor objected to both the instability of the Harrod-Domar model and the escape from it through factor substitution.[14] In his view, ready substitutability of capital for labor was impossible because of the rigidity of the technology embodied in machines. To produce a change in technology required new investment. Thus it was impossible to have technological change depend on time alone. The escape from instability in his view lay through the relations running between technical progress and the capital/output ratio. If technical progress were to get ahead, this would increase the marginal productivity of capital and lead to more investment. On the contrary, if capital investment were to gain on technical progress, the marginal product of capital would fall, so that investment would have to wait for technology to catch up. The relationship is illustrated in Figure 3.7 where labor productivity Y/L is plotted against the capital/labor ratio K/L. One production function F_t shows the technical position in period t. The curve levels out as increasing ratios of capital to labor contribute less and less to total output with a fixed supply of labor. When the curve is flat, the marginal product of capital is zero. If technical progress moves the function from F_t to $F_t + 1$, this raises the marginal product of capital, the tangent to $F_t + 1$ at w being steeper than that to F_t at s. Further investment is likely to take place to restore the

[14] Nicholas Kaldor, "A Model of Economic Growth," *Economic Journal*, December, 1957, pp. 591–624, reprinted in his *Essays in Economic Stability and Growth*, Duckworth, London, 1960.

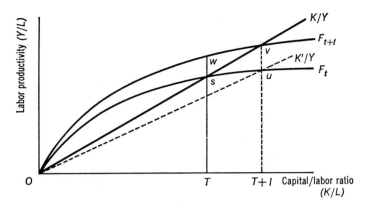

Figure 3.7 | The relationships among labor productivity, the capital/labor ratio, technical progress and the capital/output ratio in a Kaldor model.

marginal productivity of capital, and the capital/output ratio at v. If, on the other hand, capital investment had gained on technical progress, and the K/L ratio has increased along the horizontal axis from t to $t + 1$, with the production function F_t still operating, the decline in the marginal productivity of capital would tend to discourage investment until the capital/output ratio was restored by technical progress to $O - v$. The consequence is that economic growth, in the Kaldor view, tends to work along an equilibrium path in which the growth rates for the capital stock, for total output, and for labor productivity are all equal.

The differences between the Kaldor position, which emphasizes the relationships between technical progress and investment but relies on the capital/output ratio, and the neoclassical view, which permits factor substitution, are not resolved. Solow has come part of the way toward such a resolution in a paper which notes that some technical progress is "embodied" in capital equipment, i.e., cannot be realized without new investment, whereas other advances may be "disembodied."[15] But the central issue remains.

MORE COMPLEX MODELS

The student should note that a great deal of the activity of many economists is devoted to perfecting the simple models of economic

[15] Robert Solow, "Technical Progress, Capital Formation and Economic Growth," *American Economic Review, Proceedings,* May, 1962, pp. 76–86.

growth and moving on to the more complex sort. Additional complexity which can be handled only by mathematics beyond the limited powers of the writer takes the analysis in a number of different directions:

a. into a number of sectors, such as industry, agriculture, social overhead capital, and services, with different incomes, demands, rates of technical change, factor endowments, and propensities such as the marginal propensity to save
b. into the allocation process between sectors
c. into the question of initial conditions and desired end equipment, the latter largely the question whether a society is interested in building capital for future generations or is willing to let capital stock run down
d. into intermediate goods, i.e., goods which are not in themselves final production (consumption or investment goods) but are used to produce final products
e. further into the relations among inputs in the productive process, such as Kaldor's links between the capital investment and technical change

It is evident that there is room for great diversity as well as complexity among growth models. This book touches lightly on a few of these complexities in referring to various models. For the most part, however, they are left for the advanced student.

EMPIRICAL VERIFICATION

The Ricardian model in which economic growth was brought to a halt by the poverty of natural resources was disproved by nineteenth-century history of Western Europe, the United States, and the British Dominions (though it may still apply in other circumstances today). The next step was to test the Harrod-Domar model in which capital was the engine of growth. This has been done by a number of students. Some, like Maddison, find a capital theory of growth supported in history.[16] Others, notably Moses Abramovitz[17] and Robert Solow,[18] are persuaded that the historical record shows much more economic growth for the United States than can be explained by inputs of capital

[16] A. Maddison, "Economic Growth in Western Europe, 1870–1957," *Banca Nazionale del Lavoro Quarterly Review*, March, 1959, pp. 58–102.
[17] M. Abramovitz, "Resource and Output Trends in the United States since 1870," *American Economic Review, Proceedings*, May, 1956, pp. 5–23.
[18] Robert Solow, "Technical Change and the Aggregate Production Function," *Review of Economics and Statistics*, August, 1957, pp. 312–320.

and labor. Their findings have been confirmed by other studies.[19] The question then becomes what accounts for the more rapid growth of output than of inputs of land, capital, and labor.

The initial candidate of Solow was technical progress. Since that time, however, a variety of rivals have been nominated: education, or investment in human capital,[20] which is neglected in concentrating on investment in capital equipment (and even regarded in national-income accounts as consumption); managerial capacity;[21] economies of scale.[22] It is on this account that these ingredients in the growth process must be studied in the chapters that follow Land and Capital. One student is said to have used eight variables in a multiple-regression exercise, and accounted with them for only 45 per cent of the variations in growth among a list of countries. The unexplained residual he attributed to "government policy," which evades expression in equation form or analysis by computer.[23]

STAGE THEORIES

The sorts of models we have been examining thus far deal with growth as an ongoing process, i.e., with growth rather than with development. But there are theories which go beyond this task to try to account for successive changes in rates of growth and in the structure of the economy, i.e., with development proper. The most notable are the so-called "stage" theories, derived from economic history, which suggest that the growth of an economy may follow a fairly uniform pattern, passing through a series of stages.

The German historical school in particular went in for stages, with different individuals emphasizing transition along different lines of development. Perhaps the best known are those of Marx, who postulated change of economic institutions: feudalism, capitalism, and socialism. Other writers and their designated stages may be listed as follows:

List: savagery; pastoral life; agriculture; agriculture and manufactures; agriculture, manufactures, and trade
Hildebrand: barter, money, credit

[19] See, for example, E. O. Domar, "On the Measurement of Technological Change," *Economic Journal,* December, 1961, pp. 709–729.
[20] See Chap. 6.
[21] See Chap. 7.
[22] See Chap. 9.
[23] I have this on the authority of Egbert deVries.

Bücker: household economy (independent production and consumption), town economy (custom production), national economy (production for inventory and wholesale distribution)
Ashley: household system, guild, domestic system, factory
Gras: village, town, nation, world

A thoroughly worked-out theory and a recent one, by W. W. Rostow,[24] has excited great interest and a certain amount of critical comment. Rostow's system has five stages: traditional society, preconditions, takeoff, the drive to maturity, and high mass consumption. The traditional society rests in static equilibrium until it is disturbed by some such mechanism as that postulated by Hagen.[25] Techniques are fixed, diminishing returns prevail, population is stabilized along Malthusian lines.

The preconditions stage involves slow changes, especially in attitudes and organization. The idea of economic improvement takes hold, and with it the frozen traditional rigidity breaks up to allow for occupational, geographic, and social mobility. Transport becomes cheaper, and commerce spreads. New production functions are adopted in agriculture and industry. But the pace is slow.

Takeoff is the great watershed. Resistances and blocks to development are overcome, particularly in one or more leading sectors where technical change is strongly felt. The rate of investment jumps from about 5 per cent to more than 10 to raise the overall rate of growth on the compound interest (Harrod-Domar) principle. Takeoff involves such a rapid increase in the rate of change as to involve a discontinuity.

Following takeoff comes the drive to maturity, the spread of technical change, and improved efficiency from the leading sectors to all parts of the economy, with habits of growth becoming ingrained in the economy. Rates of growth outstrip population increase to raise income per head. Maturity is reached when every sector has built regular growth into its habits.

From maturity, the economy moves with growth to high mass consumption, the stage at which durable consumers' goods, life in the suburbs, college education for one-third to one-half the population come within reach. Arrival at high mass consumption may be delayed for one reason or another: it may have to wait for a diversion of energy to social legislation or national aggrandizement, or for the invention of the automobile and the electric refrigerator. Typically, however, all economic growth follows a Gompertz, S, or learning curve in

[24] *Op. cit.*
[25] See Chap. 2.

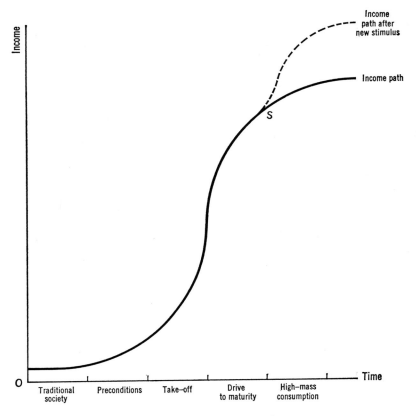

Figure 3.8 | Gompertz or S curve used to illustrate Rostow's stages of growth.

which, as in Figure 3.8, growth starts off slowly, picks up gradually, and then proceeds very rapidly before slowing down at some late stage to become asymptotic at some limit or ceiling.

The difficulty at an early point in the process is to predict how far any one stage will carry, and whether after an initial slowdown at such a point as S, another spurt is not possible, as along the dotted line. The growth of the human body, for example, follows the S curve in the stages of infancy and early childhood, but then reaches another period of spurt in adolescence. To know the shape of only the idealized curve is no help in prediction.

Rostow calls his book "a non-Communist Manifesto" and means it to counter the deeply pessimistic economic determinism of Marx. He is careful to insist that his way of looking at development is limited, arbitrary, and in no absolute sense correct, though he cites historical detail in support of his system. The book does, however, bear the marks of an economic determinism which suggests, for example, that the Soviet Union will arrive, like the United States, at station wagons and swimming pools (and therefore at a peaceable view of the world about it). Rostow's facts are questioned by some historians, and the inevitability of the transitions from one stage to the next is questioned by historians and economists alike. But his emphasis on the discontinuity between the static equilibrium of the traditional society and the dynamics of growth, i.e., on "takeoff," has attracted widespread attention and hope.

Alexander Gerschenkron[26] has a stage theory of his own with two significant differences from Rostow. There are similarities, such as the emphasis on discontinuity—in Gerschenkron's system a "big spurt"—and preconditions. But the preconditions are for the most part neither necessary nor sufficient. A few may be necessary, such as the abolition of serfdom in czarist Russia to provide mobility. In the main, however, they can substitute for one another. Just as one factor can substitute for another in the neoclassical growth model, so in the absence of one usual condition facilitating growth, more of some others can substitute. Given a lack of entrepreneurship, government can provide the organizational leadership needed.

The other difference is crucial. Growth, according to Gerschenkron, need not trace through the same set of stages in each country. The big spurt can occur at different levels of development and with different patterns, depending upon the level. The more backward the country is when it starts its development, the more likely it is to rely on governmental decision-making, as against private, and the more readily it can short-cut the slow growth path of the leaders. The Harrod-Domar model emphasizes the value of the head start, since the more income a country has, the higher its savings, the larger its investment, the faster (other things equal) its growth. Gerschenkron finds advantages in backwardness which permit the late starter to catch up or at least narrow the distance between it and the pioneers.

THE STATISTICAL APPROACH

Model building and stage making as theories of economic growth can be completed by noting the work of the statistical investigator. Occasionally, the data are trotted forth only to test a model or a theory.

[26] Alexander Gerschenkron, *Economic Backwardness in Historical Perspective*, Harvard, Cambridge, Mass., 1962.

But economic growth and development also hold fascination for the scholar immersed in statistics. Occasionally he is antitheoretical, finding theoretical speculation too easy and undisciplined in the absence of hard fact. Infrequently he will find some uniformity in the data and elevate it into a law of development, such as Walther Hoffmann's theories of stages, based upon the relationship of industrial production of consumers' goods to capital goods,[27] or Colin Clark's relationships among the primary (agriculture), secondary (manufacturing, mining, and construction), and tertiary sectors.[28] (Too often these uniformities lead via the *post hoc ergo propter hoc* fallacy to the policy conclusion that the way to development is to add capital-goods industries or manufacturing.) Generally, he subscribes to the classical division of labor and gathers material for the testing of theories, leaving the testing to others.

The best of these investigators gather their data in the light of the theoretical analysis, with which they are familiar, and seek to bring together the inductive and the deductive approaches. Among the foremost of these, Simon Kuznets has not only undertaken a series of international investigations of his own,[29] but has launched another deeper study of the statistical data in historical depth, with a view to providing further tests.[30] Some of the material he and others have brought together will be used to illustrate various propositions in scatter diagrams in subsequent pages. Theory without facts and facts without theory are both vapid. Both theory and the gathering and analysis of facts have long distances to go before economics can construct a single, unified, and tested theory of growth useful for prediction.

[27] Walther G. Hoffmann, *The Growth of Industrial Economics* (German original, 1931), expanded and revised English version, Manchester University Press, Manchester, 1958.
[28] Colin Clark, *The Conditions of Economic Progress*, 3d ed., St. Martin's, New York, 1957.
[29] See S. Kuznets, "Quantitative Aspects of the Economic Growth of Nations," in special supplements to regular issues, *Economic Development and Cultural Change*, including: I. "Levels and Variability of Rates of Growth," October, 1956; II. "Industrial Distribution of National Product and Labor Force," July, 1957; III. "Industrial Distribution of Income and Labor Force by States, United States, 1919–21 to 1955," July, 1958; IV. "Distribution of National Income by Factor Shares," April, 1959; V. "Capital Formation Proportions: International Comparisons for Recent Years," July, 1960; VI. "Long-term Trends in Capital Formation Proportions," July, 1961; VII. "The Share and Structure of Consumption," January, 1962.
[30] See, for example, Phyllis Deane and W. A. Cole, *British Economic Growth, 1688–1959: Trends and Structure*, Cambridge, New York, 1962.

SUMMARY

Models of economic growth are useful for isolating and emphasizing critical variables in the growth process. In the Ricardian growth model the major limitation on growth is imposed by land, which sets the price of food, and thus the supply of labor. In the Harrod-Domar model, growth is a result of the interaction between saving and the capital/output ratio, with capital as the engine of growth. Intended savings and the capital/output ratio lay out an equilibrium growth path from which it is easy to stray through too much or too little demand.

The Harrod-Domar model has been modified in the neoclassical direction by Solow and Meade, who provide for substitution among factors, rather than the fixed proportions assumed by the Harrod-Domar model, and by a technical-progress function related to investment, by Kaldor.

Attempts to verify the Harrod-Domar or the neoclassical model statistically have left an important proportion of historical growth unexplained. Various explanations of this "residual" have been offered: technical progress, investment in human capital, increasing organizational efficiency, increasing returns to scale, and even government policies.

Economic history has produced a variety of stage theories, of which the most widely discussed currently is Rostow's listing of traditional society, preconditions, takeoff, drive to maturity, and high mass consumption.

In addition to theorists and historians, statisticians who have gathered masses of data in time series for the economic history of particular countries and cross-section analysis between countries have also undertaken an attack on the riddle of economic growth.

All three attacks are necessary, but they have not yet produced a single theory of growth.

BIBLIOGRAPHY

The major items have been set out in the footnotes. In models special attention should be paid to Harrod (footnote 7), Domar (footnote 10), Solow (footnotes 11, 15), Meade (footnote 13) and Kaldor (footnote 14). For brief excerpts from the classic authors, see Okun and Richardson (eds.) selections 2–10. An excellent but mathematical discussion of the classic theorists and modern model builders is contained in Irma Adelman, *Theories of Economic Growth and Development,* Stanford, Stanford, Calif., 1961. See also Bert F. Hoselitz and others, *Theories of Economic Growth,* Free Press, New York, 1960. A useful and handy article is H. W. Singer, "The Mechanics of Economic Development," *Indian Economic Review,* August, 1952, reprinted in Agarwala and Singh (eds.), part 6.

On stage theories, see the Rostow and Gerschenkron titles (footnotes 9 and 26, respectively). Papers of Rostow on the stages as a whole and on takeoff are contained in Okun and Richardson (ed.), selection 16; Agarwala and Singh (eds.), part 2; and Supple (ed.), selection 3. His views are widely criticized. See, e.g., Gerschenkron, *op. cit.,* pp. 353ff.; in Kuznets' paper reproduced in Morgan, Betz, and Choudhry (eds.), selection 19; E. E. Hagen, *On the Theory of Social Change,* Dorsey Press, Homewood, Ill., 1962, appendix II; and A. K. Cairncross, *Factors in Economic Development,* G. Allen, London, 1962, chap. 8.

On the approach to theory through measurement, see the Kuznets essays listed in footnote 28, his essay on income inequality in Okun and Richardson (eds.), selection 17, and S. J. Patel, "Rates of Industrial Growth in the Last Century, 1860–1958," *Economic Development and Cultural Change,* April, 1961, reproduced in Supple (ed.), selection 2.

INTRODUCTORY

How important to economic development are resources, or land in the familiar triad of factors of production, land, capital, and labor? A variety of conflicting opinion exists. Many people regard physical resources as a rather unimportant ingredient in growth, either because any land base is sufficient to get growth started[1] or because, while the quantity of land may affect the level of national income, land is a fixed factor and is therefore unrelated to the growth rate.[2] Others, having in mind that most temperate countries are developed and most tropical are not, believe that resources, at least in the climatic aspect, are crucial.[3] We have referred to the historical debate whether the French family firm or the thinness of French coal seams did more to shape the level and rate of growth of nineteenth-century France.[4] At the limit, the resources side of this debate is maintained by W. N. Parker, an economic historian, who objects to studying economic history by countries, but prefers to do so by resource areas. By implication northern France, Belgium, and the Ruhr, connected by a single system of coal beds, should be regarded as a separate entity, apart

[1] S. Kuznets, "Toward a Theory of Economic Growth," in R. Lekachman (ed.), *National Policy for Economic Welfare at Home and Abroad*, Doubleday, Garden City, N.Y., 1955, p. 36: "Every country has some natural resources. . . . The factors that induce formation of reproducible capital adequate as a basis for economic growth are unlikely to be inhibited by an absolute lack of natural resources." This remark is qualified to a degree in a footnote.

[2] See J. E. Meade, *A Neo-Classical Theory of Economic Growth*, Oxford, Fair Lawn, N.J., 1961, p. 10: "We assume that the amount of land or natural resources available to the community is fixed, so that there is no change in N to affect Y"; and J. Tinbergen and H. C. Bos, *Mathematical Models of Economic Growth*, McGraw-Hill, New York, 1962, p. 11: "Land does not need so much attention in a study of development, which is essentially a process in time, because in time the quantity of land proper hardly changes."

[3] See especially E. Huntington, *Civilization and Climate*, Yale, New Haven, Conn., 1915.

[4] See p. 18.

from France and Germany.[5] We have also referred to the Ricardian view that lack of land set limits to attainable levels of development,[6] a view historically upset by increasing returns and technical progress. The time has come to examine in some detail the importance of resources in the development process.

A prima facie case can be made that resources are important at an early stage of growth. With the basic neoclassical development model

$$Y = F(K,L,R,T)$$

(where T stands for technology, rather than time), an underdeveloped country's level of income and growth is dependent upon R or resources when capital K is limited and technology rudimentary. At later stages, the importance of unchanged resources, if they be unchanged, declines.

A problem is posed by the difficulty in the real world of separating resources, or land, the indestructible gift of nature, from capital, from culture, and from technology. Cleared land, for example, may be identical in agricultural productivity with acreage that once formed part of the virgin plain. The first is partly land, partly capital, since the process of clearing involves production but not consumption, i.e., saving; the latter is all land. Or two mines of equally rich ore may be located, one outside a city with easy access to its factories and the other at a distance through rough country. If a road is put through to the latter to make both equally accessible, they remain different as economic land, even though physically the same, since some of the return from the distant mine must be imputed to the road, a capital investment.

That land as a resource can be intertwined with cultural institutions can be understood by contemplating the difference made in the productivity of land by a change from primogeniture, in which one son inherits a farm (and the others leave), to equal inheritance, where the land must be divided among all sons (or all children) at each generation.[7]

Finally, the availability of physical land for the growth process can

[5] See W. N. Parker, "Comment," in J. J. Spengler (ed.), *Natural Resources and Economic Growth,* Resources for the Future, Washington, D.C., 1961, p. 190. Professor Parker refers specifically to the nineteenth century when technology had not gone so far to reduce the role of resources and states: "Resources—mineral, agricultural and transport . . . were largely responsible for the direction and speed of nineteenth century development among Western countries."
[6] See pp. 41ff.
[7] H. J. Habakkuk, "The Historical Experience on the Basic Conditions of Economic Progress," in L. H. Dupriez (ed.), *Economic Progress,* Institut de Recherches Économiques et Sociales, Louvain, 1955, pp. 157–158.

be altered not only by investment and cultural change but by technological improvement. Deeper drilling turns barren land into oil-bearing, as does seismographic exploration or the development of the Texas tower for drilling on the coastal shelf. It is possible to regard the technological change as capital—the result of research and development—and to attribute the entire increase in productivity to capital, and none to land. Or some portion of output can be regarded as the product of previously no-rent land which had been increased by discovery. This is the difficult "imputation" problem of dividing responsibility for a joint product to the separate inputs. But the relation of technology to land can be seen from the postwar importance of uranium-bearing ores.[8]

The relation of land to economic development is a many-sided matter, since land itself has a variety of aspects, both physical and economic. In the rest of this chapter we shall discuss resources as an agricultural input, as an industrial input, and as a barrier to transport, and in relation to social institutions, capital, and technology.

RESOURCES AS AN AGRICULTURAL INPUT

The productivity of land in agriculture varies greatly, whether it be measured in terms of crude output per acre, which may be called the land/output ratio, or in terms of marginal physical products of land, in which the outputs of two pieces of land are compared, with all other factor inputs identical or after deduction for the contribution of other inputs. Soils differ widely in their productivity, owing to physical and chemical properties, temperature, rainfall, hours of light, and accessibility both to markets and other inputs. Moreover, importance attaches in these aspects of land not only to averages but also to variability through time.[9]

The contrast runs between the desert portions of the world, many of which are uninhabited, and the rich plains of Iowa or the polders of the Netherlands. Where the desert is inhabited by poor people lacking capital and advanced techniques, the land/population ratio is

[8] Cf. the following quotation from B. Neumann, *Die Metalle*, Halle a. S., 1904, p. 408: "Metallic uranium has practically no uses. On this account, there are no production statistics" [author's translation].
[9] See, for example, Albert O. Hirschman, *Journeys toward Progress: Studies of Economic Policy-making in Latin America*, Twentieth Century Fund, New York, 1963, on Brazil's Northeast where the problem is droughts. These occur on the average once every ten years, and last one to three years. In a normal year the rainfall amounts to 27 inches, compared with London's 24, but 90 per cent of it falls in the last five months of the year (pp. 13–14).

likely to be near the Malthusian limit. Such is the case for many parts of Africa, for example, where the fertility of 8 or 9 square miles of average land south of the Sahara and north of the Union of South Africa is equivalent to that of 1 acre of Iowa soil. In addition some of the African areas are subject to plagues of locusts, which bring famine, or are unable to raise cattle or draft animals because of the tsetse fly.

Land productivity can be high in relatively low-income countries, such as Burma with its great rice bowl, as well as in desert country, provided it is irrigated and fertilized, as in Israel; and it can be low in high-income areas where land is the abundant factor. Labor-intensive Danish agriculture produces three times the average yield per acre of the United States in wheat[10] and a much higher multiple than "dry-farming" areas such as Montana where a single farm will stretch to the horizon and be worked with a small amount of labor and masses of equipment. The marginal product per man or per unit of capital can be high, provided there is enough land, even when the land/output ratio is low.

The productivity of land is a function not only of its physical characteristics, its climatic setting, and the availability of other factors; it is also closely related to technology. The capacity of land to support added numbers of people, or the same numbers at higher levels of living, has grown continuously through history. Discovery adds to land. Technological change expands it as surely. Some economic historians attribute the Renaissance to the discovery of hay, which enabled farm animals to winter over successfully and to start the spring in good condition,[11] or to the invention of the horse collar, which permitted horses to plow without choking.[12] The Industrial Revolution was preceded and possibly initiated by a new crop rotation in British agriculture, including the turnip, in the 1740s and 1750s. Deep plowing and better drainage produced another improvement one hundred years later.[13] The introduction of the potato into Ireland in the eighteenth century made possible a large increase in population as a

[10] It produced more than three times as much in the 1930s and less than three times as much after World War II. See, for example, L. D. Stamp, *Land for Tomorrow*, Indiana University Press, Bloomington, Ind., 1952, p. 94 (using data available in the FAO *Yearbook of Food and Agricultural Statistics*). The change was due to the increased application of fertilizer in the United States after the war.

[11] V. G. Simkhovitch, "Hay and History," *Political Science Quarterly*, September, 1913, pp. 385–403.

[12] F. Delaisi, *Les Deux Europes,* Payot, Paris, 1929, p. 29.

[13] Lord Ernle (R. E. Prothero), *English Farming, Past and Present,* 4th ed., Longmans, London, 1937.

given population could be supported with half the land.[14] The major improvement in French agriculture in the nineteenth century was the introduction of cleaning crops—sugar beets in the North and Indian corn in the South, which made it possible to dispense with the fallow and to use land four successive years instead of three out of four.[15]

This variability in the functioning of land and its change through combination with other factors make it difficult to speak of the relationship between agricultural land and economic development. One possibility open to countries with capital and skilled labor is to dispense altogether with homegrown food, and to import it, as New York City does. Figure 4.1 shows very little correlation between arable land per capita, measured in hectares, and income per capita. The United States, Australia, Canada, and Argentina are high-income countries with high land/labor ratios; but much of this land is suitable only for grazing. For the rest, at every stage of development one can find countries of the same level of income, one having ten times the arable land per capita of the other—1 hectare per capita to 0.1 hectare: Australia and Switzerland: Syria and Barbados; Tunisia and Formosa.

Unfortunately, the data do not extend to some of the countries poorest in terms of arable land, such as Jordan in the Middle East and Somalia in Africa, or to virtually uninhabitable areas of tundra, desert, badlands, and the like. Statistics of growth inevitably relate to places where people live.

There is a considerable difference between the two statements: (1) any existing country is likely to have enough resources to enable it to feed itself in the course of development, whether by agriculture, hydroponics, or trade; and (2) there are places in the world where it would be virtually impossible for a group of people large enough to constitute a country to establish what would ultimately be a viable, self-sustaining economy. A minimum of resources may be needed; but every existing country has the minimum.

More and better agricultural resources are better than less. This not very profound observation is needed to correct the impression that land may not be important. A rich country like the Netherlands can do well with limited land—in fact, it has created land which is generally regarded as a fixed resource—but it could use more; and the Netherlands land/labor ratio has been declining through time because of increases in population after the country had already achieved a considerable economic growth. A poor country with a high ratio of people to land is under a severe handicap. Not only does it lack the

[14] K. H. Connell, *The Population of Ireland, 1750–1845*, Clarendon Press, Oxford, 1945, chap. V.
[15] Jean Fauchon, *Economie de l'agriculture française*, Génin, Paris, 1954.

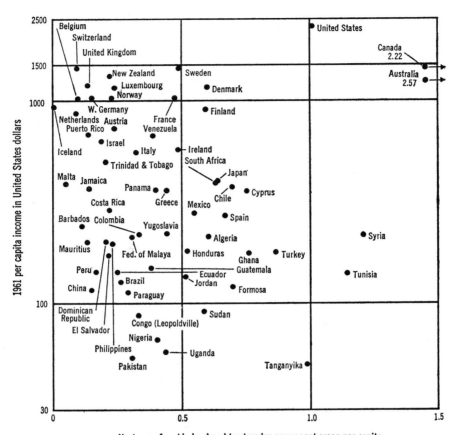

Figure 4.1 | Hectares of arable land and land under permanent crops per capita compared with income per capita, about 1961. SOURCES: Arable land and land under permanent crops, *Production Yearbook, 1961,* vol. 15, Food and Agriculture Organization of the United Nations, Rome, 1962, pp. 3–7; population, *Monthly Bulletin of Statistics,* United Nations, New York, May, 1963, pp. 1–4; income per capita, table 1.1, Average Income per Capita in Selected Countries, 1949 and 1961.

technical capacity and capital that can be substituted for land, but it can confidently expect with development a further expansion of population and a further decline in the ratio of land to mouths. It is undoubtedly true that India has a considerable amount of unused land, and that it could, with capital projects and improved techniques, extend the productivity of its land. But India is crowded, and a population of half the present numbers on the present land would have a better chance of economic development, other things more or less equal.

The existence of virtually unlimited supplies of rich land gives the lucky country (the United States, Canada, Australia, New Zealand, et al.—sometimes called the empty lands, or regions of recent settlement) much more freedom of action. Countries with masses of people crowded together on thin soil have fewer options open to them. They have a difficult time using labor efficiently, because they lack the necessary complementary factor, land. The empty lands, however, were obliged to use their labor efficiently in industry because it always had the choice of quitting the factory or town and moving to new land where it could earn a living. We shall later encounter a model of "economic development with unlimited supplies of labor";[16] how much happier at the beginning stages of development is the country with "unlimited supplies of land," as Ricardo recognized.

Abundant resources are not a sufficient condition for economic development or sustained growth, as Argentina and Burma perhaps prove. But they help it begin and support the ongoing process. To get started at all on capital formation a people must produce a surplus

[16] See Chap. 10.

Figure 4.2 | Countries with different resources and income levels, growing at the same rate.

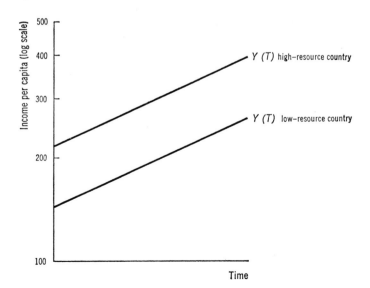

above the mere subsistence level. At the earliest stages of growth capital is food. An agricultural surplus may be necessary for takeoff (a subject we probe deeper into in Chapter 12). But once growth is started, resources may not affect the rate of growth so much as the level from which growth is started, and the level which will ultimately be attained. In Figure 4.2, a stylized comparison is given of two countries with very different resources growing at the same rate. It may serve to illustrate the growth of such countries as Australia and Japan, until the postwar Japanese spurt.

LAND AS AN INDUSTRIAL INPUT

Land differs in its ability to provide industrial materials as well as in its capacity to produce food. Certain types of industrial materials are ubiquitous, such as limestone; and some, like diamonds, are rare. Major importance attaches to the existence of high-value materials, readily transported, or of lower-value products that are accessible. The economic value of an industrial resource in its natural state depends in an obvious way upon its grade (and the difficulty of refining or purifying it to normal market standards); its transportability; and its accessibility to means of transport, to other materials, and to markets. If iron ore is sufficiently abundant and high grade, a railroad will be built into the wilderness to bring it to the St. Lawrence River. But coal in the Antarctic is not an economic resource; nor are hydroelectric sites in the Andes, since the costs of their product and its transport outweigh the value at any possible market. A country needs not only high-grade mineral resources but easy transport to bring them together, as in the case of coal, iron ore, and limestone, or to bring them to population centers or export harbors, as in the case of energy. In many instances, as will be pointed out presently, cheap transport is more important than high-grade minerals.

The significance of natural resources for industrial development is twofold. On the one hand, the country may produce and sell raw materials to other countries. Iran, Iraq, Saudi Arabia, and Kuwait produce and sell oil. Liberia, Labrador, Brazil, and Spain export iron ore. Chile, the Congo, and Northern Rhodesia are the largest producers of copper outside of the United States. These obvious examples suggest that the possession of industrial resources is not a sufficient condition of economic development.

Or a country may produce materials for consumption in its own industry. But we have a number of examples suggesting that the possession of a raw-materials base is not a necessary condition of devel-

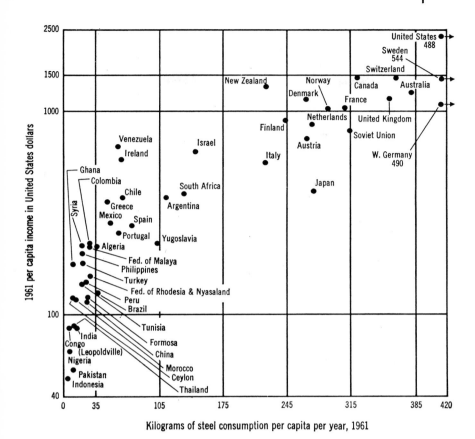

Figure 4.3 | Steel consumption per capita compared with national income per capita, about 1961. SOURCES: Steel consumption, *Statistical Yearbook, 1962,* United Nations, New York, 1963, pp. 337–338; income per capita, table 1.1, Average Income per Capita in Selected Countries, 1949 and 1961.

opment: New England with no domestic supplies of energy, no steel industry, no mines; Britain with no oil or nonferrous metals; Switzerland with only hydroelectric power; Japan with inadequate coal and few raw materials; New Zealand with no industrial raw materials to speak of.

It is nonetheless a fact that economic development implies big increases in the consumption of many industrial materials. Among the most important are steel and energy. Figures 4.3 and 4.4 show unambiguously that consumption per capita increases in these respects; and here the data suggest that the rate of consumption picks up as develop-

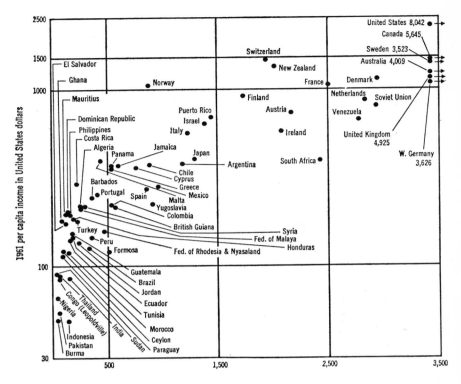

Energy consumed per capita per year in kilograms of coal equivalent, 1961

Figure 4.4 | Energy consumption per capita in coal equivalent compared with income per capita, about 1961. SOURCES: Energy consumption, *Statistical Yearbook, 1962*, United Nations, New York, 1963, pp. 290–292; income per capita, table 1.1, Average Income per Capita in Selected Countries, 1949 and 1961.

ment gets beyond a certain point ($375). Since iron ore, coal, and oil are bulky products and relatively expensive to transport in relation to their value, is it possible for a country to develop with none of these materials in its industrial base and without hydroelectric sites? The issue is currently important both for countries such as Argentina and Brazil which are devoting a significant amount of resources to explorations, and to India and other countries, which have decided to expand their steel industries.

The reduction in transport costs in international trade by the introduction of the screw propeller, the iron ship, and the reciprocating engine, to say nothing of the subsequent diesel, the 100,000-ton tanker, and the international pipeline, has made possession of specialized energy and mineral resources less and less important. Trade can substitute for energy and iron, as it can for arable land (although a country cannot import all its particular needs without exporting anything in return). It is possible for a country to specialize entirely in agricultural products, services, and the light products and to import its energy and steel. Switzerland, Denmark, Iceland, and New Zealand, to take four high-income countries, testify to the possibility of economic development without possession of the major forms of energy and metals. Such countries must have a higher dependence on foreign trade than those which contain natural resources in greater abundance and variety within their borders, a point which will be discussed in a later chapter. But the absence of energy or any other particular resource need not fatally reduce a country's opportunity for development.

But it is not necessary to deal with these issues in any ultimate sense, since a number of more immediate points can be made. First, most underdeveloped, and even a number of developed, countries have an inadequate idea of what their natural resources are. Technological innovations in the arts of geological prospecting, plus intensive exploration, have discovered new oil resources in Italy, France, and the Netherlands, for example, as well as the Alberta oil fields in Canada and the Williston Basin in the United States.[17] In underdeveloped countries the possibilities are wide open. While it is true that the frontier is gone in the sense of vast territories in which civilized men have not set foot, many countries lack knowledge of existing resources.

Second, much development is possible on the basis of known resources and known technology, awaiting only the application of capital, labor, and entrepreneurship. Waste natural gas is being burned in the Middle East, Indonesia, and Venezuela for lack of pipelines or complementary resources. The copper resources of Northern Rhodesia and the Congo are capable of vast expansion. Venezuela has been holding back oil fields for later exploitation.

Finally, it is likely that after known resources have been developed, and new ones discovered and put to use, changes in technology will broaden the industrial base. The range of substitutability to overcome missing specialized resources is continuously widening. Capital and labor can substitute for land in producing a given good. Intermediate

[17] In the United States, it should be noted, exploration in oil since World War I, except for 1957, has annually proved additional reserves equal to or greater than the reserves exhausted during the year. The limits of geological knowledge in petroleum, and perhaps to a lesser extent in other minerals, have been kept just about as far in the future, despite continuously expanding production.

products traded domestically or internationally can replace a missing factor. Or substitution may take place in consumption. Wartime blockades showed how specific resource bottlenecks could be overcome and translated into general strain on total resources, especially manpower and capital. The German shortage of copper, it will be recalled, finally produced the dismantling of high-power transmission lines and the replacement of copper with (abundant) aluminum wire, with some expense in aluminum and great cost in skilled labor. But the particular shortage was overcome.

All this does not dismiss resource problems as inconsequential. It is always better to have more resources rather than less. Countries that discover oil, like Iran and Venezuela, have a better prospect of economic development than if they had not, even though their prospects may not automatically be greater than those of countries that do not produce oil.[18] Moreover, in Venezuela, the conscious policy of reinvesting royalties from oil in capital assets—called "sowing the petroleum"—and in Iraq, the program to turn over 75 per cent of the taxes and royalties on oil to the Development Board provide sources of saving. But oil is not sufficient. In Saudi Arabia, average income is low; development is slow. A great deal of the revenue from oil is spent on consumption.

Much attention has been given to the resource preconditions for an iron and steel industry.[19] Steel is heavy and therefore difficult and expensive to import. Where coal of the appropriate quality for coking and good-grade iron ore are found in relative juxtaposition, steel can be produced more cheaply than it can be bought from abroad for an equivalent investment of capital and labor in the export commodity; or what amounts to the same thing, a greater quantity of iron and steel, and hence higher levels of consumption and investment capital formation, can be obtained from the same inputs. Coal and iron ore are not a condition of economic development. Their absence can be compensated for by other inputs, to give the same level of output at greater cost, or by other resources that will enable the developing country to buy expensive steel with its low-cost products in other lines. But other things being equal, coal and iron ore help. And

[18] Venezuela enjoys a much higher average income per capita in United States dollars than, say, Brazil, which lacks enough petroleum and coal for its own needs, but Brazilian development has been rapid. Lebanon, without oil production, is developing at a more rapid rate than Iran and Iraq.

[19] See, for example, *Coal and Iron Ore Resources of Asia and the Far East*, United Nations Economic Commission for Asia and the Far East, Bangkok, 1952; *World Iron Ore Resources*, United Nations Department of Economic Affairs, New York, 1950.

lacking coal, it is possible to build a steel industry with iron ore, as in Brazil at Volta Redonda; or lacking iron ore, it is possible to follow the example of the Ruhr or Pittsburgh. Or in a few cases, with good location close to the market, it is possible to import both iron ore and coal, as at Sparrow's Point in Baltimore or Morrisville, Pennsylvania, and still get steel cheaply in finished form. The enormous strides of Italian and Japanese steel in the absence of adequate supplies of coal and iron ore, and substituting technical proficiency and cheap transport for localized resources, provide still other illustrations.

The same considerations hold true of energy. It is better to have sources of energy than not; but it is not fatal to development to be obliged to import energy.

Lack of steel-making materials or of energy means that economic development must be accompanied by large-scale exporting; and this, as we shall see in Chapter 16, involves certain risks. But similar risks are involved in the development of domestic resources, as the ghost towns of Colorado and the less romantic hard-coal region of Pennsylvania indicate. The existence of rich resources is not a sufficient condition for developed industry, nor even a necessary one. But it helps.

LAND AS A COMMUNICATION NETWORK

An important aspect of land for economic development is the way it lends itself to transport and communication. Mountains are a barrier to transport. The language boundaries in Europe run along the divides. Rivers are generally highways that speed trade and communication. Plains present few obstacles to transport, whether by road, railroad, or canals connecting rivers. A seacoast cut by frequent natural harbors permits ready and inexpensive communication.

These generalizations and their corollaries require little demonstration. Countries that are badly broken up topographically labor under a serious handicap in economic development. This is illustrated most strikingly perhaps by Bolivia, Colombia,[20] Ecuador, and Peru on the west coast of Latin America where the Andes divide each country

[20] International Bank for Reconstruction and Development, *The Basis of a Development Program for Colombia,* Johns Hopkins, Baltimore, 1950, has a relief map as a frontispiece, which conveys some idea of the difficulty of transport in the country. The difficulties of internal transport have acted like a protective tariff within Colombia to spread her economic development evenly over the four main zones, each with a metropolitan focal point (Bogotá, Barranquilla, Medellín, and Cali). But in Bolivia the eastern lowlands, across the Andes, are fertile but relatively unsettled and inaccessible from the high, dry, and barren altiplano, where the bulk of the population lives.

into three sections, which can be unified economically only with great cost. The fact that Switzerland manages to overcome this handicap and achieve a high state of development offers some encouragement to countries similarly broken topographically; but the development problems of Yugoslavia, Colombia, and Nepal are different in degree from those of Poland, Argentina, and Ceylon.

Broad rivers, such as those which cut the European plain, offer great assistance to transport, and hence to development. Some rivers are better than others. The Hudson happens to flow from the agricultural regions to the industrial and commercial. The Danube runs from the industrial centers of population to the agricultural bottomlands; this means that bulk cargoes typically have to move against the current. In British Guiana and Surinam, the rivers that punctuate the coast are even a barrier: because of jungle, habitation is limited to a narrow strip along the coast. Lateral movement is impeded by the broad mouths of the rivers, now ferried, and one day, if development continues far enough, to be bridged or tunneled. Nor is Africa blessed with broadly navigable rivers: the cataracts of the Nile, the sand shallows of the Niger, and the rapids of the Zambesi, to say nothing of the Victoria Falls, make long-distance movement of bulk products difficult.

Access to the sea is important for cheap transport in international trade. It was a great British advantage that no point in the British Isles lies more than 110 miles from a seaport.[21] But it is important to combine this with interior lines of communication, as on an island. In Chile, Libya, and Indonesia a long seacoast may inhibit economic development if local producers have little transport advantage over foreign.[22] Where transport was constructed early in the period of commercial expansion, it frequently linked interior sources of bulk materials to ports, rather than connecting centers of population. The earliest lines in India were entirely separated, one running from the interior, north of Delhi, to the port of Calcutta on the east, the other, well to the south, from Bombay to Hyderabad to the east coast.[23] In Bolivia, railroads were built from the mines to ports in Peru and Chile, but were not joined, and so provided no internal communication.

As in agriculture and industry, the relation of land to communication is a function of innovation as well as inputs of capital and labor.

---

[21] The contrast runs with France. See A. L. Dunham, *The Industrial Revolution in France, 1818–1848*, Exposition Press, New York, 1955.

[22] *Processes and Problems of Industrialization in Underdeveloped Countries*, United Nations, New York, 1955, p. 14.

[23] See the frontispiece map in Daniel Thorner, *Investment in Empire*, University of Pennsylvania Press, Philadelphia, 1950.

Such innovation may be technological—the change from sail to steam, from wooden vessel to ironclad, railroad, automobile, and airplane; or it may consist in dramatic changes in transport routes, such as those involved in the construction of the Panama and Suez Canals and the Simplon Tunnel. The economic development of California and British Columbia, for example, initiated by the transcontinental railroads, received new and striking stimulation from the completion of the Panama Canal. The French steel industry expects similar dramatic cost-reducing impetus from the canalization of the Moselle River to permit cheaper transport of Ruhr coal to Lorraine. The world has seen a secular decline in transport costs relative to primary products. As transport costs approach zero, the importance of resources will decline still further. Geographic specialization will be based on the relative abundance of capital and labor, especially labor skills (assuming something approaching a world capital market). Resources will be important to poor countries, for lack of skill and capital. But once a critical point in the development process has been reached, land becomes of secondary interest.

LAND, LABOR, AND CULTURE

Land and labor can substitute for one another in the production process, within certain limits, and labor skills can substitute for labor numbers. The land/labor ratio indicates very little about the level of income per capita if we compare Latin-American Indians with Danish dairymen or pig and egg producers.

Chinese pre-scientific agriculture, it is said,[24] achieved the most efficient possible level in terms of wasting nothing of the fertility of the land. Everything, literally everything, was consumed or put back into the soil. The Netherlands, Israel, and Japan have developed the equivalent preoccupation with the conservation of natural resources, but on a scientific basis. The contrast is with "slash and burn" agriculture in Latin America, where land is cleared by fire, using up much of the fertility of the soil, and then the plot is abandoned in a couple of years to revert to jungle or brush because it will no longer produce an adequate yield.[25]

More significant than the variation in mere numbers, however, is the interaction between the character and amount of land and the culture.

[24] See G. M. Winfield, *China: The Land and the People*, Sloane, New York, 1948, p. 60.
[25] In China, in the prescientific period, straw was burned but only for the purpose of cooking, and then in limited handfuls.

On the one hand, purely cultural factors, such as the form of inheritance of land, determine, along with the rate of population increase, the size of the farm unit. On the other hand, the types of crops produced react in turn on the social structure. In most parts of the world, in the past, there has been either a tendency for farms to get smaller and smaller as equal division of land among children or among male children is the ruling family practice, or for farms to get bigger and bigger with primogeniture, under which the oldest son inherits and occasional families die out. The system of inheritance is by no means the sole determinant of farm size. Other factors include the availability of uncleared land, of machinery, and of farm credit, and the nature of the land and the possible crops that can be grown on it, etc. But in Europe, with no uncleared land, and in Asia, with limited amounts of it, farms become big or small, with few maintaining an intermediate size. In France farms grew bigger and bigger up to the Revolution, after which, with the abolition of primogeniture, they became smaller and smaller. Only in Denmark, by a series of apparently unconnected and unconscious events, did the middle-sized farm prevail.[26]

The significance of this for economic development is apparent. Large farms tend to produce for export. They specialize in single crops, sold for cash. Consumption by the agricultural worker is limited. It is even possible to form capital, although this is often consumed by the landowner or, in the case of plantations, remitted as profits to another country. In small-scale farming, on the other hand, the principal object is subsistence. Production is diversified among field crops and animal products. If the land is very rich, as in Iowa, or production is very capital- and labor-intensive, as in Iowa and Denmark, there will be exports of animal products.

Moreover, different crops have different impacts on the population. In the Caribbean, for example, sugar and tobacco develop completely different rhythms of life and social patterns. Sugar is produced on a sizable scale with capital and unskilled labor in a highly seasonal burst of work, followed by a "dead season" of four or five months. Tobacco, on the other hand, calls for skilled labor, working all year round; a worker has a chance to develop his creative powers. In sugar production, the land has traditionally been owned by large companies, and it is impossible for a worker to move up the economic scale through acquiring land.[27]

[26] See C. P. Kindleberger, "Group Behavior and International Trade," *Journal of Political Economy*, February, 1951, pp. 30–46.

[27] F. Ortiz, *Cuban Counterpoint*, Knopf, New York, 1947, part I. See also R. A. Manners and J. A. Steward, "The Cultural Study of Contemporary Societies: Puerto Rico," *American Journal of Sociology*, September, 1953, pp. 123–130, for

The nature of the crop may have an impact on the rate of technological change. Tree crops, like rubber, cocoa, and coffee, take a long time to bear their first harvest, and they last for years in production. They do not encourage agricultural experimentation by the individual farmer, as do annual crops. Moreover, whether farmers will adopt changed techniques depends in part on how closely they are in touch with one another. The adoption of new and higher-yielding rice in Indonesia, Egbert de Vries has said, followed a pattern dictated by the road layout.

For the most part agriculture is an isolated occupation. Farm labor is attached to the land and immobile, with communication limited.[28] In Africa, especially, with thin soil capable of supporting very few families per 100 acres, the density of settlement is limited, and the creation of a vigorous village life is difficult. The same is true of animal husbandry—the cattle raising of the pampas and the West of the United States and the sheep raising of the Out-Back in Australia. In a small country such as Denmark, with a labor-intensive agriculture, it is possible to maintain a communicating society by special efforts, such as the Folk High Schools started in the nineteenth century by Bishop Grundtvig,[29] or by a high level of living, which will give farmers radios, television, and automobiles.

The impact of people on land has a long-run aspect. Land can become worn out through overuse. In the pre-scientific agriculture of China, as much nutriment was being put back into the land as was taken out, but this situation had been reached through necessity, after deforestation, erosion, and overcropping had mined the soil of all its excess productive capacity. Man can make the desert bloom like the rose, but the necessity to do so arises in many cases from neglect and waste.

---

a discussion of the subcultural differences among sugar, tobacco, and coffee. Coffee, like tobacco, is a high-value product, which can be brought to market by muleback. Accordingly, the coffee worker can live in isolation far from roads. Bananas, plantains, yams, etc., however, as well as sugar, can be raised for the market only along roads. The low status of sugar workers, a result of their lack of opportunities, may account for the fact that in Puerto Rico and Cuba agrarian reform led to shortages of workers for the cane harvest.

[28] There are exceptions, which are a function of land tenure. In Europe there are two types of agriculture, one organized into villages, the other, in which the farmer lives on his land along a road, as in the United States. Where land is owned in large latifundia, as in southern Italy, the "villages" may be very large —occasionally as large as 50,000 inhabitants. They are still called villages rather than cities because of the failure to add new functions such as commerce, transport, etc.

[29] For references see Kindleberger, *op. cit.*

Interaction of land and people occurs in agriculture. But the problem is more general. The significant question is that posed by Huntington in his view that climate determines the level of civilization. Huntington attributed the difference in level of civilization between the tropics and the temperate zones to the average temperature and to moderate changes in temperature from one day to the next, which are a function of storms. Not only do moderate temperatures and storm patterns account for differences in civilization today. He explained further that the path of ancient civilizations, starting in the Middle East and Far East and working westward through the Mediterranean, followed the path of storm peak density. In the Toynbee version, creativity requires a challenge and response. In the tropics the challenge is too weak; in the Arctic zones, too great.

It is argued in opposition to these views that the temperate-zone visitor in the tropics is listless not because of the temperature but because of his inability to adjust culturally. He wears too many clothes and eats the wrong foods. The white man's burden is that of his own culture, which he carries into the alien environment of the tropics. The resources of the tropics are not inadequate; they are culture-bound.[30] Thus the "laziness" of the native is explained as well as the tendency of the visitor to go native. A. J. Brown ascribes much of the "laziness and lack of ambition" to malnutrition and disease, the rest to the "traditional outlook" engendered in other ways by the social setting.[31]

It is impossible for an economist to resolve these issues. The arguments against Huntington are telling, but the fact remains that no tropical country in modern times has achieved a high state of economic development. This establishes some sort of presumptive case—for the end result, if not for the means.

LAND AND CAPITAL

It was noted above that there is some difficulty in distinguishing land and capital, comparing plain with cleared forest. The difficulty, however, goes deeper. Land and capital are substitutes for each other.

---

[30] M. Bates, *Where Winter Never Comes*, Scribner, New York, 1952, p. 162. This work is an attack on the views of Huntington and Toynbee, with the thesis that the tropical blight on civilization is cultural rather than climatic. See T. S. Simey, *Welfare and Planning in the West Indies*, Clarendon Press, Oxford, 1946, pp. 112–113, who also disputes the Huntington thesis and attributes part of the deterioration of the white man in the tropics to the negative attitude toward life of men who choose to go to the tropics. This characterization does not apply to missionaries who perform more effectively than government officials.

[31] *Industrialization and Trade*, Oxford, Fair Lawn, N.J., 1943, p. 27.

Land depleted from its original state can be restored to some extent through capital formation. Chemicals replace depleted fertility; reforestation restores the capacity of land to hold water; irrigation restores desert to cultivation. Capital is a substitute for land. In the limiting case, it would be possible to raise food in factories, by hydroponics, just as poultry products are now being produced with a minimal input of land. It is also possible to find substitutes for scarce land, using capital and abundant labor. Lower-grade iron ore and bauxite can be used, with more capital to reduce them to pig iron and aluminum. Synthetics can replace wool normally produced by large inputs of grazing land. When the most accessible hydroelectric sites are used, as in the Alps, new and more capital-using projects are undertaken, including bringing streams from one side of the watershed to the other through a tunnel in the mountain. Even fresh water, the basic requirement for human life, can be produced from the sea by the use of capital and energy.

The fact that capital can be substituted for land does not make land unimportant, however. This substitution is limited by capital availability and by capacity to apply the appropriate technology. The less developed a country, the smaller its supply of capital and the more important the amount and character of the land it possesses. And vice versa. Contrary to the view widely held in this country, the United States does not confront a problem in the adequacy of its resources, at least in the foreseeable future. Short-run events affecting supply or demand, such as drought or war scares, may give rise to short-run difficulties of economic adjustment. And the social and political questions concerning resources—depletion, public versus private management, etc.—will try our capacities for equitable and efficient solutions. But there is little or no problem of the adequacy of resources in the long run.

The only possible economic test of a shortage of natural resources in a developed country is their cost. Barnett and Morse have shown that the average real cost of resource-products output in the United States has been falling steadily over the period since 1890 for which it is possible to effect measurement.[32] This is true not only of output as a whole, but of separate classes of resource products, with the single exception of forest products.[33] The real costs of other extractive products might have risen because of diminishing physical scarcity had it not been that foreign trade, with cheap transport, made it possible to import resource products at lower costs (i.e., lower relative prices) or

[32] H. J. Barnett and C. Morse, *Scarcity and Growth: The Economics of Natural Resource Availability,* Johns Hopkins, Baltimore, 1963, p. 157.
[33] *Ibid.,* p. 184.

abundant capital and effective technology made it possible to procure them by new processes or to substitute new products for them.

A major resource problem is presented by water, which is running short in the Southwest of the United States, and which may become more expensive in other developed areas in this country and abroad. There is no substitute for water. But water can be produced from energy and sea water, and energy from shale, if not from the sun, and atomic fission is available in considerable abundance at only slightly higher cost than our present sources of energy supply.

With underdeveloped countries, however, resource problems are much more significant in the absence of cheap capital. The most striking example of a country lacking land is Israel, which is substituting capital and labor resourcefulness for it—with difficulty. There, too, the problem proves to be not lack of land, but lack of water, especially in the south, with transport of water long distances from the north an expensive solution. Much farm produce has a water content 24 to 40 per cent of its value, even with government subsidies on the cost of water.[34] In countries such as Iraq, the problem is not to provide water or land, but to control the water by means of irrigation, drainage, and flood control, and in areas of irrigation, by means of deeper canals to avoid progressive salination of the soil.[35] Acquiring and transporting water, or controlling it, requires large amounts of capital and diverts this useful factor from other productive employments. On the farm, agriculture tends to be capital-saving in underdeveloped countries, and capital-intensive in developed. But if more usable land is needed by an underdeveloped country, the capital to provide it is likely to be required on a sizable scale.

LAND AND TECHNOLOGY

We have already indicated how changes in technology can affect land as an agricultural or industrial input. Technology is discussed in a later chapter, but it can be mentioned here that resources are alleged to have an impact on technological change. It was the abundance of resources and the scarcity of labor, according to Habakkuk, which made the United States concentrate on labor-saving inventions, such as movable parts, in the nineteenth century, as contrasted with Britain, which had an abundance of labor and a relative scarcity of resources

[34] Alex Rubner, *The Economy of Israel: The First Ten Years*, Frederick A. Praeger, Inc., New York, 1959, p. 117.
[35] Fahim I. Qubain, *The Reconstruction of Iraq, 1950–57*, Frederick A. Praeger, Inc., New York, 1958, chap. 4.

and which developed resource-saving inventions, such as the steam engine, recycling of heat in the blast furnace, and the reciprocating engine.[36] (Interestingly enough, the French thought that the British were favored by dear labor and cheap coal, as compared with them.)[37] The resource endowment can be altered then by technical progress, and can give rise to it.

SUMMARY

We conclude that it is difficult to define land unambiguously, and as distinct from capital on the one hand and technology on the other; that land is relatively unimportant for a developed country that has abundant capital to alter the character and capacity of its existing resources and human drive and creativeness to substitute for the niggardliness of nature; but that, other things equal, more and more varied land is better than less and less varied; that land is particularly important to underdeveloped countries with their paucity of capital and innovational skill; and that to ask the question, whether small differences in land or small differences in social structure are more significant in boosting or halting economic development, is to outrun the capacity of the discipline for answering questions. Many of us have opinions; no one knows. To the particular question whether France would have grown as fast as Germany after 1870 if it had had the Ruhr, one can only reply that partial-equilibrium analysis, which assumes other things equal, is not very useful in tracing through long stages in development, when other things change. If France had had the Ruhr, other things would have changed along with the price of coal.

BIBLIOGRAPHY

A center engaged in work on the role of resources in economic development is Resources for the Future, Inc., of Washington, D.C., which supported the work of Barnett and Morse on *Scarcity and Growth: The Economics of Natural Resource Availability* cited in footnote 32). Among the many other useful publications from the same source, one most directly related to this chapter is J. J. Spengler, (ed.), *Natural*

[36] See H. J. Habakkuk, *American and British Technology in the Nineteenth Century,* Cambridge, New York, 1962.
[37] See R. E. Cameron, "Profit, croissance, et stagnation en France au XIX⁰ siècle," *Economie Appliquée,* April–September, 1957, p. 442.

Resources and Economic Growth (mentioned in footnote 5). For a useful series of maps and data on resources, see Norton Ginsburg, *An Atlas of Economic Development,* The University of Chicago Press, Chicago, 1961. For a discussion of the adequacy of raw materials in the free world, see Edward S. Mason, "Raw Materials and Economic Development," *Quarterly Journal of Economics,* August, 1952, pp. 327–341, reproduced in Okun and Richardson (eds.), selection 23.

THE ROLE OF CAPITAL

In the view of many economists, capital occupies the central position in the theory of economic development.[1] Development brings with it, as we shall see in detail below, an increase in population and in the labor force. Since land is fixed, barring discovery or a frontier, the land/labor ratio must decline. An increase in output per worker, therefore, would appear to call for an increase in the capital/labor ratio. In this view, the process of economic development is one of replacing shovels with bulldozers, scythes with reapers, three horsepower of machinery per worker with ten horsepower. As we shall note below, this view implies a fixed state of the arts, i.e., no changes in technology.

Capital is regarded not only as central to the process of development but also as strategic. In the Harrod-Domar model, which emphasizes capital, the process of capital formation is interacting and cumulative: capital formation increases income, which makes possible more capital formation. At low stages of development, poverty precludes the saving necessary to form capital. Once the process is started, however, it feeds on itself. "The rich get richer and the poor get children."

Not all economists assign first place to capital. The econometric studies which find more growth than can be attributed to capital investment (or other factors, too, for that matter) have been men-

---

[1] See, for example, Walter Heller, "Fiscal Policies for Underdeveloped Countries," in H. Wald (ed.), *Agricultural Taxation and Economic Development*, Harvard University Law School, Cambridge, Mass., 1954, p. 62; he calls it the "main key to economic development." M. Abramovitz puts it in a tie for first place: "It is probably safe to say that only the discovery and exploitation of new knowledge rivals capital formation as a cause of economic progress." See his essay, "Economics of Growth," in B. Haley (ed.), *A Survey of Contemporary Economics*, Irwin, Homewood, Ill., 1952, vol. II, p. 146. Buchanan and Ellis express the point negatively in calling a deficiency of capital the most nearly omnipresent limiting factor, and one that is frequently also the most severe: see N. S. Buchanan and H. S. Ellis, *Approaches to Economic Development*, Twentieth Century Fund, New York, 1955, p. 67.

tioned.[2] A number of quotations running capital down can be assembled: "Capital, like Patriotism, is not enough."[3] "There is greater danger that the importance of capital in relation to economic progress will be exaggerated than that it will be underrated."[4] In Indonesia, according to Paauw, the greatest short-run need is not capital.[5] Among Letwin's development fallacies, number 2 is that "more capital is better than less capital."[6] But the matter cannot be settled by counting noses on the differing sides of the debate. Our task is to discuss the types of capital, to analyze the significance of the capital/output ratio in the Harrod-Domar model, to see what criteria should be substituted for the capital/output ratio, if that is inadequate, and finally to touch on the capital-formation process.

The definition of capital is arbitrary under any circumstances, but somewhat more arbitrary in underdeveloped than in developed countries. Education, for example, is classified as consumption, though as we shall observe in the next chapter, it is increasingly regarded as "investment in human capital." Research and development are defined as intermediate goods which enter into the cost of final product, and they, too, could be capitalized as investment. In economies of a fairly low state of development, where food, clothing, and shelter will increase the productivity of underfed and badly housed labor, and simple comforts like tobacco are used as incentive goods, it is difficult to draw a line between capital and consumption. The definition of investment arbitrarily excludes all consumer purchases except houses and allocates other durable consumers' goods to consumption, even though they may give off services for periods to twenty years.

If it be admitted that the definition of capital is arbitrary, capital can be classified in a variety of ways, depending on physical characteristics, economic function, and ownership. Some systems of classification use a combination of these schemes of categorization. For present purposes, we distinguish social overhead capital, plant and equipment,

---

[2] See pp. 53–54.

[3] E. Nevin, *Capital Funds in Underdeveloped Countries*, St Martin's, New York, 1961, p. xi.

[4] A. K. Cairncross, "The Place of Capital in Economic Progress," in L. H. Dupriez (ed.), *Economic Progress*, Institut de Recherches Économiques et Sociales, Louvain, 1955, reprinted in A. K. Cairncross (ed.), *Factors in Economic Development*, G. Allen, London, 1962, p. 88.

[5] Douglas S. Paauw, *Financing Economic Development: The Indonesian Case*, Free Press, New York, 1960, pp. 77–78.

[6] William Letwin, "Four Fallacies about Economic Development," *Daedalus*, Summer, 1963, p. 403. The others: (1) manufacturing is more productive than agriculture; (3) more roads are better than fewer roads; (4) rapid economic development is better than slow economic development.

and inventories, and occasionally that part of agricultural capital which consists in improvements to·land. Social overhead capital is occasionally but not generally divided into economic investment which is needed to enable other production for the market to take place, and purely social capital, which improves well-being directly. When the distinction is made, economic overhead capital consists of public utilities—transport, including ports, roads, and railroads, electricity and gas production capacity, pipelines, transmission lines, communication networks, etc.; one can also include the buildings needed for government, fire and police protection, facilities to maintain roads, etc. Strictly social overhead capital includes the plant and equipment required for shelter, education, and public health.

Plant and equipment in industry and agriculture need little explanation. This category also includes a large component of fixed capital equipment, sometimes slighted, in office space for business administration, insurance, banking, advertising, selling, wholesale and retail trade. The inventory component of capital is another item that tends to be neglected. Leaving out consumers' inventories, it is important to count the stocks of intermediate goods and goods in process, as well as finished goods at various stages in distribution from producer to consumer.

Table 5.1 shows the composition of gross domestic capital formation in the United States for 1961 by types of capital goods, industrial use, and ownership. The total by industrial use falls below totals on the other two bases because of the exclusion of certain outlays charged as consumption and others of banks, insurance companies, professional persons, etc. The table makes clear, however, how large a proportion of total capital formation in the United States goes into dwellings— more than a fourth—the importance of capital formation in the service industries, items 1*d*, and 1*e* in the second part of the table, to which would be added 1*f* if an estimate had been available, and the considerable proportion of government capital formation in a private enterprise economy. A single year is unlikely to be representative, of course, and 1961 suffers particularly from the low net increases in inventories (stocks); these rose less than normally because of the 1961 recession.

Inventories, like office buildings, storage capacity, and stores, tend to be neglected since their productivity is not dramatically apparent. In the United States in 1949, inventories amounted to 11 per cent of total capital stock (including durable consumers' goods), i.e., $81 billion out of a total capital stock of $720 billion.[7] Almost a quarter of

[7] See R. W. Goldsmith, *A Study of Savings in the United States,* Princeton, Princeton, N.J., 1955, vol. II, pp. 14–15.

Table 5.1 | *Composition of United States Gross Domestic Capital Formation, 1961*
(in millions of dollars at current market prices)

By type of capital good	
1. Fixed capital formation	82,396
a. Dwellings	22,861
b. Nonresidential buildings	16,424
c. Other construction and works	17,568
d. Transport equipment	} 25,543
e. Machinery and other equipment	
2. Increase in stocks	1,827
Gross domestic capital formation	84,223

By industrial use	
1. Fixed capital formation	75,116
a. Agriculture, forestry, and fishing	3,445
b. Mining and quarrying	980
c. Manufacturing	13,680
d. Electricity, gas, and water	5,520
e. Transportation, storage, and communication	5,740
f. Banking, insurance, and real estate	
g. Ownership of dwellings	22,861
h. Public administration	14,430
i. Service industries	8,460
2. Increase in stocks	1,827
a. Agriculture, forestry, and fishing	286
b. Mining, manufacturing, and construction	1,434
c. Wholesale trade	406
d. Retail trade	−78
e. Public administration and defense	−304
f. Other	83
Gross domestic capital formation	76,943

By type of purchaser	
1. Fixed capital formation	82,396
a. Private enterprises	67,126
b. Public corporations	} 2,166
c. Government enterprises	
d. General government	13,104
2. Increase in stocks	1,827
a. Private enterprises	2,131
b. Public corporations	
c. Government enterprises	} −304
d. General government	
Gross domestic capital formation	84,223

NOTE: The estimates of gross domestic fixed capital formation by type of capital good and by type of purchaser are not comparable with the estimates by industrial use. This is due to the exclusion in the latter estimates of (1) certain capital outlays charged to current expenditures and (2) certain capital outlays of institutions, banks, insurance and real estate firms, and professional persons.
SOURCE: *Yearbook of National Account Statistics, 1962,* United Nations, New York, 1963, pp. 282–283.

this was farm inventories, which tend to be high; most crops are harvested once a year and consumed evenly over the twelve months, which makes for an average inventory of half a year's production. But it is easy to overlook both the capital intensity of processes which require a smooth flow of material from one stage to the next[8] and the productivity which inventories provide in smoothing out interruptions in the flow of materials and output through the stages of production and distribution. The Soviet bloc view of national income makes no allowance for the productivity of the transport and distribution processes, as contrasted with the production of material goods, and tends in consequence to find plant standing idle, with zero product, because of lack of materials or work in process, or consumers wasting time and effort before empty shops.

THE CAPITAL/OUTPUT RATIO

Chapter 3 has already introduced us to the Harrod-Domar growth model and the capital/output ratio which plays such a big role in it. Here we discuss the statistical derivation of the ratio and its usefulness. If the capital/output ratio be rejected as a basis for allocating investment in a multisectoral (or disaggregated) model where choices must be made, what better investment criterion can be devised?

For most purposes, it is the marginal or incremental capital/output ratio (ICOR) which is wanted, rather than the average (ACOR). We want to know how much additional output will be obtained for an additional amount of investment. Let us suppose that there is no difficulty in defining national production or capital formation. Is there then any problem in calculating the ICOR? The answer, as one might expect, is yes.

First, suppose we have three observations of capital and output, as in Figure 5.1a. Is it possible, by drawing a line between them and extending it to the origin, to conclude that the ICOR is the same as the ACOR, and steady? It is not. To leap to this conclusion is possible only if other things are equal. If technology has been changing, as in Figure 5.1b, the ACOR and the ICOR may each be steady, but widely different. Or technology may be unchanged, as in Figure 5.1c, but with very different ICORs in each period and the same ACOR. The model assumes other things equal; in the real world, other things change.

---

[8] It is said that one of the big arguments against cottage weaving in India is the heavy cost of inventories in thousands of scattered locations. With bigger scale, the ratio of inventories to output can be reduced, and capital saved. (The other big argument is quality control.)

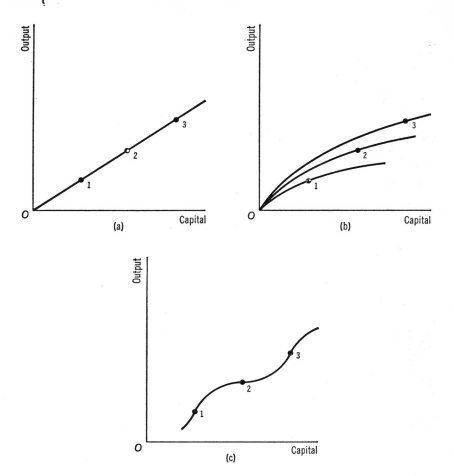

Figure 5.1 | Estimating the capital/output ratio from historical data.

Second, should we take ICOR gross of depreciation or net? It evidently makes a considerable difference since, unless D or depreciation is very small

$$\frac{I}{dY} < \frac{I+D}{dY+D}$$

Assume there are two projects, each costing $100 but of very different lives: one lasting twenty years, the other four. Suppose that there is no ambiguity about what depreciation should be charged and that straight-line cost is the appropriate basis, physically as well as financially. Then as the table shows, the gross ICORs favor project B, the net ICORs project A.

Table 5.2 | *Gross and Net ICORs for Two Projects Costing $100*

Project	Life (years)	Gross Yield (dollars)	Gross ICOR	Annual Depreci- ation (dollars)	Net Yield (dollars)	Net ICOR
A	20	35	2.86	5	30	3.3
B	4	50	2.0	25	25	4.0

The answer to the question which one ought to take, like the answers to so many questions in economics, is, "It depends." Here, it depends on whether the capital structure is likely to be fairly stable or whether transformations in the structure of the economy, discussed below, are frequent. With stability, it is sufficient to deal with net output, since depreciation allowances are not needed to shift capital to other sectors. If there is a large possibility that capital will be shifted into other industries, however, as transformation occurs, then gross production is the relevant concept.

Another aspect of this distinction is raised by the question whether one ought to consider the capital or the current cost of the capital input in choosing between two competing investments. Assuming a single rate of interest, the initial and the current costs of two capital projects bear the same relation to one another if the current cost is figured net of depreciation. Thus two investments of $50,000, at 6 per cent interest, cost the same whether one uses the capital expense of $50,000 or the current net cost of $3,000. But if the current cost is gross, this is no longer true. The longer the life of the capital, the smaller the depreciation charge in any one year and the lower the capital cost, calculated gross. But this type of reasoning may lead into danger, since it favors long-lived capital.

A number of other significant questions are raised by depreciation. For one, there is no fixed scientific basis for calculating depreciation for a given capital asset; in most instances, depreciation is charged fairly uniformly through the life of the assets, either in a straight line or with constant percentage formula. Physically, however, some capital tends to wear out more rapidly at the end of its life than in the beginning. It is possible, therefore, in a growing economy, to reinvest depreciation allowances from recent investments in new capital formation and rely on the greater productivity of the economy later when development has proceeded some distance to make good the physical exhaustion of capital. If an economy is consistently growing, moreover, straight-line depreciation will continuously provide more depreciation allowance than is needed to make good physical wearing out. But this is a simple property of geometric growth.

Third, there is the drastic oversimplification involved in comparing this year's investment to this year's increase in output. This is a helpful device but analytically unsatisfactory. Some additional reality can be introduced by a lagged model, in which inputs in period t lead to outputs in period $t + 1$, and inputs in period $t + 1$ yield their outputs in period $t + 2$. But even this remains a drastic oversimplification: investment in the High Dam at Aswan will take place over ten years or so before any output is achieved, and in the business cycle a large increase in output can occur in a given year with no capital investment.

In the real world, the relation between inputs and outputs exhibits wide variety. Some inputs, like planted trees and wine to be aged, occur at one point in time and produce their outputs at a considerably later point in time. In other cases, such as inventories, inputs and outputs are both continuous. In still others, illustrated by producers' durable goods, inputs are made at a point in time and outputs are continuous. The rate of output may be constant or may vary; it may start immediately or begin only after a lag. The imputation of a given output to a given input thus becomes impossible. When an economy undertakes all three types of investment—point-input, point-output; continuous-input, continuous-output; and point-input, continuous-output—the capital/output ratio that relates this year's output to this year's investment is evidently wide of the mark.

In a system of instantaneous production, or with a fixed lag, it is appropriate to take account of the capital/output ratio. When output is received in a different time sequence, however, the investment problem becomes one of comparing the cost of a given input with the present value of its future output. This requires applying a discount to future benefits. Where output is constant, begins immediately, and continues to infinity, the present benefit can be calculated from the formula

$$V = \frac{Y}{r}$$

where V is the capitalized value of the stream of income Y at the rate of interest r. Where there is a lag in outputs, and variability, it becomes necessary to go back to the underlying series

$$V = \frac{Y_1}{1 + r} + \frac{Y_2}{(1 + r)^2} + \frac{Y_3}{(1 + r)^3} \cdots \frac{Y_n}{(1 + r)^n}$$

The longer the delay in receiving the initial outputs and the smaller they are in relation to the ultimate level of output, the lower the present value V of an investment which must be compared with its cost C. This is because the present value of the nearer outputs is higher than that of those further in the future, which are more heavily discounted. The progression above is a declining series in which the early terms, omitted in an investment with a long gestation period, are higher than the succeeding ones.

There may arise a question whether to use a simple or a compound interest formula in comparing the present value of two investments with different time profiles of income. Simple interest, as given in the preceding formula, assumes that there is no necessity to calculate the yield on the yield, whereas compound interest allows for interest to be earned on the interest. Professor Rosenstein-Rodan has suggested a compromise.[9] If the marginal rate of savings in the economy is 20 per cent, the compound interest formula should be applied to this much of the income foregone, and simple interest to the rest. This assumes that an investment in which returns are delayed or low in the early years should earn enough later to make up not only for the income actually foregone in the early period, but also that income which one could have expected the economy to earn on the portion of income foregone which would normally have been saved.

Fourth, in a disaggregated model, the task of imputation involved in associating given outputs with given inputs becomes still more difficult as a result of complementarities and external economies. It may be true that manufacturing and distribution have ICORs as low as 2:1, compared with 16:1 for electricity and railways. But beyond the point of full employment of electrical and transport capacity, the basic industries must be expanded in order to take advantage of the opportunity to invest capital "efficiently" in the low-ratio sectors. The manufacturing sector has a low ratio only if it be assumed that markets have already been linked by transport, that materials can be cheaply assembled, and that energy is available as needed. To the extent that each sector uses intermediate products and services from other sectors, the sectoral capital/output ratios have limited meaning.

Despite these objections—assuming other things equal when they

[9] In a private communication to the author.

are not, inability to decide between the gross and net measurements and the difficulty of imputing outputs to inputs, either in time or by sectors,—the ICOR is widely calculated and widely used as an overall device for projecting outputs from estimates of investment. Its predictability as suggested is weak. In the short run, it is markedly variable. But over longer periods of time, averaging the annual marginal rate appears to produce meaningful overall results. This is in large part, no doubt, the result of the law of large numbers in which opposing movements cancel out. The ICOR has in fact been remarkably similar in a large number of countries, averaging somewhere near 3.3:1.

THE INVESTMENT CRITERIA

In the early days of the Harrod-Domar model it was thought that one could use the capital/output ratio as the basis for choice of investment projects in an investment program. If $G = \dfrac{s}{k}$, the lower the k the higher the G. The first approximation to a criterion for investment choice was a project's ICOR.

This criterion did not stand up for long, however. Initial dissatisfaction with it was based on the objection made to the Harrod-Domar model in Chapter 3: that it assumed a capital theory of value, i.e., that no other inputs were needed or that they were free of cost. If this condition is not met, it becomes necessary to switch to the marginal product of capital which takes into account the relative contribution of other factors. If this is calculated by discounting the stream of future benefits V_p and the stream of future costs of other factors C_p it becomes

$$\frac{V_p - C_p}{K}$$

Only under certain conditions can this marginal productivity of capital serve as the criterion for investment, under which all projects should be undertaken in order of their

$$\frac{V_p - C_p}{K}\, s,$$

so long as any

$$\frac{V_p - C_p}{K}$$

is greater than the rate of interest. This is the private marginal productivity of capital and assumes no imperfections of the market. There are two underlying assumptions—the existence of competition and the absence of external economies or diseconomies. The former ensures that the return to a factor equals its marginal product, and the latter (to be discussed in Chapter 9) ensures that the private marginal product is equivalent to social marginal product. The distorting effects of taxes, tariffs, and subsidies are assumed away. If there exist discrepancies between actual price and competitive price—external economies or diseconomies and distortions—then private marginal product must be modified to a third criterion, social marginal product (SMP), or

$$\frac{V_p - C_p + E_p}{K}$$

where E_p is the present value of the stream of distortions, plus or minus, between private and social profitability.[10] One can of course bundle up taxes and subsidies and distortions from social value in V_p and C_p, reserving pure external economies and diseconomies for E_p. Where this is done, benefits and costs are calculated at a "shadow price," rather than a market price, i.e., a price which departs from the market price so as to reflect the true social benefit or cost. This again is a subject to be discussed in greater detail below. The shadow price of benefits may be higher or lower than the market price, depending on the direction of the distortion. Equally, the divergence may be in either direction for costs. An overvalued exchange rate may underestimate the cost of imported equipment or materials. And in the presence of large numbers of unemployed, the going wage rate may overstate the social cost of labor. At the limit, if the shadow price of labor is zero and no other distortion or externality exists, substituting social marginal product for private marginal product may have the effect of returning us to the capital/output ratio.

The shift from capital/output ratio to marginal physical product to social marginal product does not exhaust the alternatives. Galenson and Leibenstein[11] have suggested that the project should be chosen which maximizes growth, not in the short run, but over a longer period of time. In a disaggregated growth model, different projects not only

[10] H. B. Chenery, "The Application of the Investment Criterion," *Quarterly Journal of Economics,* February, 1953, pp. 76–96.
[11] W. Galenson and H. Leibenstein, "Investment Criteria, Productivity and Economic Development," *Quarterly Journal of Economics,* August, 1955, pp. 343–370.

have different outputs immediately because of differences in productivity. They may also have different impacts on future investment because the productivity of each is associated with a different marginal propensity to save. If one project is labor-intensive and results in large wage payments, whereas another has a high proportion of income accruing to rent or to interest and dividends, the amount reinvested in the future from the income produced is likely to be higher from the second than from the first. Its "marginal per capita reinvestment quotient" (MPCRQ) is higher. If it be assumed that the marginal propensity to save is positive, but that no savings occur until after a certain level of income has been reached (i.e., the intercept is negative), the investment criterion becomes

$$\frac{Y_p - C_w}{K}$$

where C_w is wage costs. (This formula could be corrected for externalities and distortions without changing the principle.) To maximize growth, one should equalize in every use not the marginal productivity of capital (nor the SMP) but the MPCRQ. In particular, one should favor capital-intensive over labor-intensive projects on the ground that the former produce more savings than the latter.

Galenson and Leibenstein favor skewed income distributions as an outcome of investment decisions, partly because they are concerned with the impact of higher employment and wages on population growth, still to be discussed in Chapter 15. But note that income skewness may not be enough if the marginal propensity to save differs between factor shares, as Ricardo thought. Ricardo, it will be recalled, believed that reinvestment came from profits, but that rent was entirely spent on consumption. In a three-factor model, one should emphasize the high return to profits, not the low return to labor, since historically low wages combined with high rents have not led to growth to the same extent, for example, as high wages, high profits, and low rent, the model of economic development with unlimited supplies of land.[12]

The Galenson-Leibenstein model has been criticized further for its

[12] See D. C. North, "Location Theory and Regional Economic Growth," *Journal of Political Economy*, June, 1955, pp. 243–258, where growth occurred with high wages (starting in the Oregon lumber industry), and his "Agriculture in Regional Economic Growth," *Journal of Farm Economics*, December, 1959, pp. 943–951, where economic growth did not occur in the cotton South, despite subsistence wages (in slavery) and high returns to land, because the rents were consumed or invested outside the region.

readiness to sacrifice present for future consumption, at heavy social cost for today's population. It has been pointed out, however, that the SMP criterion of Chenery and the MPCRQ criterion are related in a way which depends on the rate of interest. When the rate of interest is very low, and approaches zero, future output is valued nearly as much as today's. Social marginal product will then be maximized by choosing very capital-intensive projects which accelerate growth; the SMP formula becomes close to the MPCRQ. With high rates of interest, on the other hand, growth in the future is much less valued than growth in the short run, and the Galenson-Leibenstein gloss on the Chenery criterion has little if any significance. The investment-criterion discussion thus gets back to the classical economics of interest theory.

CHANNELS OF INVESTMENT

As a preliminary discussion of sources of saving for capital formation, it is desirable to examine the agencies engaged in making investments. It is generally felt that the limiting factor in capital formation is the volume of savings and that all the savings accumulated can be readily invested. More recently, however, this view has been disputed. The International Bank for Reconstruction and Development has suggested that the bottleneck is not funds, but projects which are sufficiently advanced in planning to warrant investment consideration. Another lack may be businessmen ready and willing to undertake the investment functions of the entrepreneur.

Investment in a developing society is undertaken by farmers, by domestic and foreign entrepreneurs, and by government. Where housing is owned by the occupants, as in the United States, rather than rented from landlords or government, there is another channel of investment—the consumer—who is also responsible, of course, for investment in consumers' durables if these are included in capital.

Farmers are responsible for all but the largest investment projects in agriculture. Government is clearly obligated to furnish social overhead and economic overhead capital except in rare instances. These will occur when a large and rich company, generally foreign, undertakes a big investment in a poor country and wants to raise the efficiency of its workers through investment in education and health (the Arabian American Oil Company in Saudi Arabia, or the United Fruit Company in many countries of Central America) or when transport and housing facilities are totally absent, as is likely in mining regions, in which case the company railroad and the company town may be constructed privately.

Difficult questions arise in the area of productive investment when entrepreneurship is weak and government is inadequately equipped by training and experience to substitute for it. The range of issues involved will be explored in Chapters 8 and 11.

When the private entrepreneur is the channel of investment, it does not follow that he is the sole decision-maker in the process. If he has accumulated his own capital, and obeys the laws, he may be. But in the majority of instances, the entrepreneur employs borrowed or external capital, and the decision to lend to him may be more significant than his readiness to take the risk. While the problem in a number of underdeveloped countries today is to find enough able would-be entrepreneurs, more difficulty was encountered in the history of Western Europe and the United States in deciding which of an unlimited array of potential investors was to be entrusted with capital. In this decision-making, the role of banks has been of great importance historically.

It is a little old-fashioned today to pay much attention to the bank as a director of the flow of capital. Corporations in the United States have largely freed themselves of the dependence on banks characteristic of the three or four centuries before World War I. Reinvestment of corporate profits and sale of securities to the public through investment bankers, or directly to insurance companies, have lessened the extent to which large business in the United States depends on the good will of the commercial banks. In contrast, however, are the banks in Western Europe in all of modern times, particularly in the nineteenth century. Entrepreneurs proposed; banks disposed.

It appears unlikely that the commercial bank will play the decisive role in channeling capital in economic development in those countries now underdeveloped. This role is probably assigned to government, even though the investment be in the private sector and with private funds. The foreign entrepreneur with capital must still obtain a license to qualify under laws concerning foreign investment, and to this end he must submit his proposals for government approval. The domestic entrepreneur may be financed by a development bank, using government funds (and perhaps some International Bank capital). Large domestic enterprises which want access to foreign capital must obtain the approval of government to borrow, and in some cases, its guarantee. Whether the capital is privately or publicly owned may make little difference in this respect; government directs investment in the private as well as the public sector.

SOURCES OF CAPITAL

In a fundamental sense, capital formation is possible only when a society produces a surplus of consumers' goods sufficient to satisfy the wants of the workers engaged in producing capital, i.e., producing goods which are not themselves consumed during the period. In primitive economies this surplus consists largely of food and to a lesser extent of clothing. The problem of capital formation in these societies is seen as one of feeding (and clothing) the labor taken away from the production of food and clothing and put to work to produce capital. In more developed societies, which live further from the margin of subsistence, essentially the same problem presents itself in another form: how to get the savings out of current production to form capital. These savings may be regarded as consumption goods produced but not consumed by their producers or as capital goods produced and offset by the savings of their producers, which reduces their demand for consumers' goods.

Saving may be undertaken by business, by households, or by government in the domestic economy, or it may come from abroad. These savings may be voluntary, or they may be the involuntary result of inflation. The question of foreign borrowing will be left for later discussion, as will a number of aspects of government capital formation. Here, however, it is appropriate to indicate some of the major factors affecting personal and business savings.

In agriculture, saving frequently takes place in kind. The farmer clears land, repairs buildings, builds fences. This is simultaneously saving and investment. To a limited extent saving in kind can take place in the nonagricultural sector, particularly perhaps in the accumulation of inventories and in owner-constructed housing. For the most part, however, saving takes place through investment of income received in money form.

A variety of influences affects the volume of personal savings. The rate of saving is a function of level of income; its distribution; the prevalence of institutions which make for saving, such as the habit of life insurance, the practice of amortizing mortgages, the horizontal family in which each generation is expected to provide for its own security; and the existence of incentives and opportunities for social advance through economic betterment. A separate item should perhaps be made of the value system of the society which may attach special importance to the accumulation of wealth, whether for religious or secular motives. It is difficult to assign relative priorities to these and other contributing factors, partly because a factor may be of different significance under different circumstances. In a closed society in which social mobility is impossible, a highly skewed income distribution may not lead to a high level of saving; and the saving that does occur may take a nonproductive form in jewelry, precious metals, and luxurious dwellings. In a society, however, in which social advance comes from economic success, the more highly skewed the distribution of income, the higher the capital formation. Lewis has pointed out that in a society where 10 per cent of the population receives 40 per cent of the income, as is true of many underdeveloped countries, it should be easy

Figure 5.2 | Gross domestic capital formation as a percentage of gross domestic product compared with income per capita, about 1961. sources: Gross domestic capital formation as a percentage of gross domestic product derived from data in *Yearbook of National Accounts Statistics, 1962,* United Nations, New York, 1963; income per capita, table 1.1, Average Income per Capita in Selected Countries, 1949 and 1961.

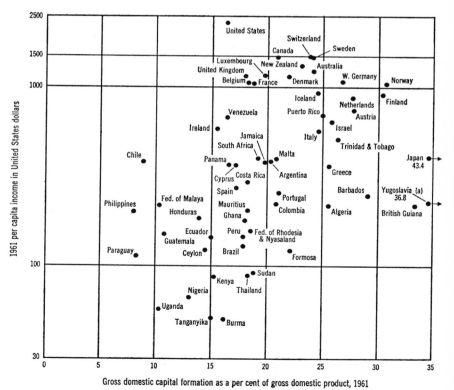

(a) For gross material product

to increase savings to 20 per cent of national income.[13] This would appear to make the level of income less important than its distribution.

There is, in fact, only the loosest correlation between rates of capital formation and level of income, as shown in Figure 5.2. The correlation between rates of capital formation and rates of growth is undoubtedly higher, although even this is not perfect: Japan with a rate of gross capital formation over 40 per cent in 1961 has a high rate of growth, but the next highest figures recorded—for British Guiana and Norway —are associated with much lower growth rates. And France and the United Kingdom have the same proportions of gross capital formation, but France has a much higher growth rate.

If the connection between levels of income and total investment is loose, that between income and the source of savings is somewhat clearer. Figure 5.3 gives household savings as a proportion of gross domestic capital formation, compared with income per capita, based on figures assembled by Simon Kuznets. The data are not unambiguous or free of error, since in a number of countries household savings are estimated as a residual and refer not only to consumption units but also to unincorporated enterprises. But insofar as figures can be believed, they show that with some exceptions households provide an increasing portion of savings as incomes grow. In the poorer countries, the largest proportion of savings is likely to come from government, and in rapidly growing economies, from corporations. Taking an historical look at the United States, and using Goldsmith data, Kuznets found that nonagricultural individuals (as distinct from farmers, unincorporated businesses, business corporations, and government) have been responsible for 50 to 70 per cent of United States savings, as compared with the figure of 29 per cent for households given in Figure 5.3 for 1961; business corporations for approximately 25 per cent, over the period from 1897 to 1949, and giving little weight to the depression decade 1930–1939. For the rest, the share of farmers and unincorporated businesses has declined; that of government, risen.

There is no reason, however, to regard these proportions as typical. Nor is it always clear in a country how sharp the distinction is between individuals and businesses.

Business savings come out of profits. Some considerable amount of gross investment, of course, comes from depreciation and depletion allowances. Depreciation is naturally much higher as a percentage of income in a developed country with a large stock of capital than in a country beginning its economic growth. Moreover, depreciation is a source of capital formation in a sense if the capital replacement is

[13] *Op. cit.*, p. 236.

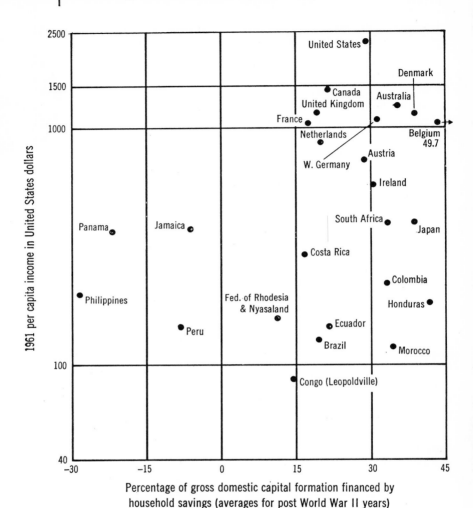

Figure 5.3 | Percentage of gross domestic capital formation financed by household savings (averages of post-World War II years) compared with per capita income, about 1961. SOURCES: Percentage of gross domestic capital formation financed by household savings, Simon Kuznets, "Quantitative Aspects of the Growth of Nations, V. Capital Formation Proportions: International Comparisons for Recent Years," appendix table 6, pp. 92–94, in *Economic Development and Cultural Change,* July, 1960, part II; income per capita, table 1.1, Average Income per Capita in Selected Countries, 1949 and 1961.

more productive than the capital worn out. But net savings come from profits.

W. A. Lewis believes that the secret to the rapid increase from 5 per cent of income saved in a stagnant country to 10 to 15 per cent in a growing economy is to be found in a high rate of profit.[14] High incomes as such are not significant: rich landlords are limited in their capacity to expand, likely to be satisfied with their social status, and are usually high consumers. But high profits, whether retained by businesses or passed along in dividends to individuals, lead to reinvestment, expansion, development, growth, at least if the economic growth takes place under capitalistic institutions.

Government as an investor may finance its capital formation with internal savings or with external savings acquired from households or business. Internal savings represent the difference between taxes and expenditure for governmental expenditures other than those for capital formation. These savings, of course, can exceed the amount of government investment and become available for investment by private business. If government taxes the economy to finance its investment, it may seem ironic to call the result government saving, but such is the practice. If, on the other hand, government finances its investment through a deficit, the saving is done in other sectors. The saving may be voluntary, and take the form of an expansion of holdings of government debt by households and business, including, it may be well to note, government debt in bank notes. Or, if the deficit is financed in inflationary fashion, the saving is involuntary and represented by the reduction in consumption caused by the rise in prices, as the government bids resources away from the other sectors. The merits, if any, and demerits of deficit financing by governments will be discussed further below. At this point, however, it can be indicated merely that economic development can occur on this basis, as the example of the Soviet Union bears out.

CAPITAL AS A KEY

Is capital formation the key to economic development? Many think so. Capital can substitute for resources; capital can substitute for labor.

[14] *Op. cit.*, pp. 234ff. In his earlier article, "Economic Development with Unlimited Supplies of Labour," *The Manchester School*, May, 1954, pp. 139–191, reprinted in Agarwala and Singh (eds.), selection 6; Morgan, Betz, and Choudhry (eds.), selection 20; Okun and Richardson (eds.), selection 24, Lewis calls the problem of explaining the increase of saving from 4 to 5 per cent of national income to 12 to 15 per cent the "central problem in the theory of economic development."

Given a capital/output ratio of some sort, capital formation leads to more output, which provides a surplus for further investment and further increases in output. But there are several reasons for believing that capital formation, while necessary, cannot explain economic development. First is the fact that the takeoff, in Rostow's phrase, from 4 to 5 per cent to 12 to 15 per cent, to use Lewis's figures, is often (but not always) abrupt. To explain it, one must go beyond the geometric-growth type of model in which capital leads to growth in income which leads to more capital. Second, the growth takes place at rates which are higher than can be explained on the basis of capital formation alone. Third, as economic growth picks up, the rate of capital formation levels off, which requires more explanation than is provided by a theory which gives the central role to capital.

It is true that capital formation is a tender plant. Its germination may be frustrated by poverty, by taboos on lending, by a preference for investment in housing, bidding up the prices of agricultural land and commodity stocks on the part of those with wealth. Once started, its growth may be stunted by hoarding, by the export of capital to financial centers, by distortions introduced by inflation, by conspicuous consumption. Or savings available for external financing may not be loaned to investors through the mechanism of the banking system and capital markets. Finally, once investment takes place, there are important problems of ensuring that it finds its way into the most productive lines which will lead to further output and growth. Accordingly, it is appropriate to spend time on problems of capital formation.

But capital formation is not the only ingredient of the growth process.

SUMMARY

Economic growth requires and depends on inputs of capital. The rate of growth implied by a given rate of capital formation is a function of the capital/output ratio and the rate of population increase. The capital/output ratio and the marginal efficiency of capital, identical when other factors are redundant and receive no incomes, normally differ. The capital/output ratio represents the relationship between all or increments of capital with total or incremental output, without regard to other factors, whether unchanged or variable. The marginal efficiency of capital, on the other hand, is the incremental output associated with an increment of investment when all other factors are held constant. The capital/output ratio is widely used in economic-development discussion, but serves principally as a handy, rough measure which is not useful for fine work. Its drawbacks include ambiguity over whether to take output net or gross; the problem of associating given outputs with given investment, whether by sectors or in time; and disassociating simple growth based on capital investment from changes in output produced by changing technology, discoveries of land, etc.

The process of growth involves savings to create a surplus for capital investment. The source of voluntary saving is intricately bound up in social attitudes toward economic mobility; in income distribution, by sectors and factor shares; and in the level of income. Saving can be undertaken by government, and can be forced on households and corporations by inflation. One of the mysteries about economic development is what makes the rate of saving rise in the early stages and decline in the late.

BIBLIOGRAPHY

The best summary of the various investment criteria is Hollis B. Chenery's "Comparative Advantage and Development Policy," *American Economic Review*, March, 1961, pp. 18–51, reprinted in Morgan, Betz, and Choudhry (eds.), selection 17, with its useful set of bibliographical references, including those on the investment criteria cited in footnotes 10 and 11. See also A. K. Sen, "Some Notes on the Choice of Capital Intensity in Development Planning," *Quarterly Journal of Economics*, November, 1957, pp. 561–574; Ragnar Nurkse, *Problems of Capital Formation in Underdeveloped Countries*, Blackwell, Oxford, 1953, which is commented on by Celso Furtado in "Capital Formation and Economic Development," original in Portugese, reprinted in Agarwala and Singh (eds.), selection 5.

For a useful discussion of the accumulation of capital through financial institutions, see Edward Nevin, *Capital Funds in Underdeveloped Countries*, St Martin's, New York, 1961. See also William Diamond, *Development Banks*, Johns Hopkins, Baltimore, 1957.

6 | *Labor*

THE QUANTITY AND QUALITY OF LABOR

Initial interest in discussions of economic growth turned on the quantity of labor and ignored the important dimension of quality. Quantity and quality were both considered in the discussion of capital, after a fashion, because capital is measured in value terms—in dollars. But labor is measured in numbers of people, occasionally divided between men and women and rarely between unskilled and skilled. The input in a production function was usually merely numbers.

This disregard for quality has recently ceased. As mentioned earlier, there are economists who believe that changes in the quality of the work force are the fundamental explanation of the fact that economic growth proceeds in advanced countries more rapidly than can be accounted for by the record of inputs of capital and labor. Moreover, differences between levels of development between countries may be explicable in the same terms. Kuznets has lumped technology and the capacity of labor together as more important than physical equipment:

> The major capital stock of an industrially advanced country is not its physical equipment: it is the body of knowledge amassed from tested findings and discoveries of empirical science, and the capacity and training of its population to use this knowledge effectively.[1]

The point may be put more sharply by contrasting two situations: one in which a country has had its physical capital destroyed, but has a highly trained and energetic labor force; the other with the latest capital equipment in abundance, but only unskilled labor with, say, two years of secondary schooling. An economy can be reequipped with capital plant in a remarkably short period—as the experience of Japanese and German economic recovery after World War II suggests.[2]

[1] "Toward a Theory of Economic Growth," in R. Lekachman (ed.), *National Policy for Economic Welfare at Home and Abroad,* Doubleday, Garden City, N.Y., 1955, p. 39.
[2] See T. W. Schultz, "Investment in Human Capital," *American Economic Review,* March, 1961, pp. 6, 7, reprinted in Morgan, Betz, and Choudhry (eds.), selection 18.

It is likely that it would take far longer to get the other economy going. Starting from scratch, it is more time consuming to build a skilled labor force than to construct a steel mill.

The quality of the labor force means more than simply technical skill. It includes "the will to economize," interest in output for the sake of output, the spirit of teamwork, and other elusive noneconomic qualities. It has been said that a modern fishing trawler with the latest equipment is manned in Norway by 7 men, in Japan by 12 to 14, and in India by 20 to 25. Each task to be performed by the small crew can be carried out by someone on the large. But the organization of the Norwegians, to be discussed further in Chapter 8, plus their versatility, energy, and appetite for income make their labor much more productive.

THE TRANSITION FROM THE TRADITIONAL SOCIETY TO INDUSTRIALIZATION

Chapter 2 has referred to the need to alter the social matrix in which men work in a traditional society. The shift from this society to what we may characterize as the factory system—recognizing that only a relatively small proportion of men work in actual factories in advanced economies—has been analyzed in stages. Kerr, Harbison, Dunlop, and Myers[3] have broken the process down into recruitment, commitment, advancement, and maintenance. Recruitment is selecting, hiring, and assigning people to jobs. Commitment means achieving the workers' permanent attachment to industrial employment as a way of life. Advancement is the process of building skills, work habits, and incentives for productive employment. Maintenance covers the various arrangements to provide security on and off the job—social security, including medical care, unemployment insurance, old-age pensions, etc.

The process of recruitment is closely linked to commitment. If we assume that entrepreneurs are able to organize their operations to maintain a steady flow of work, and do not prefer to rely on casual labor, hired daily (as in a few remaining industries in advanced countries, notably the docks), recruitment may take place indirectly through a system of compradors, or village foremen, who guarantee to supply so many hands. Or hiring may be direct. With either the comprador system or direct hiring, if there is no commitment on the part of labor to town and factory life, recruiting becomes a continuous

[3] Clark Kerr, Frederick Harbison, John T. Dunlop, and Charles A. Myers, *Industrialism and Industrial Man*, Harvard, Cambridge, Mass., 1960.

problem. Absenteeism is likely to be high as the labor returns to the farm or village for the harvest (a particular problem in India) or turnover rates very large as labor saves up a given amount in the town and quits—to buy a farm or a bride (a special problem in tropical Africa).[4] In its extreme form, this consists in the phenomenon known as a backward-bending supply curve, under which higher prices for labor produce not more offers of work but less (and lower wages not less but more). The backward-bending supply curve arises from a desire to achieve a certain level of income and no more. It gives way to the more normal upward-sloping curve when labor acquires an appetite for goods.

The comprador system, high rates of turnover, or high absenteeism interferes with the organization of work in a plant and raises labor costs. Occasionally a rather special system of organizing labor will grow up to stabilize the situation, as in the Japanese textile factories where young women used to work for a few years before marriage, living in dormitories under discipline organized by the factory. For the most part, however, the task is to achieve a commitment to the pattern of industrial life and the discipline of regular work. This poses serious problems where the new recruit feels keenly his loss of freedom and the support of his kinship group.

It is thought that the labor unions in underdeveloped countries may be able to assist in the processes of recruitment and, especially, commitment. Labor unions evolved late in Western industrial society as a reaction and protest against industrial capitalism and to redress the discrepancy in bargaining power in the market between workers and employers.[5] In underdeveloped countries, however, they emerged at an early stage, achieved political power, and became embroiled in national problems extending beyond wages and conditions of work in separate factories. In particular they have raised protests against the evils of industrialization generally and played a political role in the development process, along with government, legislators, and military and religious leaders, helping to shape decisions over social security, investment, national allocations, and the ownership of enterprise. In some instances, such as the Histadrut in Israel, a union owns and operates a variety of housing and community services and invests in business enterprises, along with its prominent political role.

Recruitment of labor could be helped if institutions more forward-looking than the comprador were available to replace the solidarity of

---

[4] E. J. Berg, "Backward-sloping Labor Supply Functions in Dual Economies: The Africa Case," *Quarterly Journal of Economics*, August, 1961, pp. 468–492.

[5] C. Kerr, F. H. Harbison, J. T. Dunlop and C. A. Myers, "The Labour Problem in Economic Development," *International Labour Review*, March, 1955, p. 6.

the tribe or village and to assuage the anxieties of the industrial system for the individual. The labor union in particular is expected to assist in effecting the commitment of labor to industrial life. Instead of simply bargaining for higher wages, it is urged to teach that higher incomes wait on productivity and that profit performs a function in encouraging investment. But to ask a union to undertake this task is to convert it into an overseer and to undermine its appeal to workers which is based on protest against the worker's loss of freedom and leisure, his lack of security, and his inability to satisfy his wants.

If special arrangements, or trade unions, do not speed the process of achieving commitment, time will. Time weakens the links to the traditional society and encourages submission to the discipline of factory and town. Where there are large supplies of labor or where the process of growth is slow, the task is difficult. Agricultural workers may be crowded into the tar-paper shacks of the towns, unable to find jobs to which they are willing to be committed, and left to earn a precarious living shining shoes, collecting old clothes, or pumping up bicycle tires. If growth gets under way, however, interest in high living standards is likely to induce workers to submit to the exigencies of industrial life.

INVESTMENT IN HUMAN CAPITAL

It is not enough to recruit a large industrial labor force and induce it to accept the values of industrial society. Beyond a minimal stage of development, the major requirement is for foremen, technicians, supervisors, maintenance and production mechanics, and engineers.[6] The capacity to handle modern technology in the United States does not reside in a small group of business and engineering school graduates, but is diffused throughout the culture. The great majority of employees are interested in productivity, and their early training, formal and informal, is machine-, production-, and team-directed. In underdeveloped countries, therefore, it is not enough to cultivate a handful of entrepreneurs and business executives. This means upgrading any existing labor force in a less developed country to provide the junior officers and sergeants and corporals to fill in the organization between the privates and generals.

That part of advancement, as it is called by Kerr et al., which consists of building productive skills, is by no means limited to the place of work. On-the-job training is an important element in "investment

---

[6] United Nations, *Processes and Problems of Industrialization in Underdeveloped Countries,* United Nations, New York, 1955, pp. 41ff.

in human capital," and a neglected one.[7] Other forms of such investment, however, include formal schooling, adult education, health, migration, and labor-market information.

Let us start with formal education. Professor Schultz recognizes that the cost of education includes, along with investment in human capital, a good deal of consumption and some expenditure which is partly consumption, partly investment.[8] In principle, he suggests, this objection could be overcome by capitalizing the yield on education, i.e., the difference in incomes received on the average by people of different levels of education. This procedure, however, has drawbacks: it makes no allowance for differences in native ability which are highly correlated with formal education and it fails to take account of short-run market conditions which may create divergence between cost and the capitalized value of yield. The return on a Ph.D. in English or history is lower than that on a doctorate in electronics, though the costs may be the same. And while it may be true that part of the reason Negroes and women typically earn less than whites and males is that they have less education or a lower level of health, in cases where educational levels and health are the same, their earnings still differ.

Schultz's calculations run mainly in terms of costs, rather than yields. These costs, it should be pointed out, include not only operating costs of educational institutions and interest on the plant, but also the income foregone by students. In the United States, this opportunity cost borne by the student amounts to more than half the total. Schultz observes that the stock of education embodied in the labor force (not the population as a whole) rose about 8½ times from 1900 to 1956, whereas the stock of reproducible capital rose 4½ times.[9] This is his explanation for the "residual."[10] But this stock, as we have indicated, includes courses in English literature, foreign languages, music, art, and so on, which, unless taught to prospective teachers of the subjects, are largely consumption.

After formal education comes on-the-job training. These are to some

[7] Gary S. Becker, "Investment in Human Capital: A Theoretical Analysis," *Journal of Political Economy,* October, 1962, supplement, p. 10.

[8] *Op. cit.,* p. 8. The distinction between consumption and investment in education is not that between general and vocational education. Peter H. Odegard (see "The Specialist and the Citizen," *The Key Reporter,* Summer, 1962, p. 3) properly insists that general education has a vocational utility. In addition, it possesses an external economy in which the private benefit of general education simultaneously benefits the society. This is the justification for making so much of education a public expenditure.

[9] *Op. cit.,* p. 11.

[10] See p. 54.

degree substitutes, but largely complements. There are no estimates of the costs or benefits of this training, but even outside of direct expenses, there is a considerable indirect cost in situations where a salary is paid from the beginning, though the productivity of the new worker is low. Becker points out that in competitive labor markets, the cost of training is borne by the worker who accepts a lower salary than he could earn in another line of work because of the opportunity to obtain training.[11] To the extent that this is so, it undermines the view that on-the-job training is an external economy, the benefit accruing to the person trained and the economy as a whole, but escaping the command of the firm. It seems likely that practice will differ from industry to industry and from profession to profession since the world is not perfectly competitive. Scottish accountants will work for two years without pay to learn their profession, but graduates of the Harvard Business School will start at $1,000 a month.

In Western Europe, apprenticeship used to be the method of learning a trade and of creating the cadres of skilled workers on which the economy depends. Schultz believes that apprenticeship has declined not only because of the rise of formal schooling, but also because of the difficulty of enforcing apprenticeship agreements during their later years when the value of the apprentice's services are worth more than he is paid.[12]

The importance of on-the-job training, including the apprentice system, is stressed by R. C. Blitz, commenting upon the role of education in Chilean economic growth.[13] Chile is not well equipped with highly trained professional personnel, such as engineers and doctors, owing to the limitation of education to the upper classes, but it is worse off in the skilled subprofessional grades. In engineering the ratio of engineers to technicians is 1:1.65 compared with a more normal ratio of 1:3 or 1:4. This gap is attributed to the fact that Chile borrowed feudalism from Spain, but without the guild system of industry with its apprenticeship for training.

An important part of on-the-job training is carried out in countries of all levels of development through military service. Here the need for skills is felt in the armed forces, but with limited periods of service, upgraded workers are supplied to the civilian economy in a continuous stream. The more highly mechanized and electrified the

[11] Becker, *op. cit.*, p. 16.
[12] Schultz, *op. cit.*, pp. 9, 10.
[13] See "Some Observations about the Chilean Educational System and Its Relation to Economic Growth," paper (mimeographed) submitted to the Conference on the Role of Education in Early Stages of Economic Development, University of Chicago, April, 1963, pp. 15–18.

armed services, the greater the training requirement and the greater the subsequent civilian benefit. Where the military has difficulty in retaining enough specialists for its own use, it can use economic incentives, such as reenlistment bonuses. In some poor countries, however, a deliberate policy for producing skilled mechanics, electricians, electronic technicians, and medical attendants—to limit the list—has much to recommend it. The military benefits of a peacetime army are at best contingent. To use the large numbers of hours of low military productivity to give further training to men whose formal education has stopped is not only to benefit them but also to stimulate growth.

On-the-job training is fairly pure investment. So are adult education after working hours, the costs of migration undergone to obtain a higher-paying job, and the provision of information on the labor market enabling a better matching of employers and would-be employees. Adult education is largely a private affair, undertaken by the worker in night school, correspondence school, or agricultural off-season courses. The costs of migration are usually private, although some employers, in a tight market, may pay the costs of moving and settling. Improving the functioning of the labor market by the provision of more information is often a governmental activity, but may be done privately, with costs borne either by the employer or employee. (It is not always possible to tell where these costs are borne, except in a highly competitive labor market when they are likely to be openly met by the employee or pushed on him through lower wage rates.)

The provision of health services is partly a public, partly a private, function, but like education, it contains a complex mixture of consumption and investment. Investments in health can be made not only in health programs, but also in the form of food, housing, recreation, and clothing,[14] which emphasizes the consumption aspects. Where diet is inadequate, health undermined by insalubrious housing, and so on, it is clear that investment in food and housing will improve productivity and will have a yield comparable to that of an investment. Yields can be calculated on investments to reduce the incidence of tuberculosis, malaria, hookworm, and similar debilitating diseases, and will in most cases be found to be positive and high.

A major difficulty of the investment-in-human-wealth approach, as exemplified in health programs, however, is that the benefits are frequently negative, i.e., preventing losses, whereas the costs are positive. Or the economy as a whole is asked to make investments on the basis of yields which accrue as consumption and increased productivity to private individuals. Where the individual invests and benefits,

[14] See Selma J. Mushkin, "Health as an Investment," *Journal of Political Economy,* October, 1962, supplement, p. 130.

as in private schooling, adult education, migration, and on-the-job training, to the extent the costs are pushed off on the employee, the expenditure can evidently be thought of as a proper investment, subject to the economic rules of maximization, minimization, and equalization. But where the state invests, with an arbitrary distribution of benefits relative to taxes, the analogy between investment in material plant and equipment and investment in human beings weakens.

HUMAN WEALTH AS A CRITERION FOR INVESTMENT IN EDUCATION

The concept of investment in human beings has been found stimulating and even "exciting" by its originators. Is it more than that? Is it specifically a guide to investment in education? Should governments invest in education until the yield from such investment equals the rate of interest or the return available in lines of material investment? Should private decisions affecting investment in human beings be aided by provision of more information, to correct for myopia, uncertainty, and high personal rates of time discount, and by improvement of capital markets to allow people without access to capital, but with good prospective returns to education, to borrow?

Most economists who have concerned themselves with the problem have thought useful the provision of information and better borrowing facilities. In view of the uncertainty attaching to any particular education being put to productive use, there being some variability about the averages, it has sometimes been suggested that educational loans be made conditional upon achievement of a certain income. But the controversial issue is whether investment in human wealth provides a guide to educational policy.

To the extent that the concept calls attention to the payoff to education, overcomes neglect, and urges more rather than less education, it is generally useful. In most underdeveloped countries, more education is better than less. To use the concept for more precise work, at this stage of analysis, is probably impossible. As already noted, the consumption elements of education are inseparable from the investment. The private consumption element is also completely entangled in the public. There is no adequate measure of cost or scarcity value, such as would emerge from an equilibrium price system. These reasons, plus the political complication that much of the investment is private, the yield public but inalienable, have led some economists to regard the approach as unworkable in its present form. There is no real way of deciding whether another university will have a higher payoff than an equal expenditure on malaria control or on an irrigation dam. An alternative approach to educational needs must be sought, in this view, in estimating skilled manpower requirements.[15]

ESTIMATING EDUCATIONAL REQUIREMENTS

Manpower requirements are calculated from projections of employment in different industries, multiplied by coefficients of educational requirements of particular jobs and industries. As an illustration of the latter, the U.S. Department of Labor has compiled lists of the "specific vocational preparation" (SVP) (on-job training or experience) and "general educational development" (GED) (years of formal education) of a wide number of jobs in the United States.[16] The SVP ratings run from 1, which requires only a short demonstration, to 9, which takes more than ten years, with the median rating 5 representing six months to a year of training; the GED categories are seven in all, ranging from zero years of schooling to eighteen years, or two years beyond college, with the median of 4 at ten years of schooling, or two years of high school. When the United States labor force for 1950 is divided by GED and SVP categories, it emerges as in Table 6.1. From this sort of table, prepared to suit local conditions of a country, it is thought that estimates of requirements for various levels of education can be made. Note how limited the average requirement for specialized preparation is in all but mining, construction (the building trades), and business and repairs (pulled up by accountants and automobile repairs, both with three-quarters of their number of category 7). Note also that two years of high school is enough for 99 per cent of agriculture, 75 per cent of manufacturing, and two-thirds of the population as a whole.

The underlying table has no detail for teachers. Here is one of the many fields in economic development where it is necessary to start with a big push. Nigeria, according to Harbison,[17] needs to fill 80,000 jobs with high-level manpower in the next five years, 20,000 representing the senior group with university degrees, and 60,000 representing

[15] See, for example, R. S. Eckaus, "Economic Criteria for Education and Training," *Review of Economics and Statistics,* vol. 45, no. 2 (May 1964), pp. 181–190.

[16] U.S. Department of Labor, Bureau of Employment, *Estimates of Worker Trait Requirements for 4,000 Jobs* (no date).

[17] See chap. 1 of *Investment in Education: The Report of the Commission on Post-school Certificate and Higher Education in Nigeria,* Federal Government Printer, Lagos, 1960.

Table 6.1 | *Distribution of Selected Categories of the United States Labor Force According to General Education and Special Vocational Preparation in 1950*

General Education

Categories	Years of schooling	Agriculture, forestry, and fisheries	Mining (per cent)	Construction	Manufacturing	Transportation, communication, other utilities	Trade	Business and repair services	Public administration	Total
1	0	....	a	a	0.2	0.1	0.1	0.9	0.3	0.2
2	4	34.2	0.9	0.3	0.9	3.0	0.4	2.3	0.2	5.7
3	7	2.5	8.8	25.2	12.7	28.1	18.7	4.7	14.7	16.5
4	10	62.2	17.2	16.5	59.2	36.8	48.9	21.6	48.3	44.7
5	12	0.8	69.6	54.4	22.9	29.1	28.5	61.2	25.2	25.5
6	16	0.3	1.2	1.3	1.6	1.3	3.2	7.5	8.0	5.1
7	18	0.1	2.4	2.4	2.5	1.5	0.3	1.7	3.4	2.4
Average years of schooling		7.9	11.3	10.6	10.3	9.8	10.2	11.4	10.8	10.1

Special Vocational Preparation

Categories	Period of training	Agriculture, forestry, and fisheries	Mining	Construction	Manufacturing	Transportation, communication, other utilities	Trade	Business and repair services	Public administration	Total
1	0	....	a	a	0.2	0.1	0.1	0.9	0.3	0.5
2	0 to 1 month	1.6	4.1	20.1	13.9	21.0	43.4	8.1	8.2	21.0
3	1 to 3 months	34.2	0.8	1.3	1.2	10.7	3.9	1.3	13.7	7.7
4	3 to 6 months	1.1	8.7	9.7	49.7	28.3	12.7	13.4	44.4	23.7
5	6 to 12 months	0.2	5.9	2.3	5.2	10.9	3.7	7.3	5.6	5.1
6	1 to 2 years	62.0	5.1	3.1	5.4	3.5	3.7	1.4	2.2	14.4
7	2 to 4 years	0.9	73.6	56.0	18.9	20.9	32.1	65.7	21.6	23.5
8	4 to 10 years	0.2	2.0	7.6	5.6	4.8	0.5	2.0	4.1	4.2
Average (in years)		1.0	2.5	2.3	1.3	1.2	1.1	2.2	1.2	1.4

a less than 0.05.
SOURCE: R. S. Eckaus, *op. cit.*, pp. 21–31.

intermediate manpower with secondary education. These figures are inflated by the demand for teachers, to expand the Nigerian educational system, and compare with the current annual flow of 300 graduates annually from Nigerian colleges and universities, 700 graduates from abroad, and 1,000 graduates of secondary schools.

Calculating manpower requirements, moreover, may lend an air of exactness which the subject lacks. Not every person educated to a given level takes a job at that level. It is difficult to get the right proportion of skills and to end up with enough graduate engineers and not too many graduate lawyers, given the cultural value system. There may well be a great many unemployed high school graduates looking for work in government bureaus and not enough willing and capable of working in automotive repair shops. As every father of small boys knows, it is necessary to have four bags of marbles under the furniture, behind the door, and down the air register in order to have one full bag available for play.

NEGATIVE EFFECTS OF EDUCATION

There is then no certain system of estimating educational requirements or how much scarce capital should be put into educational plant, how much current income should be spent on education as consumption-cum-investment. Work to improve the data and the analysis goes forward to clarify the choices to be made. The need for more education is clear in underdeveloped countries at least,[18] even though the amounts to be sought cannot be quantified.

A word is useful on the possible sources of loss. More education for villagers sometimes makes them dissatisfied with the village and unwilling to return to it, adding to the educated unemployed in the city and robbing the village of its best intellects, rather than raising the level of village education. Education abroad, too, runs risks. The exposure to foreign standards of living (or marriage abroad) may lead to emigration at high cost in foreign exchange to the country which sponsored the education, to dissatisfaction with conditions upon return, or even, when the domestic educational system is dominated by a system of local patronage which foreign study threatens, to failure to get a job. There are no easy answers to how best to manage the

---

[18] But see D. M. Blank and G. J. Stigler, *The Demand and Supply of Scientific Personnel*, National Bureau of Economic Research, New York, 1957, which suggests that the need in the United States is less for more engineers than for better utilization of the existing supply.

large educational job which underdeveloped countries face, but perhaps this much is valid: education by foreigners is more productive for the underdeveloped country if it takes place in the country itself by foreign teachers, or if the student goes abroad, he does so later, for shorter periods, and after he has obtained his career start at home. It is reported, for example, that while there are 2,000 United States citizens teaching abroad at various levels, there are 4,000 people from the less developed countries teaching in the United States. Many of these are graduate students who undertake teaching as part of their training. Some, however, have been beguiled by higher pay and better working conditions into postponing, perhaps for a long time, their return.

SUMMARY

The quality of labor is important, as well as the quantity. The change from the traditional society to industrialization proceeds, insofar as it affects labor, by steps recognized as recruitment, commitment, advancement, and maintenance. The recruitment process in a primitive economy may have to contend with a backward-bending supply curve. Commitment is a difficult process, needed to overcome high rates of turnover and absenteeism. Trade unions can sometimes help in this. Advancement raises the question of training, called by Schultz investment in human capital.

Investment in human capital can take the form of formal schooling, on-the-job training, adult education, expanded efforts in health, migration, and information about the job market. In a number of these, it is difficult to separate the elements of consumption from investment, and the public good from the private. A shift from costs to yield does not escape these dilemmas, since costs and values are not equated in the long run in the imperfect market for education.

An alternative formula for estimating educational requirements is to calculate manpower needs and the educational levels needed in different occupations. This method has some distance to go before it will yield precise answers. It is generally recognized that more education is needed, rather than less, i.e., that the payoff to education of the right sort (which begs the issue) is higher than that to many other types of expenditure on development. There is, however, some danger that educating a portion of the people in underdeveloped countries will increase wants faster than they can be satisfied and thus lead to dissatisfaction, and in some cases emigration, thus wasting the investment.

The discussion of maintenance is postponed to Chapter 20.

BIBLIOGRAPHY

Three works stand out, all mentioned in the footnotes: Kerr, Harbison, Dunlop, and Myers, *Industrialism and Industrial Man* (footnote 3); Schultz, "Investment in Human Capital" [footnote 2, and Morgan, Betz, and Choudhry (eds.), selection 18], and the symposium, introduced by Schultz, and including the outstanding essay by Becker (footnote 6), in the supplement to the *Journal of Political Economy* for October, 1962.

For the problems of labor in primitive countries, see the essay by Berg (cited in footnote 4) and the manpower estimates of Harbison for Nigeria (footnote 17). W. E. Moore's *Industrialization and Labor*, Cornell, Ithaca, N.Y., 1951, is a basic study of problems of labor recruitment. Many case studies exist of how factories have overcome the problems of labor commitment. Manning Nash's *Machine Age Maya*, supplement to the April, 1958, *American Anthropologist*, and J. C. Abegglen, *The Japanese Factory*, Free Press, New York, 1958, are two of the most famous. The journal *Human Organization* contains other such cases.

THE NEED FOR ORGANIZATION

One form of labor is sufficiently important to be worth a separate chapter. This is the labor which tells the rest of labor what to do and sees that it gets done. The man engaged in this kind of work can be called the entrepreneur, the manager, the risk-taker, the decision-maker, the administrator, the boss. Each of these conveys something of the idea, and occasionally something that goes beyond it. Following Harbison,[1] we propose to regard the man as an organizer and the task as organization. It is not enough to say that growth is a function of land, capital, labor, and technology. There must be some element or factor which combines these in the right proportions, sets the task, and sees to its accomplishment.

In Schumpeter's view, the function of the entrepreneur was innovation, the introduction of new combinations of factors in new processes or for new outputs. Technical change is an important function of the organizer or organization, which we treat in the next chapter. But Schumpeter distinguished between the entrepreneur and the manager, whose task involved routine decision-making and control.[2] He looked for the gradual supplanting of the entrepreneur by bureaucratized management, with technical change routinely produced and applied. "Management" would do as a term, though it implies both private enterprise (as opposed to "administration," which carries a slight tinge of public enterprise about it) and exclusively routine direction, instead of both new combinations and their management. Risk-taking is certainly one function of the economic process, but in large corporations, and especially in public undertakings, the risks may

---

[1] Frederick Harbison, "Entrepreneurial Organization, as a Factor in Economic Development," *Quarterly Journal of Economics*, August, 1956, pp. 364–379, reprinted in Okun and Richardson (eds.), selection 26. Harbison's emphasis is on the complex organization rather than on the more general organizing process which admits of the simple organizer.

[2] See H. Hartmann, "Managers and Entrepreneurs: A Useful Distinction?" *Administrative Science Quarterly*, March, 1959, p. 431.

reside elsewhere than in the group which is directing the productive and distributive processes. Organization carries with it perhaps a connotation more of starting than of continuous direction of an aggregation of economic resources. But organization can be defined to include the initial organization and continuous management of an economic activity, with such risk-bearing and innovation aspects as may be involved in any particular case. It follows that organization embraces decision-making, of critical and routine sorts, and also the difficult-to-describe task of making sure that the decisions made result in work performed.

Organization can be included as a separate factor in the production function, or it can be left as a special subclass of labor. But between organization and other factors, if we take the former view, there is an important distinction: all other factors tend to be substitutable one for another. Capital can be substituted for labor, or labor for land, or technology for land, and vice versa, etc., but organization is a complement rather than a substitute. The more capital a firm has, the more, rather than the less, organization, i.e., managers, decision-makers, administrators, it needs.[3] The same is equally true for land and for labor. There are no theorems, or any experimental data, of which the writer is aware, which suggest how organization needs to be increased with an increase in scale of all factors: whether it must be increased more rapidly than land-plus-labor-plus-capital in the early stages, for example, and less so after some critical size has been reached because of increasing returns to organization. But if any one factor is added, and the factor combination is changed, it seems evident that more organization is always needed, not less.

Harbison offers another conclusion: that differences in organization explain differences in labor productivity.[4] He notes that in modern Egyptian factories, technologically the equal of those in the United States, labor productivity is one-sixth to one-fourth that of the United States, and he attributes the difference to quantity and quality of organizations: in Egypt "managerial resources are scarce and managerial methods are quite primitive." Again there seems to be no reason to limit the analysis to a single factor. It is probable that significant portions of differences in the capital/output ratio or the land/output ratio, i.e., capital productivity and land productivity, can be ascribed to differences in the quality of organization, when, in the case of land, this can be distinguished from labor.

Improvements in the quality of management may provide some or even a considerable amount of the explanation of the residuals in the

[3] Harbison, *op. cit.*, pp. 368–371.
[4] *Ibid.*, pp. 371–373.

statistical estimation of production functions, i.e., the fact that growth has outstripped the rate of increase of inputs of land, labor, and capital. In Mexico the output of the manufacturing sector improved 40 per cent between 1939 and 1946 with no increase in capital.[5] Some of this was owing to unused capacity. There may have been room for improvement in the quality of capital, within the limits made possible by reinvested depreciation allowances (although machinery was difficult to obtain outside the major industrial countries during the war). Some upgrading of labor skills may have taken place (although not much time was available for education, and foreign expertise was then fully engaged at home). It seems likely that Mexican manufacturing management bore down on waste, inefficiency, and underutilization, applying more control. That there is room for improvement in efficiency even in the best-run companies is well known. It takes doing. More output can be obtained from given plant, equipment, and labor in the short run as a consequence of increased managerial effort, even in developed countries. The opportunities for doing so in underdeveloped countries must be substantial.

THE NATURE OF ORGANIZATION

To those brought up in the laissez-faire tradition, it would seem as though the previous section dealt entirely with private enterprise. But there is no need to limit it so. Organization can be provided by banks and by government. Public organization is usually called administration, and its importance is well recognized: "The heart of economic development is the reform and creation of an administrative system capable of carrying it out."[6] But discussion of the possible contribution of banks had been limited to capital until Gerschenkron pointed out the extent to which industrial banks, beginning with the Crédit Mobilier in 1852, not only provided capital, but started companies and managed them.[7] Gerschenkron has now gone further to suggest that the organizational drive for development was provided in the early

[5] Report of the Combined Mexican Working Party, *The Economic Development of Mexico*, published for the International Bank for Reconstruction and Development by Johns Hopkins, Baltimore, 1953, pp. 62–63.
[6] Sir Arthur Salter, *The Development of Iraq: A Plan for Action*, Caxton Press, London, 1955, p. 96.
[7] A. Gerschenkron, "Economic Backwardness in Historical Perspective" in Bert F. Hoselitz (ed.), *The Progress of Underdeveloped Areas*, The University of Chicago Press, Chicago, 1952, pp. 3–29, reprinted in A. Gerschenkron, *Economic Backwardness in Historical Perspective: A Book of Essays*, Harvard, Cambridge, Mass., 1962, pp. 5–30.

stages by firms, banks, or government, depending upon how backward the country was when it entered the development process. Advanced areas start the first stage of development with the factory (firm) in the organizational lead; areas of moderate backwardness with banks, and areas of extreme backwardness with government.[8] This is an empirical observation for which Gerschenkron does not offer an explanation. The possibility that business enterprise, banks, and government can each supply organization, however, is enough to justify separate treatment.

THE BUSINESS ENTERPRISE

Systematic change in the character of business enterprise has been explored by a school of economic history interested in entrepreneurship. A leader of this school originally classified stages of entrepreneurship into "rule of thumb," "informed," and "sophisticated," as business leaders increasingly introduced information and rationality into the decision-making process. More recently he has offered a substitute classification along a different dimension than cognition, focusing on the entrepreneur's consciousness of the impact of his decisions. In the early stages of development, entrepreneurs are community-oriented— aware, that is, only of their impact on local markets for labor and goods. Later they become conscious of their particular industry as a whole, and interested in its technical progress, their share of output, their standing. At some still later stage, entrepreneurs become nation-oriented.[9]

For many purposes the evolution of the business organizer can be usefully analyzed in terms of the growth of his horizon and of his changing consciousness of his impact. It would be too bad, however, to throw away the first set of stages which deal with maximizing procedures. If to this is added discussion of what is maximized, we have a useful approach to the organization of the firm for the less developed countries.

We may digress briefly to touch upon the interesting questions of where the businessmen come from and whether they enter business from traditional motives in order better to maximize income, or because of some need for achievement which comes from respect with-

---

[8] See Gerschenkron, *Economic Backwardness in Historical Perspective, ibid.,* p. 355.
[9] A. H. Cole, "A New Set of Stages," *Explorations in Entrepreneurial History,* December, 1955, pp. 99–107.

drawal at some earlier generation.[10] Entrepreneurship frequently takes on a highly national or cultural shape. In a number of instances—Britain, the United States, and Turkey—the ranks of industrial entrepreneurs will be filled from commerce: the putting-out system evolves slowly into the factory in the same trade in Britain; the New England merchant who made a killing in rum turned to textiles during the 1806 embargo; the leaders of new industry in Turkey are drawn from the merchants who piled up profits in chrome and dried fruits during World War II. In Japan it was the samurai who turned to industry and kept their social structure intact by the expedient of adopting vigorous young businessmen or taking them into the family through marriage.[11] India developed a peculiar institution, the managing agency, through which foreign capitalists not resident in India could have their projects watched over despite the scarcity of entrepreneurial talent. A managing agency would undertake the direction of a series of firms either in one industry or in different industries.[12] Landes claims that the French family firm, concerned for dynastic continuity, is unique in its financial independence, liquidity, avoidance of risk, and refusal to grow. His critics, on the other hand, claim that the family firm is a phenomenon which transcends national boundaries and represents a stage which is ultimately outgrown.[13]

In writing about German entrepreneurs, Parker has suggested that the success of German large enterprise was due to its extensive division of entrepreneurial labor, a high degree of specialist training, sufficient social mobility to permit some matching of talent with job responsibility, despite the prestige accorded to soldiers, state officials, and academic people.[14] He observes, however, that high prestige for German entrepreneurs was limited to those fields in which Germany had a world reputation—exports and armament production—and that there was no kudos in working for the home market or for consumption.[15] Ranis has noted the existence in Japan of a further type of

---

[10] See Chap. 2.

[11] M. J. Levy, "Contrasting Factors in the Modernization of China and Japan," in S. Kuznets, W. E. Moore, and J. J. Spengler (eds.), *Economic Growth: Brazil, India, Japan,* Duke, Durham, N.C., 1955, p. 516.

[12] A. F. Brimmer, "The Setting of Entrepreneurship in India," *Quarterly Journal of Economics,* November, 1955, pp. 553–576.

[13] See footnote 1, p. 18, and E. J. Hobsbawm, review of E. M. Earle (ed.), *Modern France,* in *Economic History Review,* 2d ser., December, 1951, pp. 258–260.

[14] W. N. Parker, "Entrepreneurial Opportunities and Response in the German Economy," *Explorations in Entrepreneurial History,* October, 1954, pp. 28–29.

[15] *Ibid.*

entrepreneur who is community-minded, rather than self-centered, and who seeks to accumulate wealth and power for his neighbors along with himself.[16] On the showing of this sort of evidence, it can be said that the entrepreneur is not a fixed type, whether the "business-like man" emphasized by Phelps Brown,[17] the exploitive or hoarding personality manipulator distinguished by Erich Fromm (from the productive entrepreneur),[18] or the Schumpeterian innovator. National, cultural, and even personal characteristics intervene to shape the person and through him the business enterprise.

To return to the evolution of some average entrepreneur: at an early stage of development, the functions of a given person in organizing production include assembling materials and labor, capital provision and risk-bearing, management, and possibly innovation.[19] The entrepreneur must be less stereotyped; he cannot afford to be as professionalized as in developed countries. He lacks the help of markets for components, materials, labor, capital—markets which have already standardized products and trained workers as well as organized them in readiness. He also lacks the communications network —specialized industrial newspapers and magazines, not to mention governmentally collected statistics, which apprise him of availabilities of inputs, outlets for outputs, and technological progress.

All this would seem to supervene before the organizer could operate by rules of thumb. Gradually through on-the-job training, imitation of other organizers, not to mention some adult education, and in the rare case formal education of the business school type, he reduces his need to make decisions by applying rigid rules of behavior. If he is a risk-averter, his initial rule to the call of new business opportunities will be to say no; if he is a risk-embracer, the burden of proof will be in favor. Such maximizing as he undertakes will be within limited horizons, both geographically and in terms of products with which he is familiar. If he fails to develop into a highly rational, wide-horizon, profit-maximizing entrepreneur, it may be because he has his attention diverted to some other variable, converting his rules of thumb into those which give him a quiet life or the greatest possibilities for avoiding losses which might threaten the continuity of the family

[16] G. Ranis, "The Community Centered Entrepreneur in Japanese Development," *Explorations in Entrepreneurial History*, December, 1955, p. 81.
[17] E. H. Phelps Brown, *Economic Growth and Human Welfare*, Ranjit, New Delhi, 1953.
[18] E. Fromm, *Man for Himself*, Rinehart, New York, 1947, pp. 62ff. Fromm also regards the market orientation as "nonproductive."
[19] *Processes and Problems of Industrialization in Underdeveloped Countries*, United Nations, New York, 1955, pp. 30–31.

from generation to generation. When entrepreneurship does become diverted from the path of profit maximization, returning, as it were, to the stability of the traditional society, the effect is to slow down growth.

Where growth of the firm occurs, old rules of thumb must be discarded for sophisticated rationality, which means specialization, and the growth of organization. The management team must itself be managed, divided into line operators with authority and staff experts with specialized knowledge. Responsibility must be delegated and decentralized. Parker has observed that in Germany decision-making was broken down in a highly specialized way in large firms; the cartel worried about price, banks about finance, managers about production, and business executives about investment and plant location.[20]

How developing countries should enlarge their ranks of entrepreneurial organizers is very much an open question. Some are seeking to follow the route of formal education, bringing business schools to the country and sending young men to business schools abroad. Others are establishing industrial banks as seed corn. Interest attaches to particular forms of management, such as the managing agency.

A suggestion has been put forward by Albert Hirschman that development plans should deliberately create imbalance so as to underline the existence of business opportunities for businessmen.[21] In his view the scarcest talent in developing countries is decision-making. Decision-making capacity grows with practice, in a learning process. If the central authorities can induce pressures for decision-making, they will advance growth by breaking critical bottlenecks. The exact mechanism by which Hirschman's proposal works, drawing attention to investment opportunities through creating shortages, on the one hand, or cheap inputs, on the other, belongs to Chapter 11. Its central purpose finds a place here, however, in the connection with organizational capacity.

INDUSTRIAL BANKS

The normal rule in developed countries is for business to propose, and for banks to decide through the mechanism of granting or withholding credit. Typically, in the Anglo-Saxon tradition, emulated even in

---

[20] W. N. Parker, *op. cit.*, pp. 28–29.
[21] Albert O. Hirschman, *The Strategy of Economic Development*, Yale, New Haven, Conn., 1958, chap. 4.

France, this mechanism works through short-term debt, three- or six-month paper, which is discounted at the bank. Of late, somewhat longer accommodation has been available in Anglo-Saxon countries as term loans.

Industrial banking, as developed in France by the Crédit Mobilier and adopted in Central Europe, Italy, and Spain, went much further. In the early stages after the Crédit Mobilier was started by the Pereire brothers, and widely imitated by newly formed and existing private banks, the industrial bank was much more of an organizer. Along with finance of equity or long-term debt, it often provided the vision which led to new enterprise. In France the industrial banks turned away from organization into pure security promotion, largely of governmental bonds, but in Germany and Italy the links between the industrial banks and industry were intimate and sustained. Bank officers would be appointed to the boards of industrial enterprises and would deal not only with finance but with the whole gamut of business decision.

Outside Central Europe this significance of banking in industrial decision tended to decline. Men like Ford tried to free themselves from dependence on banks, and the rise of the market for equity stocks in Wall Street led other companies to achieve their freedom in a world of capital abundance. Only in particular industries, such as motion pictures, where profits are insecure, do banks exercise great authority.

But in underdeveloped countries there is a revival of industrial banking, partly for the sake of decision-making in the allocation of investment, partly to seek out credit-worthy private enterprise and get it going. State banks were first established for this purpose in Turkey. Since World War II, there has been a wave of interest in the subject on the part of foundations,[22] the United Nations,[23] and the International Bank for Reconstruction and Development,[24] which has made loans to industrial development banks.

[22] Carroll Wilson of M.I.T.'s School of Industrial Management, for example, has arranged foundation support and personnel assistance for a series of such industrial banks in the newly independent countries of Africa.

[23] See *Processes and Problems of Industrialization in Underdeveloped Countries, op. cit.*, pp. 95ff.

[24] See the books by IBRD staff members William Diamond, *Development Banks,* Johns Hopkins, Baltimore, 1957; and Shirley Boskey, *Problems and Practices of Development Banks,* Johns Hopkins, Baltimore, 1959. The work of the International Bank for Reconstruction and Development with development banks has lately been turned over to the International Finance Corporation, a sister organization established to facilitate investment in private companies, where it is organized into a Development Bank Service Department.

THE ECONOMIC ROLES OF GOVERNMENT

The traditional economic roles of government can be listed succinctly: first, the provision of "public goods," such as police and fire protection, national defense, flood control, public health measures, roads, bridges, parks, and so on, where use by one consumer, up to very high limits, leaves unchanged the amount of the good available for others; second, the construction of schools, hospitals, and possibly housing, where there are external economies in consumption and the consumer is compelled (as in elementary education) or encouraged to adopt appropriate standards; third, the prevention of external diseconomies by private concerns, in erosion, pollution or depletion of natural resources, the proliferation of standards, with consequent lack of interchangeability; fourth, the prevention of wasteful competition, such as duplicate railroads between two cities, or duplicate electric, gas, or telephone companies. In the last two cases there is dispute whether regulation or government ownership and operation of productive facilities is the better solution, but no one questions the necessity for government to concern itself.

When it comes to monopolies based on considerations other than natural indivisibilities, as in railroads, electricity, gas, and so on, there is more controversy. Socialists have long argued for public ownership of the means of production to prevent monopoly profits and what they regard as an undesirable distribution of income in favor of entrepreneurs. Sometimes they call for government operation of an entire industry, occasionally only for one or more government plants to compete with the private potential monopolists, set standards of service, and bring profits down to the competitive level.

While socialist theory argues for public ownership of industries which exhibit great strength, socialization occurs in developed countries largely because of the failures of private entrepreneurship—leaving out the natural monopolies of rail, post, telephone, telegraph, electricity, etc. Coal, airplanes, and Renault automobiles in France, and coal, steel, and road transport in Britain were nationalized not so much to capture monopoly profits for the public as to increase efficiency. Failure of private enterprise in these fields (plus political retribution as a dominant factor in Renault and an element in British steel) led to the substitution of governmental organization for the private entrepreneur. Similarly, in underdeveloped countries the main basis for governmental organization of enterprise outside the traditional fields is not that private enterprise works so well, but that it performs, or is expected to perform, so badly.[25] Whether public enterprise is good or bad in a country is an empirical question, rather than a matter for doctrine, and turns on the advantages and disadvantages of private enterprise and government, in general, and the particular circumstances. Our discussion leaves aside public goods, public external economies, and private external diseconomies, and touches only lightly on two other possible governmental economic functions: the provision of savings by the government (because private individuals want growth though they are unwilling to save themselves) and substantial income redistribution. Government saving is possible without governmental investment, as in Norway, if the savings are made available to private entrepreneurs. The redistribution function will be touched upon later in Chapter 20.

ADVANTAGES OF GOVERNMENT ORGANIZATION

Government may have an advantage over private enterprise in risk-taking because of the spread of risk over the economy as a whole rather than its concentration on one or a handful of individuals; it may have an advantage in risk-taking, innovation, and decision-making because of access to better information, which enables it more effectively to calculate; but the real edge of government over private enterprise in underdeveloped countries comes from its advantage in recruiting men of ability and energy needed to get growth under way. This advantage, where it exists, will differ in extent from country to country.

There are two sides to the question of risk-bearing. The fact that the risks are not borne privately may make public servants—politicians and civil administrators—underestimate the risk of loss and may lead to waste. On the other hand, where productive projects are lumpy, i.e., involve substantial amounts of capital, where private entrepreneurs are risk-averters, or where they lack information to calculate properly the mean of the probability distribution of a project's success, government may take desirable risks which private enterprise would ignore.

In innovation and decision-making, government is likely to have access to more and better information, to evaluate it more professionally, and to scan a wider range of alternatives, because it looks beyond

---

[25] It is possible, of course, to have both monopolistic behavior and poor performance in industries with easy entry. This leads to high prices and unused capacity, as in restaurants and corner retail stores. But these industries are rarely socialized.

even the sum of the narrow horizons of private enterprise. This is by no means certain. The more rudimentary the economy, the more likely that specialized, professional services needed for effective organization on any substantial scale will be available only or primarily in government.

But the major advantage of government is in recruitment. Where feudal traditions remain, government is associated with power and enjoys a degree of social approval not accorded to private enterprise. Government can attract intelligence, training, and energy in many countries in ways which private enterprise cannot. In developed countries, the tradition is often otherwise, and so is the practice in some underdeveloped countries: vigor and drive are associated with private undertakings, and government is believed to be manned by the shiftless, not to mention the corrupt. Both can be true simultaneously, of course, with energy and idealism embodied in a portion of the government, but weighed down by masses of civil servants who hold sinecures.

The outcome will differ from country to country. In India, high civil service morale is legendary. In Burma, workdays in government are no more than 150 a year; the day starts at 9:30, ends at 4:00, and is punctuated with newspapers, gossip, and tea.[26] "Egypt has a large and comparatively well trained body of civil servants, while Iraq is handicapped by an acute shortage of high-talent manpower in government."[27] "The [Indonesian] government has shown neither the will nor the disposition to impose the discipline required for economic development under socialism."[28] But even though the results are varied, the advantage of government over private industry in recruitment is often real.

DISADVANTAGES OF GOVERNMENT ORGANIZATION

The major weaknesses of government in economic development are overcentralized decision-making, attempting too much, concern for monumental projects, and maximizing the wrong variable.

[26] Louis J. Walinsky, *Economic Development in Burma, 1951–60*, Twentieth Century Fund, New York, 1962, p. 393. Walinsky's major conclusion is that Burmese development waits on good government to provide law, order, honesty, and responsibility (*ibid.*, p. 585).
[27] Frederick Harbison, "Two Centers of Arab Power," *Foreign Affairs*, July, 1959, pp. 4–5.
[28] Don D. Humphrey, "Indonesia's National Plan for Economic Development," *Asian Survey*, December, 1962, p. 20.

The balance between centralized and decentralized decision-making is sometimes delicate. Mistakes are made in development, inevitably. Many are called; few chosen. Bankruptcy of private entrepreneurs purges the system of a deadweight load of debt unsupported by productive assets. Given uncertainty as to the exact nature of the blocks to development, probing along a broad front in reconnaissance makes more sense than committing all one's force to a single salient which may prove unyielding. As one Indian visitor put it in discussing irrigation, and with a hydraulic as well as an economic point, "Little-dam foolishness is better than big-dam foolishness."

But it is equally true that a light reconnaissance may be unable to make an initial breakthrough which can later be profitably exploited, when an adequate force can. If increasing returns to scale are available, it is a mistake to commit too little. We have still to discuss the theories of the "Big Push" and "Critical Minimum Effort," but the strong believer in economies of scale is unmoved by mention of too many eggs in one basket or of the grand failure of the Tanganyika groundnut scheme.[29]

While there is something to be said on both sides, there is an accepted principle which favors decentralization. The presumption of external diseconomies to centralized decision-making is probably stronger than the likelihood of positive economies to the Big Push. Effective organization delegates to the maximum possible extent both in decision-making and in administration. Development from above runs the risk of all plans and no implementation. Development from below can be private or public, but the spontaneous private is clearly easier to organize, when it exists, than the contrived public.[30]

There is little need to discuss the proclivity of public organizers to attempt too much. The material risks of loss rest on the public; the political payoff to success is great. The temptation is always to overstate the benefits and underestimate the costs. It is particularly easy to overestimate administrative capacity. In announcing the first Five-Year Plan of Pakistan, Mohammed Ali indicated that the chief bottleneck in its execution was the dearth of skilled manpower and the shortage of technical and administrative talent. In the first two years of the plan, only $160 million of the $230 million earmarked for various developmental purposes was spent; the reason was "our inability to

---

[29] S. H. Frankel, *The Economic Impact on Under-developed Societies,* Harvard, Cambridge, Mass., 1953, chap. 8.

[30] See Walinsky, *op. cit.,* p. 586: "Implementation is more important than plans," and U. K. Hicks, *Development from Below: Local Government and Finance in Developing Countries of the Commonwealth,* Clarendon Press, Oxford, 1961, for an analysis of the problems of local government in developing countries.

pursue several projects through to completion primarily because of a lack of qualified personnel to carry them out."[31]

The penchant of government for the development showpiece has been widely remarked. Monuments to political glory, industrial cathedrals, these massive undertakings which lend themselves to cornerstone laying, ribbon cutting, and foreign visiting are regarded by Hirschman as the weakness particularly of "strong" governments. Democratic governments, on the other hand, in his view have a bias for undue dispersion of investment in all regions of a country in the effort to mend fences. Hirschman goes on to observe that the biases of foreign experts and even international lending agencies frequently work in the same direction as those of the government. The former are in the country for only a short time, and therefore try to change the face of the country rather than its people. The latter look for shortcuts and permit themselves to be persuaded that they may be found in this or that project.[32] Whether based on local or foreign suggestion, the massive project tends to have a lower social marginal product of capital than the petty economies involved in the New England virtues of repair, mend, and make-do, which fail to come naturally to government officials. The mean value of the risk they involve is also probably higher than the sum of that of a myriad separate undertakings.

In its proneness for monumental investment, government is maximizing the wrong variable. The more widely significant illustration, however, is provided in the field of pricing. Government as a political body is inevitably interested in income redistribution. One way to achieve this is to hold prices below the economic level which rations scarce resources into their most valuable uses. Not only does government typically underprice transport and energy, thus ensuring their inefficient use, but frequently it imposes price controls on the private sector, which distorts output. High profits in private enterprise are widely held in underdeveloped countries to be unaesthetic, indecent, or obscene. They have, however, an economic function, which is to attract additional resources into a use that is valued. More than that, where entrepreneurs save and reinvest, and entry is not restricted, profits serve to forward growth. It can even be argued that capital formation through private profit is less painful to society as a whole than government taxation, because purchases are voluntary whereas

[31] "Pakistan Issues First 5-Year Plan," *New York Times,* May 15, 1956 (direct quotation in original).
[3] A. O. Hirschman, "Economic and Investment Planning: Reflections Based on Experience in Colombia," in *Investment Criteria and Economic Growth,* Asia Publishing House, New York, 1961, p. 43.

taxes are compulsory. In addition, there is likely to be public pressure for lower pricing by governmental enterprises, because the private profit motive is accepted, whereas the government's embracing of economic pricing in preference to income redistribution is not. "Railroad transportation and electric power are underpriced. Hence, equipment is not replaced and too much power is consumed by households."[33] The overcrowded Indian railways and the brownouts in electricity distribution in Latin America are notorious examples of the same phenomenon.

THE VACUUM THEORY OF GOVERNMENT

But government has one great virtue to its credit. It is charged with the public interest, whereas private enterprise is preoccupied with its own. Where the public interest, as well as the private, is being adequately served by private enterprise, there is good reason for government to leave organization in private hands. Where it cannot be, as in public goods, external economies and diseconomies, and monopoly, or where it does not, government must fill the void. It is fatuous to be doctrinaire on the question of private versus public enterprise, as some capitalists and socialists are. There is a slight presumption that private decentralized organization is better in directly productive activities, but the presumption is minimal and liable to be upset by a slight change in fact. Where private enterprise won't or can't proceed with the business of development, there is every reason for government to move in.

This of course is just a little too pat. It may happen that private enterprise and government agree about what is to be done, but disagree upon the terms. Private enterprise, let us assume, can build and operate the Bokaro steel plant in India (though the Tata private steel company has stated that neither it nor any other private firm, domestic or foreign, can provide the capital),[34] but it demands guarantees of profits, or tax exemptions, or access to cheap capital. The decision between private and public organization has elements of bargaining in it, as well as efficiency, though they lie outside the range of the present discussion.

One serious problem: to substitute government for missing private organization may encounter the obstacle in some countries that the supply of government organization is limited and correlated positively,

[33] D. D. Humphrey, *op. cit.*, p. 19.
[34] See "Aid Chief Banks India Steel Loan but Sees Problems," *New York Times*, June 19, 1963, p. 14.

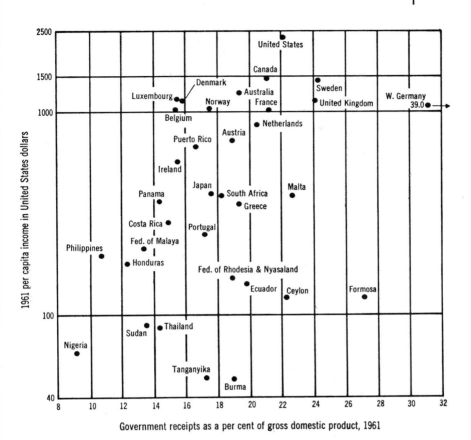

Government receipts as a per cent of gross domestic product, 1961

Figure 7.1 | Government expenditure as a percentage of gross domestic product compared with income per capita, about 1961. SOURCES: Government expenditure as a percentage of gross domestic product calculated from data in *Yearbook of National Accounts Statistics, 1962,* United Nations, New York, 1963; income per capita, table 1.1, Average Income per Capita in Selected Countries, 1949 and 1961. NOTE: Government expenditure is the sum of "general government consumption expenditure" and fixed capital formation of the "general government" and "government enterprises."

not negatively, with the supply of entrepreneurship. Figure 7.1, which shows government expenditure as a percentage of gross domestic product broadly rising with the level of income, provides only a crude illustration of the point, since other functions than organization, such as income redistribution, help account for the trend. Typically, however, entrepreneurs and top civil servants are both drawn from the same social and economic class. This class may be so small that the possibilities of remedying deficiencies in private organization by the use of public organization are not great. Expansion must be undertaken in both. The gap in government will probably be more readily filled than that in the private sector; this is the explanation for the empirical uniformity found by Gerschenkron, that the more backward the country when it embarks on development, the more heavily it relies on government. More important than the task of whether firms, banks, or government provide the organization is improvement in quality in all three.

SUMMARY

Along with land, labor, capital, and technology is needed the organization to combine them for production and distribution—the mechanism for managing, bearing risks, innovating in technology, and making decisions. Organization is perhaps only a special form of labor, but it cannot be substituted for, as the other factors can. Differences in the quantity and quality of organization help explain differences in output among countries; and improvements in quality of organization may explain why growth proceeds faster than is accounted for by factor inputs.

Organization is frequently thought of as private enterprise, but banks and government can also provide the service. The efficacy of enterprise is based partly on cultural characteristics, partly on experience. Some enterprises maximize profits; others maximize different variables, such as the quiet life or the time span of a family dynasty. The possibilities of expanding the numbers and quality of private organizers are touched upon.

Industrial banks may direct businesses as well as validate their applications for credit. Development banks are a promising modern version of the nineteenth-century German and Italian banking organization.

Government organization has certain fairly clear-cut functions in the field of public goods and in industries with external economies and diseconomies. In other lines, where it would be more directly competitive with private enterprise, government has advantages of risk-spreading, better information, and ease in recruitment, but the disadvantages of overcentralized decision-making, a proneness for the monumental, and a tendency to get diverted from economic objectives into welfare redistribution. A special weakness of government is that it tends to underprice its output.

In general, it is unwise to be doctrinaire about insisting on either private enterprise or government, but to reserve government for what private enterprise with decentralized decision-making cannot do. Unhappily for the organization needs of less developed countries, administrative capacity in government may be scarce in the very countries that lack vigorous profit-maximizing enterprise.

BIBLIOGRAPHY

The general need for organizational inputs is well stated by Frederick Harbison in "Entrepreneurial Organization as a Factor in Economic Development," *Quarterly Journal of Economics,* August, 1956, pp. 364–379, reprinted in Okun and Richardson (eds.), selection 26. On private enterprise, see Frederick Harbison and Charles A. Myers, *Management in the Industrial World,* McGraw-Hill, New York, 1959, which deals with the general subject and with management in a number of developed and underdeveloped countries. Gerschenkron's view that banks and government substitute for private enterprise in backward countries is set out in *Economic Backwardness in Historical Perspective,* Harvard, Cambridge, Mass., 1962, esp. the postscript, pp. 353ff.

For a useful insight into problems of public administration in underdeveloped countries, see A. H. Hanson, *Public Enterprise and Economic Development,* Routledge, London, 1959. The role of government in developing countries is discussed more generally in H. G. J. Aitken (ed.), *The State and Economic Growth,* Social Science Research Council, New York, 1959.

8 | *Technology*

THE PROCESS OF TECHNICAL CHANGE

Previous chapters have brought technological change into discussion more than once—as an autonomous ingredient in the production function, as an ingredient dependent upon the passage of time, as one which is tied up with capital investment, and in less formal terms, as a major explanation of the "residual" growth which cannot be accounted for statistically by the record of the growth of inputs of measurable factors. The time has come to bring the analysis together, to look at the process of technical change as it has been described by Schumpeter and his followers, and to make an assessment, if possible, of the factors which govern it. First, however, it may be observed, in keeping with the practice of other chapters, that technical change is not just one aspect of growth in some systems, but the central one. To Schumpeter, for example:

> The slow and continuous increase in time of the national supply of productive means and savings is obviously an important factor in explaining the course of economic history through the centuries, but it is completely overshadowed by the fact that development consists primarily in employing existing resources in a different way, in doing new things with them, irrespective of whether those resources increase or not.[1]

Dewhurst, referring to the United States, writes: "Technology, in fact, can be thought of as the primary resource."[2]

As a preliminary, note that technical change is represented in the two-input–one-output production function used earlier, by a shift of the isoquants toward the origin. Figure 8.1*a* shows a single isoquant *I*, a solid line, which, subsequent to technical change, shifts to I_a. The

[1] J. A. Schumpeter, *The Theory of Economic Development*, Harvard, Cambridge, Mass., 1949, p. 68.
[2] J. F. Dewhurst, *America's Needs and Resources: A New Survey*, Twentieth Century Fund, New York, 1955, chap. 24 and p. 834.

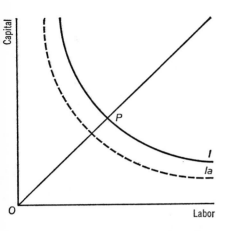

Figure 8.1a | Neutral technological innovation.

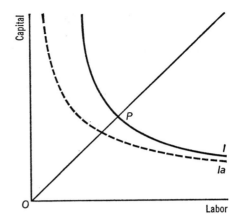

Figure 8.1b | Labor-saving innovation.

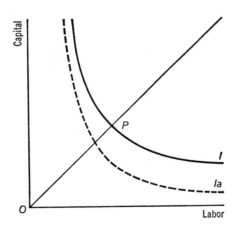

Figure 8.1c | Capital-saving innovation.

same output can now be produced with fewer inputs. If at previously existing factor prices, i.e., the same slope tangent to the isoquant at P, the factors would be used in the same proportion after technical change as before, the change is regarded as neutral with respect to factor saving. If, on the other hand, as in Figure 8.1b, the same factor price calls for less labor, the change is called labor-saving, or, if less capital, capital-saving (Figure 8.1c). (Whether a labor-saving innovation is at the same time capital-using, or a capital-saving innovation labor-using, is not predetermined. An innovation can save one factor more than the other at the old factor price, i.e., not be neutral, but still save both.)

Kaldor's objection to regarding technical progress as an independent source of growth, it will be recalled from Chapter 3, is that in his model technical progress is embodied in capital. It would be unlikely under this circumstance to achieve neutral technical improvement (Figure 8.1a) because the change is necessarily embodied in new capital equipment. This same objection can be raised for land and labor as well. Land, as noted in Chapter 4, cannot be defined separately from a given state of technology. A change in technique will change the economic, if not the physical, quantity of land. And the same is true of labor: new techniques cannot be applied without new or improved technicians. Investment in human capital may need to accompany technical change. And as automation reminds us, technical change may even reduce the quality, if not the quantity, of the labor supply by rendering obsolete old machinery and skills. So the notion of technical progress independent of land, labor, and capital cannot be entertained.

In the early days of President Truman's Point Four it was widely thought that technical assistance, by itself, would result in economic development. The means was to impart the secret of advanced technology to the less developed areas. Longer hoes, row planting, improved seed, and the diffusion of agricultural techniques through extension services (or on the shop floor, improved plant layouts which sped the flow of materials and reduced the physical strain on machine operators) were thought to be sufficient. There has been, is, and may be disembodied technical progress. Mordecai Ezekiel has said that it is probably mostly to be found in agriculture where yields per man, per acre, and per dollar of machinery employed have been raised by simple changes in method involving no or minimal additional inputs. Even here, however, there may be small changes in inputs such as the addition of hormones, sulfa drugs, or research to produce hybrid seed.

The task of this chapter is to describe, characterize, and examine the sources of technical change, and especially of imitation. Schumpeter's primary interest was in the development of new technology through invention and innovation. The task for underdeveloped countries today is to apply such portions of existing technology as are economic for them. But since such application is best when it is adaptive, it behooves us to look at innovation and invention along with imitation.

INVENTION AND INNOVATION

Schumpeter made a fundamental distinction between invention, which was the discovery of new technique, and innovation, which consists in the practical application of an invention in production for the market. Somewhat analogously, Rostow distinguishes the propensity to develop pure science and that to apply science in output for the market. In Schumpeter's view, invention was performed by inventors, and innovation was the task of the entrepreneur. In Rostow's version these propensities could exist together or separately in a given country: in the nineteenth century France had a high propensity for pure science, but inventions first reached the market in Britain. Today the British role is largely reversed. British scientists and inventors have no reason to be ashamed of their record in mathematics, physics, chemistry, or in radar, jet propulsion, etc. But mass production in these areas is frequently first reached by the United States. Atomic energy is instructive as an example: the bulk of the theoretical work was done by Europeans; the construction of the first pile and first bomb, by American teams.

Usher has pointed out that the distinction between invention and innovation is too sharp and that limiting the field of technological change to the physical sciences and their applications is unduly restrictive. Using modern psychology, he notes that all action can be divided into three types: (1) innate activities, which are unlearned and instinctual; (2) acts of skill, which are learned, whether through formal training or individual imitation; and (3) inventive acts of insight, resulting in new organizations of prior knowledge and experience.[3] Usher insists that inventive acts occur in fields of conceptual activity, involving interpretations of codes, rules for group behavior, and the execution of policies for individual or group activity. He is fearful that Schumpeter's distinction between the inventor and the innovator, and identification of the entrepreneur with the latter, may be misleading, since it suggests that the inventor has a monopoly on inventive acts of insight. This is not the case. It should also be said that acts of skill frequently require abilities of a high order and that at higher levels, acts of skill and acts of insight become interwoven to an extent that they cannot readily be distinguished.[4]

---

[3] A. P. Usher, "Technical Change and Capital Formation," in *Capital Formation and Economic Growth*, Princeton, Princeton, N.J., 1956, pp. 523–550.

[4] One difficulty with Usher's distinction is that, under modern research methods, invention becomes an act of skill rather than an act of insight. It may be neces-

This emphasis further stands as a corrective to Rostow's narrow view of the propensities in terms of science and its application to production. Usher does separate fundamental science from applications, designating as primary, inventions not carried to the stage of commercial application; secondary, those which open up new practical uses; and tertiary, improvements in a given device which do not extend the field. But inventions can occur well outside physical science—in commerce, industrial administration, government, communication, even advertising. More significant than the presence of discrete classes of inventors and of entrepreneurs is the spirit in a society which is prepared to devise new means to solve problems at all levels, whether by trial and error, intuition, or operational research, and whether in the laboratory or on the shop floor.

Not all inventions are economic to the point where they can use the services of the innovator, to continue to use the Schumpeterian terminology in qualified form. Atomic energy provides one striking example. Here many groups have confidence that the long-run cost curve is bound either to fall or be reduced to the point where it will be able to compete with coal and hydroelectric power in locations of economic significance. But there are others. Modern alchemists can contrive a million chemical and physical miracles which run afoul of the economic disability that the inputs cost more than the output can be sold for. The insight which converts an invention from uneconomic to profitable may be trivial in scientific terms.

That necessity is the mother of invention, like most proverbs, contains an element of truth. The most striking economic development occurs where demand for a new good in consumption meets an innovation which permits it to be satisfied with new efficiency in production. Swedish economic development after 1870, for example, had its roots in the substantial increase in demand for lumber and wood products, including particularly paper, plus a series of peculiarly Swedish inventions in the chemical processing of wood pulp which reduced its price.[5] The Danish response to the fall in the price of grain after 1870 was not only the marketing cooperative, but also the invention of the mechanical cream separator, which made possible the production of a standardized butter on a large scale for the hearty breakfast of the British

---

sary to separate the class of inventions which were produced to order from those which resulted from random insights or from research into fundamental science with no practical applications contemplated.

[5] See E. F. Heckscher, *An Economic History of Sweden,* Harvard, Cambridge, Mass., 1954, pp. 228ff.

middle class.[6] In Canada, opening of the prairie provinces after 1900 required improvement of cultivation techniques, particularly in dry farming and summer fallow, which permitted a profitable harvest where none could be grown before, and appeared as a response to the reduction in freight rates of the Crow's Nest Pass Agreement of 1897.[7] But necessity is not always fruitful in such timely fashion. British industry lost some of its lead in steel production when the Bessemer process, announced in 1854, proved unsuitable to iron ores with high phosphorus content. Not until 1878, with the development of the Thomas process, did Britain with its limited supplies of hematite ores have an opportunity to regain its lead. By this time German competition had gotten well under way. The threat of orlon and dynel to wool in Australia after World War II was met—at least for a time—by an improvement of productivity, reducing costs as much as 30 per cent through myxomytosis, the disease which wiped out the jack rabbit and left more grass for the sheep. But Japanese silk, Chilean nitrates, and similar products needed similar *dei ex machina* and waited in vain. There is an element of luck in whether new inventions will be forthcoming to exploit opportunities or defend economic positions; but beyond this random element there is the capacity of the society to respond to the situation by producing a new insight.

IMITATION

Brozen observes that there is a difference among (*a*) what is technologically possible; (*b*) the technical capacity of the leading firms; and (*c*) the technology used by the economy as a whole.[8] The first exceeds the second; the second, the third. Even in the United States, handicraft firms to a surprising degree in a surprising number of industries and trades, exist side by side with firms using modern machine techniques. The question arises, why does not imitation—i.e., the learned act of skill—raise the technology of the total to the level of technological possibilities? The existence of technological possibilities better than those in use obviates the necessity for a large part of the difficult tasks of invention and innovation.

[6] See C. P. Kindleberger, "Group Behavior and International Trade," *Journal of Political Economy*, February, 1951, p. 36.
[7] P. C. Hartland, "Factors in Economic Growth of Canada," *Journal of Economic History*, 1955, no. 1, p. 19.
[8] Y. Brozen, "Invention, Innovation and Imitation," *American Economic Review, Papers and Proceedings*, May, 1951, pp. 239–257.

A wide variety of answers is given to this question. Ignorance, legal restriction, the fact that existing equipment is interrelated with other equipment in the economy, managerial irrationality, and maximization of the wrong variable are among the reasons cited for technological dispersion.[9] Or it may be simply that the new technique must earn enough to cover its fixed and variable costs plus a normal return, whereas the old capital need cover only its variable costs.[10]

Some analysts lay stress on lack of competition.[11] Where the leading firm is interested in lowering prices, expanding its share of the market, improving product and production efficiency, the industry as a whole is necessarily required to imitate, innovate, or perish. The electronics industry in the United States illustrates this condition fully. But where the leading firms are nonaggressive, secretive, content to live and let live, and where entry into markets is restricted by weight of the product, inadequate transport, lack of large sums of capital needed to make a start, or a class structure which keeps people in their place, imitation languishes. But, as this last list suggests, the character of the competition may lead back into social structure or into capital formation.

DEMAND–INCREASING AND COST–REDUCING INNOVATION

Innovations are of two types: there are new goods and new ways to produce old goods. The distinction is a loose one. Synthetic rubber is mostly a new way of producing an old good, but partly a new good; equally mixed is the automobile, which is partly horse-and-buggy— i.e., local transport on the former limited scale—and partly an entirely new item of consumption. To the extent that inventions take place in new goods—particularly consumption items—invention is the mother of necessity.

In discussing Brozen's paper, Scoville points out that, while competition may be vital for the spread of imitation in new ways of pro-

---

[9] See C. P. Kindleberger, "Obsolescence and Technical Change," *Bulletin of the Oxford University Institute of Statistics*, August, 1961, pp. 281–297.

[10] See W. E. G. Salter, *Productivity and Technical Change*, Cambridge, New York, 1960.

[11] Brozen, *op. cit.* See also H. J. Habakkuk, "The Historical Experience on the Basic Conditions of Economic Progress," in L. H. Dupriez (ed.), *Economic Progress*, Institut de Recherches Economiques et Sociales, Louvain, 1955, pp. 149–169 [reprinted in Supple (ed.), selection 4], although he is disposed to believe that producers who responded to an increase in demand were as important as innovators in the early Industrial Revolution.

ducing old goods, i.e., cost reductions, it is not equally clear that this holds for new goods, i.e., demand-increasing innovation.[12] It is sometimes charged that large companies slow down the rate of innovation, holding inventions off the market—the perpetual match is most frequently cited in the folklore. But large companies with records of high profits also have the resources for research and experimental projects and frequently a bias in favor of introducing new products. In part this may be wasteful product differentiation without significant difference, as in oligopolistic competition in gasolines, cigarettes, soaps, etc. Beyond this, however, is the record of new products in chemicals, aluminum, oil, automobiles, where the attempt is made to develop a broad market for a new product.

The appeal of new goods to the consumer has been a powerful factor in economic development, but may currently be even more powerful. Nurkse, in particular, has called attention to the "demonstration effect," following a lead of Duesenberry in domestic trade.[13] Domestically, this effect is used to explain why increases in consumption use up most of the increase in real income and more, and savings tend to remain relatively steady or decline. New goods satisfy new wants; appetite grows with eating. The demonstration effect in the domestic area operates as a stabilizing influence to maintain expenditure and output. With consumption growing continuously, it can be argued that economic development depends on consumers as much as or more than on entrepreneurs.

In the international realm, however, the demonstration effect injects an element of instability and disequilibrium. Classic economic theory operated on the assumption that opening of trade between two countries left tastes unchanged and had its effects in inducing shifts in production. With the demonstration effect, however, the impact of new trade may be to shift demands even before any impact on the allocation of resources. Before trade, the underdeveloped countries consume native foodstuffs, local products, and go without the material trappings of the developed country. With trade introduced, there occurs a substantial change in patterns of taste and a shift in demand in favor of imported goods and against the goods produced with a comparative advantage.

There is much dispute about the existence of the demonstration effect. It is possible to adduce evidence on both sides of the question. A distinguished economist visiting Latin America insists that the demonstration effect is a figment of an overdeveloped imagination. A keen

[12] *American Economic Review, Proceedings,* May, 1951, pp. 275–279.
[13] R. Nurkse, *Problems of Capital Formation of Underdeveloped Countries,* Blackwell, Oxford, 1953, pp 58, 63–67, etc.

observer of the French scene noted that the American way of life penetrated a certain depth into cities, but that the countryside was for a long time unaffected.[14] On the other hand, there is a wealth of testimony to the effect that, especially since World War II, the entire world has been moving toward the adoption of United States and Western European standards in food, dress, amusements, and even literary and artistic taste, as well as in durable consumer goods. One can find evidence on both sides of the question to prove that there are places where the demonstration effect exists as well as places where it does not. The question is how widely is it prevalent, and how intense. That the effect is spotty is probably undeniable. There is little trace of it, for example, in Lewis's account of Mexican village life;[15] whereas Simey can say about Jamaica:[16]

> It would be relatively easy (given the necessary basis of research) to define standards which are capable of attainment in the West Indies which would allow mankind a reasonable chance of a happy and useful life without fear of "outside" comparisons. But the opportunity to lead their own lives in their own way is a slender one. . . . "Outside" standards are applied through the medium of the middle and upper classes, who in a materialistic and competitive age see no alternatives to the standards of living which have been set by the urban communities of Great Britain and North America. The motor car, the refrigerator, the suburban house of a type quite grotesquely unsuited to a tropic climate, all these are the hallmark of success in the West Indies.

Standards of food consumption are particularly important. The incorporation of milk in the Indonesian diet, the substitution of wheat for rice in Japan, the adoption of the European breakfast in place of fish and soybean soup in Thailand[17] work against comparative advantage and often reduce dietary levels.

Often the objects of consumption are symbolic rather than useful.

[14] This observation of the 1950s does not stand up in the present decade. See Laurence Wylie's essay, "Social Change at the Grass Roots," in Stanley Hoffmann et al., *In Search of France*, Harvard, Cambridge, Mass., 1963, pp. 159–234.

[15] Oscar Lewis, *Life in a Mexican Village*, The University of Illinois Press, Urbana, Ill., 1951 (but see the exception in *ibid.*, p. 182).

[16] T. S. Simey, *Welfare and Planning in the West Indies*, Clarendon Press, Oxford, 1946, p. 160.

[17] *New York Times*, July 4, 1955. See also the quotation in J. Biesanz and M. Biesanz, *Costa Rican Life*, Columbia, New York, 1946, p. 35, from Chacon Trajos, *Tradiciones Costarricenses:* "Our zeal to imitate the foreigner has made us abandon our good food. . . . We have lost our classic, more nutritious and savory national cooking."

Grattan observes that the underdeveloped world prizes above all American fountain pens, Swiss watches, and British bicycles.[18] The last has primarily a utilitarian flavor, but the pen is as much a symbol of literacy as an article of writing, and the watch exemplifies a shift from the timeless world of the peasant to the split-second, synchronized universe of the machine. It seems safe to conclude that the spread of interest in the Western standard of living has occurred in many areas of the world, and everywhere among government officials, and that the demonstration effect is to this extent an important factor creating interest in economic development.

DEMONSTRATION EFFECT IN PRODUCTION VERSUS DEMONSTRATION EFFECT IN CONSUMPTION

Wallich has drawn the contrast between Schumpeterian development in which the leadership is taken by the entrepreneur, imitating or creating new ways of production, and Duesenberry development with its emphasis on consumption.[19] In the one, the leadership comes from supply; in the other, demand. In Riesman's terminology, Schumpeterian development is inner-directed; consumption-oriented development produced by the demonstration effect, other-directed. In the former, savings and capital formation are fairly readily produced from the fortunes of driven and dedicated men, who have no time for consumption; in the latter, government is called upon to lead investment, and savings are difficult to accumulate because consumption tends to parallel or outdistance increases in productivity.

The distinction lies between growth through innovation and growth through imitation. It is reminiscent of the question whether growth is led by supply or by demand, as raised in Chapter 3. Schumpeterian supply-led growth may have been easier in countries which experienced the Industrial Revolution before they acquired democratic institutions, whereas Duesenberry growth may be a consequence of democracy earlier than the Industrial Revolution in other countries.

This issue has perhaps only historical interest. The more operational question is whether demonstration effect is stronger in production than in consumption, or the contrary, in countries now con-

[18] H. Grattan, "The Things the World Wants," *Harper's Magazine,* November, 1956, pp. 57–60.
[19] See H. C. Wallich, "Some Notes toward a Theory of Derived Development," in Agarwala and Singh (eds.), selection 3.

sciously embarked on economic growth. These differences are small in relation to the totals, as Micawber observed in *David Copperfield,* but they carry significance.

TECHNICAL CHANGE IN DEVELOPED COUNTRIES

The rate and character of technical change in developed countries have occupied the attention of economists without producing agreed answers. A brief confrontation between the major views and the facts may be suggestive.

First is Meade's assumption for the purposes of his model that technical progress is a linear or monotonic function of time: every year or every five years, technical progress proceeds at a rate of x or y per cent. Convenient in a model, this notion of technical change fails to meet the test of history. Almost all the major innovations in the cotton textile industry in the eighteenth century were bunched in a single decade around 1770. British farming underwent two waves of improvement in technology, one in the 1740s, another in the 1840s. Or in a narrower context, there was no improvement in the technical capacity of locomotives on the Great Western Railway in Britain from the 1840s to 1891, after which there was a new type of locomotive every three years, until 1906, after which nothing until 1945.[20]

Schumpeter was well aware that innovation came in fits and starts.[21] But his theories called for innovation to be correlated with the depression phase of business cycles. This was a time when entrepreneurs sought to reduce costs, to increase their share of the market, with the result that innovations were bunched in depressions.

The historical evidence in support of this contention is weak. If anything, innovation is associated with the boom phase of the cycle. In the 1840s and 1850s the introduction of new techniques took place on a large scale, stimulated in part by the pressure of demand, short supplies, and high profits engendered by the railroad boom. In a seller's market, producers stretch their ingenuity. The process was repeated in France, Germany, and the United States in the boom from 1896 to 1913. But the great depression from 1873 to 1896 was not without its innovations, even though the rate of productivity increase in Britain began to slow down.

[20] See Humphrey Cole, "Great Western Locomotive Replacement," unpublished manuscript, Oxford Institute of Statistics. The spurts were due to the genius, successively, of Brunel and Churchward and the timidity of their successors.
[21] J. A. Schumpeter, *Business Cycles*, McGraw-Hill, New York, 1959, vol. I, p. 102.

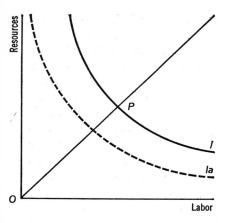

Figure 8.2a | Labor-saving innovation, which is also resource-saving.

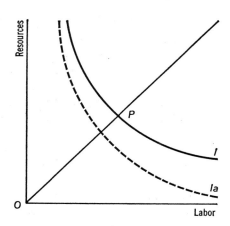

Figure 8.2b | Resource-saving innovation, which is labor-using.

The possibility exists that innovation is entirely random through time, being connected with such noneconomic aspects of society as individual (rather than cultural) personality. In view of the bunching already mentioned, this seems unlikely.

On this showing it seems that the pressure of demand is the best explanation of the timing of innovation, but it is neither necessary nor sufficient.

Another aspect of innovation which has occupied economists and historians is whether it is biased in systematic ways. As already noticed in Chapter 4, Habakkuk thinks that American innovation sought to save labor, which was relatively expensive in the United States as compared with Britain, and Britain sought to save resources, which were relatively scarce in that country. The reason for the difference rested in the abundance of land in the United States, which made labor scarce and high priced (since it could always earn a good living farming), and of labor relative to land in Britain, which made resource products relatively high priced.[22] In his judgment, this gave the United States an important advantage in growth, since labor-saving innovations, he asserts, are likely to be saving of all resources, whereas resource-saving innovations save resources alone. The possibilities are illustrated in Figures 8.2a and 8.2b. Labor-saving innovation in the first of these has resulted in a shift of isoquant I to the I_a position, to save, at the old factor price, both labor and resources, whereas in

[22] Note how this differs from the Ricardo model, in which wages were determined by the quantity of agricultural land, not by the abundance of workers who were always in excess.

Figure 8.2*b* the resource-saving innovation required the use of more labor. This analysis may have applied to specific innovations. Interchangeable parts were perhaps a more powerful innovation than recycling of heat in the blast furnace. But it is hard to see that this is a function of their relative factor intensity. The steam engine which conserved water power was surely a more powerful innovation than such a labor-saving innovation as the mule jenny. On a priori grounds there would seem to be no reason to have innovations which saved different factors biased in one direction or the other. In addition, the French believed that they suffered from cheap labor and dear coal, which biased their entrepreneurs against the introduction of machinery. As compared with France, Britain had perhaps cheap resources and dear labor, which could be used to explain a different pattern of innovation. Factors are dear or cheap only in relation to some other country (since there are many other countries, they cannot be dear or cheap in any absolute sense) or in relation to some past position. In a closed economy with fixed factors, no factor is cheap or dear, and it is hard to see that there is any bias to innovational incentive. Even with abundant labor it will still pay to save labor if the cost in capital is not great and if one can save enough of it.

The other view of bias is derived deductively. Fellner reasons, from the Harrod-Domar model and from Keynes's views of the likelihood of the long-run rate of interest approaching zero as capital accumulates, that technical innovation must historically have been capital-using (and labor-saving) or the rate of interest would have exhibited a more strongly declining trend.[23] In a two-factor model this conclusion is unexceptional. The capital-labor ratio in the United States has risen from what was probably close to $100 per head in colonial times to an average approaching $10,000, without reducing the rate of interest by much more than half. But whether innovation has been more land-saving or land-using is hard to say, since much of it is land-creating, and whether the labor-saving bias inheres in the nature of factor proportions or the nature of the innovation process is another riddle.

DISSEMINATION OF TECHNOLOGY

More central to our interest in the less developed countries is the process of imitation and how it works. Here again economic history

[23] W. Fellner, "Individual Investment Projects in Growing Economies: General Characteristics of the Problem and Comments on the Conference Papers," pp. 122–123, in *Investment Criteria and Economic Growth,* Asia Publishing House, New York, 1961.

may teach something. The international spread of technology is not new. British wool was initially exported. Not until the British acquired weaving skills brought by immigrants from Flanders in the sixteenth century was a woolen industry established. The Industrial Revolution spread over the Continent originally through workers and master craftsmen operating in Europe, later through a series of means. British companies were established across the channel, especially in Belgium and northern France; French businessmen paid visits to British plants; British machines were smuggled out of the country despite a prohibition against the export of machinery, repealed only in 1828.[24] Later, when the French Industrial Revolution had been largely accomplished and the organizational device of the Crédit Mobilier had been developed, French bankers teamed up with French engineers to bring modern construction and construction techniques to Germany, Italy, Spain, Switzerland, and Austria.[25]

The record of experience in the United States has been briefly summarized by Handlin, who notes that the imported skill was initially highly valued, but later replaced by domestic talent partly because of cost, sometimes because of further innovation, and frequently because of its technological conservatism which resisted further evolutionary change.[26] The speed with which this displacement took place in the United States was of course a function of the country's receptivity to the ideas brought by the technician immigrants and the country's capacity for innovation and adaptive imitation.

Perhaps the classic case of growth through imitation of foreign technology is the Japanese. Originally the country earned a somewhat derisive reputation for slavish copying, even duplicating, equipment the use of which was not understood. With time, however, and especially after World War II, Japanese imitation became highly adaptive to local conditions and ultimately gave way to an independent capacity to innovate. In such technical fields as photography, after starting out to reproduce the German models, the Japanese developed their own independent and high-quality innovations.

Imitation, like innovation, is best when it is selective and creative, i.e., when it takes local conditions and requirements fully into account. This is sometimes a physical necessity, for example, when the machinery of developed countries must be made to function under

[24] See, e.g., W. O. Henderson, *Britain and Industrial Europe, 1750–1870,* University Press of Liverpool, Liverpool, 1954. For a lurid account of one such operation, see Charles Ballot, *L'Introduction du machinisme dans l'industrie française,* Rieder, Paris, 1923, pp. 100ff.

[25] See Rondo E. Cameron, *France and the Economic Development of Europe, 1800–1914,* Princeton, Princeton, N.J., 1961.

[26] See Oscar Handlin, "International Migration of the Acquisition of New Skills," *The Progress of Underdeveloped Areas,* pp. 54–59.

special conditions of cold, heat, sand, humidity, etc., which exist in underdeveloped areas. In other instances, it is economic to improve the efficiency of modern technology by cutting its costs or raising its output in particular circumstances. One major issue in this area, whether underdeveloped countries should borrow the latest technical devices or the more simple, older ones—i.e., whether the technology developed in the capital-intensive countries is suitable for simple adaptation to labor- or land-intensive economies—is worth extended discussion, given in Chapter 14. But the presumption is always against straightforward borrowing and in favor of adaptation.

Underlying the receptivity of a country to the diffusion of new technology is the rationality of the culture, the level of literacy and education, the existence of channels of communication and techniques of demonstration. If illiteracy is prevalent, there may be a long way to go, especially in certain cases, as Simey points out, because it is not worthwhile to provide education for people who are hungry.[27] Basic to speed of learning is the desire to learn.

A special problem exists in agriculture because of the lack of means of easy communication in many countries. Peasants and farmers are more tradition-minded, especially in the Middle East, Africa, and Asia, which means more resistant to change, more illiterate, and more difficult to reach by communication. On the first two scores, it is believed that demonstration techniques hold more promise than the written or spoken word. Because of the last, experience in technical cooperation suggests the wisdom, in countries such as Brazil, of combining the usual type of technical assistance in health, education, and agriculture with credit in a single package.[28]

SUMMARY

Technological change is a principal contributor to economic growth. The pace of innovation is not entirely understood—i.e., whether it is a simple function of time, is tied to gross investment, moves counter-cyclically, is positively correlated with periods of high demand, or follows an independent path linked to noneconomic variables. In addition, there is no satisfactory answer whether such change responds in character to factor proportions in a systematic way.

Invention can be separated from innovation in advanced countries

---

[27] Simey, *op. cit.*, p. 92.
[28] A. T. Mosher, "The Agricultural Program of ACAR in Brazil," pamphlet in series on *Technical Cooperation in Latin America,* National Planning Association, Washington, D.C., 1955.

and imitation in the less developed. Innovation can take the form of new processes or new products. Imitation in consumption, called "demonstration effect" by Nurkse, tends to run a close race with imitation, or demonstration effect, in production. Innovation is most effective when it responds to emergent needs; imitation contributes the most, in its turn, when it is adaptive.

BIBLIOGRAPHY

General discussion of the contribution of technical change to economic development is limited. One useful article, which refers to a certain amount of the literature in its footnotes is W. R. Maclaurin, "The Sequence from Invention to Innovation and Its Relation to Economic Growth," *Quarterly Journal of Economics*, February, 1953, reproduced in Okun and Richardson (eds.), selection 27. The Habakkuk historical volume referred to in the text with reference to Chap. 4 is *American and British Technology in the Nineteenth Century*, Cambridge, New York, 1962, and is an interesting, sophisticated but not yet fully agreed, interpretation. For a discussion of the role of technological change in the United States, see the papers by Schmookler, Brownlee, and Gustafson in the *American Economic Review*, May, 1962.

9 | *Scale*

THE SIZE OF THE MARKET

The engine of economic development before the days of governmental planning was the market. Some economic historians describe the process of growth as one of increasing the size of the market. Adam Smith believed that the core of increased productivity was specialization, which in turn was limited by the size of the market. But modern economists also believe in the market as a road to growth, and in external economies. In a well-known essay entitled "Increasing Returns and Economic Progress," the late Allyn Young wrote:

> It is dangerous to assign to any single factor the leading role in that continuous economic evolution which has taken the modern world so far away from the world of a few hundred years ago. But is there any other factor which has a better claim to that role than the persisting search for markets? No other hypothesis so well unites economic history and economic theory.[1]

And Paul Rosenstein-Rodan of the Massachusetts Institute of Technology believes that the "residual" growth, which cannot be explained by inputs of land, capital, and labor, is the result of external economies of scale in the growth process.

Certainly the market was central when growth was an unconscious process. In primitive stages of development, households were largely self-sufficient and did little trading in the village. Thereafter village trade picked up, possibly with markets on special days in special places, but with most produce local, and little but salt, kerosene, matches, or iron pots, machetes, and axes bought from outside. At a further stage of development, the village was joined to the metropolitan system. The market moved from village square to stores, which were open regularly. Barter and exchange of gifts gave way to use of

---

[1] *Economic Journal*, December, 1928, p. 536, reprinted in R. V. Clemence (ed.), *Readings in Economic Analysis*, Addison-Wesley, Cambridge, Mass., 1950, vol. 1, chap. 5.

money. And increased specialization in production made possible more output and required exchange. At a final stage, goods which are valuable and transportable in some appropriate combination, in which a low mark on one score is compensated by a high grade on the other, are traded all over the world. But there are still countries where rural life is self-sufficient. The higher the stage of development, the higher the proportion of consumption represented by purchases—with appropriate qualification for owner-occupied houses and a few hobbies such as gardening. Wisconsin farmers can no longer afford to eat butter produced in their dairies, buying instead margarine made from cottonseed oil originating more than 500 miles away; and Italian peasants buy and sell olive oil, exchanging their high-quality product for the inexpensive variety they consume.

With widening of the market, and in part a result of it, comes the spread of the money habit. The more developed a country, the larger the proportion of its income earned in money form, which is the simple obverse of the statement made in the previous paragraph. And the more it needs monetary institutions. The major factor initially separating markets is the cost of overcoming distance between them. Investment and technological change in transport and communication reduce this cost and are a prime cause of linking and enlarging markets. Finally, fusion of markets has significant repercussions on entrepreneurs and labor. It is perhaps not too much to say that commercial revolution is a vital and almost a necessary step on the way to industrial revolution as it sets the preconditions for rapid economic growth.

ECONOMIES OF SCALE[2]

Economic theorists debate at length questions of economies of scale. Much in this debate need not concern us, since under the conditions of markets in underdeveloped countries the existence and importance of economies are hard to doubt. But it is appropriate to recapitulate the categories of economies and diseconomies of scale.

The first distinction is between external and internal economies; the second, between pecuniary and technological. Internal economies are those within the firm; external economies are external to the firm but available to other firms in the same industry or in other industries or sectors. Pecuniary economies arise from a change in the price of a factor or an intermediate good or a cost of marketing. Technological

[2] This discussion relies heavily on a manuscript of R. L. Bishop.

economies are realized when a higher scale of output permits a lower input per unit of output to be realized in physical terms.

Much of the emphasis in economic development is on external economies on the ground that internal economies cannot exist under competitive conditions. Moreover, there is the tendency of some theorists to go further and to dismiss external technological economies as bucolic in character—the classic example is beekeeping and the growing of fruit, where the two industries provide external economies for each other—of little importance under modern conditions. It is even doubted whether the pollination of fruit by the bees and the gathering of honey from fruit trees should be regarded as true externalities so much as "inappropriabilities," an inability of the beekeeper to charge the fruitgrower for the services of his bees, because of imperfections of the market mechanism, and of the fruitgrower to charge the beekeeper. Finally, it is suggested that external pecuniary economies are typically the result of internal economies in another industry where the increased efficiency is passed along in the form of lower prices for intermediate goods. If this be so, and if internal economies due to monopoly are ruled out, economies of scale would seem to be pretty well disposed of. Not only are external economies dismissed as realistically unimportant. They are also attacked as ideology. Liberal economists, if we use that adjective in the classic laissez-faire sense, are inclined to regard external economies as improbable and as a figment of the imagination of the interventionist.[3]

But this is inappropriate in economic development. Internal economies of scale are important in this area, since markets frequently are monopolistic rather than purely competitive. Even if it is necessary to dismiss external technological economies as idyllic, and internal pecuniary economies, which occur when a firm can buy factor and material inputs more cheaply as its scale of output increases, as rare, internal technological and external pecuniary economies have real importance. So has the irreversible downward shift of supply curves, which theoretically differ from reversible economies of scale but which resemble them in the real world. Costs and prices decline as the scale of output increases with development. The monopolistic character of the market in underdeveloped countries, which makes possible internal economies of scale, is the result of difficulties of new entry into profit-

[3] This is pointed out by Karl deSchweinitz, Jr., in his "Industrialization, Labor Controls, and Democracy," *Economic Development and Cultural Change*, July, 1959, p. 387, note citing P. T. Bauer and B. S. Yamey, *The Economics of Underdeveloped Countries*, The University of Chicago Press, Chicago, 1957, p. 244, as evidence for the liberal position, and P. A. Baran, *The Political Economy of Backwardness*, Monthly Review Press, 1957, pp. 190–194.

able industry and limitations on the expansion of production due to high costs of transport, ignorance of market opportunities, lack of capital, unavailability of inputs, etc.

Internal technological economies are those resulting from the division of labor, the use of specialized machinery and other capital equipment with considerable capacity, the opportunity for using the insurance principle in massing inventories, and certain once-for-all contributions, such as new design. The machinery and the design are said to be "lumpy" capital investments in that they are not infinitely divisible to permit all possible scales. A minimum efficient scale of operation exists for every investment, and it is sometimes very large. The division of labor was extolled by Adam Smith in his classic example of how ten men can make more than ten times as many pins as one man. The savings inherent in the division of labor derive from the increased physical efficiency in work that comes with repetition, increased knowledge of the job, and avoidance of waste of time and motion in moving from one task to another, as required of the generalist. If enough can be sold to keep men and machines fully employed at the appropriate scale determined by the lowest common multiple of their separate individual efficiency rates, considerable gains in efficiency and lower costs can be achieved.

Offsetting technological economies, in some part, are technological diseconomies. These are largely a function of the increased difficulty of organizing, administering, and supervising work as its scale increases. One man can keep himself busy and active. With division of labor, administrative personnel is needed to keep the work flowing smoothly and to see that the workers stay up with their tasks.

Division of labor can take place within and between firms. Within the firm, various sets of individuals or shops may concentrate on various stages of production and achieve efficiency in the production of components. If, however, the organizational problem leads to diseconomy, there is the possibility of vertical disintegration and exchange of components through the market mechanism. Buying and selling of standardized components at prices determined by the market may be easier to organize than the administration of the necessary men in one unit to produce them locally.

One important external pecuniary economy in underdeveloped countries arises from the improved organization of the market itself. When markets are fragmented and small, it is necessary to incur marketing costs to move production. Marketing costs can be regarded either as an input or as the reduction of an output, i.e., a subtraction from price. As marketing facilities grow, some markets become organized on a formal basis, with a building where buyers and sellers gather and with rules for trading. In other goods and services firms in different industries selling to similar customers gather to assist the buyer, whether in insurance, entertainment, garments, cloth, securities, or diamonds, to indicate some of the market areas in New York City. The external economy is realized through reducing marketing costs or, what is the same thing, an increased selling price realized by the producer. The organization of formal and informal markets in cities —for factors and intermediate goods as well as final product—plays an important role in the achievement of scale. In the opinion of some economists, however, reduction in cost to the consumer is not a true economy of scale but an irreversible downward shift of the supply curve arising from the breaking down of monopoly with new entry. It has the same effect.

GROWTH OF MARKETS

Markets may grow through increases in real income of the people of an area which enable them to buy more. Where markets are now worldwide, this and taste changes are the only means of expanding demand. But short of those commodities where the market is already the world, and historically of greatest importance, markets grow because of improvements in transport and communication. The market is originally local and small. Demand is restricted by the cost of getting goods out of the village and ignorance of whether they can be sold outside; supply is limited by the cost of getting goods into the village and ignorance of how much they can be bought for outside. In these circumstances, markets grow through increases in transport and communication. The expansion becomes cumulative. Increased outlets for a commodity give rise to increased real income which in turn raises the demand for other products. As new supplies of these come on the market, in turn, incomes grow further. The linkage of markets by an improvement in transportation or by an improvement in a product, which makes it lighter and more readily transported, becomes part of a developmental process.

In these circumstances, it is not surprising that economic development is correlated positively with transport facilities. Figures 9.1 and 9.2 relating railroad and highway construction per capita to income per capita give only a rough approximation of this, since qualification is needed for the density of population by area, responsible for the outstanding results in the case of Australia and Canada, and for other means of transport such as canal boat, seagoing vessel, etc.

It is unnecessary to dwell upon the means by which changes in

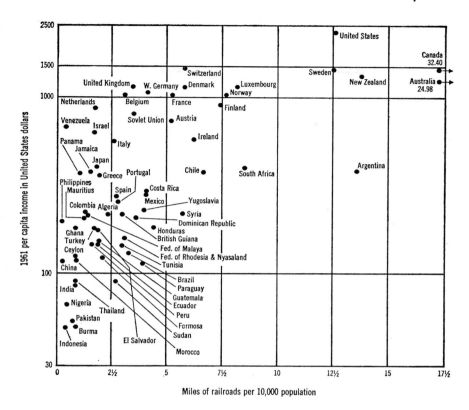

Figure 9.1 | Density of railroad lines (miles per 10,000 population), compared with income per capita, about 1961. SOURCES: Railroad mileage, *The Statesman's Yearbook, 1962–1963,* St Martin's Press, New York, 1962, *passim;* population, *Monthly Bulletin of Statistics,* United Nations, New York, May, 1963, pp. 1–4; income per capita, table 1.1, Average Income per Capita in Selected Countries, 1949 and 1961.

transport link markets and produce their expansion. These changes may be simple extensions or transport innovation. A striking example of extension was the spur given to economic development in Turkey by road building. The Truman Doctrine of military support for Greece and Turkey included in Turkey a major program of building military roads to render troops mobile. To these trunk lines were joined feeders, a good many built under Point Four assistance. The results were startling, in social terms[4] and in the linkage of markets for wheat pro-

[4] See D. Lerner, "The Grocer and the Chief," *Harper's Magazine,* September, 1955, pp. 47–56.

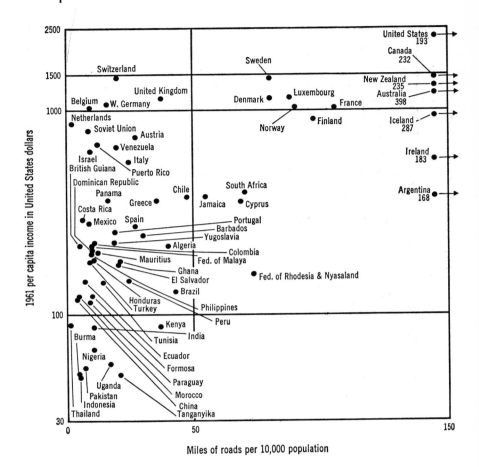

Figure 9.2 | Density of roads (miles per 10,000 population), compared with income per capita, about 1961. SOURCES: Road mileage, *The Statesman's Yearbook, 1962–1963*, St Martin's Press, New York, 1962, *passim* (in a few cases, some roads are not usable by motor vehicles throughout the year); population, *Monthly Bulletin of Statistics,* United Nations, New York, May, 1963, pp. 1–4; income per capita, table 1.1, Average Income per Capita in Selected Countries, 1949 and 1961.

duced in the interior and manufactures and imports available in the towns.

Development literature is full of such examples of the impact of roads. In some cases the emphasis is on the social changes; in others, on the possibilities provided for expansion of production, and economies of scale in the division of labor, through access to a new market. A significant handicap in southern Italy has been lack of communication. *Christ Stopped at Eboli*[5] tells that Christ stopped on His way south from Rome because the road network petered out. In Brazil the subsistence farmer has great difficulty in bringing his coffee to market, and the technical assistance mission visiting the farmer has to use jeep, boat, mule, and shank's mare.[6] In Oscar Lewis's account of *Life in a Mexican Village* frequent reference is made to the changes introduced when the road was built.[7] In Bolivia the building of the Santa Cruz–Cochabamba highway allowed a rapid increase in the commercial production of rice and sugar.

In the history of developed countries, great impact has been made by technological change in transport, particularly innovations of railroad, ironclad vessel, automobile and truck, and most recently the airplane, as well as cost-reducing investments, such as the Suez and Panama Canals and the Simplon Tunnel. The rise of the world economy is generally dated from 1870 after transcontinental railroad construction in the United States and similar construction in other areas combined with the general transoceanic haulage by ironclad steam vessel to bring the produce of the Western Hemisphere, India, and Africa to European ports on a substantial scale.

Too little attention is generally paid in these accounts to the spread of communication needed to link markets. Face-to-face trading in which the producer or his agent must deal directly with the buyer or his agent imposes a considerable limitation on the extent of the market. The peddler is an inefficient marketer compared with the traveling salesman who follows up leads derived from direct mail advertising, telephone canvas, or records of previous sales. Provision must be made especially for communication of price information so that the village trader can tell whether and when he chooses to take his plums to which city. In modern markets there has grown up a paraphernalia of market quotations in the general and specialized press, telephonic and telegraph communication, including ticker tapes, avalanches of discussion by mail of specifications, price, and delivery dates. These media are being adopted as means to development in a number of countries. Uruguayan radio broadcasts of agricultural prices are a

[5] This is the title of the book by Carlo Levi (Farrar, Straus & Cudahy, New York, 1947) which gives a vivid account of life in southern Italy in the 1930s.
[6] See A. T. Mosher, "The Agricultural Program of ACAR in Brazil," pamphlet in series on *Technical Cooperation in Latin America*, National Planning Association, Washington, D.C., 1955.
[7] The University of Illinois Press, Urbana, Ill., 1951, pp. xv, 36, 165, etc.

good example. Along with transport, or rather some distance in advance of capacity to transport, there must be a network of communication, which is vital to market operation.

A quantitative impression of the growth in numbers of people engaged in the distribution of goods, which is positively correlated with economic growth generally, is given in the next chapter, and particularly in Figures 10.4 and 10.6. That chapter also suggests some reasons why the figures of occupational distribution should be treated skeptically in very underdeveloped countries. Nonetheless, there can be no doubt that, as development proceeds, it takes more and more people to distribute goods, and less and less, proportionately, to make them. Production may be less significant than marketing and the services of transport and communication which spring up around it.

THE CHANGE IN CHARACTER OF MARKETS

With the growth in numbers of people in a market comes an inevitable change in its character. The major change is in the elasticities of demand and supply. It is a familiar observation in economics that, whereas the demand of an individual for a given commodity may be low, or the supply of a given producer, when linkage of markets takes place under competitive conditions, the elasticities of demand and supply facing the individual seller or buyer increase manyfold, and under pure competition, become infinite. The buyer in the village learns about alternative sources of supply. The seller is conscious of alternative outlets. For labor there are alternative occupations into which it becomes possible to move. The landowner cannot move his land but can contemplate its use in other than the traditional ways.

This increase in elasticity of demand and supply is vital to the effective working of the price system, discussed in Chapter 11 below. Here it may be said, however, that a number of economists consider that a primary distinction between developed and underdeveloped economies lies in the efficacy of their price systems. In underdeveloped economies, it is sometimes said, the price system is ineffective. An increase in the demand for a given product elicits no response because supply is inelastic, frequently at zero output. A decrease in price, moreover, produces no increased consumption because the limited number of buyers does not extend consumption at lower prices and no more buyers are added to their number. Only structural changes are capable of producing changes on the needed scale. In this circumstance, the nature of the economic analysis applicable to underdeveloped countries differs sharply from the marginal analysis associated with the price system of the developed countries.[8]

There may be differences in elasticities of demand and supply between developed and underdeveloped countries which are not solely a function of the size of markets as determined by transport and communication networks. Lack of interest in increased material well-being, so that consumption is unchanged at all levels of income, is one such feature which may be found in some underdeveloped countries. The existence of economies of scale external to the firm which cannot be turned into profit opportunities, and therefore do not lead to private investment undertakings, may be another. Still other factors play an important part, such as lack of capital, information, and skill which inhibits entry into new industries and reduces elasticity of supply, and the low level of income which inhibits demand. But a significant part of the difference in the character of developed and underdeveloped markets lies in the number of buyers and sellers, which again is frequently a function of their physical extent in space. The linking of local into regional and regional into national and world markets through the spread of transport and communications is a step in the direction of a more effective price system.

THE GROWTH OF MARKETS AND NATIONAL INCOME PER CAPITA

It should not be forgotten that growth of markets and the increased division of labor made possible thereby also directly increase income. Kuznets has pointed out that income in currently developed countries was higher prior to the Industrial Revolution than levels existing today in the underdeveloped parts of the world.[9] Using Colin Clark's crude figures of International Units (I.U.–dollars of United States purchasing power during 1925–1934) per occupied worker (not per capita), he notes that in Britain the level was more than 300 in 1800 and even in 1688, as compared with 230 to 250 for India in the 1930s and 1940s. Other countries which achieved levels of more than 300 I.U. prior to intensive industrialization were the United States in 1830, France in

---

[8] If lower price does not bring increased volume, it is sensible for producers and distributors to maintain the highest possible markup. See J. J. Spengler, "IBRD Mission Economic Growth Theory," *American Economic Review, Papers and Proceedings,* May, 1954, p. 590.

[9] S. Kuznets, "Toward a Theory of Economic Growth," in R. Lekachman (ed.), *National Policy for Economic Welfare at Home and Abroad,* Doubleday, Garden City, N.Y., 1955, p. 27.

the 1840s, Belgium in 1854, Germany in 1854, Sweden in 1860. By contrast, Brazil was scored at 153 in 1928 and rose rapidly to 297 by 1946.[10]

Kuznets forbears to attribute these relatively high levels of income to any particular cause. He is not even certain that they came from increases in output per worker, although this is regarded as probable. But, while the data which prove the point conclusively have not been gathered, it is a foregone conclusion that the answer is that to which Adam Smith attached so much importance—the division of labor. British agriculture benefited from technological improvement as well, but in part this depended again on the merging of markets, the concentration on cash crops instead of general-purpose subsistence or mixed farming, and production on a basis involving scale.

MARKETS AND MONEY

Specialization and exchange require the parallel growth of the money mechanism. With the commercial revolution inevitably come the development of paper money and checking instead of specie and coin, the evolution of credit instruments to finance roundabout production and the holding of stocks, and finally techniques for regulating the amount of money in the system. As the subsistence economy shrinks and the proportion of total income exchanged against money enlarges, a concomitant expansion in the money supply must take place. This expansion is indicated in the correlation between income per capita and money supply per capita given in Figure 9.3. This diagram reveals more than merely the increased demand for money for transactions. As first-year students of economics now know, money is sought for transactions, as a precaution against the unexpected, and for liquidity. Within the transactions portion of the total money supply, the widening of the proportion of real income earned in money form may be partly or wholly offset by increased efficiency in the use of money, leaving the major explanation of the growth of money in response to income to the precautionary and liquidity demands. But on whatever score, Figure 9.3 shows that within a rather wide range of variation, money increases as a percentage of national income with growth.

The question whether monetary policy can make an active contribution to growth or whether the best monetary policy can merely prevent inflationary losses is left for Chapter 13. Here it is enough to make the point that the monetary mechanism must be developed in parallel with linkage of markets and expanded use of money. At an

[10] *Ibid.*

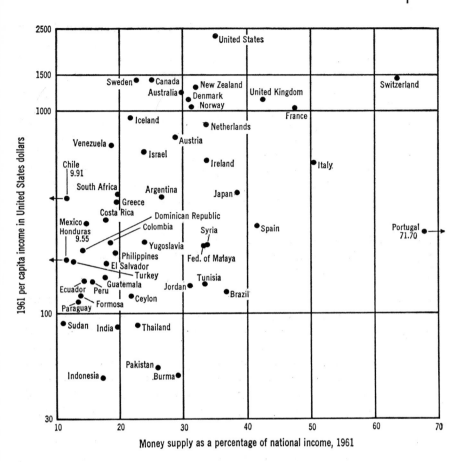

Figure 9.3 | Money supply as a percentage of national income compared with income per capita, about 1961. SOURCES: Money supply as a percentage of national income derived from figures for money supply (pp. 520–524) and national income (pp. 478–488), both in *Statistical Yearbook, 1962,* United Nations, New York, 1963; income per capita, table 1.1, Average Income per Capita in Selected Countries, 1949 and 1961.

early stage moneylenders are supplanted by commercial banks. Later a central bank is needed. And the money supply must grow in some relation to the growth of markets. Ordinarily, in the closed economy, this requirement will not be very different from the requirement of stability measured in terms of prices and/or employment. In an open economy, however, there may be failure of articulation between the monetary policy, which would maintain the foreign-exchange value of the currency, and the appropriate rate of monetary expansion, having in mind the rate of economic growth. In a number of such instances, however, the conflict between external and internal stability, including within the latter the requirements of growth, goes much deeper than any conflict between growth alone and external or internal requirements.[11]

Considerable debate has occurred historically over the appropriate rate of monetary expansion in the course of development. In addition to the overall rate of inflation or deflation, the sectoral distribution of income has been at issue. In caricature, Wall Street has been for deflation; mortgaged farmers and producers of commodities, for inflation or for a more rapid rate of monetary expansion.

IMPACT OF THE MARKET ON ENTREPRENEURS, LABOR, CAPITAL FORMATION

In some societies, trade is regarded as a low-status occupation and is handed over to foreign groups. Where this is not the case, however, the growth of markets performs an important role in preparing members of the society for economic development. Part of this preparation consists in training potential entrepreneurs. Traders develop capacity to maximize, sufficient literacy to calculate. More than this, however, the expansion of trading is preparatory for the degree of rationality, universalism, and functional specificity required of a developed economy.

In underdeveloped economies, trade is frequently partly a test of skill and partly an experience in social intercourse. The initial asking price is not "the price" but a stylized opening in an act or game. The rules of the game are few and far between, but the game is played partly for its own sake, as well as to be won, which explains the disappointment of some sellers when a Western tourist buys an article at the asking price. *Caveat emptor* applies—let the buyer beware. If he is cheated, it is his own fault. The seller expects no retribution, no repeat sales, and has no interest in building a reputation or good will.

It is a condition of markets which spread beyond face-to-face contacts, however, that these rules of the game be modified. Standardization of product and grading make possible the sale of goods halfway around the world, without the danger that the seller will misrepresent. In some commodities, such as wool and furs, it is impossible to grade

[11] See H. C. Wallich, *Monetary Problems of an Export Economy*, Harvard, Cambridge, Mass., 1950.

and standardize, so world markets are operated by auction with buyers present. But to sell its wheat without discount, Turkey found itself obliged to standardize and grade, to clean it of stones and mice. Before Denmark could sell butter on a large scale to Britain, the flavorful but frequently surprising "peasant butter" had to be brought to the standard consistency of "manor butter." And so on with native and estate rubber and a host of other products. Among the most notable of recent additions to the list is Indian khadi, or handwoven cloth, which it is believed would find a ready market in the United States but for the fact that more than half of it is found, upon arrival, to be below the specified standard, and is therefore shipped back to India.

At a later stage entrepreneurial talent is expended in differentiating products to increase the demand for the product of the firm. In an early stage the requirement of market standards, spread by wholesalers and jobbers back to producers, inculcates some of the training for mass production needed as a precondition of the industrial revolution.

Not only does the growth of markets train the entrepreneur: it eases his tasks. As the labor market grows, he can call upon it rather than beat the bushes for his workers. The same is true for capital and for intermediate goods. His need to hold large inventories of materials is reduced if these can be readily acquired in organized markets. His incentive to standardize, moreover, is that he can reduce his marketing problem, the task of showing the ultimate consumer exactly what his wares are. Production to the specifications of the market simplifies his task in another of its myriad facets.

The commercial revolution does more. It starts the accumulation of capital. Inventories and ships are two early objects of and outlets for capital accumulation. The productivity of capital becomes evident, the habit of saving spreads, and accumulations of capital capable of being converted to industrial use come gradually into existence.

The impact of commerce extends beyond the entrepreneur. Markets are located in cities, which are breeders of a different attitude toward tradition and material rewards. Production for the market requires division and organization of labor, whether in the small shop or on the plantation, which begin the inculcation of the discipline necessary for factory production.

On this showing there is a strong argument to be made for the proposition that economic development through industrialization should be preceded by commercialization, and the industrial by the commercial revolution. To short-cut the evolutionary process and attempt forthwith to turn a subsistence into an industrial economy may find the society badly equipped in capacity for transport and distribution. It may well be possible to abbreviate greatly the commercial period in the West, which lasted perhaps three hundred or four hundred years, but whether the process can be eliminated altogether is open to question. Especially is this the case in those countries which have relied on foreign traders to perform the necessary commerce over long periods of time: the Chinese merchant of the Philippines, Malaya, and Indonesia; the Armenian, Jew, and Greek in Turkey. A powerful case can be made that the rapid rate of growth in Turkey in recent years depended not only on the construction of trunk military and farm-to-market roads, but on the fact that Turkish citizens were forced, after the great transfers of population in 1921, to perform trading functions, and so were prepared for their later increased responsibilities.

The Japanese example may be put in the balance on the other side. Industrialization moved very rapidly and capacity at marketing increased *pari passu* rather than in advance. Government preserved order, provided the necessary expansion of money, but marketing grew up along with capacity at administering production, without the necessity for prior conditioning. This is a remarkable case. In my judgment, however, it provides the exception rather than the pattern. Attention to commerce and marketing is an important element in a design for development.

BLOCKS TO DEVELOPMENT IN MARKET ECONOMIES

It must not be thought that the linkage of markets which ultimately connects the interior village with the world economy is a cumulative process, which, well started, leads inevitably to industrialization. Many economies, for reasons not always clear, make an effective start along the commercial revolution and reach a stage at which further progress of a spontaneous character seems impossible. At least two elements in such situations can be observed: undue concern with the profit rate and widespread adoption of the speculative psychology.

A number of countries in Europe remained blocked essentially at a mercantilist stage of development for long periods. Markets developed and were traded in. But marketers became bemused by their rate of profit per unit sold rather than by the total profit per capital invested or some other rational criterion. High profits per unit tended to keep turnover small and were maintained only by limiting entry. Where it was impossible to limit entry, the combination of free entry and price fixing led to overcapacity and underutilization, the affliction which beset retail trade particularly in Belgium and France.

What seemed to be missing from this scene was the entrepreneur's interest in innovation for the sake of increasing his profits. The *petit bourgeoisie* ran its tiny cafe or *épicerie* (small corner grocery store) much the same way immediately after World War II as it had in 1870. As a member of the *bourgeoisie,* the owner had status. He was content. He grumbled that his level of living was no higher, and in France he might have been beguiled by the Poujade movement into taking political action. But these countries had failed to pass the stage of mercantilism prior to about 1955 largely because the pattern of trade had become frozen. This suggests that, while commercial revolution may be a necessary prelude to industrial development, it may not be sufficient.

A second form of marketing pathology is speculative fever. In Western Europe and the United States this disability has not been unknown, but its incidence has been sharp and short. The South Sea Bubble, Crédit Mobilier, and the Ponzi scheme are part of the economic history of the West, but they do not dominate it.

In the Middle East and in many parts of Latin America, social status is accorded to wealth, but wealth appears to be the result of luck rather than work. A corner on the Alexandria cotton market, a squeeze in wheat, or a relatively small movement in the price of coffee, rubber, sugar, or tin can produce sizable fortunes from trading on organized commodity markets. In Western Europe and the United States, such speculation has by no means been unknown, but a considerable part of speculative interest has attached to corporation securities, and the speculative position of the owner of a block of shares can be improved by effective production on the part of the corporation and by effective innovation.

Stabilizing speculation performs a useful economic function in providing additional demand when supplies are heavy and additional supply when this is needed. Speculation, however, may be destabilizing, exaggerating the swing of prices and interfering with orderly production and distribution. More significant, perhaps, for economic development in the long run, it creates a speculative psychology which tends to denigrate success through work and thrift and to elevate the role of luck. Western development has never been free of predation, but it has been based on work. Where fortunes can be made far more readily, and with less effort, through speculative excesses, interest in horse races, football pools, and the national lottery, the incentive to continuous application diminishes. The authors of the International

Bank study on prerevolutionary Cuba referred to speculative interest in sugar in that country as economic diabetes.

DISTRIBUTION AND DEVELOPMENT

The emphasis on markets in spontaneous or private enterprise development must not lead anyone to believe that no comparable set of problems exists in, say, the Soviet Union. There the allocation of resources to distribution is clear: apart from private marketing arrangements, there must be transport, workers, and administrators, plus the state stores, whose task it is to distribute goods. In spontaneous development, growth of size of market through the fusion of smaller markets, with improved transport and communication, has been an engine assisting in the process of development. One is obliged to say an engine, rather than the engine, since there are cases on record of development and no substantial fusion of markets (Japan) and commercial revolutions which did not roll forward into industrial development.

But whether markets pull development or lag behind it, it is evident that much planning in the area of economic development today neglects distribution. The lessons concerning transport and communication have been learned in the ordinary planning effort, as discussed below in Chapter 11. But marketing means more than this. Storage facilities in particular tend to be neglected, and encouragement to middlemen, wholesalers, jobbers, who are too often regarded as parasites because of the distasteful record of the market manipulator. Product standardization may also be an outlet for energy and resources with a high payout in terms of permitting more effective scales of production and reducing costs of distribution.

Distribution is inescapable. The Western economist has always been fascinated with how swiftly, efficiently, and with how little direction free markets can perform this function. Whether the fusion of local into larger markets be encouraged for its transforming function, or the movement of goods and services into consumption and investment be tackled directly according to plan, distribution takes resources. It cannot be overlooked.

SUMMARY

Efficiency of production is partly a function of its scale, which in turn is limited by the size of the market. The larger the scale, the cheaper the cost of the product when there exist economies external to the firm. In economic development, moreover, one expects to meet opportunities for internal economies of scale blocked by the existence of monopolies where entry is limited by lack of knowledge, capital, skill, etc.

The growth process can be led by a widening of the market, which in turn may result from increased efficiency in transport or communications. Cheapening transport fuses markets, bringing additional buyers and sellers into contact one with another, increasing elasticities of demand and supply. Or markets can grow through an increase in efficiency and income in any commodity, which increases the effective demand for other products and spreads in cumulative fashion. Even where the growth process is led by efficiency in production, however, the requirements of distribution are inescapable.

BIBLIOGRAPHY

Most of the literature emphasizes external economies rather than the spread of the market. See especially Tibor Scitovsky, "Two Concepts of External Economies," *Journal of Political Economy*, August, 1954, pp. 143–151, reprinted in both Agarwala and Singh (eds.), selection 14, and Morgan, Betz, and Choudhry (eds.), selection 13; Marcus Fleming, "External Economies and the Doctrine of Balanced Growth," *Economic Journal*, June, 1955, pp. 241–256, reprinted in both Agarwala and Singh (eds.), selection 13, and Okun and Richardson (eds.), selection 13; Rosenstein-Rodan, "Notes on the Theory of the 'Big Push'" in Ellis and Wallich (eds.), *Economic Development for Latin America*, St Martin's, New York, 1961, pp. 57–81 (with discussion).

Among the few works on marketing are W. H. Nicholls, "Domestic Trade in an Underdeveloped Country: Turkey," *Journal of Political Economy*, December, 1951, pp. 463–480, and J. K. Galbraith and R. H. Holton, *Marketing Efficiency in Puerto Rico*, Harvard, Cambridge, Mass., 1955.

10 | *Transformation*

THE MULTISECTORAL ECONOMY

Thus far we have dealt almost entirely with the subject of growth—more output in a single-good economy. The time has come to take cognizance of the fact that economic development involves change—change in structure, function, resource allocation, which we sum up in the word "transformation."[1]

Transformation is required because of the physiological and psychological limits to increased consumption in any one good. The one-commodity world of growth we have been exploring cannot take us far because it requires unit-income elasticity of demand for the one commodity: demand for the product increases with capacity to turn it out. If there were more than one good, it would be arbitrary to assume that income-elasticity for each was unitary. Even in the one-good model, one is tempted to admit diminishing returns in consumption, which requires the introduction of a second good—savings, or leisure. Moreover, enough is known about the behavior of demand to enable one to make some fairly realistic assumptions. Transformation is required because, with increased output and income, the demand for some products increases less than proportionately, and the demand for others, including in this category leisure and savings, more than proportionately. While the demand for all goods and services excluding savings and leisure can be less than unity, it cannot if these are included.

ENGEL'S LAW

It is well known that the Prussian statistician Ernst Engel discovered the uniformity that, with the growth of income above a certain mini-

---

[1] I. Svennilson, *Growth and Stagnation in the European Economy*, United Nations, Economic Commission for Europe, Geneva, 1954, p. 7, uses the word transformation to cover capital deepening, innovations, and changes in the relation of foreign

mum, consumption of food decreases as a percentage of income, even though the absolute amount of food consumption increases. A considerable difference is made, to be sure, whether one counts food as it leaves the farm in its rudimentary state or food served on the table at home or in a restaurant. Engel's law applies to both, but to basic food more than to food plus services embodied in it in the finished state. Moreover, the demand for simple food energy in calories responds more quickly to the law than protein or protective foods.

Unfortunately the data on income-elasticities of demand for various types of food are not sufficiently extensive to enable us to furnish measurements of income-elasticity for food for countries at various stages of growth. It is believed that the income-elasticity of demand for food is close to unity in a number of densely populated and under-developed countries: this would mean that most or all of an increase in income would be spent for increased consumption of food. And it is known that in the United States only a small proportion of an increase in income is spent in ways which increase the sales of farmers.[2] But adequate comparative studies are lacking. The best that can be done is to use budget studies for given countries to illustrate how demand alters with rising income within a given culture. Figure 10.1 furnishes data from the Food and Agriculture Organization in Rome on income-elasticities of demand for food for various areas in the world, along with average per capita incomes in dollars of 1955 purchasing power. Between the poorest area, Asia, and the richest, North America, the income-elasticity for food declines from 0.9 to 0.16.

Engel's law was worked out for food consumption, but it applies much more widely. Like production, consumption follows a Gompertz curve of growth. The physical demand for any product will have an upper limit, so that no matter what happens to per capita income, the rate of growth of demand for a given product will not expand faster than the rate of population increase when this limit has been reached. Moreover, the limit is approached asymptotically, so that the demand pattern for any new good which wins public acceptance is likely to show a slow rate of increase as this acceptance is being won, a high income-elasticity in the middle stages, and thereafter a decline in income-elasticity as the physical limit of consumption is approached.

This law of consumption has great importance for economic growth.

---

trade to domestic output, as well as the redistribution of labor among industries. The present view is more narrow. Svennilson's inspiration is acknowledged, especially his view that barriers to transformation will block growth.

[2] For particular (inferior) goods, income-elasticity can of course be negative. But no class of consumption such as food is inferior as a whole.

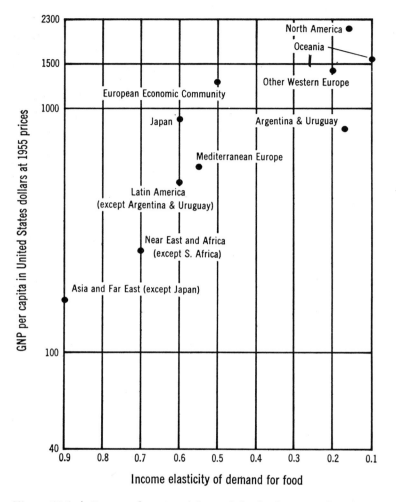

Figure 10.1 | Income-elasticity of demand for food compared with GNP per capita in selected areas, 1957–1959. SOURCES: Income-elasticity and GNP per capita (1957–1959) from the Food and Agricultural Organization, *Agricultural Commodities: Projections for 1970,* Rome, 1962, p. A-2.

To illustrate with a closed economy, if transformation is impossible, economic growth will fail at some stage because of lack of demand. Without new goods, and without new entrepreneurs to arrange the transfer of capital and labor into their production, economic development must slow down with the decline of demand for old products.

PRIMARY, SECONDARY, AND TERTIARY PRODUCTION

An early contributor to the modern discussion of economic development was A. G. B. Fisher, who introduced the concept of primary, secondary, and tertiary occupations.[3] Fisher observed that countries could be classified with respect to the proportions of their total labor force engaged in these sectors. Primary production was defined originally to include agricultural and pastoral production, and, in some versions, mining. Secondary production comprised manufacturing, generally mining, and, as a rule, construction. Tertiary industry consisted in transport and communications, trade, government, personal and domestic service, and in some versions, construction.

Fisher's insight was originally supported by the wide-ranging and imaginative statistical research of Colin Clark,[4] who calculated sectoral labor inputs and total outputs. Figures 10.2 to 10.4, derived from somewhat more up-to-date figures, show the percentage of the economically active population engaged in the primary, secondary, and tertiary sectors, and support Fisher's insight in a general way. The proportion of the labor force in agriculture declines as a country advances, with some adjustment for foreign trade, from 80 per cent for the least developed to 11 to 12 per cent for the most developed, and 5 per cent in the case of Britain which imports a considerable proportion of its food. The proportion of labor engaged in secondary industry increases with growth, but levels out short of 50 per cent, and closer, in the usual case, to 40 per cent. The sector with the highest income-elasticity, which still grows after agriculture and industry have evened out, is services.

The statistics bearing on this transformation will be criticized in a minute. Here, however, it is important to indicate that the total allocation of resources by sectors should not be measured by the single factor, labor. Factor proportions not only may differ by sectors; they must do so, since secondary industry uses much less land than primary, and tertiary industry virtually none. Even if the marginal products of land, labor, and capital are identical in all three sectors, resource allocation is inadequately measured by a single factor and presents an

---

[3] A. G. B. Fishei, "Economic Implications of Material Progress," *International Labour Review*, July, 1935, pp. 5–18; and "Primary, Secondary and Tertiary Production," *Economic Record*, June, 1939, pp. 24–38.

[4] C. Clark, *The Conditions of Economic Progress*, 1st ed., St Martin's, New York, 1940, chap. V; 2d ed. (completely rewritten), St Martin's, New York, 1951, chap. IX; 3d ed., St Martin's, New York, 1957, chap. VII.

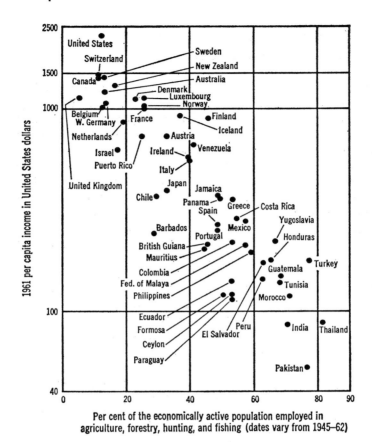

Figure 10.2 | Percentage of economically active population engaged in primary production (agriculture, forestry, fishing), various dates, 1945 to 1962, compared with income per capita in 1961. SOURCES: Percentage of economically active population engaged in agriculture, forestry, hunting, fishing derived from *Yearbook of Labor Statistics, 1962,* International Labor Office, Geneva, 1962, table 4, pp. 14–59; income per capita, table 1.1, Average Income per Capita in Selected Countries, 1949 and 1961.

index-number problem if the attempt is made to measure the total resource input. The more of a given factor input, the lower its marginal product, and the lower weight its quantity input is accorded. The higher the marginal product, the higher the price weight of the scarce factor. Because of this index-number difficulty in measuring capital/

labor ratios between countries it is hard to obtain meaningful results. The country with abundant capital and scarce labor has a low value for the one and a high for the other; and vice versa for the country with little capital. Unless the measure is put in physical terms, such as horsepower or acres per head, international comparison of factor proportions and of total factor inputs is a blind alley.

Figure 10.3 | Percentage of economically active population engaged in secondary production (manufacturing, mining, and construction), various dates, 1945 to 1962, compared with income per capita in 1961. SOURCES: Percentage of economically active population engaged in manufacturing, mining, and construction derived from *Yearbook of Labor Statistics, 1962*, International Labor Office, Geneva, 1962, table 4, pp. 14–59; income per capita, table 1.1, Average Income per Capita in Selected Countries, 1949 and 1961.

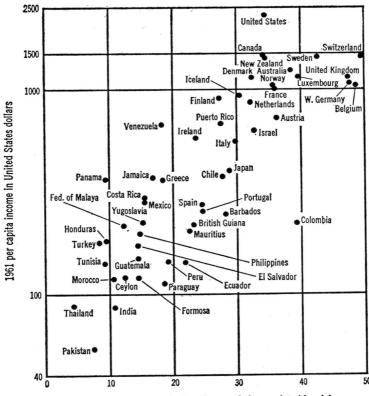

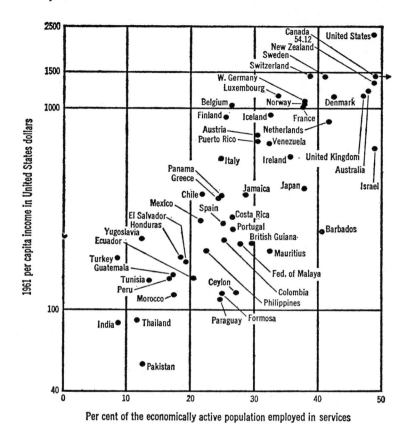

Figure 10.4 | Percentage of economically active population engaged in tertiary production (services, including electricity, gas, water, sanitary services, commerce, transport, storage, communication, etc.), various dates, 1945 to 1962, compared with income per capita in 1961. SOURCES: Percentages of economically active population in services derived from *Yearbook of Labor Statistics, 1962,* International Labor Office, Geneva, 1962, table 4, pp. 14–59; income per capita, table 1.1, Average Income per Capita in Selected Countries, 1949 and 1961.

These difficulties apply where the marginal product of each factor is identical among sectors. But this is more nearly approached in developed than in underdeveloped countries. In underdeveloped countries factor as well as goods markets are localized, separate, monopolistically competitive. Some factors may not be marketed at all, but are allocated by tradition. Perroux has called underdeveloped economies "disarticulated" with this aspect in mind, and Myrdal approaches the same concept from a different direction when he suggests that economic development is a precondition of "economic integration." In his sense, integration means equalization of factor prices with the elimination of all noncompeting groups (or quasi rents) except those based on physical attributes of factors, including in labor, intelligence as well as dexterity, mechanical aptitude, etc.[5] If labor can earn more in industry than in agriculture, but does not move, there is a presumptive case for reallocation. This is equally the case if capital can earn more in agriculture than in industry. Colin Clark has propounded the "law" that labor will move from agricultural occupations into industry when the return in industry is twice as high as in agriculture, the wide difference being needed to compensate for nonwage benefits in agriculture and costs of urban living, as well as to overcome inertia.

A widespread view among economists is that labor in agriculture in overpopulated, underdeveloped countries is often redundant to the point where it contributes no marginal product at all. The marginal productivity of the last worker could in fact be negative: he produced nothing and got in the way of others who would be more productive without him. This is called "disguised unemployment." The men appear to be employed, but make no contribution to output. The concept of disguised unemployment is debated. It is not agreed whether it should be reserved for cases where the marginal physical product of labor is zero, or negative, e.g., where the addition of more labor does not lift production to a higher isoquant on a production function because the economy is already working at a point where the isoquant is horizontal (as at point w in Figure 3.1) or merely for those cases in which it is well below other occupations; whether the highly seasonal character of much agricultural work is a form of disguised unemployment or merely an inescapable condition; and whether in any particular area or country—Latin America, India, southern Italy—there is in actuality disguised unemployment, and how much. Where disguised unemployment may be said to exist, because the marginal product of labor is zero or approaches zero, labor nonetheless receives a return—the subsistence wage at a minimum—but generally as a transfer from another factor share, presumably rent. It may, in fact, receive its average product, which is positive, when its marginal product is zero. This would mean that total product would be divided among all workers, leaving nothing for rent or interest.

Conceptually, of course, one can have disguised unemployment of

[5] G. Myrdal, "Toward a More Closely Integrated Free-world Economy," in R. Lekachman (ed.), *National Policy for Economic Welfare at Home and Abroad,* Doubleday, Garden City, N.Y., 1955, pp. 235–292; and *An International Economy,* Harper, New York, 1956, esp. chaps. 1–4.

labor in industry. At one stage in the postwar period it was stated that too much labor had moved from farms to towns in Yugoslavia, to the point where the marginal productivity of labor was higher in agriculture with unused land than in industry, where workers were getting in one another's way. The more typical phenomenon, however, is the movement from disguised unemployment in agriculture to open unemployment in towns.

Transformation, then, may have two aspects in the course of economic development: first, resource reallocation as a consequence of the improved functioning of factor markets, even without any increase of inputs or increased efficiency of existing inputs; and second, as demand changes, resource reallocation with the growth of income for whatever reason. The equalization of marginal product of factors has gone further in Britain than in the United States, it may be observed. In Britain, net labor productivity is as high in agriculture as in industry. In the United States this is not the case. This country has in fact not one agriculture but two: an efficient, capital-intensive, commercial agriculture, located for the most part in the Middle West, Texas, and California, together with parts of the South; and a subsistence, labor-intensive, impoverished agriculture, largely in the South, in the hills of the border states, and in parts of New England.[6] In this respect, development has not brought about economic articulation.

MEASUREMENT OF PRIMARY, SECONDARY, AND TERTIARY PRODUCTION

The data on the allocation of resources in Figures 10.2 to 10.4 are an approximation only, for a variety of reasons. Some of these have been referred to obliquely already. Where labor productivity is lower in agriculture than in industry, a choice is presented between using income generated by sectors and numbers of gainfully employed. In an average underdeveloped country, 80 per cent of the working population may be engaged in agriculture; but since their productivity on the average is as little as one-third that of people engaged in secondary and tertiary production, the proportion of income generated in that sector will amount to less than that. With the numbers chosen,

[6] See T. W. Schultz, "Reflections on Poverty within Agriculture," *Journal of Political Economy*, February, 1950, pp. 1–15.

this proportion will be 57 per cent, since $80/[80 + (20 \cdot 3)] = 57\%$.[7]

A second qualification is needed for foreign trade. The allocation of resources adequately measures the state of demand in a closed economy, since production and consumption are identical, except for changes in stocks which differ from one sector to another. But in an open economy, primary products may be exchanged for manufactures in foreign trade, or vice versa, with the result that the allocation of resources by sectors does not reflect the state of demand. Resources which are engaged in primary production which is exported, as in Turkey, are really engaged in satisfying the demand for secondary products, while contrariwise in Britain, manufacturing industry is needed to feed the population through the exchange of exports of secondary products for imports of primary.

A third difficulty is due to the nature of the data and the fact that they, like other statistical measures developed by mature economies, do not neatly fit underdeveloped countries. Bauer and Yamey have pointed out that occupational differentiation is carried much less distance in underdeveloped countries than in developed.[8] Specialization is imperfect. People reported to be engaged in agriculture spend time in trading and are partly idle for lack of complementary resources or during the dead season. The assignment of whole men to specific sectors presupposes a division of labor which has not been attained, with the result that the figures for tertiary industry are vastly understated and those for agriculture overstated. Nor is imperfect specialization confined to agriculture: enterpreneurs in underdeveloped countries double in brass in a dozen capacities. And Bauer and Yamey note that even "doctors, lawyers, and leading chiefs (in Nigeria) have extensive trading interests."

Finally, it should be mentioned that Fisher's generalization lumps under tertiary production a variety of services and that the demand for these is by no means uniform from service to service. This of course is not surprising. Demand for various foods differs widely, from negative income-elasticities in potatoes and rye bread to very high

---

[7] For figures on the comparative productivity in agriculture and the rest of the economy, see E. M. Ojala, *Agriculture and Economic Progress*, Oxford, Fair Lawn, N.J., 1952, table LI.

[8] See P. T. Bauer and B. S. Yamey, "Economic Progress and Occupational Distribution," *Economic Journal*, December, 1951, pp. 74–85, reprinted in Morgan, Betz, and Choudhry (eds.), selection 26, and in Okun and Richardson (eds.), selection 18; A. G. B. Fisher, "A Note on Tertiary Production," *Economic Journal*, December, 1952, pp. 830–834; S. Rottenberg, "Note on Economic Progress and Occupational Distribution," *Review of Economics and Statistics*, May, 1953, pp. 168–170.

ones in lobster and champagne. Similarly with secondary production, which includes both necessities of low income-elasticity (work clothing) and luxury products (sports cars). But tertiary production seems even more disparate in its behavior. Most services—education, government, entertainment, transport and communication, commerce—have high income-elasticities at early stages of economic development and

Figure 10.5 | Percentage of United States labor force engaged in primary, secondary, and tertiary production, 1820–1940. SOURCE: S. Kuznets, appendix to "Toward a Theory of Economic Growth," in R. Lekachman (ed.), *National Policy for Economic Welfare at Home and Abroad*, Doubleday, Garden City, N.Y., 1955, based on Colin Clark, *The Conditions of Economic Progress*, St Martin's, New York, 1951, chap. IX.

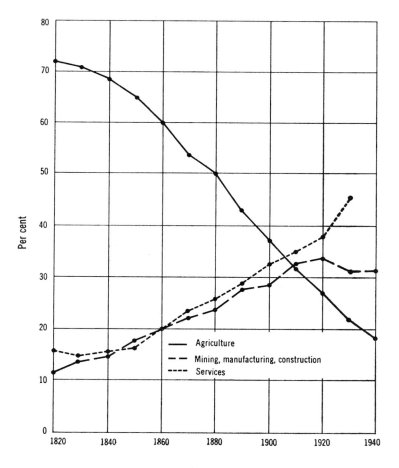

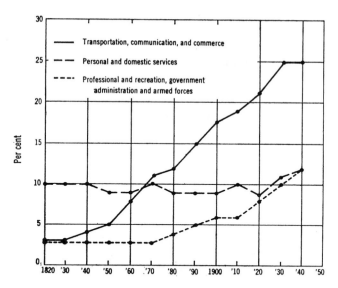

Figure 10.6 | Percentage of United States labor force engaged in various branches of tertiary production, 1820–1940. SOURCE: S. Kuznets, appendix to "Toward a Theory of Economic Growth," in R. Lekachman (ed.), *National Policy for Economic Welfare at Home and Abroad*, Doubleday, Garden City, N.Y., 1955, based on Colin Clark, *The Conditions of Economic Progress*, St Martin's, New York, 1951, chap. IX.

grow faster than total output. But others, particularly domestic service, follow mixed trends, depending upon the level of income, its distribution, and social attitudes toward the occupation. Domestic service in households is not separated in the statistics from hotel services, although both tend to follow different patterns of demand with respect to income. In Britain the composite group declines sharply with development, from 17 per cent of the gainfully occupied in 1880 to 11 per cent in 1940. In Belgium from 1880 to 1930, the decline was from 20 to 5 per cent. In the United States, on the other hand, the total fell from 10 per cent in 1870 to 9 per cent in 1900 and the same in 1920, before rising to 12 per cent in 1940. And in India the level was 8 per cent in 1880, and appears to have risen between 1910 and 1930 from 7 to 10 per cent.[9] This suggests that demand patterns, at least in the field of tertiary production, are by no means identical from country to

[9] All figures are from C. Clark, *The Conditions of Economic Progress*, 2d ed., St Martin's, New York, 1951, chap. IX.

country, and that, even if all countries experience the same growth in income per capita, their requirements as to transformation may significantly differ. The data for the United States for all sectors, and for separate activities within the tertiary sector, are shown in Figures 10.5 and 10.6.

SYSTEMATIC PRODUCTIVITY DIFFERENCES BY SECTORS

The French statistician, J. Fourastié, who is much interested in productivity, has suggested a model of economic development which combines systematic differences in productivity by sectors with the pattern of income-elasticity of demand implied by Engel's law.[10] In his exposition, potatoes are chosen as an example of a primary good, bicycles of secondary, and a hotel room of tertiary output. Labor productivity in the first is said to have increased from 100 in 1800 to 130 in 1950. Consumption rose continuously throughout the period to the 1920s, but has recently developed negative income-elasticity with per capita consumption 250 per cent of the 1800 level. In bicycles, it is necessary to take 1900 as a base year, since the product is relatively new: productivity increased from 100 in 1900 to 700 in 1950, and is still increasing. Consumption has gone up nine times in the same period, but is beginning to level off. In hotel rooms, labor productivity remained practically unchanged from 1800 to 1950, but demand brought about an increase in consumption from 100 in 1800 to 10,000 in 1950. Fourastié uses these systematic differences in productivity and demand by sectors to project systematic changes in the terms of trade which favor tertiary industry over primary, and both over secondary.

It is by no means clear that the productivity differences between sectors are everywhere as sharp as in this example. In the United States, labor productivity or output per worker has been rising as rapidly in agriculture as in industry in recent years—or more rapidly —owing partly to increased investment of capital and partly to higher real productivity. Moreover, productivity in tertiary industry is not stationary. Many tertiary occupations are labor-intensive, with a given state of the arts; and, with only small amounts of capital, limits of productivity of labor are quickly reached. But in the United States substantial changes in production functions have occurred in retailing and administration, to say nothing of transport and communication. Economies of scale are being achieved in the large-scale shopping

---

[10] See J. Fourastié, *La Productivité*, Presses Universitaires de France, Paris, 1952.

center, with a substantial investment in land for parking as well as area of building; automation is increasing capital-intensity in administration and improving the productivity of labor and of total resources.

Without commitment to any values of systematic changes in productivity by sectors, therefore, it may still be possible to suggest broadly that, on balance, labor productivity tends to be higher in secondary than in primary production, and higher in primary production than in tertiary production as a whole, though not in the capital-intensive branches of transport and communication. This, of course, is the gross productivity of labor, i.e., total output divided by the number of workers, or the inverse of the labor/output ratio, and differs from marginal productivity of labor which makes allowance for the contribution of other factors. To the extent that this is true, and demand for tertiary production is more income-elastic than that for manufactured products turned out by secondary industry, transformation requires first a fairly slow transfer of labor from agriculture to industry, and then a much faster movement to tertiary production. Since much of the demand for tertiary production, however, in commerce as in transport and communication, is complementary to secondary production, the movement of labor into secondary and tertiary production is not sequential but simultaneous, which smooths out the process.

ECONOMIC DEVELOPMENT WITH UNLIMITED SUPPLIES OF LABOR

An important model of economic development by W. Arthur Lewis focuses upon the transformation of the economy from purely agricultural to industry and agriculture, starting from the position of unlimited supplies of labor in agriculture.[11] This model, refined by G. Ranis and J. C. H. Fei,[12] is not only intellectually elegant, but has considerable explanatory power in economic history and in the growth of developed countries.

The process starts with an autonomous expansion in demand in industry. Labor shifts from agriculture into industry, but since there is disguised unemployment in agriculture, the supply price of labor does not rise there. Redundant supplies of labor at existing wages hold

---

[11] "Economic Development with Unlimited Supplies of Labor," *Manchester School*, May, 1954, pp. 131–191, reprinted in Agarwala and Singh (eds.), selection 6; Morgan, Betz, and Choudhry (eds.), selection 20; Okun and Richardson (eds.), selection 24.

[12] "A Theory of Economic Development," *American Economic Review*, September, 1961, pp. 533–565.

down labor costs in industry. Higher demand and higher prices in industry therefore mean higher profits, which are plowed back into capital formation, more demand for industrial output, further shifts of labor out of agriculture into industry. The process halts only when disguised unemployment in agriculture has been eliminated by this transfer, thus effecting the equalization of marginal productivities of labor in the two sectors.

Note that this model is close to the Ricardian, except that it neglects the central concern of Ricardo—how the price of food is to be held down. We return to this vital issue in the next several chapters. If it be assumed, however, that the supply of labor to industry is infinitely elastic at a steady wage for a considerable distance because of redundant labor in agriculture, this can help explain "takeoff," which comes to an end when wages start to rise with increased capital formation.

Historically, one effect stands out which is not explicit in the Lewis or the Ranis and Fei models: as labor leaves agriculture, raising wages there, it applies pressure for rationalization of agricultural technology, for the introduction of machinery and other capital-intensive methods, such as fertilizer. Productivity increases in industry interact with productivity increases in agriculture after the supply of labor has been drawn down. This is why Mrs. Lutz believes that the economic development of southern Italy requires not only the movement of capital from north to south, but the movement of labor from south to north, as is in fact happening.[13]

This model fits nineteenth-century Britain fairly well, as Habakkuk has pointed out.[14] In the first half of the century, after the enclosures and with the decline of domestic industry, the supply of labor available from agriculture was very large. There is debate whether the level of living rose or fell down to 1850, but if it moved in either direction, it was not far. Redundant farm workers streamed into manufacturing, mining, and services at constant wages, to keep profits, capital formation, and growth all high. After the middle of the century, there was a boom, with rising wages to 1873 as the labor supply became limited, and still further rising real wages, but no boom, because of squeezed profits, to the end of the century.

In postwar Europe, too, the rapid expansion on the Continent was fed from 1950 to the early 1960s by unlimited supplies of labor coming from East Germany as refugees, from southern Italy, from French

[13] Vera C. Lutz, *Italy: A Study in Economic Development*, Oxford, Fair Lawn, N.J., 1962.
[14] See H. J. Habakkuk, *American and British Technology in the Nineteenth Century*, Cambridge, New York, 1962, chap. V, esp. p. 140.

agriculture, and from the cutting off of Dutch emigration. Until about 1960, wages lagged behind increases in productivity and profits were maintained at high levels, with strong pressure for reinvestment of industrial profits. When the labor supply began to dry up, wage rates rose rapidly, profits fell, and rates of growth slowed down.

A somewhat analogous model of growth has been explored by Nurkse, who contemplates using redundant workers in agriculture to contribute to capital formation.[15] If their productivity in agriculture were zero, and could be positive in road building, the economy would gain and grow from transferring them from agriculture to road building. But this model, like Lewis's, encounters the formidable difficulty that these men are fed when they are on the farm and may not be when they leave—a subject we defer mainly for Chapter 12.

OTHER SEQUENCES IN TRANSFORMATION

These models assume that growth begins with an increase in demand in the industrial sector or in government capital formation. There is no need to start there. The process might begin with a general increase in productivity, which would call for reallocation of resources in accordance with income-elasticities; or with particular supply changes. Whether a particular supply change attracts resources to the industry or releases resources for other industries depends upon the elasticity of demand for its product, as well as the supply elasticity. If the good is widely used with an elastic demand, perhaps an industrial product, lower costs leading to price reductions (because of an elastic, competitive supply) will expand output and require resources to move into the industry. But if cost reduction encounters an inelastic demand, perhaps because it occurs in food, it will release resources for use elsewhere in the economy in accordance with the incremental spending of consumers who now spend less on the cheaper commodity.

Clark's emphasis on changing proportions of primary, secondary, and tertiary production has led to the fallacy of *post hoc, ergo propter hoc:* developed countries have large sectors of secondary and tertiary production; our country will be developed by expanding secondary and tertiary production. Frequently tertiary production is ignored altogether and development is identified with industrialization. It is the corrective to this attitude which has led to the emphasis on "balanced growth" discussed in the next chapter.

But whether the increase in productivity leads and stimulates de-

[15] R. Nurkse, *Problems of Capital Formation in Underdeveloped Countries,* Blackwell, Oxford, 1953.

mand or an increase in demand induces a rise in productivity—or whether the two are nearly simultaneous as in the examples of Sweden and Denmark referred to in early chapters—certain requirements must be met. There must be a new group of entrepreneurs or entry by old entrepreneurs into new lines of activity and exit from the old. The flow of capital must be redirected into new lines. New labor skills must be developed, or old converted. Occupational and possibly spatial mobility must permit recruitment of the new labor force. Innovation is needed, or effective and frequently adaptive imitation of examples already extant. It may be necessary, as indicated earlier, to undertake some innovation in the field of economic and social institutions.

BARRIERS TO TRANSFORMATION

A variety of barriers to transformation is suggested by the last paragraph. Lack of entrepreneurship, labor immobility, rigid and inappropriate institutions pose obstacles to the evolution of the structure of the economy in the direction required by the shifting of demand. The prices of old outputs decline; those of new rise. But nothing happens. Supply is inelastic in the face of falling prices in the first case, despite rising prices in the second. Monopoly profits elicit no expansion of old firms, and no entry of new. The system becomes inured to high returns in one area and to low in another.

This takes us back to noneconomic factors, such as the system of land tenure, under which equal inheritance will immobilize agricultural workers on the farm. The classic case is nineteenth-century France. Here the immobility of French labor on the farm meant that industry was attracted to rural locations, using female or part-time male labor which continued to work the land. This system had one advantage—it eliminated the necessity of constructing dwellings in cities—but this was unimportant compared with the major disadvantage—that industry and agriculture mutually discouraged, rather than stimulated, each other. Part-time labor was cheap, so that industry was under no incentive to invest in labor-saving machinery. Farm workers supplemented their income in the factory, so they felt no pressure to improve agricultural efficiency. Where there was a strong enough pull to the city—as around Paris and in the north—the immobility of the farmer was overcome and there developed efficient industry in the cities and efficient agriculture in the countryside. Elsewhere, in Alsace, in central France and in the south and west, transformation was inhibited by worker immobility.

The slowing down of European economic growth between the world wars, in Svennilson's view, resulted from a temporary incapacity to transform the economic structure in line with the increased economic potential made possible by the higher technology and from an inability to adjust to the changes in world structure which had taken place during the war. The rest of the world had developed capacity in textiles, matches, basic steel, and energy. Europe insisted on continuing to produce and sell to the world textiles, matches, basic steel, and coal. The new industries of automobiles, engineering, chemicals, and electrical equipment were slow in developing; textiles and coal were slow in transferring their resources into other occupations. Management in iron and steel, matches, and similar industries clung to old methods and tried to hold their position by organizing world cartels. After World War II, Europe achieved a more effective reorganization of the economic structure; textile and coal industries were permitted to shrink. The modernized engineering, chemical, and electrical industries expanded their employment. Increased supplies of Middle East oil and heightened investment in hydroelectric facilities permitted a substitution of new sources of energy for the coal.

In underdeveloped countries, lack of capital, unskilled labor, absence of entrepreneurship, and social structure which emphasizes traditional irrationality, particularism, and diffuse functional relationships are all barriers to transformation. There is also a danger that a governmental program will plan too drastic a restructuring of capital investment, which will fail for lack of the social capacity to carry it out. Economic development is a product of many interlocking and articulated changes. Construction of a hundred factories, together with connecting transport and public utilities, will not by itself convert an agricultural to an industrial state.

SOCIAL TRANSFORMATION — URBANIZATION

It is appropriate to tie discussion of change in economic structure to the parallel social change and, in particular, to the growth of cities in development. The two movements are interconnected in a variety of ways. Specialization and exchange based on markets give the first impetus to increased production. Markets require cities. Pirenne explains that by the ninth century the earlier cities of Europe virtually disappeared. Their revival was initially due to the requirements of defense and of administration, particularly ecclesiastical, with its requirement of cathedrals. But beyond this, and more significant, the city was the home of the merchant and of the rising middle class which he represented.[16]

Cities have been classified as eotechnic, paleotechnic, and neotechnic—the first preindustrial, the second industrial, and the third the modern metropolitan city.[17] Perhaps the more important distinction is that between the first two, the mercantile city and the industrial city: the former growing up around markets and developing services ancillary to its original functions and to meet needs of merchants buying from and selling to the wider community, and the latter springing up around factories and evolving services of repair, maintenance, equipment, supplies, and research needed by factories as external division of labor takes place or internal division followed by vertical disintegration. Manchester is cited as the classic example of an industrial city, rising out of mere villages, to rival or outstrip in size long-standing commercial towns. The Ruhr, where industrial communities reach out to merge into one another, Pittsburgh, Cleveland, and Cincinnati provide later examples.

In some metropolitan cities—London, Paris, Berlin—administration and commerce are combined. In others specialization takes place, as between Washington and New York, Ottawa and Montreal (and Toronto), Rome and Milan, The Hague and Amsterdam, Bern and Zurich. Higher education may be combined in the metropolitan city or separated out in an Oxford or Cambridge.

The distinction between the industrial and the mercantile, administrative, and education city is regarded as important by some writers. Hoselitz started with the view that "one may therefore look to the cities as the crucial places in underdeveloped countries in which the adaptation to new ways, new technologies, new consumption and production patterns, and new social institutions is achieved."[18] In a later article he is disposed to believe that industrial cities perform these functions less effectively in underdeveloped countries than cities as a whole, including industrial cities, have done in developed areas.[19] In developed countries, cities have evolved self-government, with some political activity and consciousness on the part of their inhabitants. In addition, there has developed attachment to urban life, while in under-

---

[16] Henri Pirenne, *Medieval Cities*, Princeton, Princeton, N.J., 1923, chaps. 2 and 3.

[17] P. Geddes, *Cities in Evolution* (London, 1915), cited by E. E. Lampard, "The History of Cities in Economically Advanced Areas," *Economic Development and Cultural Change*, January, 1955, pp. 81–136.

[18] B. F. Hoselitz, "The Role of Cities in the Economic Growth of Underdeveloped Countries," *Journal of Political Economy*, June, 1953, pp. 195–208.

[19] B. F. Hoselitz, "The City, the Factory and Economic Growth," *American Economic Review, Proceedings*, May, 1955, pp. 166–184.

developed countries a sense of community is generally lacking. Various quarters of the city form self-contained villages spiritually connected to the rural area from which the migrants came. Cities with a strong sense of unity, such as Mecca, resist industrialization rather than promote it. The rapid urbanization now taking place all over the underdeveloped world has its origin less in the pull of economic opportunity in the city than in the disruption of life in the countryside. The transfer is not economic transformation in the sense of a change in economic function, but a shift from disguised unemployment in agriculture to open unemployment in what are variously called shantytowns, bidonvilles, favelas, barriados, and so on. Shacks are built out of flattened-out

Figure 10.7 | Percentage of total population in urban areas, various dates, 1947–1960, compared with income per capita, 1961. SOURCES: Percentage of population in urban areas (under different definitions), *Demographic Yearbook, 1960,* United Nations, New York, 1960, pp. 373–395; income per capita, table 1.1, Income per Capita for Selected Countries, 1949 and 1961.

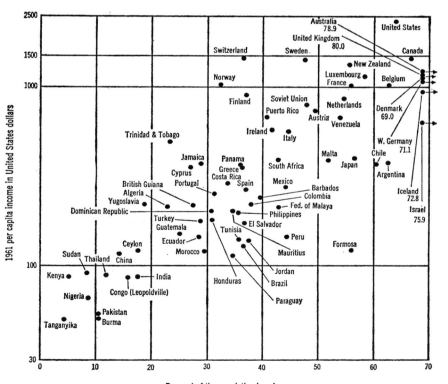

Per cent of the population in urban areas

gasoline tins (*bidons*), tar paper, old doors, or any material which comes to hand. The unlimited supplies of labor have moved to industry in advance of the capacity of the economy to take them up. Life in these shantytowns is economically precarious, demoralizing, incapable of training the inhabitants for industry or providing them with the commitment to modern economic life.[20] By all accounts the extreme of such pathological conditions is reached in Calcutta, where 200,000 persons, at an estimate, live without housing, on the streets, and another 60,000 are reported to live in the main railroad station. In these circumstances, the city has little to contribute as a civilizer, and the factory must inculcate such values as it needs and can.

Whether the movement to the city follows or precedes the economic transformation from useful employment in agriculture to manufacturing and services, there is no doubt that there is a high correlation of development with urbanization. Data shown in Figure 10.7 suffer from the variety of definitions used. Urban localities are defined by some minimum number in a given political area, the number varying between more than 1,000 in New Zealand to more than 20,000 for the Netherlands and 30,000 for Japan. Nonetheless, the data show a fairly strong correlation between population living in "urban" areas and income per capita.

THE PROCESS OF ECONOMIC DEVELOPMENT

This, then, completes our introductory discussion of development, with its ingredients and changes. We have suggested that there is no agreement on how economic development proceeds and have implied that this is because the process is not simple. There are many variables involved, and there is a wide range of substitutability among ingredients—land, capital, the quality and quantity of labor, and technology can substitute for one another, above certain minima, although there are at the same time certain complementary relationships among them. The will to economize and organization are probably the only

---

[20] For a journalistic discussion of this phenomenon focusing on Brazil, see Jacquelyn Gross, "As the Slum Goes, So Goes the Alliance," *New York Times Magazine,* June 23, 1963; a sociological treatment, again of Brazil, is Gilberto Freyre, *The Mansions and the Shanties* (original in 1936), Knopf, New York, 1963, by the author of *The Masters and the Slaves.* See also Oscar Lewis, *The Children of Sánchez,* Random House, New York, 1961.

indispensable ingredients. For the rest, none are necessary, and none sufficient.

The writers who place greater emphasis on one ingredient or another—Hagen on the noneconomic factors which induce change, Harrod and Domar on capital, Huntington or Parker on resources, Schumpeter and Solow on technology, Rosenstein-Rodan on scale, Schultz on investment in human capital—all of them have useful insights. Even the rather rigid stage theories can illuminate the development process, just as in human growth one can propound a wide variety of sets of stages based on weight, height, ability to talk, muscular coordination, reproductive functioning, and so on. But the search for a single theory of growth, or a dominant variable, or the key to development is surely too simplistic. It may be less courageous to be eclectic, but it is also more reasonable. In a complex process with many variables and wide ranges of substitution, it is foolhardy to be a true believer in one causal pattern.

The possibility of substitution ratios among these ingredients of growth raises an interesting point. In the first chapter it was suggested that income per capita provides an approximation of growth, but that some writers wanted to discuss growth in relation to capacity for higher incomes rather than in absolute terms. Height is an inappropriate measure of relative growth if a Californian is compared with a Pygmy.

But this assumes that the capacity for development has some definitive meaning, as would be the case if there were a finite limit to it imposed by resources or by some total of inputs, including resources, capital formation, quality of population, optimum technology (assumed not to change), and optimum scale. The difficulty, however, is that capacity for development has meaning only with respect to the minimum amount of resources needed. If this minimum is present, there is no basis for determining when returns to capital formation become negative or when further economic development is impossible as a result of qualitative changes in population. An economy, unlike a student with a fixed IQ, cannot be measured in performance against a capacity standard, since in a multidimensional system, with most if not all of the inputs variable, there is no meaning to capacity.

We proceed to deal with a more manageable series of topics—issues in economic development. These are chosen particularly from the problems confronting countries which are underdeveloped today, rather than from economic history, and can follow, unfortunately, no very sensible order. Domestic issues, however, are gathered together, and international ones, separately.

SUMMARY

Transformation of resources among sectors is a requirement of growth and development in an economy of more than one output. It is called for by the fact that consumption of any one good encounters diminishing returns after a time. As income increases, old wants take smaller percentages of income, and new wants arise. In consequence, resources must be transferred to new occupations.

The major transformation is from agriculture to manufacturing and services. Productivity is likely to differ between sectors, at any level of income, and to change at different rates. Redundant labor with no (or even negative) marginal productivity is thought to exist as disguised unemployment in overpopulated, underdeveloped countries. If demand increases in the industrial sector, the transfer of this labor into industry can hold down wages, maintain profits, stimulate industrial investment, in a particular model of development "with unlimited supplies of labor." This model has historical support and relevance to the recent growth of countries in Western Europe.

Barriers to transformation may slow down growth or cause premature transfers of workers out of agriculture to the cities before there are jobs or housing for them. A social aspect of the transformation process is urbanization.

BIBLIOGRAPHY

The classic article, widely anthologized, in this subject is W. A. Lewis, "Economic Development with Unlimited Supplies of Labor," cited in footnote 11. The Bauer and Yamey article cited in footnote 8, also reprinted more than once, is a useful antidote to too strong reliance on the concept of nearly distinguishable sectors. The notion of disguised unemployment is attacked by Gottfried Haberler in "Critical Observations on Some Current Notions in the Theory of Economic Development," *L'Industria*, no. 2, 1957, reprinted in Morgan, Betz, and Choudhry (eds.), selection 21. Several studies of urbanization have been included in the UNESCO *Technology and Society* series.

PART TWO | *Domestic Policy Problems*

Direct Allocation versus Allocation
by the Price System | 11

THE ROLE OF THE PRICE SYSTEM IN ECONOMIC DEVELOPMENT

There is wide disagreement over the proper role of the price system in economic development—how much should be left to its inscrutable operation at the hands of private enterprise and how much the government should enter the economic arena and direct the allocation of resources to production and distribution. We have touched upon this question in Chapter 7 on Organization. The present chapter will refer summarily to that discussion, indicate how economic planning can replace the price system, or cooperate with it, and finally direct attention to a central problem illustrating the clash between direct allocation and the price system—the question whether administrators of developing countries should worry about "balanced growth." A detailed discussion of planning in the development process is contained in the Appendix by Richard S. Eckaus.

There is not only disagreement, but also a variety of conflicting opinion. Some economists believe that the price system can work effectively in developed and underdeveloped countries alike (and that their governments mainly make mistakes); some that the price system works adequately in developed countries, but not in underdeveloped; some that governmental planning is needed to replace pricing for both types of economies. There is the view that government allocation should proceed by simulating the competitive price system, achieving the same allocation but a different income distribution than that of private-property arrangements; another that an appropriate division of function exists between government direct allocation and private profit-maximizing decisions. There are various possible types of planning, ranging between more projections of the major components of gross national product to narrower sectoral and industry projections **193** supported by allocation machinery for credit, investment funds, or even materials to detailed orders for particular plants. The French make a distinction between "indicative planning," based on sectoral projections, and "imperative planning," which tells each factory what to do.

The chapter on organization summed up the advantages and disadvantages of private enterprise and government as organizers of output. The great advantages of private enterprise were its decentralization of decision-making, avoiding diseconomies of scale, and spreading of incentive. Its disadvantages were unwillingness to undertake activities involving external economies, incapacity to produce public goods, with their indivisibilities in consumption, and at least occasional monopolistic behavior. Government, on the other hand, had the advantage of dealing with public goods, external economies, and special diseconomies of pollution, depletion, and the like; it had access to better information for decision-making; but it tended to go in for monumental projects. These strictures may be said to hold for both developed and underdeveloped countries. What about the view that the price system works differently in the two situations?

One form of this statement is that the price system works well at the margin, but is not competent to produce the structural changes which development calls for. Once a society has some amount of activity in every line, the price system can redirect resources from one to another through small changes. It is much harder to use prices to start new industries.

Or the point is put that markets differ between developed and underdeveloped countries in size and that this difference is critical, since, as Adam Smith said, "The division of labor is limited by the extent of the market." In this circumstance, the price of a good might seem inviting, but producers in underdeveloped countries know that if they produce at that price at some normal level of output, they will saturate the market, the price will fall, and they will lose money. Or there may be a price, but no supply if one tries to buy at that price. To bid for the product would drive the price up.

Finally, the price system is likely to work less well in underdeveloped than in developed countries because the latter have far more social overhead capital, complementary factors, and intermediate goods. Labor may be cheap in India but entrepreneurs don't use it in preference to expensive Western labor because it lacks education, health, mobility, etc., and because the complementary factors needed with labor—roads, public utilities, machinery, skilled maintenance men, and so on—are missing.

THE PROVISION OF SOCIAL OVERHEAD CAPITAL

If the absence of social overhead capital were largely responsible for the malfunctioning of the price system in underdeveloped countries, the disagreement could perhaps be narrowed. Let government supply the social overhead capital for the economy, despite its high capital/output ratio, and this will provide the basis on which private enterprise can proceed with directly productive investment. The pioneering article in this field by Rosenstein-Rodan[1] wanted this, and more. Where lack of transport is a flagrant obstacle to economic progress, as in China and parts of Latin America, government investment is obviously needed. But in southeastern Europe there was no such shortage. "The quality of 'basic industries' is not confined to . . . some public utilities. . . . Complementarity makes to some extent all industries 'basic.' "[2]

The view that programming of investment must consist at a minimum of basic utilities provided in advance of private activity was widely accepted until Hirschman questioned it.[3] He asserted that the scarcest resource in underdeveloped countries was decision-making capacity—a view which echoes the emphasis of Chapter 7. It made little difference, he thought, whether social overhead capital kept ahead of directly productive activities, to provide necessary services to private business, or private business took the lead, and by creating shortages, pointed to needs for overhead capital. Governmental investment programming in Latin America was rendered simple by existing shortages of electric power and crowded roads and railways. But this view assumes that starting from an optimum mix of the two sorts of investment there is considerable room for expansion of directly productive activities. In the two-sector-one-output production function in Figure 11.1a, for example, it is perhaps desirable to proceed along the "balanced-growth" expansion path O-S, but possible to move first in one direction, and then in the other, i.e., from A to B and then to D, or from A to C and thence to D. In fact, according to Hirschman, it is better to proceed in zigzag fashion because the shortage of social over-

---

[1] P. N. Rosenstein-Rodan, "Problems of Industrialization of Eastern and Southeastern Europe," *Economic Journal*, June–September, 1943, pp. 202–211, reprinted in Agarwala and Singh (eds.), selection 4, and Okun and Richardson (eds.), selection 11.

[2] *Ibid.*, p. 208.

[3] See Albert O. Hirschman, *The Strategy of Economic Development*, Yale, New Haven, Conn., 1959.

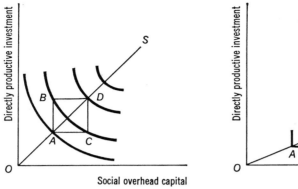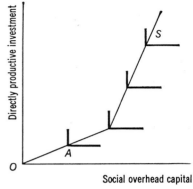

Figure 11.1a and Figure 11.1b | Expansion path between social overhead capital and directly productive activities with and without room for substitution between them.

head capital is clear at B (or that of directly productive activities at C) whereas at A decision-makers may be uncertain what to do.

The argument on the other side, however, is that the same output cannot be produced with varying combinations of social overhead capital and directly productive investment, as suggested by the isoquants in Figure 11.1a. The question is an empirical one. But suppose that the isoquants are kinked and call for fixed combinations of inputs, as in Figure 11.1b, rather than smoothly curved. There will then be only one possible expansion path, with positive prices for inputs, drawn as O-S, to indicate an early need for emphasis on social overhead capital, before switching to a preponderance of directly productive investment. To add directly productive activities at A in Figure 11.1b would yield no output. The private economy has little chance of finding the right combination of directly productive investment to go with the government's social overhead capital by the use of the price systems. Under competition there are only three prices in the system: zero for directly productive activity if production takes place on a vertical portion of an isoquant, with total output going to social overhead capital; the opposite, total output accruing to private producers and zero for government, on the horizontal portion; and a positive price for each, arbitrarily settled, at the kink. But of course with government providing the social capital there is no competition. Some services will be rendered free, others will be charged noncompetitive rates. The price system will be arbitrary in either case, and provides little indication of investment needs.

Whether economic conditions in the countries of the underdeveloped world resemble Figure 11.1a more than Figure 11.1b is, as has been said, an empirical question. The question concerns not only the choice between directly productive investment and social overhead capital, but also complementary industries within directly productive investment, and even consumption. In consumption, the isoquants have to be relabeled as consumption-indifference curves on an indifference map, rather than a production function, and the expansion path becomes an Engel's curve, which shows the path of consumption with increasing income at constant prices for two goods, such as food and manufactures. If the consumption-indifference curves are smoothly curved as in Figure 11.1a, it does not make much difference whether production starts with one good or the other. Substitution in consumption will take place in response to price changes. But if the indifference curves are kinked, meaning that consumption takes place at positive prices only in fixed combinations, and the Engel's curve shows strong income-elasticity of demand for food up to a certain point and then a switch to manufactures, the price system won't work. Prices will be indeterminate over the range between zero and infinity (i.e., at the kink); small changes in the production mix will lead to large price swings. Or if we return to production and label the axes coal and iron, the question is whether there is a range of substitutability as in Figure 11.1a so that in whichever direction we start the price system will guide us back to the expansion path by gentle price movements, or whether the coefficients of production are fixed within rigid limits, as in Figure 11.1b, so that prices swing in wide ranges and provide uncertain guidance.

Let us leave the diagrams behind. In Hirschman's system excesses and shortfalls are corrected through profit opportunities which guide entrepreneurs to the right expansion path. These he calls "linkages." A forward linkage is a profit opportunity created for a firm which uses the product of a company that has expanded and now makes the output cheaper; a backward linkage is the result of a new demand for inputs because of expansion. Both backward and forward linkages are stimuli to expansion and growth, stimuli to which it is assumed that private enterprise will respond. The contrary position is that, without planning, the increased output of an industry cannot be sold, because no other industry will respond to the opportunity to buy the goods cheaper, and that the stimulus of increased spending by an expanding industry will fail to stimulate new production by possible suppliers. In short, the increase in output, in this view, will create no forward linkage, and the increase in demand for intermediates, no backward linkage. Without planning! With planning, on the other hand, the output of firm A can be sold, because firm B, which will use it, has been started at the right time; and the input required from C will be forthcoming, because that need has also been foreseen.

The case for planning is then that the price system gives the wrong signals as a result of external economies, public goods, and monopoly, and that the economy would fail to respond to the right signals if these should be forthcoming. This is essentially the consequence of, or at least can be described in terms of, low elasticities—low elasticity of demand with respect to price, which prevents substitution taking place between consumers' goods, and low elasticity of supply, which prevents substitution taking place in production. If goods must be consumed in fixed proportions laid down by low income-elasticities and must be produced with fixed coefficients of inputs, the price system cannot work, and it is necessary to turn to planning. It is enough in any market for demand *or* supply to be elastic to produce an effective price mechanism. If demand is elastic, the adjustments will take place in consumption; if supply, in production. Elasticity in both is better, but elasticity in one is sufficient. But whether there is any elasticity to price responses in underdeveloped countries is, we repeat once again, an empirical question.

PLANNING

There is no agreed content to "planning" in economic development. At a bare minimum it may mean no more than government provision for the public goods, law and order, a stable currency, and a few external economies such as industrial standards. At a slightly higher level, it can consist in macroeconomic policies for full employment and encouragement to investment, using the general mechanisms of monetary and fiscal policy. These minimal definitions hardly qualify as planning.

Next in order of progression from the simple to the elaborate is the formulation of sectoral projections of the feasible and desirable. Projection of total income, with the help of the marginal propensity to save and a capital/output ratio involves problems of the reliability of these coefficients which have been discussed. Projection of sectoral outputs within the total has great educational value for government officials and the public alike, as it underlines the need for rationality in anticipations about growth. Output cannot expand without increased inputs or increased efficiency. Capital investment can be increased only by decreased consumption or borrowing from abroad. Labor requirements differ, depending on the combinations of outputs and technical methods of production. If borrowing from abroad is impossible, increased foreign inputs are obtainable only if exports are expanded. Government consumption and investment require tax revenue or borrowings. To disaggregate the projections of the economy is to call attention to a score of problems which arise in the development process, the solution of any one of which affects the rest of the economy. Consistency in projections means rationality in the approach to the development problem, including especially that difficult-to-learn lesson that one cannot obtain a quart from a pint pot.

Real planning, in some views, must go beyond mere projections of the disaggregated model and provide for more actual direction of resources than is normally found in the usual mixed–government-free-enterprise market economy. The first step from the disaggregated projection is perhaps the introduction of shadow prices to correct for discrepancies between market prices and social values among various outputs and inputs. The shadow pricing may be notional only, if the state is going to undertake an investment: this project does not show an appropriate ratio of benefits to costs, on the investment criterion, but the benefits should be rated higher because of external economies, or the costs should be altered, because the real value of labor is less than the market wage. Or perhaps the purpose is to maximize employment rather than growth. Or the inputs may be underpriced, as in the case of capital and imports, with the need to downgrade projects. Where shadow pricing is applied to private undertakings, however, it is necessary to go beyond the notional stage and actually apply subsidies and taxes.

Finally planning may become detailed in physical terms. Starting from an input-output table, methods of linear programming may be used to show how to maximize domestic production under various assumptions about desirable and feasible outputs and to indicate what each combination calls for in the way of inputs of factors and intermediate goods. As explained in the Appendix, an input-output table presents a picture of the interrelations among sectors or industries in an economy, in matrix form, with the rows showing where the outputs of each industry are sent and the columns showing whence each industry gets its inputs. The tables can be rudimentary—as simple as 4×4—suggesting in the typical case that most agricultural output goes to the agricultural sector—or as complex as 200×200. Where the input-output table is helpful in physical planning it suggests the requirements of intermediate goods which emerge from particular bills of final output. Rather than plan the output of steel as if the supply of coal were unchanged, in a partial-equilibrium model, or the supply of coal as if the level of steel output were fixed, the input-output table allows one to see how much coal and steel are needed, when it takes coal to make steel and steel to make coal. Where the price system fails to solve for these two unknowns, either simultaneously, or, in the Hirschman view, by successive approximations, this information, provided it is reliable, can supply the answer.

There are other meanings to the term planning. It may mean much less than the allocation of resources to alternative uses and simply the avoidance of gross mistakes, like the building of highways where there is no traffic, or irrigation ditches where rainfall is adequate, or the construction of eight-story buildings in areas lacking electricity for the elevator.[4] Or there may be project planning, the provision of economic analysis and engineering specifications for particular investment undertakings such as electricity-generation stations, steel plants, or road systems without relation to the economy as a whole. A special form is city planning, often ending in recommendations for large-scale investment to raise living standards in consumption, which will mean diversion of scarce capital from productive use. And there are surveys, such as those by International Bank missions to a number of underdeveloped countries which typically describe what an economy is like, how it might look if it were developed, but often without a description of the dynamic path between the two situations. For present purposes, however, and in the Appendix, planning refers to the central direction of resources, in contrast to the decentralized direction of the price system.

BALANCED GROWTH

The issue between direct allocation of resources through planning and the market mechanism can be illustrated by the arguments in the development literature about balanced growth. First it must be mentioned that "balance" or balanced growth has so many meanings that it is in danger of losing them all. At one extreme, it is an optimum growth path in various economic models with particular assumptions, such as a world where every capital stock grows at constant rates.[5] In the Harrod-Domar model balanced growth is that rate at which the full employment is maintained by demand expanding at the same rate as potential supply. At the other extreme, the word has purely rhetorical meaning, like "well-conceived plans" or "carefully integrated

[4] See A. O. Hirschman, "Economic and Investment Planning, Reflections Based on Experience in Colombia," in *Investment Criteria and Economic Growth,* Asia Publishing House, New York, 1961.

[5] P. A. Samuelson and R. M. Solow, "Balanced Growth under Constant Returns to Scale," *Econometrica,* July, 1953, pp. 412–424.

projects," and means little more than "successful."[6] Between, however, the term is used in a number of ways. In this chapter, we use balance in relation to the composition of output in a disaggregated model.

Apart from pure theory, there is little agreement about what balanced growth means or implies. To some it means investing in a laggard sector or industry so as to bring it abreast of the others.[7] To others, it implies that investment takes place simultaneously in all sectors or industries at once, more or less along the lines of the slogan, "You can't do anything until you can do everything."[8] In still other meanings, balance is a motto opposed to the even simpler slogan of development through the establishment of manufacturing industries, and serves primarily as a salutary reminder not to neglect agriculture. Whether balance has any particular significance depends on the context.

BALANCE IN SUPPLY

For working analytical purposes, it is useful to distinguish two broad classes of balance discussed in the literature: balance in supply and balance in demand. The first emphasizes complementarities and external economies among industries and vertical sectors in the economy; the importance of higher stages, producing energy, raw materials, intermediate products and services such as transport, to the lower industries which produce for the consumer. (The distinction between the vertical and horizontal orderings of industry is exactly parallel to that between vertical integration, among firms at different stages of

[6] See, for example, the title of the American Economic Association's discussion of the role of monetary policy in economic development, *American Economic Review, Papers and Proceedings*, May, 1955, p. iv, "The Monetary Role in Balanced Economic Growth." Only Ellis referred to the word "balanced" and this in an oblique way: "But economic growth, even balanced economic growth, as an objective of monetary policy is extraneous and potentially pernicious" (p. 208).

[7] *Taxes and Fiscal Policy in Under-developed Countries*, United Nations, New York, 1954, p. 5: "Balanced economic development depends on assigning priorities to projects according to their contribution to the productivity of the economy. . . ."

[8] See, e.g., "India's Crucial Plan," *Economist*, Feb. 25, 1956, pp. 516–517: "In an undeveloped economy everything has to be got going at once, so that the various sections can provide each other with markets and complementing facilities; a lag in any part destroys the balance of the plan." See also J. J. Spengler, "IBRD Mission Economic Growth Theory," *American Economic Review, Papers and Proceedings*, May, 1954, p. 590; he refers to "simultaneous expansion on all or most subsector fronts."

production, and horizontal integration, or mergers between companies producing the same product with the same purchased materials.) The second refers to complementarities among industries, particularly consumer-goods industries, and horizontal sectors, especially agriculture and manufacturing industry.

Like many distinctions in economics, that between the horizontal and vertical ordering of industry breaks down in practice. It becomes impossible to order all industries in a vertical array, so that the output of the higher ones would be sold only to those below it. In an input-output table this would mean that there would be no figures in the half of the table below a diagonal line running from upper left to lower right. In fact, electricity is sold to steel mills and steel to power plants, to take but one illustration, so that it is impossible to arrange industries in descending order where an industry can be said to be uniquely vertical or horizontal to all others. Nonetheless, the rough distinction is worth keeping.

The desirability of balance in supply arises from external economies. Social and economic overhead investment, themselves requiring large capital investment and producing a low rate of return, may be justified because of the fact that they make possible profitable investment in industries using skilled workers produced by education, or industries drawing on the electricity produced. In a vertically integrated industry, low rates of return in one or more branches are tolerated if they are necessary to high profits in others. In some underdeveloped countries, where large foreign companies are operating, it pays the latter to construct ports, railroads, workers' housing, etc., in order to be able to get at the primary undertaking. This problem has already been discussed above in connection with the difficulties of imputing particular returns to particular capital investments. Rosenstein-Rodan in his 1943 article pointed out that if a "sufficiently large investment unit" is established to include "all the new industries in a region, the external economies become internal profits, out of which dividends may be paid easily."[9]

In an open economy foreign trade may provide an opportunity for escaping internal balance in supply. Components can be purchased abroad, and technical assistance obtained to meet some needs for skilled labor. To the extent that imports can be substituted for domestic production, balance can be obviated. But there are some services, like power, which are required to give industry a start and which cannot be imported. Some components are too expensive. Accordingly, there is a strong argument for investing in social and economic overhead industries where these have large external economies.

[9] Rosenstein-Rodan, *op. cit.*, p. 207.

A semantic question can be raised, however, whether this calls for balance or priorities. The existence of external economies in supply clearly leads to priority for investment in those areas—generally transport, communication, education, and sometimes electric power—where external economies are largest and most potent. This differs distinctly from "getting everything going at once." Social overhead investments of low payoff directly and indirectly get postponed until the marginal efficiency of capital has been reduced by increased supply. Where existing overhead facilities have excess capacity, they are left alone. This takes us back to Figures 11.1*a* and 11.1*b*. If the isoquants were kinked, but the expansion path were a straight line, it would be necessary to "do everything at once." If, however, the expansion path follows such a course as in Figure 11.1*b*, then growth calls for priorities. If, finally, the isoquants are smoothly curved, as Hirschman implies, neither balance nor priority is called for, but a start anywhere—unbalance—which will point the way to the next step.

Rosenstein-Rodan's view that all industries are basic because of external economies, is impossible to accept if it means that all are equally basic. Analytically, perhaps, it is possible to conceive of a situation in which every industry is equally endowed with external economies at a diminishing rate, so that the optimum investment path is to divide investment among them all. In the real world, however, some industries and sectors have greater external economies than others. These may not always be the same industries in all countries; but transport, communication, education, and perhaps electric power are the most obvious candidates for examination.

It is important to avoid one particular fallacy which lies in wait for underdeveloped countries: the construction of an overhead facility to give rise to external economies, and subsequent investment which barely becomes worthwhile if it exploits all the advantages offered by the initial project. The initial investment with low output is justified by the fat profits anticipated at later stages of production, while the subsequent construction is designed to rescue capital now regarded as sunk.

An example may be furnished by the Assan hydroelectric power project in north Sumatra, to which aluminum production was to be added to use up the cheap power. The combined project would be highly capital-intensive and would make sense only at a low rate of interest. If Indonesia were to be offered capital available only for this combined project, and for no other purpose, the opportunity cost of the capital might be said to be low, and a capital-intensive project possibly economic. But if using capital in this way limited other investments in the country, it would seem, on the basis of limited information, that the project would be an example of fallacious planning, in which power was undertaken for the sake of other projects and a single other project was undertaken for the sake of using up power.

Rosenstein-Rodan combined the lumpiness of investment in social overhead capital, external economies in supply, and complementarities in demand (which called for fixed combinations in consumption[10]) into a theory of the Big Push.[11] Not only is it necessary to do everything before you can do anything; the scale on which everything is required means that a minimum critical effort is needed. Small efforts will not get the economy off dead center.

BALANCED CONSUMER DEMAND

Nurkse has made much of the point that a single manufacturer cannot undertake an investment on a large and efficient scale because only a very small amount of the income paid to productive factors will be spent on the output. He quotes Adam Smith that the division of labor is limited by the extent of the market, observes that price elasticity of demand in underdeveloped countries is low, and concludes that the only chance of starting efficient consumer-goods industries in an underdeveloped country is to start a large number of industries at once. In this eventuality, the increase in income to the factors working in each industry will be spent among them and make them all profitable.[12]

This view is based upon a breakdown or disaggregation of the Malthusian underconsumption model. It is true, of course, that final demand of producers in the consumer-goods industries will be insufficient to buy their total output if they attempt to save any part of their income. Demand from producers in the investment industries is needed to offset that part of the output of consumption goods which is not disposed of in that sector. Put another way, this surplus of consumer goods, including food, is needed to make investment possible

---

[10] Paul Streeten points out that complementarities in consumption can constitute step-by-step linkages as well as necessities to produce goods in the right combination. See his chap. V on "Unbalanced Growth" in *Economic Integration: Aspects and Problems*, Sythoff, Leyden, 1961, esp. pp. 102ff. The rise in production of automobiles led to increased output of roads, service stations, tires, etc., without the need to produce them all at once.

[11] P. N. Rosenstein-Rodan, "Notes on the Theory of the 'Big Push,' " in H. S. Ellis and H. C. Wallich (eds.), *Economic Development for Latin America*, St Martin's, New York, 1961, pp. 57–73.

[12] R. Nurkse, *Problems of Capital Formation in Underdeveloped Countries*, Blackwell, Oxford, 1953, pp. 11ff.

by supporting the producers of investment goods. Underconsumption is not a problem in underdeveloped countries: on the contrary.

The model, moreover, fails to take account of foreign markets. If the output of new investment cannot be sold at home, it may, in certain circumstances, be marketed abroad.

The more fundamental difficulties with Nurkse's model, however, as it relates to separate consumer-goods industries, are, first, it ignores price elasticity which may be fairly high in one or more products because of existing producers; second, it pays no attention to the possibility of starting with cost reductions instead of with new industries. On a practical basis, if it were true that one had to start everywhere before one could start anywhere, it would be necessary to abandon all hope of development, since the capital requirements necessary to do everything at once are beyond all dream of realization.

Suppose the new investment occurs in a good where existing consumption takes place on a substantial scale from high-cost sources. Room will be made for the investment by displacing other producers. Technological and transitional unemployment will result. If any and all unemployment are ruled out by hypothesis or political restraint on the solution to the problem, Nurkse's model may be applicable again, and no investment in any single industry can be made. But under more normal circumstances, existing resources are displaced in the market by new investments at the same time that real income is increased generally throughout the system by the resulting lower prices. This increased income, if saved, holds out the possibility of expansion in investment industries and the transfer of the displaced resources to them. If spent in accordance with the income-elasticities, it creates further employment opportunities in those industries. When the displaced resources have found new employment in industries as dictated by the income-elasticities, the result is balanced growth. But it is not necessary in this, the normal case, to undertake simultaneous investment everywhere at once.

As an alternative to the foregoing case of a single investment in an existing industry, there is the possibility of cost reduction in general. Assume that there is full employment and balanced expenditure and production by industries, and that a cost-reducing innovation occurs, or that there is a decline in the interest rate. It now becomes profitable to expand output in a variety of industries, but particularly in those which use capital in substantial amounts. This expansion takes place. Where demand is price-inelastic, this expansion will go only a limited distance, lowering price and increasing consumers' real income. Where demand is price-elastic because of competition of existing production, production will be expanded, to raise producers' real incomes, rendering some resources unemployed (as in the example in the previous paragraph). Incomes are raised, however, and will be spent or saved, whether one starts with an increase in demand, a single new investment, or a reduction in costs.

It remains true that it would be foolhardy to undertake a substantial investment in an income-elastic and high-standard-of-living item— automobiles, refrigerators, electrical equipment—in a poor country. There will, nonetheless, always be some industries which offer investment opportunities that can be taken up one at a time.

One particular form of balance in demand arises in the relations between agriculture and industry. This was touched upon earlier in the discussion of Figures 11.1a and 11.1b, when it was suggested that if these represented consumption-indifference maps between food and manufactures, the efficacy of the price system turned on whether the consumption-indifference curves were kinked or smoothly curvilinear. Where there are kinks, it may be necessary to balance the output of agriculture and industry in order to stay on the growth path. But this raises the larger question of industrialization and agriculture discussed at length in the next chapter.

BOTTLENECKS

We have taken notice of Hirschman's view that what needs to be done in underdeveloped countries is obvious because of bottlenecks. A bottleneck can perhaps be defined as a shortage which the price system is not remedying. The case for balanced growth assumes that bottlenecks are fairly evenly spread throughout the economy, that to break one would advance the economy only a short distance before a new one was encountered, and that bottlenecks must therefore be attacked on a broad front. Support of investment priorities rests implicitly on a different view of bottlenecks, that these bind deeply but are widely spaced. After breaking through a bottleneck, the economy will develop momentum of its own which will carry it a considerable distance until the next one is encountered. Incapacity to forecast leaves the economist with little knowledge of the form the next bottleneck is likely to take. Accordingly, it is appropriate to take on current bottlenecks, one by one, as they appear. A bottleneck is recognizable either because of a shortage at existing prices or a high price and high quasi rents for the limited factors engaged in its output. New investment is needed where capital earns the highest return or where shortages at existing prices are the most serious.

GROWING POINTS

Another form of the belief in investment priorities emphasizes growing points, or investments which have a high potential for development because their effects ramify in a wide area. A search of the literature on development reveals a wide use of the term, which goes back to A. G. B. Fisher,[13] but never a definition. Growing points are partly associated with external economies such as in the training of labor, partly perhaps in having strong linkages, or capacity to signal to entrepreneurs what is needed. They may be primarily industries which stimulate their entrepreneurs to produce technological change—the electronics industry today, for example, as compared with the cotton textile. Or a growing point may be distinguished by high income-elasticity of demand, which means that if income grows, it will grow too, and high price elasticity, so that improvements in production lead to expanded output.

French development literature is particularly bemused by growing points, sometimes referred to as poles of development, and a number of scholars have attempted to determine which industries constitute such points and which do not. Some argue for railroads which link markets and cut transport costs, others for electricity generation. A study of the textile industry in the nineteenth century calls it a growth pole because it stimulated the demand for coal, as an input, and the production of clothing.[14] A geographer attacks the whole notion of poles of development and wants to substitute *forces motrices,* or dynamic industries, from which he would exclude heavy and extractive industry, and include those industries with a large intellectual component and small capital requirements, such as the watch industry in Switzerland, but especially the automobile industry.[15]

As the contrast between the textile industry in the United States in the 1960s and that in France in the 1860s makes clear, however, there may be nothing consistent about an industry in every time and place which makes it behave in the same way. If all demand follows a Gompertz curve, the income-elasticity of demand for a good will decline with time and reduce in this respect its usefulness as a growing point. Or if technological change is sporadic, leading to irregular re-

[13] Production: Primary, Secondary and Tertiary," *Economic Record,* June, 1939, pp. 24–38.
[14] C. Zarka, "Un exemple de pôle de croissance: l'industrie textile du Nord de la France, 1830–1870," *Revue Économique,* January, 1958, p. 100.
[15] J.-F. Gravier, *Paris et le désert français,* Flammarion, Paris, 2d ed., 1958, pp. 148–169.

ductions in cost, the stimulus from this side will vary. One could argue that growing points consist of industries with complex interrelations of intermediate goods, buying supplies from many industries and selling materials for use in many more. This may be a necessary condition, but it surely is not sufficient.

The contribution an industry can make to growth through rapid expansion because of demand characteristics, through forward and backward linkages, and rapid technological progress is likely to vary within a wide range, thus defeating the quest for typical growing points. Moreover, expansion in an industry which has a maximum of interconnections with industries in the input-output table may not galvanize an economy if the latter is incapable of responding to the stimulus. Direct foreign investment often constitutes an enclave in underdeveloped economies, physically located within a tropical country, for example, but economically really a part of the overseas metropole.[16] Such an industry—oil, mining, even automobiles[17]—may in a different setting produce forward and backward linkages. In an underdeveloped country of low demand and supply elasticities, however, it may be obliged to sell abroad and obtain its equipment, material, skilled personnel, and even its general labor force abroad. Mining was said by Innis to be a stimulator of economic development in Canada, as contrasted with, say, furs, because it stimulated farm settlement which in turn led to railroads, etc.[18] But the development of mining in Southern Rhodesia failed to stimulate native farming, attracting rather the immigration of European white settlers to supply the needed foodstuffs. The stimulus was there, but not the response. In economic terms, the supply elasticity was higher for imported factors than for domestic.

LEADING SECTORS IN GROWTH

Closely related to the idea of growing points, *pôles de croissance*, and *forces motrices* is that of a leading sector, which Rostow worked

---

[16] See H. W. Singer, "The Distribution of Gains between Investing and Borrowing Countries," *American Economic Review*, May, 1950, pp. 473–475, reprinted in Okun and Richardson (eds.), selection 15; see also J. Levin, *The Export Economies*, Harvard, Cambridge, Mass., 1960.

[17] George Maxcy and A. Silberston, *The Motor Industry*, G. Allen, London, 1959. Note that when William Morris (later Lord Nuffield) started out to produce Morris automobiles in quantity, he was unable to place large orders for components in Britain and was obliged to order them from the United States.

[18] See H. A. Innis's various studies of staple production in Canada and the differential impact of different commodities, in, e.g., *Problems of Staple Production in Canada*, University of Toronto Press, Toronto, 1930.

into his stages theory. The sector in some cases is nothing more than an industry—cotton textiles in the British takeoff from 1783 to 1803, or railroads in France from 1830 to 1860, again during the takeoff. The evolution from maturity to high mass consumption in the United States was led by the automobile. The leading sector is not always the same from country to country, and it leads for different reasons connected with demand and supply. It may grow rapidly because of high income-elasticity of demand, or it may have a wide impact because of major cost reductions for its consumers; or on the supply side, it may stimulate output in other industries by calling for inputs, may develop techniques which can usefully be applied or adapted elsewhere in the economy, may produce external economies, and so on. A reasonable subject of historical inquiry is to ask what have been the leading sectors (fastest growing? or relatively fast growing and large? or growing and having the greatest impact on other sectors or industries?) in various periods of growth, but it seems unlikely that any regular pattern can be found which will be useful in prediction.

What can be said, however, is that the notions of growing points and leading sectors are the antithesis of balanced growth as we have discussed it, which calls for allocation of resources in the correct input mix so as to produce the correct output mix.

OPERATIONAL CHOICES

As indicated already more than once, the allocation of resources in production must be determined in the light of the empirical situation in which a country embarked on development finds itself. The essential question is whether consumers and producers economize, i.e., whether they respond to price incentives, switching products in consumption and jobs and input mixes in production when relative prices change. If the elasticities are low, present prices are no indication of what future prices will be when demand has been changed by the growth of income, and its redistribution, and supply altered by resource reallocation. Present prices, in short, are no indication of prospective prices and cannot serve as a guide to investment decisions. The marginal efficiency of capital in various uses calculated from present prices must be disregarded, since it will be substantially altered by small changes in demand or supply, which will entail large changes in price. The allocation of resources, and particularly of increments of capital, must then be guided by the dictates of balance.[19]

[19] For an interesting example under planning, see the interview with Oskar Lange of the Polish State Planning Commission in the *New York Times*, July 18, 1956: "Professor Lange gave a frank review of the shortcomings of the First Five-Year

If, on the other hand, there is responsiveness to price, more attention can be paid to shortages as revealed by current high prices. Prices will not change a great deal as a result of increments and decrements in demand and supply. It then becomes possible to calculate investment decisions not on the basis of sectoral balance, but in terms of the marginal efficiency of capital in various uses, regardless of sector. Any diversion in the composition of the increments in production from that dictated by income-elasticities of demand will be offset by shifts in consumption and production brought about by the price system.

If one had complete knowledge of all aspects of the economy—price elasticities, income-elasticities, capital/output ratios, marginal efficiencies, etc.—the distinction between balance and priorities would fade into nothing. One could feed the information to a computer, give it a few additional instructions as to what to maximize, e.g., output or employment, indicate what income distribution was wanted from the welfare point of view, and the machine would produce a balanced program of investment priorities. Information, however, is woefully incomplete. In particular, it is difficult or impossible in a closed system to forecast price changes when the elasticities are low. Accordingly, it is necessary to decide how much to rely on prices and how far to assume that the price system is ineffective so that the planning authority must ensure that the economy will produce what is demanded at whatever prices. If the price system works to an extent, investment can concentrate on the most profitable enterprises and expect the trimming and balancing to be undertaken by the economy itself. If not, the plan itself must provide balance.

SUMMARY

The distribution of function between private enterprise and government turns partly on questions of public goods (especially social over-

---

Plan. He said that the plan had been 'basically carried out' with the development of heavy industry but not with the expected rise in living standards. This he attributed to the lag in the development of agriculture and of smaller industries and handicrafts.

" 'Disproportions,' he said, 'have developed between agriculture and industry, between investment in fixed capital and availability of raw materials. Owing to a shortage of the latter, fixed capital investments have not been fully utilized,' he continued.

"Dr. Lange noted that there had also been a lack of balance between quality and quantity. . . ."

The entire interview, too long to be reproduced here, is worth reading as an indication of the problems of planning for development.

head), external economies and diseconomies, and monopoly, already discussed in Chapter 8, and also on the efficiency of the market system in allocating resources. There are various views against the use of the price system in economic development, ranging from one that the price system never works anywhere to the view that it works badly in underdeveloped countries. Examining the latter view, we contemplate two possible relationships between directly productive activities and social overhead capital. In one they can be combined in various ways around some optimum growth path, without much loss, and even with some gain in underlining investment opportunities or bottlenecks; in the other they must proceed in predetermined combinations because of physical interrelations and lack of substitutability in production. The different possibilities are generalized to suggest that the price system works if there is substitutability in consumption and production in underdeveloped countries, i.e., if the elasticities are high in either production or consumption, but not if consumption proceeds in fixed proportions, and production with fixed combinations of inputs. Where the price system works, but not well, a large movement in either direction may help to indicate what move is needed next.

The issue of balanced versus unbalanced growth is cited as a particular application. The case for a system of priorities favoring growing points, poles of development, and "motor industries" is examined and found to suffer from the fact that there is no way of establishing what industries are such growing points under any and all conditions. Even where an industry provides a strong stimulus for growth, moreover, the economy in which it is located may not be able to respond, which would suggest that under some conditions planning is called for rather than the market mechanism. The different types of planning are summarily described, but the techniques of planning are treated in the Appendix by Richard S. Eckaus.

BIBLIOGRAPHY

The major works on the question of how much to leave to the price system are P. N. Rosenstein-Rodan's papers on southeast Europe and the Big Push, cited in footnotes 1 and 11; Nurkse's *Problems of Capital Formation in Underdeveloped Countries* (footnote 12), and Hirschman's *Strategy of Economic Development* (footnote 3). Streeten's interesting paper on balanced growth, cited in footnote 10, contains a useful list of citations in its notes, and gave rise to a lively discussion in *Oxford Economic Papers* in June, 1962, and March, 1963. For an empirical defense of balanced growth, see L. J. Walinsky, *Economic Development in Burma, 1951–1960,* Twentieth Century Fund, New York, pp. 593, 594. Francis M. Bator discusses the weakness of the market in technical terms in "The Anatomy of Market Failure," *Quarterly Journal of Economics,* August, 1958, pp. 351–359.

For a bibliography on planning, see the Appendix.

A particular illustration of the balanced-growth problem, and historically an important one, is presented by sectoral balance between industry and agriculture. This can be regarded as a problem of balance in demand, if attention is paid to the income-elasticities which imply that one must produce more food in the early stages of growth because of the high income-elasticity of demand for food, or as balance in supply, if one regards food as an intermediate good needed for capital formation in social overhead or industry. But the problem goes somewhat beyond merely producing the right outputs. It is bound up with questions of relative prices between foodstuffs and manufactures and the distribution of income between farmers and city workers.

The prima facie case for industrialization is readily set out. First, developed countries have industry; therefore the way to become developed is to industrialize. (This is a fallacy of the *post hoc ergo propter hoc* variety, but it carries a powerful appeal to underdeveloped countries.) Second, the marginal value product of labor is higher in industry than in agriculture; to transfer a worker from agriculture to industry raises national output. This is especially the case when disguised unemployment exists in agriculture, so that any product out of a transferred worker in industry is better than none on the farm. Third, industrialization has external economies, whereas agriculture has not. These reside in training, in stimulating communication, interaction, demonstration effects in production as well as consumption, and so on. Rural society tends to be stagnant; urban society dynamic. Industrialization brings urbanization, therefore it is better than the stimulation of agriculture. Fourth, the improvement of agriculture waits on the availability of manufactured inputs such as fertilizer and farm machinery. In order to increase efficiency on the farm one must start in the factory.

The valid one-half to three-quarters of this reasoning makes a powerful presumptive case for starting in industry. But what about balance? In particular, when a developing country brings men from the farm to the city, how does it bring their food? On the farm they may have produced little or nothing, but at least they had a seat at the dinner table. Now they go to the city, but their food remains behind. If there is no disguised unemployment on the farm, the difficulty is compounded, because now total food production will decline as industrial production or capital formation rises, unless some *deus ex machina* intervenes.

Let us pose the problem by returning to the Lewis model of development with unlimited supplies of labor. We start from an independent increase in demand for industrial output (or capital formation) which puts pressure on industry to hire more workers. Workers transfer into industry from agriculture where they have been in disguised unemployment. So long as the price of industrial output remains high and wages stay steady, profits are made, saved, and reinvested, and the development process is underway in a positive feedback process.

But will industrial-goods prices and wages hold steady? Ricardo thought that wages were tied to the price of food, which was a function of the availability of productive land. Today it is recognized that the price of food, or the terms of trade between industrial goods and foodstuffs, depends upon a more complex set of conditions. It depends on whether the disguised unemployed are put to work producing consumers' goods or producers' goods for capital investment, what they do with their income, and what the remaining farmers do with their increased income. (Total farm output may be unchanged, and the physical product of the marginal farm worker may still be zero, but because of the reduction in workers, average product per head goes up, and with it average income.)

Assume an increased supply of consumers' goods produced by industry in a closed economy. These can be sold at unchanged prices if the remaining farmers and the newly employed workers spend the entire increase in their incomes on industrial products. In order to buy the industrial products, the farmers must market the same amounts of food as before plus the amounts previously consumed by the transferred workers. The transferred workers spend their old average income on food, which clears the food market, and the increase in income on industrial products, which, with the increase in farm spending, clears the industrial market. Prices will be unchanged.

Or if the increase in output made possible by the transfer goes entirely into capital formation, markets can clear at the old prices provided that the increases in income of both groups are saved. The farmers' savings must take the form of money or bonds or of capital formation with industrial inputs. The farmers cannot save by cutting down on production of food, devoting the labor to capital formation in real terms. This would leave no net agricultural saving available for other sectors, and workers would still be without food. Or the government can obtain the savings from the agricultural sector by levying taxes on the farmer payable in foodstuffs or in money which he obtains by marketing foodstuffs. In that case, the government pays money to the newly recruited workers from agriculture, who pay money to the farmer for food, who pays it back to government in taxes.

In an open economy, the terms of trade between industrial goods and food can be stabilized by international prices. There is still a requirement that capital formation be matched by saving in one sector or the other. If not, there will be an import surplus as total spending exceeds total output. But the industrial goods can be sold abroad and the new workers fed with imports, leaving the farmers out of the picture with the same output and more consumption, i.e., no increased farm marketing provided there are industrial savings; or the farmers can export agricultural raw materials or foodstuffs like coffee and cocoa, not consumed in large amounts by the industrial workers, save the proceeds (or spend them on industrial goods), and have the workers engaged in capital formation (or producers of consumers goods) buy food abroad. If foreign markets are inelastic with respect to price, so that increased industrial or agricultural sales depress prices (and even increased imports raise them), the problem of the closed economy is posed again. In an open economy, with elastic demands for exports and supplies of imports and provided spending is no greater than output, sectoral balance is easily achieved by foreign trade.

But the problem is a real one for developing countries—both in the past and today. The danger is that increased income in both agriculture and industry will be spent on food, given the high elasticities of demand noted in Figure 10.1, and that demand for food will expand more than the supply, while the supply of industrial products increases more than the demand.

Falling prices for industrial goods and rising for farm products could bring about the substitution of consumer manufactures for foodstuffs among farmers and the new industrial workers alike. If this were the case, the problem of balance would solve itself through the price system. At low levels of real income, however, food, clothing, and shelter tend to be complements, rather than substitutes. If farmers do not save the increase in average income resulting from the movement of their unproductive relatives to the city,[1] and will not spend it on manu-

---

[1] Note that low marginal propensities to save are implied by high income-elasticities of demand for food. Marginal propensities to save in agriculture in under-

factures, the economy can perhaps be rescued from rising agricultural prices which block expansion by balanced growth, i.e., by expanding agricultural output along with industrial, in accordance with the income-elasticities of demand. The arguments in favor of industrialization as a means of economic growth and development have to be modified to take into account the distribution of income and foodstuffs, which with low price elasticities[2] may be soluble only through increased efficiency in agriculture.

SECTORAL BALANCE IN HISTORY

Two episodes in British economic history illustrate the problem of sectoral balance. In the first, in the 1740s, an increase in farm productivity based on scientific farming, better crops, rotations, stall feeding of animals, and so on, preceded the spurt in industry known as the Industrial Revolution. Historians differ on whether improved agricultural productivity caused the Industrial Revolution, i.e., was a sufficient condition; whether it was a necessary condition; or whether it merely helped and extended it. But this is a clear example of balanced growth, or even overbalanced growth, with agriculture as a leading sector.[3]

---

developed countries have been recorded as high as 0.25, i.e., a quarter of any increase in income is saved. This would leave little income to be spent on manufactures if the income-elasticity of demand for food is 0.6 to 0.9 as in Table 10.1. The budget studies which have produced these results, however, may refer to areas where peasants had been in debt to moneylenders at usurious rates. Once the peasants became free of debt, it seems likely that the marginal propensity to save would drop to more ordinary levels, such as 0.1. But peasants in some areas, as in France in the nineteenth century, have saved in compulsive fashion to buy more land.

[2] Low price elasticities prevent calculating social marginal products for use as investment criteria, because current prices do not reflect future prices. Social marginal product is necessarily marginal value product, not marginal physical product; i.e., it involves an estimate of physical productivity times a price. But with low elasticities, the price may clear the market today but is wrong as a forecast for tomorrow. Expanded industrial production will reduce the prices of manufactures to render what initially appeared as a higher social marginal product a lower one. But where the price system does not function because of low elasticities, as noted in Chap. 11, it is necessary to undertake direct allocations.

[3] This analysis, and that of the other historical cases, will disregard the extent to which the terms of trade between agriculture and manufactures changed and succeeded in clearing the separate markets. This addition would be necessary for a complete analysis, but would be complicated. The contribution of changes in these prices was probably not great.

In the nineteenth century the main reliance was on foreign trade. Improvement in industry, and especially the resulting scarcity of labor, had a considerable influence on agricultural efficiency, through the movement known as high farming of the 1830s, 1840s, and 1850s— deep plowing, draining heavy fields, and some irrigation. But the main factor at work was the repeal of the Corn Laws, following the teaching of Ricardo. Britain clung to free trade even after a revolution in ocean transport brought the cheap grain of North America, Australia, Argentina, and Russia to British ports to ruin the British grain grower. Industrial products were sold abroad, food was imported (especially after 1846), and sectoral balance was achieved by trade.

In nineteenth-century France, the major engine of balance was savings. Foreign trade in foodstuffs was restrained by tariffs; gains in productivity were limited; but the peasant was a thrifty soul (some would say miserly), deeply concerned to buy more land, to accumulate a dowry for his daughter, and to protect himself from possible losses. He let himself be gulled into buying foreign bonds, which proved worthless in World War I, but this loss was unimportant for the sectoral-balance outcome. The peasant marketed his produce and acquired money in his wool stocking or in bonds. Industrial products were bought by foreign borrowers, and the industrial worker exchanged industrial goods for food.

Japanese experience is worth attention on two scores: big increases in productivity and high agricultural taxation.[4] They were probably related. Heavy taxes levied in money forced the Japanese peasant to become more productive in order to meet his bill. Some portion of the stabilization of food markets was brought about by rice imports, but foreign trade for the most part remedied Japanese deficiencies in materials.

The Soviet system has failed to cope successfully with the problem, as is evidenced by the periodic campaigns to excoriate the kulak, collectivize farming, extend grain production to new land, and so on. The more impressive weapon, the collective farm, is designed both to stimulate production by specialization and mechanical equipment and to limit consumption by farm workers. The Soviet Union started off with a substantial cushion of grain exports available for diversion to city workers. But collectivization has proven to be a difficult technique at best: its prospect leads to slaughtering of livestock, which peasants prefer to eat rather than see collectivized, and the addition of capital inputs seems to be more than matched by loss of interest and energy

[4] See B. F. Johnston, "Agricultural Productivity and Economic Development in Japan," *Journal of Political Economy*, December, 1951, pp. 490–513.

on the part of the peasants in an enterprise from which they cannot expect to benefit. Soviet experience illustrates both the problem of balance between industry and agriculture and the difficulties in solving it.

Finally, for present purposes, there is Chile, where increased industrial output is not matched by increases in agricultural efficiency, leading to inflation. The issue of structural versus monetary inflation will be dealt with in the next chapter. Here it is useful to say only that higher food prices do not elicit a supply response from the large landowners in the valleys, who keep cattle but do not plant crops; nor do they induce the peasants on the steep hillsides to produce more food, because they have reached Ricardian limits of nonproductive land. Accordingly, the terms of trade turn against industry and slow down expansion in that sector.

FUNCTIONS OF AGRICULTURE IN DEVELOPMENT

This analysis and the glimpse of the historical necessity for sectoral balance suggest that agriculture can play a variety of roles in economic development, and not just sit back while the development process spurs industry. In the first place, it can provide workers to industry. Second, it can furnish demand for industrial output. Third, it can provide savings for use in industry or by government in forming social overhead capital. Fourth, it may pay taxes to government, rather than lend to it. Fifth, agriculture can earn foreign exchange through exports to pay for imported capital equipment and raw materials needed in other sectors. Sixth, it can supply food for consumption by workers in industry or in capital formation. The more efficient agriculture is, the better it can perform these various functions.

Note that some of these functions are complementary, but others are competitive. If a peasant or farmer sells his output abroad, he cannot sell it at home. And if he spends his income on industrial products, he cannot save it or pay it to the government in taxes. After those workers with zero net physical product have left the farm, the farmer cannot at the same time maintain his spending, saving, and tax paying and release more labor, unless he improves either his terms of trade or his productivity; and any increase in productivity at constant terms of trade cannot be used more than once in freeing labor, adding to demand for industrial products, adding to the supply of savings, or paying more taxes.

The necessity for greater efficiency in agriculture is found not only in the positive case for growth to provide more demand, more savings, more taxes, and more labor, at constant terms of trade—plus possibly some more exports—but also in a negative one. If population is increasing on the farm, the amount of food available for the city is likely to decline, not merely stand still. A decline in average productivity—the same output with more labor on the farm—may well lead to reduced marketings, and hence lower savings, spending, and taxes. It would doubtless be easier to send more people to the shantytowns of the city, but less food. For all these reasons, it is widely believed that increased agricultural productivity can make an important contribution to economic development. Where the demand and supply elasticities are low, this contribution may have to be "balanced" to hold the terms of trade between agricultural products and manufactures steady in an economy which does not do much trading.

INCREASING AGRICULTURAL PRODUCTIVITY

Johnston and Mellor have divided the development of agriculture into three phases: one of preconditions, a second of labor-using, capital-saving techniques, a third of capital-using, labor-saving improvements.[5] By the preconditions, they mean the breakup of the traditional pattern of rural life, making the producer aware of the opportunities for increasing his income, participating in the market, acquiring mobility as between farm and town. Among the most important preconditions may well be land reform, especially if it takes land away from a feudal class, who own land for status or as a hedge against inflation but are not concerned to produce goods for market on it or to get it into the hands of people who are eager to produce. In the second stage the main instruments of advance are education to improve scientific understanding, the development of better seed and methods, the application of fertilizer, the development of rural credit institutions, marketing arrangements, and farm-to-market roads. Finally in the last stage comes mechanization.

This analysis seems to overlook the importance attached in developing countries to capital-intensive methods of extending cultivable land at the first stages of development by introducing irrigation, drainage, reclamation, and so on or by opening up new territories with roads and railroads. Feeder roads may be labor-intensive in method of construc-

---

[5] B. F. Johnston and J. W. Mellor, "The Role of Agriculture in Economic Development," *American Economic Review*, September, 1961, pp. 566–593.

tion, and it may be possible to obtain contributions of labor in the off-season from village communities. This only means, however, that the savings are furnished in kind, not that there is little capital involved. Nonetheless it is useful to follow the Johnston-Mellor schema and to pay attention particularly to land reform.

LAND REFORM

Land reform consists as a rule in the redistribution of large estates, or latifundia, into small holdings. Occasionally, as in postwar France, an attempt is made to aggregate scattered holdings of small plots into medium-sized farms of a more efficient size.[6] In most underdeveloped countries, however, the feudal heritage of the traditional society poses the other problem, to take land away from *hacendados* and latifundists and put it into the hands of small farmers who are interested in production.

The literature abounds in data showing the skewness of land distribution. In 1955, in Chile, 10 per cent of the farms had more than 200 hectares and covered 86 per cent of the farmland, while 75 per cent of the farms, of 1 to 49 hectares, accounted for 5 per cent of the arable area. In three provinces close to Santiago, where property concentration is above the national average, one-fifth of the irrigated land was not cultivated at all, and 36 per cent of all land was uncultivated because of the lack of interest of the owners. In Egypt in 1952, 72 per cent of the landowners with 1 acre or less had 13 per cent of all land, while less than ½ per cent of the owners, with 50 acres or more, had 34 per cent of all land. In Iraq in recent times, tribal lands have been appropriated as private by the sheikhs and large estates dominate the irrigation zone. The fellahin or serf who worked the land had to pay two-fifths of his produce to the sheikh, two-thirds if the sheikh furnished the seed, and five-sevenths on pump-irrigated land. A 1933 law said that the fellahin could not leave the land if he owed the sheikh on last season's operations. These conditions prevailed before the reforms of 1952 and 1958.

Land reform is said to release energy for increased production in agriculture and to furnish a stimulus to education, highway construction, labor organization, entrepreneurial initiative, and industrialization.[7] The reorganization of agriculture has been a "catalyst of a large

---

[6] See also Kenneth Thompson, *Farm Fragmentation in Greece,* Center of Economic Research, Athens, 1963.

[7] See W. P. Glade and C. W. Anderson, *The Political Economy of Mexico,* Uni-

chain of complex socio-economic movements which have pushed forward the country's over-all development."[8] On this account, the Alliance for Progress has made land reform and tax reform the touchstones of its conditions for economic assistance in Latin America.

But land reform may have its difficulties and drawbacks. It is likely to meet serious resistance, though this may be overcome by adroitness.[9] Once reformed, the land requires capital investment,[10] as individual peasants previously working with the tools of the landlord, or underemployed, seek to build house and barn and to provide their own equipment, possibly to be less efficiently used. And in Eastern Europe after World Wars I and II, land reform has generally meant a transformation from a specialized, exporting agriculture, which produces savings, to a series of mixed farms in which the peasant lives better but food surpluses for the city or export and savings decline. The exports from the specialized latifundia qualify as "hunger exports," produced by a system of production which restricts the consumption of the worker on a grain farm to a limited diet. When he gets his own land, he buys a cow, a pig, and chickens, and diverts acres from grain for sale in the city or abroad to vegetables and feed grains for his own stock. Small holdings limit the application of capital to land, and lack of capital restricts capacity to shift among crops.[11]

The conflict between the positive and negative sides of land reform takes different shape in different situations. In much of Latin America, the latifundia is not an efficient means of producing surpluses for the city but one of holding land idle. Small landowners produce the coffee export crop in Colombia, while the large estates in cattle grazing produce only 15 per cent of Colombian agricultural output because of

---

versity of Wisconsin Press, Madison, 1963, pp. 52–71. A correspondent commenting on the rather negative conclusions of the first edition reports that agricultural marketings have doubled in ten years after the land reform in 1953 in Formosa, after rents of 50 to 70 per cent of output had been replaced by purchase contracts for occupiers with a limit set to annual payments at 37.5 per cent of the crop. In an eloquent letter he quotes Arthur Young who said, "The magic of proprietorship makes sand gold."

[8] See Thomas F. Carroll, "The Land Reform Issue in Latin America," in A. O. Hirschman (ed.), *Latin American Issues,* Twentieth Century Fund, New York, 1961, p. 175.

[9] See Albert O. Hirschman's account of "Land Use and Land Reform in Colombia," *Journeys toward Progress,* Twentieth Century Fund, New York, 1963, and his conclusions on "reform-mongering," or how to achieve reforms.

[10] See Doreen Warriner, *Land Reform and Economic Development,* National Bank of Egypt, Fiftieth Anniversary Commemorative Lectures, Cairo, 1955.

[11] See W. E. Moore, *Economic Demography of Eastern and Southeastern Europe,* Princeton, Princeton, N.J., 1945, pp. 77ff.

neglect of parasitic diseases and poorly seeded pastures. In Chile, it is even necessary to import meat, while the fertile valleys are used for raising beef herds. In Kenya, on the other hand, any shift of land from the 3,000 white settlers with average farms of more than 3,500 acres to the 1.4 million African farmers with an average of less than 24 acres each would cut down on agricultural marketings and exports, five-eighths of which are provided by the European-settler farms. Redistribution of land in this circumstance—there is still a great deal of land in the Crown reserve, but the Europeans maintain leases on the best—would have to be accompanied by strenuous efforts to bring natives out of the class of subsistence farming to growing for the market to avoid a setback in development. Land reform is by no means the only precondition of improved agricultural efficiency: there is producing to standards for the market, with technical skills, education, and even the breakup of the kinship system, which hinders capital formation. The serf in Russia, the *colono* in Latin America, the African subsistence tribal farmer need more than just land before they can produce effectively like the efficient peasant agricultures of coffee in Africa and Colombia, cocoa in West Africa, or the East Pakistani rice and jute grower. Small-scale agriculture can be but is not always efficient and market-oriented.

LABOR–USING, CAPITAL–SAVING TECHNIQUES

Johnston and Mellor emphasize that the research to develop improved production possibilities, the educational extension programs, the facilities for supplying new inputs (especially improved seed and fertilizer), and the new institutions, such as credit and marketing agencies and rural bodies for organizing local collective action, must all be brought into agriculture from the outside. They cannot be supplied indigenously. Given the scarcity of administrative capacity and the costs of education, or investment in human capital, there is even a question whether the means can be called capital-saving. Yet the development of new strains of higher-producing rubber trees in Malaya or of ways of combating the swollen-shoot disease in cocoa in West Africa cannot be undertaken by spontaneous combustion among the peasants. Government must act, as it has successfully in these cases. Nor can the 600,000 villages of India be expected to organize themselves without guidance and leadership. The agricultural development of the United States was spurred by the extension service of the Department of Agriculture and the research effort of the land-grant colleges. In

Britain there was the leadership of the gentry; in Denmark, the Folk High Schools. Rural cooperatives assisted in Japan. Adaptive imitation seems to be peculiarly called for in this area, along with the general prescription of more education.

LABOR–SAVING, CAPITAL–USING TECHNIQUES

The third phase of agricultural development envisaged by Johnston and Mellor calling for mechanization and still higher efficiency is reached only when labor has moved off the farm in substantial amounts. The research of Nicholls and Tang on the Southern United States[12] makes clear that agriculture flourished best in the setting of an industrial complex. The same conclusion applied to Britain, the first country in which labor earned as much in agriculture as it did in industry, and in the efficient agriculture of France, situated for the most part in regions accessible to Paris. Nicholls emphasizes that the juxtaposition of industry and agriculture, with well-developed factor markets for labor in the town and for capital in the countryside, makes for higher farm incomes than in the isolated counties remote from industrial centers.

BALANCED GROWTH?

Is this then balanced growth? Not in the sense that you can't do anything until you can do everything. If the price system functions, and demand or supply responds to the terms of trade between agriculture and industry, there is no problem of inadequate supply of foodstuffs. On the contrary! Rising prices for agricultural produce will bring increased supplies. This must happen in the last stage, and gives rise to surpluses, as in the United States and of late in Western Europe. It presumably doesn't happen in the first stage, which is why it is necessary to undertake some steps, such as land reform, to get resources in agriculture which will respond to incentives. In the second stage, to the extent that the institution-building must be done from the outside,

[12] For a summary, see William H. Nicholls, "Industrialization, Factor Markets and Agricultural Development," *Journal of Political Economy*, August, 1961, pp. 319–340; W. H. Nicholls, *Southern Tradition and Regional Progress*, The University of North Carolina Press, Chapel Hill, N.C., 1960; Anthony M. Tang, *Economic Development in the Southern Piedmont, 1860–1950*, The University of North Carolina Press, Chapel Hill, N.C., 1958.

presumably some conscious policy of balanced growth is called for, at least to the extent that opportunities for increasing output in agriculture in return for an input of administrative attention are not neglected. But it may be that the supply elasticity in many underdeveloped countries is underestimated. West African cocoa producers seem to be maximizers, as are the jute-rice producers of East Pakistan, the cotton producers of the Sudan, highly organized in the Gezira scheme, and many others—producers of coffee in Africa, rubber in Malaya, rice in Burma, and so on. In this circumstance, the problem is not to replace the direction of the market but to improve its functioning. This calls, not for balance, but for sharpening the responses to prices where they are weak and moderating them where they are too strong.

Ultimately, industry and agriculture will interact, either in the mutual stimulation pattern found by Nicholls and others in developed countries or in mutual sterilization, which has existed as a pathological condition in parts of France. In neither case does balanced growth offer a guide to conduct. But if the slogan of balanced growth helps make the authorities examine sectoral interrelations and judge their nature, it will serve a useful purpose.

SUMMARY

A naïve view of economic development regards it as entailing industrialization. But shifting resources out of agriculture into industry or social overhead capital requires shifting food with them. If the people left in agriculture increase their consumption of food without producing any more—a possibility if those who left were disguised unemployed with zero output—and if those newly employed in towns wish to increase their food consumption, demand reaching the market rises while the marketed supply declines. The terms of trade shift against industrial products and in favor of foodstuffs. These terms of trade may be stabilized by foreign trade. If they are not, consumption may respond to the price change. But if consumption has low price elasticity and the supply of manufactures increases while that of foodstuffs falls, there is likely to be a major redistribution of income to the farm, industrial output will be unprofitable, and development may be blocked. One recommended method of repairing the damage is increased agricultural output to the point where marketing of foodstuffs and the demand for industrial products increase. In addition to expanded output and foreign trade, the problem can be solved if the agricultural sector has a high propensity to save or if it is heavily taxed. These methods may be combined, but it is evident that the problem will be eased if agricultural productivity increases.

Farm output is likely to be assisted in early stages of economic development by the breakup of the traditional methods of production, including not infrequently, land reform, which may release the energy of highly motivated farmers. But land reform in some circumstances can reduce farm marketing by substituting subsistence for commercial agriculture. In the second stage of improved agricultural efficiency, research, education, new institutions for cooperation, credit, and community endeavor are recommended on the ground that they are labor-intensive and capital-saving. In the third stage, usually under the stimulus of industrial growth, agriculture tends to become capital-using and labor-saving. It thrives best in close proximity to industrial growth.

Balanced growth is a rather empty slogan unless it means only that agriculture merits attention as well as industry.

BIBLIOGRAPHY

The most useful recent article is that by B. J. Johnston and J. W. Mellor, cited in footnote 5. This contains, moreover, a host of citations to the technical literature. The Carroll article in *Latin American Issues* (noted in footnote 8) gives a useful survey on land reform in Latin America. Doreen Warriner has written a study of *Land Reform and Development in the Middle East*, Oxford, Fair Lawn, N.J., 1962. See also United Nations, *Land Reform: Defects in the Agrarian Structure and Obstacles to Economic Development*, New York, 1951, reprinted in Morgan, Betz, and Choudhry (eds.), selection 27; the useful article by George Coutsoumaris entitled "Policy Objectives in Latin American Land Reform, with Special Reference to Venezuela" in *Inter-American Economic Affairs*, Autumn, 1962, pp. 25–40; and Philip M. Raup, "The Contribution of Land Reforms to Economic Development," in *Economic Development and Cultural Change*, October, 1963, pp. 1–21. A case study in agricultural development is Arthur Gaitskell, *Gezira: A Story of Development in the Sudan*, Faber, London, 1959.

13 | *Monetary and Fiscal-policy Issues*

It is impossible in a short chapter to cover in detail the myriad financial questions which arise in economic development. Equally is it inappropriate to limit the discussion to one or two issues. Monographs can be written on how to collect taxes from the agricultural sector or whether the quantity theory of money is valid in underdeveloped countries. Here the best we can do is discuss in a superficial way a series of issues which give rise to dispute: the harmfulness of inflation in economic development, its inevitability, the debate between the monetarist and structuralist school over the origin of inflation, the possibilities of deficit financing without or with only limited inflation, and taxation as the means of capital formation and growth. In dealing with these topics, we shall touch upon most of the issues which excite discussion, including the complications arising from the fact that many underdeveloped economies are heavily engaged in foreign trade.

Our treatment must proceed at two levels: the technical and the real. Too frequently the latter is neglected. But finance is by no means all technical, and deflation and particularly inflation have their origin not in the poor economics training of central-bank authorities and treasury officials and in error of analysis. The financial problem in economic development is to acquire resources for investment from income recipients. These resources may be saved and invested by the income recipients themselves or transferred to business or government for investment by them. Or business or government may seek to obtain resources by bidding them away from those who would use them themselves, say, in consumption, with the help of bank credit or money creation. This last case can be identified as monetary inflation. But it is not the only kind.

Where new savings are transferred for investment, the shift in expenditure from consumption goods to investment may run up against supply rigidities and produce rising prices of a nonmonetary origin. Or various classes in a society can respond to an exogenous rise in prices by demanding and obtaining (because of noncompetitive markets) increased prices for their own services or goods. When all classes in society want shares in income which aggregate to more than 100 per cent and it is impossible to run a foreign deficit for lack of credits, prices will rise, but it will not be monetary policy at the root of the difficulty. Finance may operate efficiently and neatly, or it may be inept and slow down the rate of growth. The range in which financial skill can accelerate the growth process will differ from situation to situation, but may, on the average, not be very wide. No more than anyone else can a central banker make a silk purse out of a sow's ear. It is easy in many but not in all circumstances for a governor of the central bank or a secretary of the treasury to make a botch out of a sound situation through elementary errors, but it is hard to correct supply rigidities or social tensions through the discount rate.

THE INEVITABILITY OF INFLATION WITH GROWTH

The drawbacks of inflation in economic development have been recited frequently, so they will be merely summarized here. Inflation reduces the level of voluntary savings, as income recipients are unwilling to hold money or claims payable in money of declining value. It distorts the pattern of investment by substituting for the criterion of productivity that of capacity to resist depreciation: real estate and, especially, luxury housing, hoards of specie and jewelry, and stocks of standardized commodities become prime objects of investment in contrast to industrial plant and equipment. And inflation tends to become cumulative as income recipients exercise what Walker calls extramarket power and strike for higher wages, demand governmental stabilization of farm prices or subsidies to farmers and industry, etc., to protect their incomes in real terms and to push the burden of the extra spending onto others.[1] In addition to these considerations in a closed economy, an open economy faces added disabilities of distorting incentives in favor of imports and against exports, and in favor of the use of foreign capital instead of high-priced domestic labor.[2] It serves at the same time to repel foreign capital and to encourage domestic savers to safeguard their wealth abroad. Against this list of the evils of inflation, the positive case for it is short: first, inflation is said to

[1] See C. Iversen, *Monetary Policy in Iraq,* Munksgaard, Copenhagen, 1954, chap. 9. The reference on extramarket power is to E. R. Walker, *From Economic Theory to Policy,* The University of Chicago Press, Chicago, 1943, chap. VI.
[2] See M. E. Kreinin, "Controlled Inflation in Israel, 1949–54," *Journal of Political Economy,* April, 1956, p. 117. This reflects, of course, overvaluation. If inflation is followed by depreciation, the distortion does not occur.

transfer income from consumers to investors—whether government or private enterprise; second, it leads to fuller utilization of resources, particularly where bottlenecks hold back total production and stable prices would leave large amounts of resources outside the bottleneck areas underutilized; and finally, it is easier to effect politically than taxation.[3]

But is inflation inescapable? The argument that it is rests on the notion that an economy which is going to grow must invest on the order of 12 to 15 per cent of its national income. Voluntary domestic savings will amount at best to 6 to 8 per cent. Foreign borrowing will provide another 2 or 3. The gap must be filled by "forced savings," resources bid away from the public, or taxed away. Since it is far easier to bid them away than deliberately to raise taxes, in this reasoning, inflation is inevitable.

Moreover, any economic leadership worthy of its salt must err on the side of too much expansion rather than too little. It has been said that every developing country should have a deficit in its balance of payments, just as every college treasurer manages to produce a small deficit in his accounts each year. It shows that more money is needed, although the deficit should be small enough to indicate that the task of providing it is not hopeless. It is human to overestimate benefits, especially the timing of their coming to fruition, and to underestimate cost. Developing economies therefore attempt too much. Moreover, they have borrowed their financial institutions and ideas from developed countries, allowing monetary expansion more appropriate to a large developed country, with small exposure to foreign trade, than to the typical underdeveloped country, and applying Keynesian doctrines that full employment must be maintained in a situation where the quantity theory of money would be much more appropriate since there is little or no tendency for aggregate demand to fall below the full-employment level.

Many economists have made the point that there are, proportionate to numbers, really no more cases of inflation among underdeveloped countries than there are among developed.[4] The underdeveloped cases, however, are much more virulent. Whereas the countries of Western Europe are experiencing price increases of 5 to 10 per cent a year in

[3] Roberto de Oliveira Campos, "Inflation and Balanced Growth," in H. S. Ellis and H. C. Wallich (eds.), *Economic Development for Latin America,* St Martin's, New York, 1961, pp. 86–87.
[4] See Roberto de Oliveira Campos, "Two Views on Inflation in Latin America," in A. O. Hirschman (ed.), *Latin American Issues,* Twentieth Century Fund, New York, 1961, p. 70, quoting Arthur Marget; and "Inflation and Economic Development," Federal Reserve Bank of New York, *Monthly Review,* August, 1959, p. 122.

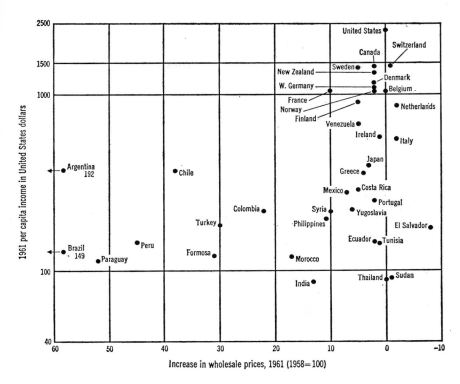

Figure 13.1 | Percentage increase in wholesale prices, 1958 to 1961, compared with income per capita. SOURCES: Percentage increase in wholesale prices, *Monthly Bulletin of Statistics,* United Nations, New York, May, 1963, pp. 118–129; income per capita, table 1.1, Average Income per Capita in Selected Countries, 1949 and 1961.

the middle 1960s, and an increase of $\frac{1}{10}$ per cent in the cost-of-living index makes the front pages of United States newspapers, countries like Brazil discuss whether the cost-of-living increase in wages of civil servants will be 40 or 60 per cent. Figure 13.1 shows the percentage increase in wholesale prices over the three-year period from 1958 to 1961, plotted against income per capita in 1961, and verifies the contention that while price rises and declines of a moderate sort can take place in rich and poor countries alike, inflation gets out of control more frequently in underdeveloped and developing countries than in those which have arrived. It is interesting that the rate of inflation seems to be higher in Latin America than in the Far East. There are evident exceptions, such as the inflationary Indonesia and stable Ecuador, but the wildest inflations are recorded in Argentina and Brazil, with prices in Peru, Chile, and Paraguay rising at rapid rates too.

If we shift from the level of income to the rate of growth, it is evident that there can be all possible combinations: stability without growth: India and Ceylon; stability with growth: Burma, Honduras, and Guatemala; inflation with growth: Mexico, Brazil and Turkey; and inflation without growth: Indonesia, Argentina, Chile, and Bolivia.[5]

KINDS OF INFLATION

Various kinds of inflation may be distinguished, depending upon, first, the origin of the inflationary stimulus, and second, the response to that stimulus of other spending and producing units. The stimulus can be an increase in total expenditure, a shift in expenditure, or even an independent rise in prices of goods or factors, including particularly wages. If there is an increase in spending it must be financed in some fashion. The response of spending units can be to spend less or more, depending upon expectations of the future course of spending and prices and upon access to financing. Producing units may offer more or less goods and factor services on the market, again depending upon expectations. One can perhaps distinguish profit inflation, in which business spending for investment out of bank credit is matched by households spending less to wait for prices to come down and firms and factors offering increased goods and services on the market. This is not at all a bad outcome. In Mexico it leads to rapid growth and is very good. Or there is cost-push inflation which starts from, say, an increase in wages, leading to increased prices of domestic goods, import restrictions to prevent an import surplus which would have dampened the price increase, more spending by households, business, and government, in an effort to maintain real consumption and investment, financed by increased velocity, bank credit, and money creation, not necessarily respectively. The major distinction under discussion today is made between the monetary school and the structuralist. Before getting to that issue, however, we should note that inflation may be purely superficial.

An astute French observer once suggested that in the Middle East and Africa it was frequently necessary to make a distinction between

[5] *Monthly Review, op. cit.,* pp. 124–125. These characterizations are from the article itself and do not agree with the impressions of growth derived from comparison of the 1949 and 1961 figures in Table 1.1. But the growth as measured in the article by deflated annual series in domestic currency provides a better guide than Table 1.1 with its currency conversions and undeflated figures.

the "façade economy" and the real economy. When oil royalty and tax payments by the Anglo-Iranian Oil Company to the Iranian government ceased, the Western world waited breathlessly for the ensuing collapse. Nothing happened. The impact of the throughput of oil, foreign exchange, and imported consumer goods had affected only a small layer of the economy. Their stoppage when payments were cut off went virtually unnoticed as the modernized sector returned to the ways of its forebears and contemporaries in the subsistence economy. Similarly, the story is told of Paul Van Zeeland visiting Lebanon to discuss the combination of persistent inflation in the surface economy and persistent growth and vitality in the real economy below. He is reported to have said that he did not know how the economy could function, given the many violations of the rules of sound finance, but since he observed that the economy was fundamentally growing at effective rates, he suggested that nothing be altered.

MONETARY VERSUS STRUCTURAL INFLATION

The debate between the monetary and structuralist economists takes place largely in Latin America and turns on the origin and mechanics of the price rises which have been so prominent in Chile, Brazil, Argentina, Bolivia, etc. The monetarist school holds that the inflation has been the consequence of the expansion of spending financed by bank credit or money creation. Business has been allowed to borrow on too easy terms; governments have been afraid to levy taxes or curb expenditure. Given business and government deficits, stability could have been maintained by voluntary savings by households. Long years of experience with inflation, however, have trained households to respond to higher prices not by more savings but by less. If the banking system were tightened up, or if government would either reduce its spending or raise taxes, or both, the inflation would be brought to a halt. In particular, central banks should make it impossible for business or government to finance spending by credit creation, as opposed to real savings.

The structuralists regard these monetary views as naïve. The changes in spending and in credit creation, in their view, are symptoms, not root causes. Even if there were no increase in total spending there would still be a possibility of inflation because of the inelasticity of the supply response of various sectors of the economy, especially agriculture, a supply response based not on monetary expectations but on physical bottlenecks to production. Assume, for example, that an attempt was made to shift workers out of agriculture into industry—in accordance with the Lewis model of development with unlimited supplies of labor—and that there was no increase in net spending, but a shift of spending from consumption to capital formation (in the industrial sector). The increased income of the remaining peasants and farmers and their increased food consumption would mean a net increase in the demand for food and a decrease in the marketed supply. The price of food would rise. This would lead to a rise in wages in the industrial sector, which would spread via increased costs to industrial-goods prices. Leaving aside the foreign-trade aspects of the problem, the increased working capital of the industrial sector would be financed by the banks, to be sure, but this could be justified on the basis of higher prices and possibly expectations of higher profits, if prices and costs rose proportionately. Government reaction to the increase in prices in the agricultural and industrial sectors is readily imagined: an immediate increase in appropriations, and an increase in taxation, if at all, only subsequently. The consequence would be a government deficit. But the borrowing of industry and the deficit of government would be passive responses to the price rise generated fundamentally by the inelasticity of supply in agriculture, not causes of the inflation.

Similar shifts can take place in industry. Suppose that population grew faster than exports. This would mean that the average propensity to import consumption goods would have to decline and that domestic substitutes for imports would have to be produced. If the supply of these was inelastic, prices would rise and the currency would have to be devalued to prevent the balance of payments turning adverse, or import controls would have to be applied. In either case, rising import prices would increase costs; industrialists would raise prices, financed by bank credit, the cost of living would inch up, and wage earners would go on strike for higher wages; agriculture would respond to higher industrial prices by withholding supplies; a government deficit would follow, and the inelasticity of supply in import-competing industry would be the root of the trouble, not monetary laxity.

Monetarists believe that the social tensions and structural rigidities are a result of extended monetary inflation, leading industrialists to buy land and hold it idle and labor unions to fight for cost-of-living clauses in union contracts as a hedge against inflation; whereas the structuralists believe the monetary phenomena are the result, and the rigidities and tensions the cause. Where there is more social cohesion among classes in the society, for example, there is agreement on tax programs to share the cost of development equitably, and the various devices by which one class and another fight to protect their real income are unnecessary. Monetarists hold that correction of inflation will lead to growth, structuralists that growth will cure inflation. The monetarists observe that developing countries which maintained stable prices showed gains in export values while those with inflation experienced declines. The structuralists hold that the causation runs from sluggish or falling exports to inflation.

The disagreement, of course, extends to policy. The monetarists all want restrictions on bank credit, on government borrowing from the banking system, and especially the central bank, and oppose price controls, overvaluation, foreign-exchange restrictions. Agreement among the structuralists is less complete. Some believe that revolution is necessary to break through the inelasticities in agriculture which are the root cause; others support land reform. Many agree with the monetarists on the need for tax reform. But there is structuralist consensus that monetary policy is fighting symptoms, and that real influences dominate over financial.[6]

DEFICIT FINANCING WITHOUT INFLATION

The structuralist position that there is no room for monetary policy is surely excessive. Monetary economists interested in growth have continuously wondered, especially in Asia and Africa where the problems of inflation (with notable exceptions) have been less severe than in Latin America, whether there was not a possibility of positive monetary expansion without inflation or with a once-and-for-all increase in prices. What is the appropriate amount of money supply in a developing country, and as that supply expands, with increased monetary use, (noted in Chapter 9 and Figure 9.3), is there not an opportunity to finance capital formation by government, without inflation?

The increased demand for money comes from a number of sources. In the first place, the extension of the money economy at the expense of the subsistence sector requires a stock of money to satisfy the transactions demand for money on the part of new entrants. To acquire these balances, the newcomers to specialization and exchange through markets must save out of current production and not hoard precious metals, jewelry, or stocks. In any event, the counterparts are available to the government or monetary authorities for capital formation. This is

[6] This section relies on the analysis of David Felix, "An Alternative View of the Monetarist-Structuralist Controversy," pp. 81–94, and Joseph Grunwald, "The 'Structuralist' School on Price Stability and Development," pp. 95–124, both in Albert O. Hirschman (ed.), *Latin American Issues,* Twentieth Century Fund, New York, 1961.

a once-and-for-all contribution of savings, and in countries any distance along the development path, it is probably no longer available. But in many countries, particularly in Asia and Africa, its significance can easily be underrated.

Next is the increase in the demand for money for ordinary transactions, as income per capita and the numbers of people rise. With no change in sophistication, this demand will grow more than proportionately with total income. After a certain stage of monetary sophistication has been reached, it will increase at a slower rate. The use of coins gives way to notes; in their turn notes are displaced by checks. The cost and the efficiency of the monetary system improve. But some expansion of coins, fiduciary money, or bank money is possible. This is a source of available savings. If coins contract, moreover, their replacement by notes adds another small item.

Thirdly, in the later stages of development, a diversification demand for money will arise. Growth brings an increase in financial assets, as deficit-spending units (which invest) issue debt or equity securities to surplus-spending units (which save). One of the major tasks of the monetary authorities in development is to support the gradual expansion and proliferation of the machinery—commercial banks, savings banks, investment banking, insurance companies, government bond market, private bond and share markets, etc.—which link surplus- and deficit-spending units. Some investment by government and business (and in housing by consumers) will be internally financed. This will not lead to the accumulation of financial assets. But some considerable part of investment is likely to be financed externally. Government and business, typically, will borrow from household units, either directly or, more typically, through financial intermediaries. As financial assets grow in this fashion, their composition is important. A diversification demand for money is likely to develop.[7]

Not much of a counterweight exists on the other side. At some stage, with the growth of confidence in other financial assets, dishoarding of coins and notes will take place. And ultimately, increased efficiency of the clearing system will reduce the ratio of money to national income. But financial assets as a whole will rise with growth, and that part of the increase which takes the form of money, and, in the case of bank money, the debt by which the increased bank money is backed, per-

---

[7] See J. G. Gurley and E. S. Shaw, "Financial Aspects of Economic Development," *American Economic Review*, September, 1955, pp. 515–538. These writers stress the similarities between money and other financial assets in the growth process, without, however, adequately noting the fact that increases in money permit investment to take place in advance of saving, whereas those in other financial assets do not.

mits and in fact requires government deficit spending or business deficit spending financed through bank credit.

Can deficit financing go beyond this close support, which takes advantage of the opportunities for increasing money required to meet demands? It is generally agreed that the underemployment or disguised unemployment in the agricultural sector or elsewhere in the economy does not constitute an adequate basis for noninflationary deficit financing.[8] Structural unemployment results from lack of complementary resources or wrong factor proportions, not from dearth of effective demand. The opportunity lies rather in the possibility of limited inflation, which permits limited deficit financing.

At the least there is something to be said for a distinction between functional price increases, which are needed to adjust relative prices for the sake of inducing movements of real resources, and inflationary price increases, which reflect the inadequacy of productive resources in the economy as a whole.[9]

To the purist, it is possible to change relative prices while keeping the general price level stable. Where any one price goes up, another can come down. Deflation expels resources, while inflation attracts. In reality, however, there is likely to be some asymmetry. Price deflation is strongly resisted, and takes a long time to drive resources out of a given sector. More than asymmetry of response is involved, however. Deficit spending for a given item will raise the price. To tax for the purpose of financing the spending is difficult in the first place, and may result in decreased savings or reduction in socially useful consumption. One-shot deficit spending as a carrot to move the donkey in a given direction, without hitting him with the directionless stick, has something to recommend it.

Government deficit spending is, of course, warranted when foreign assets are drawn down or foreign aid is received. If these assets are sterling balances owned by the government in the first place, they can be used to buy goods—the goods sold in the domestic market—and the proceeds spent in turn without danger of inflation. In the case of aid, counterpart funds must be spent to avoid deflation, unless they are deliberately sought to mop up an outstanding inflation. Where a long time lag runs between the receipt of aid and the ultimate bureaucratic approval to spend the counterpart, as in Pakistan, central banks must bestir themselves not to permit unnecessary and unwarranted monetary changes which might flow from the aid arrangements.

[8] See R. Nurkse, *Problems of Capital Formation in Underdeveloped Countries,* Blackwell, Oxford, 1953, p. 17.
[9] W. Malenbaum, *Prospects for Indian Development,* Free Press of Glencoe, New York, 1962, p. 268.

Beyond these limited instances, V. K. R. V. Rao, with the use of a mathematical model, has made a case in which a limited but continuous deficit will produce a once-and-for-all rise in prices so long as some part of the newly created money consistently comes back to the government in taxes or savings.[10] This, of course, is merely a multiplier model. The higher the marginal propensities to pay taxes and save—the latter influenced by inelastic price expectations and the price rise—the higher the possible deficit or the lower the price increase resulting.[11] But the possibility of continuous deficit financing rests, of course, on the stability of the marginal rate of tax, which is dependent on the extent and rates of income tax and on the stability of inelastic expectations which induce saving. If the fickle public gets the idea that the price rise is permanent or likely to continue, and therefore responds to higher prices by more rather than less spending, the model breaks down. Inflation results from deficit financing rather than stable prices at a higher plateau.

Beyond the Rao model there is the possibility of capital formation through the disequilibrium system, which takes us back to the structuralist position. Deficit spending creates capital; price control and rationing are invoked to prevent the inflation from becoming cumulative, to minimize the social unrest which inflationary skewness in income distribution produces, and to make the forced savings generally acceptable. During the war, it is argued, the disequilibrium system proved very effective in mobilizing resources for war. In peacetime, why should it not be turned to do battle with underdevelopment by mobilizing resources for capital formation? The Soviet Union, between monetary reforms, exemplifies the disequilibrium system in extreme form but in an economy with only limited resources under private

[10] V. K. R. V. Rao, *Deficit Financing, Capital Formation and Price Behaviour in an Under-developed Economy*, Eastern Economist Pamphlets, Delhi, 1953. See also W. A. Lewis, "Economic Development with Unlimited Supplies of Labor," *Manchester School*, May, 1954, pp. 162, 165; he calls inflation for the purpose of capital formation "self-destructive as prices are sooner or later overtaken by rising output" and states that voluntary savings out of profits grow to the level of investment.

Observe that in an earlier article, Rao had held that the deficit financing in an underdeveloped country with disguised unemployed could not be used in a noninflationary way, as in the Keynesian analysis applicable in developed countries with unemployment. See V. K. R. V. Rao, "Investment, Income and the Multiplier in an Underdeveloped Economy," *Indian Economic Review*, February, 1952, reprinted in Agarwala and Singh (eds.), selection 3.

[11] Two forces of opposing directions will be at work over long periods of time: an attempt to maintain the value of cash balances by increased savings, and an attempt to maintain real consumption. Inelastic price expectations permit consumption to decline in the short run.

control. Money becomes redundant. Interest rates have no effect in rationing credit; incomes have no effect in rationing consumption goods.

Deficit financing of this sort evidently interests the countries of Asia. The United Nations Economic Commission for Asia and the Far East is aware that there are limits on the capacity of a country to use this method and warns against operating an "excessive 'disequilibrium system.' "[12] It is perhaps not so aware as Western economists are of the fact, or impressed by it, that the disequilibrium system requires more administrative inputs to be effective than a well-run monetary equilibrium, and the chances of its becoming excessive are ever present and dangerous. Controlled inflation in Israel illustrates this.[13] Much of the effort of Western economists has been to warn against what they believe is the illusion that the disequilibrium system can be used for capital formation on a substantial scale.[14]

Finally, some attention is being paid to the sectoral impact of monetary policy. Monetary policy has an incidence, no less than taxation, and the question is sometimes put whether monetary expansion cannot be used to turn the terms of trade against the agricultural sector which tends to benefit, as we saw in Chapter 12, from expanded production in the secondary or tertiary sector. If the prices of industrial goods can be raised through inflation, without spreading to foodstuffs and raw materials, with a resultant change in the terms of trade between the two sectors, there may be an opportunity to offset the strong opposite pressures.

We have already seen how relative inflation for industrial products in overall deflation may be beneficial, but it is hard to see how monetary policy can make a positive contribution here. There is much to be done on a sectoral basis in the perfection of the monetary machinery to make credit available to agriculture through some more economical

[12] "Problems and Techniques of Planning for Economic Development," *Economic Bulletin for Asia and the Far East*, United Nations, New York, November, 1955, p. 27. See also "Deficit Financing for Economic Development with Special Reference to ECAFE Countries," *Economic Bulletin for Asia and the Far East*, United Nations, New York, November, 1954, pp. 1–19.

[13] Kreinin, *op. cit.*

[14] See E. M. Bernstein et al., *Economic Development with Stability: A Report to the Government of India by a Mission of the International Monetary Fund*, Washington, October, 1953, esp. pp. 41ff. In general, this mission appears to have been somewhat too fearful of inflation in India during the first Five-Year Plan, perhaps through underestimating the importance of new saving through the extension of the monetary sector, and because of the favorable influence of unpredictable good monsoons, and the willingness of individuals, given falling food prices, to save in money form.

institution than the moneylender and to ensure that it is used productively. This may benefit the terms of trade between country and town in behalf of the latter by expanding agricultural production. It may also be possible, through the extension of banking, to gather rural savings for urban investment, although the more likely direction of the flow is the opposite. But the notion that inflation hurts the country and helps the city sounds strange to the student of American financial history. Here the sectoral disputes ran between Wall Street and the farm, to be sure, but with opposite sides: the country wanted more and cheaper credit and an expansion of money supply to raise its prices. So long as agricultural supplies are inelastic, inflation is likely to hurt the town and hurt private capital formation, which is primarily an urban occupation. The sectoral incidence of inflation seems to be lined up against the desired solution. More effective results will probably have to be sought in shaping directly the incidence of taxation.

THE LIMITS OF INDEPENDENT MONETARY POLICY

These considerations suggest that there is little that the monetary authorities can do to stimulate capital formation beyond sustaining or increasing domestic confidence in the currency. Another limiting factor is, of course, external. This is partly a matter of confidence, and turns on the extent to which development plans or hopes revolve around foreign private capital. It goes further, however. In an export economy, Wallich has pointed out, exports are likely to be larger in relation to net geographical product than either private investment or government expenditure.[15] Moreover, investment and government expenditure are linked to exports through some sort of acceleration principle. The connection in investment is clear, and follows the normal accelerator model. In government expenditure there are two connections. Increased exports give rise to the demand for increased government expenditures to improve ports, transport, and marketing facilities associated with sales abroad. In addition, they bring in revenue through

[15] H. C. Wallich, "Underdeveloped Countries and the International Monetary Mechanism," in *Money, Trade and Economic Growth* (Essays in Honor of John H. Williams), Macmillan, New York, 1951, pp. 15–32. But see C. P. Kindleberger, *Foreign Trade and the National Economy*, Yale, New Haven, Conn., 1962, table 13-2, p. 220, which shows great variety in the relative sizes of investment, government expenditure, and private investment among developed and underdeveloped countries alike. For an impression of the openness of various economies, see Fig. 16.2, comparing imports and national income.

export taxes and, somewhat more slowly, through their general income-multiplier effect. Lacking a developed capital market, government must delay its expenditure—unless it is prepared to undertake purely inflationary finance through bank credit—until it has the funds in hand.

In places where the marginal propensity to import is high, whether because people are hungry and the country imports food or because Western-style items have been added to their standard of living, independence of monetary policy is narrowly circumscribed. Monetary expansion results in increased imports, an unfavorable balance, loss of gold reserves, etc.

Monetary stability in an export economy requires heroic measures. A country must save all the increase in income from expanded exports in periods of world prosperity in order to have foreign exchange on hand to maintain imports during periods of world depression. This means anticyclical measures of some considerable proportions.[16] The difficulties are many. Incomes expand in the export sector, and normally the expansion spreads throughout the economy through the influence of the multiplier. To use monetary measures, however, will involve the contraction of some other sector, which must cut spending in response to the contraction of monetary reserves through central bank action to offset the expansion of exports. This is virtually certain to meet resistance. In addition, one must be careful to distinguish sharply cycle from trend, and make sure that cyclical borrowings are not spent through secular inflation.

Apparent independence can be gained by the introduction of the disequilibrium system in international transactions, rationing foreign exchange for expenditure on imports, and insisting on the collection of the exchange proceeds of exports. But this independence is more apparent than real. As in the domestic disequilibrium system, it requires the substitution of strong incentives, such as patriotism or compulsion, to operate the system, plus an incorruptible civil service. Even where these ingredients happen to be present, the system will limp because of the ease of evasion.

The rediscovery of monetary policy in developed countries with the return of full employment in postwar years was not paralleled in underdeveloped countries. There money has always been more of a problem

---

[16] S. N. Sen, *Central Banking in Underdeveloped Money Markets*, Bookland, Calcutta, 1952, pp. 76–84, discusses the Argentine attempt to stabilize through monetary measures to offset balance-of-payment fluctuations. For a recent discussion of international commodity price stabilization in which Ragnar Nurkse recommended fiscal measures rather than taxes on exports and imports, see the special issue of *Kyklos*, no. 2, 1958, on "The Quest for a Stabilization Policy in Primary Producing Countries: A Symposium."

than an opportunity. That the underdeveloped countries should try to find opportunities in it is understandable. In the early stages of development, the changeover from a specie to a fiduciary coinage gives a once-and-for-all opportunity for spending, and this is followed as the monetary base grows with further opportunities. As shown earlier in Figure 9.3, the money supply grows with economic development, not only proportionately but at a rate faster than that. It must not be thought, however, that monetary manipulation offers a royal road to development. Judiciously used, it helps. Unfortunately, the difficulties of financing government capital formation through taxation induce many countries to use monetary manipulation to excess.

THE ROLE OF FISCAL POLICY IN DEVELOPMENT

Government capital formation can be backed by personal (or business) savings or by government savings, which are a surplus of tax revenue over government current expenditure. Private savings may be forced by inflation. They may be voluntary, but made in money form and therefore available indirectly to government, as in the deficit-financing possibilities discussed in the previous section; or they may be voluntary, and made directly in the form of purchase of government securities.

Possibilities of capital formation by means of inflation and by voluntary savings indirectly available have been found to be limited. Equally limited is the possibility of mopping up private savings by selling securities to investors. Capital markets for the most part are undeveloped. Private demand for savings for investment is inelastic with respect to increases in the interest rate which might shrink competitive demand. The private supply schedule of savings is equally inelastic with respect to interest rate changes. If capital from abroad is not forthcoming, major reliance must be placed on increasing governmental revenue and decreasing government expenditure for consumption. Since the latter is likely to be low and difficult to reduce, the opportunities at home for capital formation reduce themselves, in large part, to the capacity to tax.

Discussion of fiscal policy in developed countries focuses attention largely on ability to pay, the problem of equity. In underdeveloped countries, however, the relevant ability is that of the government to collect—that is, the administrative convenience and even feasibility of raising the requisite revenue. A secondary consideration, but a vital one, is to raise the revenue with the least possible hurt to productive investment. Taxation to support government capital formation and prevent inflation must restrain consumption, particularly luxury and wasteful consumption, and limit unproductive investment. But it must not at the same time discourage investment which fits into the desired growth pattern.

These considerations imply a tax program heavily weighted on the side of consumption taxes and against imposts on income. The objection to the income tax is partly its discouragement of the new men from rapid accumulation of capital and plowing back of profits, and partly administrative convenience. Personal and business income taxes require a money economy, high standards of literacy among taxpayers, the prevalence of accounting records honestly and reliably maintained, a large degree of voluntary compliance, and an honest and efficient administration.[17] Moreover, where incomes are low, cost of collection is high. Social cohesion which may be important in gathering support for the development program might be enhanced by instituting a steeply progressive income tax; and where there is skewed income distribution, with the rich indulging in luxury consumption, there is something to be said for an income tax as a diverter of resources from consumption to investment. But the tax runs the risk of weakening the incentive to invest in productive uses in the private sector, unless it be hedged with provision for accelerated depreciation on new investment and similar exemptions. Here the difficulty is to distinguish between productive and unproductive investment. A further point which argues against major reliance on a general business income tax is that where goods and factor markets are monopolistic, as is typical of not a few underdeveloped economies, the tax is likely to be passed forward or backward. It then becomes an indiscriminate tax on consumption and intermediate-goods production or on employment. While the business income tax has certain advantages of administration, it may be desirable to convert it to a direct consumption tax which can be more selective in incidence and in allocative effect.

Felipe Pazos[18] has asserted that Latin American economists have a long tradition of opposition to progressive taxation, which is partly anti-Yanqui, partly based on pride in the Latino tradition of growth with inflation, and partly rooted in the views that there are no big amounts of income which can be obtained from the upper income brackets, and such amounts as can be obtained will be at the expense of savings. According to Pazos, these views are being modified, under

[17] R. Goode, "Reconstruction of Foreign Tax Systems," *Proceedings of the 44th Annual Conference,* National Tax Association, 1951, pp. 212–222.
[18] In a seminar at M.I.T., December, 1962.

the pressure of both events and the Alliance for Progress. Studies have revealed that in Mexico and Venezuela 10 per cent of income recipients collect more than 45 per cent of personal income. Roughly the same position obtains in other countries, though outside of Mexico more of the recipients may be engaged in agriculture than in industry. A shift of 5 per cent of national income from consumption to government investment should be possible in these circumstances.

Could income taxation provide relief for savings? This is typically rejected on the grounds of feasibility—in the light of the accounting information which would be needed to enforce it—and usefulness. On the latter score, not all savings are put to effective use, and to separate savings in hoards, speculative inventories, and luxury apartments from those in productive employment, as already noted, is virtually impossible.[19] As a special example of the propensity of economists in general, and fiscal experts in particular, to recommend for adoption in underdeveloped countries devices too complex and controversial to be adopted at home, one tax authority persuaded India and Ceylon to adopt a tax on expenditure, rather than income, in an effort to discriminate in favor of savings and investment. Just as in the machinery field, untried innovations in administration pose serious practical problems, and both India and Ceylon have abandoned the experiment.

Real estate taxes are widely used in underdeveloped countries and have much to recommend them in the abstract.[20] An effective tax would be progressive where land was owned by the wealthy; it would stimulate optimal use of land for production—to say nothing of the important increase of production for the market—and rates could be adjusted to penalize luxury housing. In practice, these ideals are difficult to realize. Politically powerful landowners resist the changes necessary to keep valuations and rates abreast of the price level. Delinquencies are high. The opportunity presented by taxation of real estate fails to be seized because of the difficulties of administration in the face of interests.

The difficulty of administering the tax is indicated in Indonesia where the percentage of total taxes provided by the rural portions of the country fell from 7 per cent in 1939 to 1 per cent in 1952, despite the fact that the rural areas expanded more in income than the towns

---

[19] See Richard Goode, "Taxation and Economic Development," *Proceedings of the 46th Annual Conference,* National Tax Association, 1953, pp. 225–236, reprinted in Morgan, Betz, and Choudhry (eds.), selection 33.

[20] Douglas S. Paauw, "Financing Economic Development in Indonesia," *Economic Development and Cultural Change,* January, 1956, pp. 171–185; H. P. Wald, *Taxation of Land in Underdeveloped Economies,* Harvard, Cambridge, Mass., 1959.

and in 1952 accounted for 81 per cent of national income.[21] Part of the change was due to the substitution of the weaker Indonesian administration for the Dutch. The local nature of the administration of land taxes in Indonesia is used by Paauw as an argument for diverting governmental capital formation from the national to the local level, to increase efficiency in collection and to stimulate participation. Where the land tax is high, as in China, and can be collected in kind, it makes a contribution to capital formation at the national level by freeing resources and stabilizing the terms of trade between industrial products and foodstuffs.[22]

The unsuitability of income taxes and the weakness of taxes on land leave most of the task of raising revenue to taxes on consumption. That part raised domestically runs between one-fifth and one-third of total revenue, as a rule. Another considerable fraction represents taxes on foreign trade. Import taxes are generally paid by consumers: the tariff to improve the terms of trade plays only a small role in the imports of underdeveloped countries which buy at world prices. But export taxes may be shifted by exporters, whether forward to purchasers in sellers' markets or backward to employees through reducing wages. When they are in fact paid by the producer, which is frequently, they are a selective income tax levied against a particular sector.[23]

Consumption taxes can be made progressive, particularly if they are heavy on luxury goods. It is sometimes claimed that their incidence on consumption and production is moderate, given the inelasticities of demand and supply as dictated by tradition and lack of mobility. But consumption taxes are likely to be regressive; they impede the development of wider markets and the extension of the money economy. When levied against imports, they encourage production of luxury

---

[21] *Ibid.;* see also "Belgrade Raises Tax on Farmers," *New York Times,* Mar. 12, 1956, in which the increase in tax rates is said to be designed to stimulate production.

[22] The International Bank for Reconstruction and Development team in Iraq wanted the turnover tax on consumption which was highly regressive replaced with a tax on cultivable land, levied according to the land's productive capacity, as "ascertained through tests or control plots located in various parts of the country" (*Economic Development of Iraq,* Johns Hopkins, Baltimore, 1952, p. 96). This evidently approaches the Henry George single tax on rent and would be highly effective in enforcing better land utilization, but can readily be imagined to be administratively and politically unworkable in a country of sheikh landlords.

[23] The Iraq export taxes on animal products, unginned cotton, vegetables, fruits, barley, and licorice roots cannot be passed forward in a competitive world market and in the case of barley are estimated to reduce the fellah's income from marketings by as much as one-third (*ibid.,* p. 134).

goods at home. They distort the optimal allocation of resources, at least insofar as the market is permitted to dictate it. Nonetheless, they raise revenue.

Using the fiscal system to raise funds for capital formation runs afoul not only of the objectives of progressive redistribution of income and of efficient allocation (in the international sphere at least); it also conflicts with the objective of stabilization. As we have noticed under the earlier discussion of monetary policy, an export economy has little autonomy in income stabilization, at best. Fluctuations in the supply or demand for its raw-material exports impart sizable swings in the volume and price of its exports, which impart wider swings to money and real income throughout the economy. Export taxes, or income taxes levied on the exporting sector, can effect some stability in national income, but at the expense of substantial variability in governmental revenue. The more the country succeeds in stabilizing its national income, through taxing exports on an increasing scale when prices rise and on a declining scale when they fall, the more it is likely to accentuate the fluctuations in its revenue and balance of payments.

This conflict could be reduced if the raised export taxes were not shifted forward and if foreign-exchange proceeds were hoarded by the central authorities for disbursement as subsidies to producers in slack times. This assumes that the fluctuations take place about a long-run equilibrium level which the fiscal authorities somehow estimate. It is akin to stabilization of the export economy through monetary contraction when exports rise and expansion when they fall, but superior since the dampening occurs in the sector where the expansion and contraction originate. In this situation, however, the proceeds of export taxes above the minimum level are not available for economic development, but must be devoted entirely to stabilization. Such a standard of fiscal self-denial would be high for developed countries. In actuality, cyclical instability of export prices is inflationary in underdeveloped countries because expenditures are tied to revenues which fluctuate with export proceeds, and because projects started in the expansion phase of the cycle are pushed to completion in contraction, despite the decline of revenue.

Taxation of income (or of export proceeds) of foreign concerns with an incidence on the exporter adds to net national income of the country and provides a clear addition to possible capital formation. In Iraq, 75 per cent of taxes and royalties received from the Iraq Petroleum Company are made available for financing the development program. In Venezuela, taxes on profits from foreign oil exploitation are regarded as a national depletion allowance reinvested in productive assets. An early and rudimentary rule of thumb in Bahrein involved the division by the British resident of the local oil royalty and tax paid by the Bahrein Petroleum Company into three equal portions: one for the administration of the protectorate, one for the support of the Sheikh and his extensive entourage, and one for developmental projects. Heavy taxes on the foreign copper producers in Chile, jacked up to the point where the companies canceled their expansion plans, were said to be a reflection of frustration at the inability of the country to work out an equitable system of internal taxation. But given the domestic political difficulties of governments, it is tempting to single out the foreigners.

Multiple-exchange-rate systems can achieve the same effects as combinations of export and import taxes and subsidies. Typically, too, they have a revenue effect, as the state exchange monopoly sells foreign exchange at a higher average price than it pays. A special study of these systems[24] in connection with economic development, emphasized the extent to which special rates charged and paid to foreign investors may be used to increase revenue. Where an overvalued or undervalued exchange rate is used in connection with special taxes on exports and imports, for example, as in a multiple-exchange system, it is difficult to trace through the revenue effects and the incidence of taxation. It has been asserted by a visitor from East Pakistan, however, that the overvalued rate for the Pakistan currency, plus heavy import taxes, effectively tax the East Pakistan peasant growing jute and rice for export for the benefit of the West Pakistan citizens enjoying the capital formed by the proceeds of import taxation.

THE DEFICIT AS A SYMPTOM

A wide-ranging review of the inflationary problem in underdeveloped countries produces the simple and evident conclusion that the difficulties are not technical, but come from attempting too much. A United Nations study which summarizes the work of a number of missions proposes many small technical changes for a variety of countries in Latin America, the Middle East, and Asia. But the basic problem would seem to be that deficits run generally from 10 to 20 per cent of total expenditure.[25] Officials of the international agencies, largely the International Monetary Fund, recommend cutting down

[24] E. R. Schlesinger, *Multiple Exchange Rates and Economic Development,* Princeton, Princeton, N.J., 1952.
[25] See *Taxes and Fiscal Policy in Under-developed Countries,* United Nations, New York, 1954, part III.

the budget and applying monetary restriction. National and international officials promise international assistance if the budget be reduced and foreign obligations funded.[26] Finance ministers undertake to reform, but the real pressures, which lie in political demands for increased income and unwillingess of many groups to cut consumption so long as they believe that the burdens are not equitably shared, tend very quickly to hike up the spending and let the taxation decline.

Discussions of monetary and fiscal policy of underdeveloped countries by American and European economists almost always take on a patronizing air. Inflation would be cured if the country would cut back on expenditure or tax more heavily. But it is not so frequently recognized that the fiscal problem is more difficult in underdeveloped countries. The average rate of saving is small, the marginal rate low. The demonstration effect implies that consumption leads production or rapidly catches up with it. There is always need for further overhead capital investments to create opportunities for increasing productivity. Duesenberry asymmetry in the responses of consumers to increases and declines of income—the former being accepted, the latter resisted—and the political inability to impose austerity make the fiscal problem much more difficult. The difference in the intellectual and administrative capacities of the men operating the system are smaller, and certainly less important, than the difference in the difficulty of restraining inflation in a developed and an underdeveloped country.

In this circumstance inflation, like the working girl who has slipped, is more to be pitied than scorned. It is not exactly inevitable, since the inflationary push is much harder in some countries than others by reason of circumstances, national character, and essentially surface phenomena, but the task of consciously preventing inflation when the pressure mounts is much harder in underdeveloped countries than in countries with higher marginal propensities to save, widely spread overhead capital, and social and occupational mobility.

In these circumstances an underdeveloped country with luck or virtue can avoid inflation; but it needs more of either or both than a developed country. To try to push its luck or risk its virtue in positive programs of accelerating development through a disequilibrium system is likely to end in disaster.

[26] See any newspaper for appropriate headlines, but perhaps especially the *New York Times:* July 1, 1962, "Balanced Budget Is Sought in Iran; Premier Strives to Qualify for World Bank Loan"; May 29, 1963, "Inflation Study Ended in Brazil: Monetary Fund Said to Find Stronger Action Is Needed"; June 29, 1963, "Indonesia Moves to Spur Economy: United States Helps Outline Program to Halt Currency Decline."

SUMMARY

Inflation reduces the level of investment and distorts what investment remains. It creates problems of international adjustment. Whether it is inevitable is debated. It occurs at greater intensity in underdeveloped countries than in developed, if not more frequently, and the world offers examples of stability without growth, stability with growth, inflation without growth, inflation with growth. Inflation therefore neither ensures nor precludes growth.

Debate occurs in Latin America as to whether inflation is a monetary or a real phenomenon. The adherents of the latter school are called structuralists and believe that inflation stems from inelasticity of supply in underdeveloped countries in which monetary expansion and deficit financing play supporting rather than initiating roles.

Some room exists for deficit financing without inflation, as the money requirements of a developing economy expand. Whether deficit financing can go very far without inflation, however, is dubious.

The openness of many underdeveloped economies complicates their stability efforts through monetary and fiscal policy, since disturbance can arise abroad.

Taxation is helpful in combating inflation, but the tax problem in underdeveloped countries itself is complicated by social tensions and resistances in burden sharing. For the most part, tax systems in underdeveloped countries are regressive and bear heavily on consumption, given the political and administrative difficulties of an equitable system of progressive taxation. Taxation of land would be highly desirable, in view of the numbers of people on the land and the need to get them working for the market, but is administratively difficult. Taxation of foreign direct investment can assist the development process.

BIBLIOGRAPHY

The heated Latin American discussion of inflation is admirably set forth in the essays collected in *Economic Development for Latin America* and *Latin American Issues*, referred to in footnotes 3 and 4. Campos has essays in both, and Felix and Grunwald in the second. In addition to Grunwald's case study of Chilean inflation, see the historical approach of Hirschman in *Journeys toward Progress*, Twentieth Century Fund, New York, 1963, again dealing with Chile. For a more general statement, see E. M. Bernstein and I. G. Patel, "Inflation in Relation to Economic Development," *Staff Papers*, November, 1952, pp. 363–368, reprinted in Okun and Richardson (eds.), selection 36. On financial institutions, see Arthur I. Bloomfield, "Monetary Policy in Underdeveloped Countries," from C. J. Friederich and S. E. Harris (eds.), *Public Policy*, Harvard, Cambridge, Mass., 1956, pp. 232–274, reprinted in Morgan, Betz, and Choudhry (eds.), selection 32, and Edward Nevin, *Capital Funds in Underdeveloped Countries*, St Martin's, New York, 1961. On tax policy see the articles by Heller and Goode, referred to in footnote 1, Chap. 5, and footnotes 17 and 20, this chapter. A useful discussion of the differences between monetary policy in a developed and an open underdeveloped economy, focused on Cuban experiences from 1914 to 1947, is contained in Henry C. Wallich, *Monetary Problems of an Export Economy*, Harvard, Cambridge, Mass., 1951.

FACTOR PROPORTIONS

Economic development through time involves an increase in the capital/labor ratio and permits capital deepening. A significant question, over which some dispute has arisen in economic discussion, is whether a developing country should use the technology appropriate to its existing factor proportions, including especially its capital/labor ratio, or whether it should anticipate the relative growth of capital and begin the use of capital-intensive methods of production before its capital endowment is really suitable for this. In particular, the question is whether countries at early stages of development, with capital scarce and often with labor abundant, should take advantage of the modern technology developed by advanced countries, where capital is abundant and labor scarce, or whether they should devise a technology of their own or use production methods which are obsolete in countries abroad.

The dispute has many facets. It can be argued on a priori grounds, by appeals to history, and by reference to empirical data and current practice.

The theoretical argument for using a technology appropriate to existing factor proportions has been tartly put by Hayek:[1]

> I am profoundly convinced that we should be doing more good to the underdeveloped countries if we succeeded in spreading the understanding of elementary economics than by elaborating sophisticated theories of economic growth. If, for example, we could merely gain understanding of the simple and obvious fact that a country which cannot hope to reach within foreseeable time a capital supply equal per head to that of the United

---

[1] F. A. Hayek, comment on S. Kuznets, "Toward a Theory of Economic Growth," in R. Lekachman (ed.), *National Policy for Economic Welfare at Home and Abroad*, Doubleday, Garden City, N.Y., 1955, p. 89.

States will not use its limited resources best by imitating American production techniques, but ought to develop techniques appropriate to a thinner and wider spreading of the available capital . . . .

This is evidently a static argument. Maximization of the return on capital is achieved by equalizing its return in every use. If there are two possible ways to produce a commodity, represented by production functions in Figure 14.1, of which R_1, R_2, R_3, and R_4 are the isoquants of one, and T_1, T_2, T_3, and T_4 are the isoquants of the other, and $R_1 = T_1$, $R_2 = T_2$, etc., a country with OK capital and OL' labor would do well to use the process represented by T. To use the capital-intensive method R would reduce output from T_4 (or R_4) to R_1 and would leave unemployment at positive wages $L - L'$ of labor.

On this showing, much of the adoption of modern technology is mere demonstration effect on the side of production, the attempt to run before one can walk. Such technology wastes capital, since it uses it too intensively in a narrow sector, and requires ignoring opportunities for profitable investment. If a bulldozer costs $5,000 and shovels $2.50 each, if 1,500 men can shovel in a day as much as one man can move with a bulldozer, and if manpower is abundant, capital can be saved by buying $3,750 worth of shovels, and disguised or open unemployment avoided.

Figure 14.1 | Alternative technological means of producing the same good.

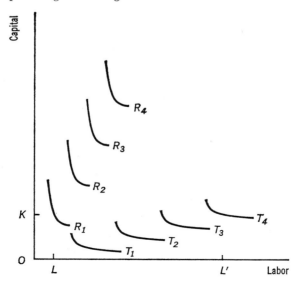

Kuznets' objection to Hayek's argument ran largely along empirical lines, discussed below.[2] But a theoretical argument may be made against it. For one thing, capital-saving technology may involve substantial innovations of a neutral variety. Suppose, for example, that isoquant R_1 was equivalent in terms of output not to T_1, but to T_5 or T_6 (not shown). To change from T_4 to R_1 would disemploy some labor but increase overall output. Or suppose R_1, R_2, etc., is the only possible way to produce the good, which has important uses. It is claimed, for example, that there are only capital-intensive ways of producing gasoline, or nitrogenous fertilizer, or electricity (although there may be a choice whether a dam for hydroelectric generation is built with giant earthmovers and concrete mixers or by thousands of workers carrying loads on their backs). The fixity of the factor proportions of modern technology is frequently exaggerated, or to put it the other way around, the range of substitution of variable costs which are typically more labor-intensive for fixed costs, which are capital-intensive, is often ignored. It is possible to produce gasoline from simple pipe stills and not always necessary or economic to install catalytic crackers. But there is something to the point that for some products it is necessary to use considerable amounts of capital to get any output at all.

In dynamic terms, Bruton has suggested that the industries which embody external economies are frequently capital-intensive. These capital-intensive investments must be undertaken before one can take advantage of opportunities for investment in labor-intensive industries. When industries are linked together in complementary interacting fashion, the capital intensity of a single industry is not an appropriate index of its suitability for investment until one has traced through and imputed to it its total return, with all the difficulties this involves.[3] This is only mildly persuasive, however, and appears to concede that in industries producing final output, a country should on theoretical grounds adopt the technology appropriate to its factor pro-

<hr />

[2] "Brief consideration suggests a much less certain diagnosis. The United States technique may be particularly well adapted to the use of large numbers of workers with relatively low levels of individual skills, unlike the less capital-intensive technologies of some European countries. American machinery may be more suitable because of an assured supply of spare parts and better servicing arrangements. In short, the validity of the principle is contingent upon a large number of items impounded in *ceteris paribus,* many of which are not casual disturbances but are integrally connected with processes of economic growth." (Kuznets, *ibid.,* p. 98.)

[3] H. J. Bruton, "Growth Models and Underdeveloped Countries," *Journal of Political Economy,* August, 1955, pp. 322–336 [reprinted in Agarwala and Singh (eds.), selection 3].

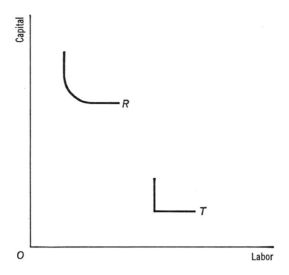

Figure 14.2 | Labor-intensive production function with fixed factor proportions, capital-intensive function permitting factor substitution.

portions after subtraction of those considerable lumps of capital needed for the overhead industries. This article further implies that labor productivity is higher in capital-intensive than in labor-intensive industries, and that this is an argument for the former. But this is not true if there is a competitive market for labor; nor, if true, is it relevant. The investment criterion is net capital productivity or gross, if labor is redundant.

We have already referred to the Galenson-Leibenstein argument that capital-intensive industries should be preferred to labor-intensive not because of their immediate productivity but because of their greater contribution to savings and hence to future growth. This is more directly an argument for investment in fast-growing industries in which entrepreneurs reinvest than it is for the adoption of capital-intensive techniques. And whether the marginal reinvestment quotient is a better criterion for investment than the social marginal product depends upon the rate of interest.[4]

Leibenstein offers another argument for using the capital-intensive technique. He suggests that in an economy which looks to the accumulation of capital faster than labor, it may be that capital can be sub-

[4] See Chap. 5.

stituted for labor in capital-intensive production methods, but not in labor-intensive. The isoquants of the two methods have different shapes, as in Figure 14.2, so that small increases in capital, unaccompanied by added labor, will yield more additional output under the *R* production function, but not under the *T*. The importance of the discontinuity between the two methods is that if an economy has expanded in the *T* direction, after a certain point it can expand further only by adopting the *R* technique on some scale, thus creating a dual economy. Moreover, technical progress is likely to be faster, Leibenstein believes, in the capital-intensive than in the labor-intensive method.[5] But these are empirical questions and it has not yet been established that the isoquants have this shape, are located in this way, and record technical progress in this biased fashion.

The theoretical case which the economic historian Gerschenkron has in mind urges the use of the latest technology in general:[6]

> Industrialization always seemed the more promising the greater the backlog of technological innovations which the backward country could take over from the more advanced country. Borrowed technology, so much and so rightly stressed by Veblen, was one of the primary factors assuring a high speed of development in a backward country entering the stage of industrialization. . . .
>
> . . . to the extent that industrialization took place, it was largely by application of the most modern and efficient techniques that backward countries could hope to achieve success. . . . The advantages inherent in the use of technologically superior equipment were not counteracted but enhanced by its labor-saving effect.

Gerschenkron uses in part an argument discussed below, that abundant labor may be expensive rather than cheap in underdeveloped countries. But his argument appears to rest mainly on growing points. He points out that growth in countries of Europe embarking on industrialization frequently took place in those industries where technological progress has been the most rapid. The use of modern technology in a limited and rapidly moving leading sector of the economy, to use Rostow's phrase, has dynamic effects in attracting entrepreneurs, developing profits from which savings produce capital, and training labor. Once development is under way, as a result of the removal of large social blocks, the existence of sufficient resources,

[5] Harvey Leibenstein, "Technical Progress, the Production Function and Dualism," *Banca Nazionale del Lavoro Quarterly Review*, December, 1960, pp. 3–18.
[6] A. Gerschenkron, *Economic Backwardness in Historical Perspective*, Harvard, Cambridge, Mass., 1962, pp. 8–9.

and presumably some capital formation, most rapid progress is made by using late technology.

We shall suggest below that the crux of the question is the capacity to distinguish between two situations of very little objective difference. In one, modern technology will lead to rapid growth and constitute an effective shortcut. In the other, the use of the latest technology fails to produce rapid development and creates no capital for use in other occupations which have been rationed on capital to make possible the capital-intensive investment. In the latter situation, an economy should make haste slowly.

FACTOR PRICES AND FACTOR EFFICIENCY

An important element in the arguments of Kuznets and Gerschenkron in favor of modern technology in underdeveloped countries is that abundant labor may not be cheap labor. Two reasons may explain this. Labor may be low in price, but lower in efficiency. Or the price of labor may be artificially bid up or raised by one or another means.

Low-priced labor may not be cheap because of malnutrition, incapacity to stand up to factory discipline, or high rates of absenteeism (possibly at a period of harvest or of religious festival). In many countries there may be not only a backward-bending supply curve of labor but also, in terms of costs, a forward-falling one, as higher wages enable a worker to raise his consumption to the physiological minimum needed for efficient factory work. But even where nutrition is not a problem, the uneducated, undisciplined worker will not be readily used in large-scale production with simple machinery, since his efficiency is too low to compensate for his low wages. In these circumstances there is an argument for labor-saving technology.

Saving one type of labor requires the assistance of another. The more automatic the machinery, the higher the training required of skilled maintenance staff, production engineers, etc. At low levels of training, and in the absence of capacity to recruit maintenance personnel abroad, neither labor-intensive nor labor-saving production may be possible.

It is possible to illustrate disparity between factor price and factor cost outside the field of labor. Hirschman calls attention to the fact that underdeveloped countries are weak on maintenance, and that it may be useful to invest in industries where maintenance is less necessary or where failure to maintain becomes more immediately evident or carries a more obvious penalty. In Colombia, airplanes function better than railroads, which perform at a mediocre standard but above that of roads. The penalty for postponing maintenance of air-planes is dramatically evident. A highway engineer recommends using bituminous surfacing on low-traveled routes instead of dirt, because holes in the road would more quickly attract attention and mainte-nance and retreatment would be less long delayed.[7]

In addition to low price but lower efficiency, another obstacle to labor-intensive technology is inefficient but high-priced workers. Where the demonstration effect has extended into the field of social services and collective bargaining, the price of labor, including wages and benefits, will be high despite low productivity. Italy provides an example of this: small-scale industry must ignore the social security system, with its heavy exactions in unemployment insurance, old-age pensions, severance pay, etc., or be unable to function. Large-scale industry can afford to hire labor, but the numbers are limited, and new workers are hired with reluctance because of the difficulty of dis-missing them should they not be needed. A labor-intensive industry such as shipbuilding is priced out of the market and subsidized back in again. The consequence is that there grow up, side by side, two separate sets of factor proportions—one, a small-scale, labor-intensive industry, in which employer and employee alike disregard the laws, and the other, a capital-intensive industry, where large amounts of capital are combined with small amounts of labor, in some consider-able part due to the high price of the latter.

Even apart from social security and high wages, labor may be ex-pensive in the domestic market because of domestic inflation, and foreign capital equipment cheap because of the overvaluation of the exchange. This combination in Israel gave entrepreneurs every in-centive to substitute machinery for labor.[8]

The disparity between factor prices and factor efficiency may ex-tend beyond labor, and particularly into the field of capital. Capital is frequently underpriced and overused, in a limited sector, with the result that it is not available for high-earning occupations outside. This may occur as a consequence of government concentration of in-vestment in industry; but even where no government interference has occurred, the capital market may be imperfect and split into segments within which demand and supply for loanable funds yield different rates of return. The credit system frequently slights agriculture and small-scale industry. Or the noncompeting groups may be regional,

[7] A. O. Hirschman, *The Strategy of Economic Development,* Yale, New Haven, Conn., 1958, chap. 8.
[8] See M. E. Kreinin, "Controlled Inflation in Israel, 1949–1954," *Journal of Political Economy,* April, 1956, p. 117.

like the South in the United States before World War I and southern Italy.

It is sometimes argued that prices of factor inputs correctly reflect factor efficiency, but that entrepreneurs adopt the wrong factor proportions because of their unwillingness or incapacity to maximize their return. On occasion this may reflect ignorance, although competitive elements should ensure that a Darwinian survival value is attached to finding the right combination, if only by trial and error. At other times, however, it may reflect a more systematic bias, such as a predilection for modern labor-saving technology, despite cheap labor and expensive capital. If so, this is demonstration effect in production.[9]

Or factor prices in various parts of the economy may fail to reflect social marginal product, even though they may accurately represent efficiency in the private sense. This was the basis for the Manoilescu recommendation of shifts of workers out of agriculture, where its private return overstated its social efficiency, into industry, where its social return was understated by the market.[10] Manoilescu failed to consider that the opposite was likely to occur in the capital market, nor did he contemplate the possibility that the shift of labor into, and of capital out of, industry called for different sets of factor proportions in industry as well as in agriculture. He was, however, one of the first to recognize that different factor proportions, or rather different combinations of factors involving labor, might exist side by side in the same economy and that this situation offered a potentiality for increasing output by factor redistribution. His interest was in increasing tariffs on industrial products to bring private marginal products more nearly into line with social, and to move labor from underemployment in agriculture into employment in industry. Like many who use the capital/output ratio as the criterion of investment, on the ground that the marginal productivity of labor is zero and the total value of the product can be imputed to capital, he worked only with labor and appeared to assume a limitless supply of capital of zero marginal efficiency.

One final source of confusion arises with foreign investment. What are the relevant factor proportions, and hence technology—those of the country of origin of the capital, those where the investment is taking place, or those where land and labor of the latter are combined with the capital of the former? To the country in which investment is

[9] A Chinese student has mentioned as examples of the demonstration effect in production, the building of two-story factories on cheap land to emulate foreign practices, and the purchase of the latest machinery in textiles while neglecting maintenance and repair. The Chinese source cited was dated June, 1937.

[10] See M. Manoilescu, *The Theory of Protection*, King, London, 1932.

taking place, all but the second will involve factor proportions different from those of purely domestic industry; but for the investing firm
or country, only factor proportions consonant with those of the country of investment represent maximization of return. It is convenient
to use the same technology as in the home country and to pay high
wages, despite the fact that labor is abundant. In addition to managerial inertia, it is possible to justify the practice in terms of earning
good will in the local population. But this is not the outcome under
competitive conditions, or conditions of short-run income maximization.

For the country of investment, capital invested in this way may be
regarded as cheap because its opportunity cost may be zero. An oil
company may put in a refinery, an aluminum company a reduction
plant, a chemical company a fertilizer installation; but the alternative
to these investments is no capital. If capital is available for a given
project and for nothing else, its opportunity cost is zero, and from an
economic point of view it may be properly used in most capital-
intensive fashion. This was the original basis for the great electricity
and aluminum installation[11] planned for the lower Volta in Ghana,
which was to be constructed by the Aluminium Company of Canada
(Alcan) with its own funds. Later, however, as the costs of the
project rose and the supply of aluminum seemed to be catching up
with the demand, Alcan backed out. Ghana wanted very much to go
ahead, since its prestige became involved. But this time it was much
more expensive. A private entrepreneur, the Kaiser Aluminum Company was interested, but it insisted on guarantees from the United
States government to cover economic as well as political risks. The
Agency for International Development (AID) put in some money, as
did the International Bank for Reconstruction and Development
(IBRD) and the Ghana government itself. All these sums except
what Kaiser risks for its own account have an opportunity cost which
is positive, because the more that is put into the Volta project the less
there is available for other Ghanaian investment. This is self-evident

---

[11] Hydroelectric power and alumina reduction are of course highly capital-intensive. Bauxite mining presumably could be undertaken on a labor-intensive or
on a capital-intensive basis. In Jamaica a few years ago three bauxite firms had
$70 million of capital and only 3,000 workers, or a capital/labor ratio of some
$23,000 per head.

In the construction stages, hydroelectric dams and aluminum plants can be
built with a high or a low capital/labor ratio, depending upon whether one uses
modern construction equipment or not. In many parts of India highly labor-intensive methods are used. But where manpower is used for simple energy, in
traditional methods of construction, the ramifying effects of training and discipline
may not be large.

for Ghana's own money; but it applies as well to the AID and IBRD loans and to the guarantees. It could happen that AID would reduce its loans to a country because of a large private investment, but this is unlikely. It will certainly make fewer other commitments when it moves in to take on a project which private enterprise dropped on an unguaranteed basis.

DUAL ECONOMY

The result of the introduction of modern or even reasonably efficient technology in some cases may be to develop what has come to be called a dual economy, i.e., an economy with different marginal efficiencies of identical factors in different parts of the economy. Different factor proportions and equal marginal factor product can exist side by side, of course, if production functions have different shapes in different sectors and industries. But in dual economy the marginal efficiency of labor and capital will be different in different sectors, different industries, and frequently, as the examples of native and plantation rubber and bananas show, in the same industry.

A dual society may be distinguished from a plural society or economy, and not in the numbers of different markets for identical factors. A plural economy is generally also a dual economy in the foregoing sense of having more than one factor market for a factor, but the differences in factor markets are based on race, such as characterize a plural society. The major literature in this field has developed over Indonesia.[12]

It is sometimes argued that the difficulty of a dual society is that, even where the gap is not based on a social difference, too wide a gap in the return to labor in the two-factor markets will paralyze rather than stimulate development. It is claimed, and denied, that high rates of wages paid by oil companies in Venezuela discourage work, thrift, and innovation. It is easier to take one's chances of getting a job with the oil company. Like speculative psychology in market economies, which undermines ambition to advance through socially productive channels, the modern sector of a dual economy may cause people to queue up for good jobs rather than demonstrate the advantages of capital accumulation and modern technology for diffusion throughout

[12] See B. Higgins, "The 'Dualistic Theory' of Underdeveloped Areas," *Economic Development and Cultural Change,* January, 1956, pp. 95–115; J. H. Boeke, *Economics and Economic Policy in Dual Societies,* Institute of Pacific Relations, New York, 1953; and J. S. Furnivall, *Netherlands India: A Study of Plural Economy,* Cambridge, New York, 1939.

the society. Where the dual economy is also a plural society, more rigid barriers to enter the high-priced labor market are likely to be accompanied by less incentive to the lower-priced factor to contemplate change.

Apart from significant social influences, it seems likely that small differences in the spread of wage rates in a dual market may result in opposite effects—in one case, stimulating the lower-priced factor to catch up, in the other, leading it to sink back. The degree of stimulation arising from foreign investment is subject to influence through policy, as discussed below. But, just as the existence of a middle class stimulates social mobility through narrowing the gap between the aristocrats and the workers, giving the former somewhere to go short of sinking to the lowest class and the latter a steppingstone up, so a narrow gap in factor proportions between the leading and lagging sectors in development may stimulate growth, whereas too wide a gap, above a critical level, may slow it down. Research is needed to ascertain whether this is the case and what the critical levels for stagnation or progress may be from country to country.

OBJECTIVE: OUTPUT OR EMPLOYMENT

When unemployment exists, disguised or obvious, the choice of factor proportions may be complicated by a confusion, or merging of objectives, between maximum rate of advance in output and maximum employment.[13] With constant returns to scale, two factors and one output, the problem does not arise: the maximum output can be obtained by using capital in such a way as to employ the most labor. But if there are variable returns, with two factors and one output, there may be a conflict, and with more than one output and external economies, there is almost certain to be one.

Increasing returns to scale from capital investment which involves capital deepening puts the problem for a single output. In two or more industries, investment in one may give more income, in the other, more employment. This may be true in each case, both directly and with external economies under which income and employment prospects created in other industries are imputed back to the original investment. In making these calculations, one should take into account the cost of distribution involved in getting consumption goods to the

---

[13] See R. S. Eckaus, "The Factor Proportions Problem in Underdeveloped Areas," *American Economic Review*, September, 1955, (reprinted in Agarwala and Singh (eds.), selection 5), esp. p. 553.

locus of the investment outlay. This cost may be borne by the workers, in the form of higher prices of consumption goods than they anticipated when they accepted employment, or by the employer, in the form of subsidies to a commissariat or other means of distributing goods. As our discussion of planning balance emphasized, however, moving the under- or unemployed to new lines of work may give rise to substantial distributional costs.

Much depends on the nature of the unemployment and the long-run prospects of its correction. It is assumed that it is structural and arises from employing capital in part of the economy with a technology that requires capital/labor ratios which cannot be generalized. The range of choice includes capital deepening in the capital-intensive sector, capital widening which would enlarge that sector relative to the labor-intensive, and improving the capital/labor ratio in the labor-intensive sector. Which is undertaken may turn on whether the capital/labor ratio in the capital-intensive sector is one which would be too capital-intensive in any prospective pattern of the economy's development. In this situation, it makes little sense to widen or deepen capital in this sector, even if this should give greater output.

In the final analysis, the choice between maximum output and maximum employment is not one which the economist can make, although he may be able to tell the political decision-makers how much of one must be given up for a fixed amount of the other. Where unemployment is destroying morale and undermining the society, a strong argument can be made for modifying the usual goal of economic development, which is highest possible output. But if the institutions of the society have adjusted themselves so as to make the problem uncritical, there may be much to be said for undertaking development first and solving the unemployment second.

Where employment becomes a primary and output a secondary objective, it is still necessary to use capital as efficiently as possible. The experience of the United States during the days of the Works Progress Administration has been studied in this connection and demonstrates that the modifications in technology necessary to maximize employment may call for some significant large-scale units of capital which can be intensively used, such as the trucks to haul men and their shovels to work on the construction site.

COMMUNITY DEVELOPMENT AND COTTAGE INDUSTRY

One solution which compromises the objectives of employment and output is that of community development and cottage industry. This was tried first in Southeast Asia, which is highly labor-intensive, and it has more recently been promoted there and elsewhere by the Peace Corps. The effort is made to keep underemployed workers in the village (and avoid the distribution problem), rather than transfer them to the city, but nonetheless to give them useful, labor-intensive tasks to perform. In community development the emphasis is on local public works, such as roads and schools. In some cases this is designed as a counterweight to seasonal unemployment in agriculture, and represents an introduction, or frequently an extension, of taxes in the form of services. Elsewhere an attempt is made to build a new community spirit and to let it choose the direction and character of the community works. Where the necessary community enthusiasm exists or can be developed, this sort of development has much to recommend it. It involves no fiscal or inflationary problems, since the investment and saving take place simultaneously. It invokes widespread local participation in a national movement, with the effects both of enlisting support and of training. And insofar as it concentrates on roads and schools, it contributes to the growth process at its core.[14]

Community development takes place outside the market. Cottage industry, on the other hand, represents production for the market which takes place in the village instead of in the factory. Cottage industry represents a return to the putting-out system from which the factory originated, a system in Britain in the sixteenth and seventeenth centuries under which middlemen bought supplies and put them out to be worked up into yarn and cloth in cottages. One modern descendant of the putting-out system may be said to be the watch industry of Switzerland.[15] Here there are many small and highly specialized "factories" in mountain towns, which supply parts through highly organized markets to assemblers. This characterization, which has produced objection, may be somewhat exaggerated, but it serves to indicate the essence of the cottage system—small producing units and efficient distribution through organized markets and middlemen.

The most interesting and major issue over cottage industry is that in India. In the second Five-Year Plan, provision was made for restraining factory production of cloth, through taxation, in order to

---

[14] T. S. Simey, *Welfare and Planning in the West Indies*, Clarendon Press, Oxford, 1946, opposes reliance on any one social institution such as schools or orphanages, emphasizes, the importance of local decisions on objectives of community effort, and warns that food, clothing, and shelter are the primary concerns of people (pp. 192, 200). "It is absolutely no use . . . providing educational services for adults whose chief thought is of food" (p. 92).

[15] *Processes and Problems of Industrialization*, United Nations, New York, 1955, p. 50, notes that Danish efficient small-scale industry evolves only a short distance from cottage industry.

enlarge the area of cottage production. Capital investment was roughly $20,000 per person employed in the steel industry; about $4,000 to $5,000 in other heavy industries; $2,000 to $2,500 in consumer-goods factories; but only $120 to $140 per artisan family in cottage industry.[16] But as suggested in Chapter 5 these figures on cottage industry may relate only to fixed equipment and neglect the substantial requirements of the industry in inventories of raw materials, goods in process, and finished output. The figures also neglect the facts that raw cotton is capital-intensive and that the extra costs of distribution through the various stages plus spoilage more than make up for the gain in lower labor costs. One analysis concludes that the scheme for hand spinning by the specially designed machine known as *ambar charka* would pay the workers only the value of the government subsidy, with no allowance for capital costs.[17] Reddaway draws a distinction between labor-intensive methods in a highly organized factory or plantation and dispersed cottage industry with problems of distribution and collection, maintenance of standards, use of capital-intensive materials, and so on. But factory organization requires investment in urban living, which may be an external diseconomy of efficient private operation.

It is possible to emphasize hand methods of production throughout industry insofar as this is technologically feasible. In the prevailing thought in India, however, capital-intensive efficient production is required for the capital-goods industries and for export;[18] but labor-intensive methods are applied in the field of home consumption. This is contrived dual economy. It makes some sense if there is an initial division of capital between that for capital-goods industries, for use in further expansion of capital, and a smaller sum available for home production, combined with a decision to employ only "modern technology" in the capital-goods industries and a desire for optimum employment in consumption goods. The capital-goods industries are important. No risks can be taken with them. If there is any risk in adopting a labor-intensive technology for the sake of employment

[16] P. C. Mahalanobis, "Role of Household and Small Industries," *Indian Finance,* Sept. 24, 1955, p. 626.
[17] See the interesting discussion of labor techniques by W. B. Reddaway in *The Development of the Indian Economy,* Irwin, Homewood, Ill., 1962, pp. 71–78.
[18] It should be noted that labor in the factory textile industry is strongly opposed to the rationalization of the industry with more labor-saving machinery, despite the fact that many industrialists and some economists believe that this is necessary if India is going to maintain its recently won place in the export market. See C. A. Myers, "Labour Problems of Rationalization: The Experience of India," in *International Labour Review,* January, 1956, pp. 1–20.

and to reduce the amount of building needed in cities, by all means let such risk be taken in the area of consumption.

MODERN TECHNOLOGY

The observation has frequently been made that the technology developed in the most advanced countries is not suited to the factor proportions of the underdeveloped. By the time a country is developed, its capital/labor ratio means that capital is cheap and labor expensive, and its inventions and innovations proceed in an awareness of this situation. But labor-saving, capital-using inventions are not appropriate to the factor proportions of underdeveloped countries. They have the choice of ignoring this fact, adopting an obsolete technology already abandoned in the leading country, or devising a new capital-saving, labor-using technology of their own.

In some areas obsolete technologies are used, frequently coupled, indeed, with obsolete equipment. The Japanese textile industry grew to power on secondhand British machines; the Burmese industry had a faltering start with the most modern. Kaiser-Frazer automotive equipment dismantled in Willow Run was reassembled in Tel Aviv and in Argentina.

But the availability of obsolescent equipment at low prices is not the essence. Obsolete techniques are less capital-intensive. Even if the equipment must be constructed *de novo*, it will frequently pay to do so rather than to buy the latest product on the market. The technique is tested, even though there may be some difficulty in finding manufacturers with experience in producing the equipment. A current example is the windmill, long abandoned for pumping water and generating electricity in the United States and Western Europe, but adopted in India under the second Five-Year Plan. In Iran a jump has been made straight to diesels from pumping with bullocks and the water wheel. The cheapness of fuel, and possibly the absence of winds of the requisite velocity, may justify this decision. An imported windmill originally cost $600 to $800 in India, but an attempt was made to cut this by the use of local materials.

One interesting experiment under way to bring extra power to the villages of India, to enable peasants to pump water at seasonal peaks in greater quantities than can be supplied by their draft animals, and perhaps to provide a modest amount of light is to develop a small-scale, foolproof, electric-generating unit which can be turned out in quantity and will use local materials. Something on the order of the converse of a refrigerator with its sealed-in unit is being tried; the purpose is to put heat into the heat exchanger to develop electricity, rather than to put electricity into it to take heat out of a box. If such a unit could be devised with a sealed-in heat exchanger and if it could use any ubiquitous fuel—instead of the standby gasoline electric generator in the United States which may be the right size in terms of output but burns expensive fuel—the increase in agricultural output might be substantial.

The notion that underdeveloped countries should fashion their own technology has been widely advocated and widely condemned. The introduction of new techniques is risky, and underdeveloped countries cannot afford to take the risks. As the quotation from Kuznets, above, indicates, the user would not be assured of parts and servicing arrangements. More significant, however, is whether the actual performance of the machine would bear out the promise of pilot studies. The experimentation necessary to develop a process through its *Kinderkrankheiten* (teething troubles) is appropriate to a very large company or a small and dogged innovator trying to win a place for himself. There seems to be fairly general agreement that, while in theory it would be useful to develop a special technology for underdeveloped countries, in practice there are strong resistances which prevent this. Communist China in the course of the "Great Leap Forward" undertook the fascinating experiment of trying to produce steel in thousands of small furnaces all over the countryside, but apparently abandoned the effort as a failure. The exact nature of the expensive mistake is not well understood in this country, but the problems seem to have been in the quality of steel, which was uneven and typically poor.

Several compromise solutions are available. In some industries the developed countries may offer a variety of technologies. Side by side with the integrated steel mill with linked stages of smelting, refining, and rolling, the United States is also producing steel in various parts of the country in separate stages which more nearly fit the conditions of some underdeveloped countries.[19] One such stage is rerolling, where semifinished steel shapes—slabs, blooms, or billets—are rerolled, after heating, into rods or light structural shapes. This operation can be undertaken efficiently on a small scale. From this stage it is an easy step to actual production of steel from scrap or pig iron in small furnaces of no more than 100,000 tons of annual capacity, fired by gas, oil, or electricity. This type of furnace has become widely popular in the United States because of costs of transport, both of scrap to the

---

[19] From an unpublished memorandum by Kenneth Bohr of the International Bank for Reconstruction and Development.

integrated mill and of finished product to the consumer. Scrap is scarce in underdeveloped countries, to be sure, but some is available or purchasable, and the smaller efficient scale may make this steel operation more desirable than the more dramatic, modern prestige-conveying integrated mill. In Colombia, the International Bank mission recommended a small mill for treating scrap, but the Colombian government turned down this recommendation in favor of the integrated mill.

Another compromise is to separate technology and factor proportions by stages, and to use capital-intensive methods when increasing returns to scale are available in any stage, but to cling to labor-intensive elsewhere, even in the same industry. Machinery to cut metal makes more sense than machinery to move it. The expensive capital involved in in-plant conveyor systems has little merit in light engineering in underdeveloped countries. Whether it would pay to break down the steps in continuous-process, integrated steel, chemical, or oil refining operations is a difficult question. In general, however, these industries seem unusually capital-intensive to have a prominent role in the plans of underdeveloped countries.[20]

Unfortunately, too many instances exist of no thought being given to the existence of variable factor proportions between countries. The Hoover Commission Task Force Report, *Overseas Economic Operation*,[21] argues that large industry cannot provide employment in underdeveloped countries because in the United States an investment of $100 million is needed to provide 10,000 jobs ($10,000 per job). This is half of the Mahalanobis figure for steel for India cited above, but double his figure for other heavy industry. More fundamentally, the statement ignores the possibility of modifications of technique to take advantage of lower rates for labor and to economize on higher-priced capital. A more extraordinary example is furnished by a "Report on Utilization of Waste Gases in Saudi Arabia."[22] This study calculates the costs of an Arabian venture to produce synthetic fertilizer by using American processes and converting to Arabian costs. In capital requirements, conversion uses a factor of 2 to take account of the average added expenses of *American* companies doing business in Saudi Arabia. In labor charges, a factor of 1½ is used, again based on the experience of United States firms in the area. Identical rates of

[20] But note the Soviet Union, Red China, and the second Indian Five-Year Plan.
[21] Government Printing Office, June, 1955, p. 50.
[22] By a Special Panel of the Advisory Committee on International Technical Assistance, published by the Division of Engineering and Industrial Research, National Academy of Science, National Research Council, Washington, D.C., July 14, 1954.

interest on capital are assumed, and identical depreciation. To an economist, these elaborate calculations overlook the essential problem, which is whether, given cheap labor and high capital costs for an Arabian concern, it would be possible to modify American capital-intensive methods of producing synthetic fertilizer from waste gases, substituting labor for capital. All too frequently it is the technologically culture-bound expert from the developed country, rather than the politicians of the underdeveloped, who needs to receive Hayek's understanding of elementary economics.

TECHNICAL ASSISTANCE

These lessons have been learned, albeit often painfully, in the spread of technical assistance in economic development which started with President Truman's Inaugural Speech of January, 1949, with its Point Four program. Technical assistance was initially conceived of as the sole engine of development, but it was quickly appreciated that the expert from the developed country has to be malleable to be of use in backward areas. Capital is not available to take advantage of all, or even many, opportunities for increased output, and what capital is available must be used with great economy and spread thinly. In Latin America, public health, education, and agriculture absorb more than 80 per cent of the efforts of the United States and probably a similar proportion of those of the United Nations. In these fields the expert has been obliged to recall obsolete techniques, which use little equipment, and where he could, to concentrate attention on methods which involve little or no equipment but only changed ways of doing things, even at the expense of some effort.

The initial tendency of the expert to be bemused by the technology and factor proportions of his own country has led recently in the United Nations and in the Colombo Plan area to an attempt to narrow the technological gap between giver and receiver of technical assistance. In India the Japanese technique of rice planting is taught instead of the American. It is more effort to plant rice in rows than to scatter the seed broadside in the paddies; but the row-planting method pays off in a way that the American, less-effort way of broadcasting seed from an airplane would not. Similarly in public health in rural Brazil, the need is for privies, not tiled bathrooms.

When it comes to direct investment by developed countries, the merit of modifying advanced technology is not so obvious, if indeed it is evident at all. Inertia, habit, and a sense of the proper way to do things lead foreign direct investment to bring its own technology with it unmodified. The prestige of the underdeveloped country pushes in the same direction: its politicians want to be able to point with pride to the modernity of the foreign plants. As a symbol, capital-intensive foreign industry may have value in encouraging dissatisfaction with old ways and interest in change. But the lesson is directly applied on a narrow front.

SUMMARY

If a country were doomed not to develop or to experience a change in its capital/labor ratio, it would maximize its existing income over time, or more probably minimize the rate of decline in income per capita, by equating the marginal efficiency of capital in every occupation. The marginal efficiency of capital is high in a really underdeveloped country, although perhaps not so high as in one which has started its development. It is uneconomical, therefore, to use capital anywhere where it cannot earn the high return.

When a country is successfully developing, it makes sense to employ capital more intensively in a leading sector than elsewhere (taking into account the differences in production functions). But the gap should not be too wide or the educative effect may not take hold, and dual economy may even turn into a block.

Finally, where growth is not yet started or has barely begun, the possibility of direct foreign investment in highly capital-intensive industries requires a weighing of two considerations: the opportunity cost of the capital, i.e., whether it would be available at all if it were not used where it was going, and the possibility of dual economy. If the foreign capital would not be available for any other use with a higher return, its opportunity cost is zero, which would justify investment in any industry at any set of factor proportions above the prevailing level. The prospect of dual economy, on the other hand, may be favorable or unfavorable, depending upon whether the up-to-date technology serves as a source of training and stimulation to labor— a growing point—or inhibits productive effort because the gap is too wide.

BIBLIOGRAPHY

The standard theoretical article is that by Richard Eckaus mentioned in footnote 13. Other articles are Vera C. Lutz, "The Growth Process in a 'Dual' Economic System," *Banca Nazionale del Lavoro Quarterly*

Review, September, 1958, pp. 279–324; and Albert O. Hirschman, "Investment Policies and Dualism in Underdeveloped Countries," *American Economic Review,* September, 1957, pp. 550–570. The most interesting practical case is perhaps India, on which see Reddaway, *The Development of the Indian Economy,* cited in footnote 17, and John P. Lewis, *Quiet Crisis in India,* Brookings Institution, Washington, D.C., 1962, chap. 3.

INTRODUCTION

For the last 150 years, since Malthus, the world has been conscious of the race between output and number of people. Optimists emphasize the increase in output and can point as a demonstration of their view to the experience of Western Europe and the United States, where population has grown rapidly but output has gone ahead faster. Pessimists, on the other hand, point to many other parts of the world, where income per capita has been steady or falling because population increase has outstripped the growth of total income. They may no longer agree with Malthus that output grows at an arithmetic rate, while population expansion is geometric. But they have new worries— the cheap cost of controlling malaria and other epidemic and endemic man-killers with present-day chemicals and drugs which bring down death rates, expand population, and increase the pressure of population on resources. And in the view of some, present exploitation of natural resources is close to ultimate limits, so that Malthusian concern for diminishing returns is not altogether unwarranted.

Too little attention has been given to the fact that the population problem is not encountered everywhere. Some countries which are growing at rates in excess of 3 per cent per year, a high rate, are not densely populated—Costa Rica and Venezuela, for example. In fact, apart from a number of Caribbean islands, Latin America is not over-populated, and Africa and substantial parts of Asia—Burma, Siam, Malaya, Sumatra, and Borneo—are not.[1] Moreover, in some areas, such as India, East Pakistan, and China, the density of present population

---

[1] See W. A. Lewis, comment on J. Viner, "The Role of the United States in the World Economy," in R. Lekachman (ed.), *National Policy for Economic Welfare at Home and Abroad*, Doubleday, Garden City, N.Y., 1955, p. 211. Another development economist who is disposed to regard the population issue as exaggerated is Everett Hagen. See his "Population and Economic Growth," *American Economic Review*, June, 1959, pp. 310–327. On the other hand, H. H. Villard makes population the central focus of concern. See his *Economic Development*, rev. ed., Holt, New York, 1963, chaps. 16 and 17.

is more significant than rates of increase, which are moderate. Nonetheless, in one way or another, population does represent a barrier to development in many countries.

We may return to the significance of the rate of population increase for income per capita, which we touched on in Chapter 3. At a capital/output ratio of 4:1, a 1 per cent per annum increase in output per capita requires 4 per cent of income saved if population is stable; 8 per cent at a 1 per cent per annum rate of population growth; 12 per cent at a 2 per cent rate of population growth; and 16 per cent at a 3 per cent rate of population increase. Starting with a 4 per cent rate of saving, a 1 per cent per annum population increase, and zero increase in income per capita, a program of investment which leads to increased income is likely to compound its difficulties by reducing the death rate and raising the rate of population increase.

These simple models suggest even more pessimistic conclusions if they are disaggregated by sectors. The agricultural sector is likely to have the faster rate of population growth, the higher capital/output ratio, and the lower rate of investment. In these circumstances, disguised unemployment may grow at a rapid rate.

This chapter has little to add to the general discussion of a well-worn topic and will attempt succinctly to recapitulate the familiar. It will treat, in order, the death rate, birth rate, and resultant rate of increase, the change in age distribution of the population, the role of migration, the impact of population change in demand and supply for goods and services, and population density.

DEATH RATES

Figure 15.1 gives crude death rates for a number of countries correlated with income per capita. The data relate to about 1961. The correlation is not nearly so high as one would suppose, if in fact it is positive, and this for two reasons. In the first place, demographic data are very poor in underdeveloped countries because of serious underreporting of births and deaths, as well as difficulties of taking a census. In Colombia, for example, a serious student found that birth statistics were 40 per cent understated and death statistics, 50 per cent. Instead of a birth rate of 33 per thousand and a death rate of 15, the recalculated rates, derived from the application of fertility ratios and death rates for different age groups to the population breakdown, gave figures of 46 per thousand and 24.[2]

Alvaro Lopez, "Problems of Stable Population Theory," unpublished doctoral

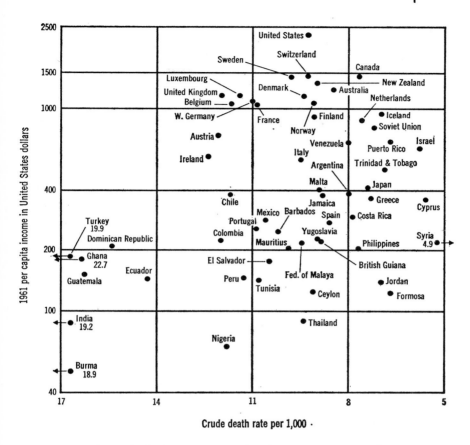

Figure 15.1 | Crude death rates compared with income per capita, about 1961.
SOURCES: Crude death rates per 1,000 inhabitants, *Statistical Yearbook, 1962,*
United Nations, New York, 1963, pp. 46–49, and *Demographic Yearbook, 1961,*
United Nations, New York, 1962, pp. 264–278; income per capita, table 1.1,
Average Income per Capita in Selected Countries, 1949 and 1961.

In the second place, however, since the end of World War II there
has been a widespread reduction in death rates in underdeveloped
countries owing to the spread of scientific understanding of disease and
its treatment, medical cooperation, and inexpensive public health
programs. K. Davis has calculated the decline in the crude death rate

thesis, Princeton University, Princeton, N.J., 1961. But see Philip M. Hauser,
"Demographic Indicators of Economic Development," *Economic Development and
Cultural Change,* January, 1959, pp. 98–116, who holds that mortality data are
one of the best indicators of the level of development and growth.

for eighteen underdeveloped countries by five-year periods showing the striking impact of the years after World War II to the middle of the last decade:[3]

Years compared	Per cent of decline in crude death rate
1935 with 1940	8.3
1940 with 1945	5.6
1945 with 1950	24.2
1950 with 1954 or 1953	14.0

While the years from 1940 to 1945 were perhaps not representative in these countries, few of which were in war areas, the threefold increase in the rate of decline between 1935–1940 and 1945–1950 is eloquent. In Ceylon, the crude death rate fell by 34 per cent in one year, from 1946 to 1947, as a result of the use of DDT against endemic malaria. Over a period of nine years the death rate fell from 22.2 per thousand to 10.4, or 53 per cent. During the 1940–1950 decade the death rate declined by 46 per cent in Puerto Rico, 43 per cent in Formosa, and 23 per cent in Jamaica. The result of these spectacular changes has been to bring recorded crude death rates in underdeveloped countries down to the level of those in urban developed countries.

The crude death rate, it should be noticed, does not adequately reflect differences in mortality experience because of the different average-age composition of population. With identical age-specific death rates, the country with the younger average population—the underdeveloped country—would show a lower crude death rate than the older country.[4] Conversely, the somewhat higher crude death rates of underdeveloped countries with populations which are younger on the average reflect higher mortality rates at a given age.

This is true of certain crude death rates which remain correlated with income per capita, and in particular of the infant-mortality rate. While data are scanty and unreporting is widespread in underdeveloped countries, so that the figures are minimal, it is clear from Figure 15.2 that the correlation is high. There is a wide divergence between the rates around 15 of Sweden, Norway, Iceland, the Netherlands, and France (sic!) on the one hand and the recorded data of more than 100 in Chile, the Dominican Republic, and Ghana. Earlier figures have

[3] K. Davis, "The Amazing Decline of Mortality in Underdeveloped Areas," *American Economic Review*, May, 1956, p. 307, reprinted in Morgan, Betz, and Choudhry (eds.), selection 18.
[4] *Ibid.*, p. 310.

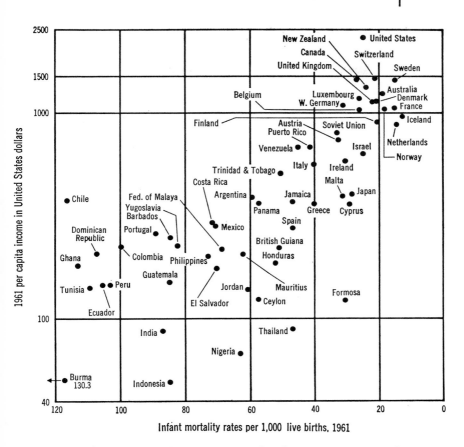

Figure 15.2 | Infant mortality rates compared with income per capita, about 1961. SOURCES: Infant mortality (deaths of infants under one year of age per 1,000 live births), *Statistical Yearbook, 1962,* United Nations, New York, 1963, pp. 50–52, and *Demographic Yearbook, 1961,* United Nations, New York, 1962, pp. 222–235; income per capita, table 1.1, Average Income per Capita in Selected Countries, 1949 and 1961.

reached as high as 231 per 1,000 live births in Burma (in 1953), and it is said that in Nigeria 50 per cent of the babies die before they are five days old, another 50 per cent of the remaining children die before they are five years old, and women over forty-five on the average have given birth to 11 children, of whom only 3 are alive.[5]

[5] Stated by R. G. Gustavson at a conference on the Role of Natural Resources in International Development, Resources for the Future, Washington, D.C., January, 1963.

In nonepidemic, nonfamine, nonwar years, the premodern death rate was somewhat higher than 25 per 1,000,[6] which is just about double the central tendency of the rates shown on Figure 15.1. The inclusion of epidemics, wars, and famines raised the *average* death rate to something nearer 30 per thousand. In modern societies, however, whether industrialized or underdeveloped, the rate is approaching its long-term limit, which is not far from 9 or 10 per thousand.[7]

BIRTH RATES

Birth rates are much more closely connected with the state of economic development. Figure 15.3 shows the position for a number of countries for which data are available near 1961. Some exceptional figures appear on Figure 15.3, but for the most part the correlation between birth rate and income per capita is a close one.

The connections, of course, are highly complex. In developed countries birth rates declined in the nineteenth century for different reasons and by different means. In some countries, such as Ireland, the reason was the scarcity of land, and family limitation took place in rural areas. In others, England and the United States, for example, the impetus to family limitation came from the desire for higher standards of living. And the mechanism could be either delayed marriage, as in Ireland and on the European Continent except for France, or restriction within the family. In some instances in developed countries and in underdeveloped countries as a whole, the linkage between birth rates and economic growth runs to the cultural pattern—age of marriage, status of women, urban-rural position, and nature of the family system. With agricultural production, ancestor worship, and the extended family, a man begets children to increase output currently (after a five- or six-year lag), to add social security in his old age, and to enhance his standing in the afterworld. When factory acts prevent children working at an early age and universal education is not only enacted but enforced, the economic utility of children declines. Where population pressure on resources grows high, such practices as abortion, exposure of girl infants, taboo against re-

[6] Kuznets, "Toward a Theory of Economic Growth," in R. Lekachman (ed.), *op. cit.*, p. 20.

[7] Ten per 1,000 would be the limit if everyone lived to be 100 years old and the population were stable. The fact that life expectancies are lower than 100 years raises this rate somewhat less than it is lowered by the fact that the population is growing.

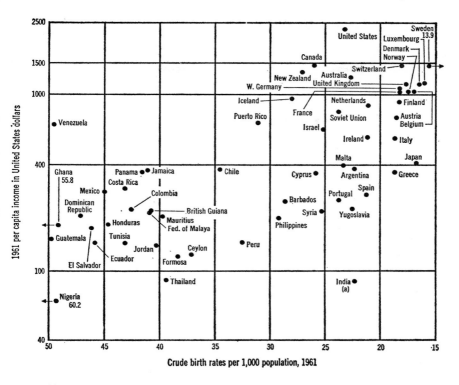

(a) Registration area

Figure 15.3 | Crude birth rates compared with income per capita, about 1961.
SOURCES: Crude birth rates per 1,000 inhabitants, *Statistical Yearbook, 1962,*
United Nations, New York, 1963, pp. 42–45, and *Demographic Yearbook, 1961,*
United Nations, New York, 1962, pp. 162–177; income per capita, table 1.1,
Average Income per Capita in Selected Countries, 1949 and 1961.

marriage of Hindu widows, or delayed marriage, as in Ireland, may
slow down population increase.

Most cultures set a high store on children, in the abstract, and hold
infertility in low esteem.[8] As the culture becomes urbanized and in-

[8] See M. Mead (ed.), *Cultural Patterns and Technical Change,* UNESCO, Paris,
1953, p. 125: "A Tiv married to get children. The production of numerous children was the main function in life." Also, *ibid.,* pp. 57, 96. See also J. Biesanz and
M. Biesanz, *Costa Rican Life,* Columbia, New York, 1944, p. 75: ". . . blessing
to have a large family." And T. S. Simey, *Welfare and Planning in the West
Indies,* Clarendon Press, Oxford, 1946, p. 15: "Children are highly prized and
warmly loved."

creases in economic development, however, emphasis shifts from quantity to quality of children. In Britain, the decline in the birth rate has been linked in the upper classes to primogeniture, and in the middle class, to the increase in education.[9] The reasons underlying the halt in the rate of French population growth in the nineteenth century—in what was a Catholic rural society—are not clear. In the view of some, the shortage of land, French distaste for emigration, and the abandonment of primogeniture in favor of equal inheritance slowly brought about an interest in family limitation. To others, the enormous bloodletting of the Napoleonic Wars induced the women of France to produce fewer soldiers. The population explosion in Egypt, which currently threatens the economic prospects of that country, had its beginning in the first half of the nineteenth century simultaneously with the introduction of cotton culture. But whether the added income from growing cotton on irrigated land enabled the prolific workers to afford larger families or whether the spurt in population was a response to the increased demand for field hands for a labor-intensive crop is an unanswered question.[10]

More surprising than unexplained declines in the birth rate, perhaps, is the demographic counterrevolution which occurred during and after World War II. In the 1930s, demographers in developed countries worried lest they be overtaken by population decline, as birth rates threatened to slide below death rates and the net reproduction rate below 1. As Figure 15.6 (on p. 279) indicates, however, birth rates in the United States and Britain turned sharply upward after the war. In part, the increase made up for the postponements of marriage, which occurred during the depression, and of births, which occurred during the war. For a time, demographers were inclined to dismiss it on these counts. But in the United States at least, and elsewhere in Western Europe if not in the United Kingdom, it seems that what has occurred is an increase in family size, a return from the modal two-plus children per family during the 1930s to something more nearly approaching four. Rather than raise fewer children to a higher standard of living the family began to include more children as part of its standard of living. The phenomenon was most remarkable

---

[9] K. B. Smellie, *The British Way of Life*, Heinemann, London, 1955, chap. 2. See also T. H. Marshall, "The Population of England and Wales from the Industrial Revolution to the World War," *Economic History Review*, April, 1935, pp. 65–78, reprinted in E. M. Carus-Wilson (ed.), *Essays in Economic History*, E. Arnold, London, 1954, vol. I, pp. 331–343.

[10] See C. Issawi, *Egypt at Mid-Century*, Oxford, Fair Lawn, N.J., 1954, chap. IV: "The high birth rate in Egypt now seems to be built into the culture. While the divorce rate in 1947 was 31 per cent of the marriages, less than 1 per cent of the divorces occurred where women had three or more children" (p. 56).

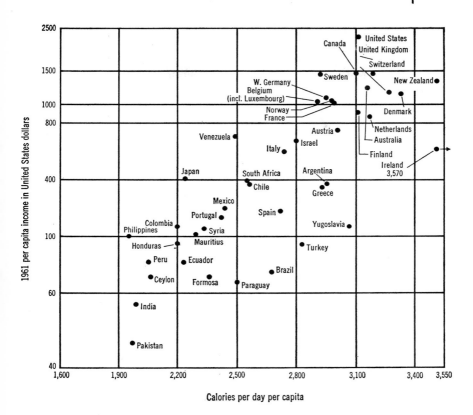

Figure 15.4 | Calories per day per capita compared with income per capita, about 1961. SOURCES: Calories per day per capita, *Statistical Yearbook, 1962,* United Nations, New York, 1963, pp. 330–333; income per capita, table 1.1, Average Income per Capita in Selected Countries, 1949 and 1961.

in France which reversed a downward trend in birth rates that had extended from 1750 to 1936. The change occurred simultaneously with revival of the French economy which broke with the prewar past; the two phenomena are doubtless connected, though probably through dependence on a third factor—a thorough-going change in the attitude of the Frenchman toward the family, the future, and economic expansion.[11] But demography remains a complex social science, and the causes of population rise and fall are by no means completely understood.

One interesting hypothesis has been advanced to explain some part

[11] C. Kindleberger, "The Postwar Resurgence of the French Economy," in Stanley Hoffmann *et al., In Search of France,* Harvard, Cambridge, Mass., 1963, pp. 131ff.

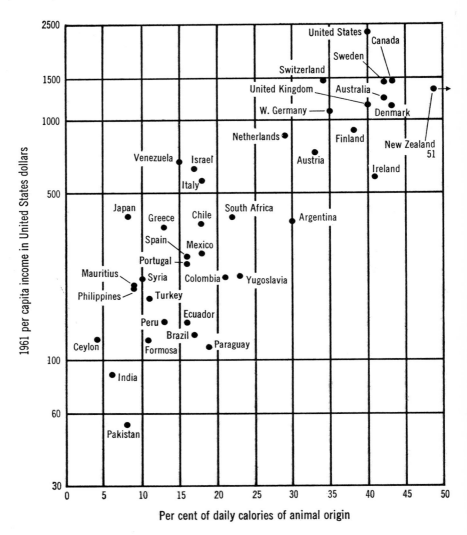

Figure 15.5 | Percentage of daily calories of animal origin compared with income per capita, about 1961. SOURCES: Percentage of daily calories of animal origin, *Statistical Yearbook, 1962,* United Nations, New York, 1963, pp. 330–333; income per capita, table 1.1, Average Income per Capita in Selected Countries, 1949 and 1961.

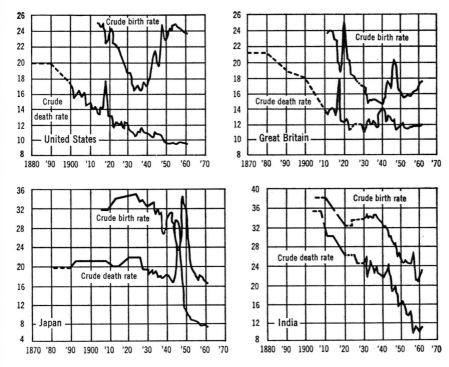

Figure 15.6 | Crude birth and death rates for the United States, the United Kingdom, Japan, and India. SOURCES: *Demographic Yearbook, 1950, 1951, 1954, 1961,* United Nations, New York, 1962; *Statistical Abstract of the United States,* 1936; W. S. Woytinsky and E. S. Woytinsky, *World Population and Production,* Twentieth Century Fund, New York, 1953.

of the decline in birth rates in developing economies on physiological rather than cultural grounds. J. de Castro, retired chairman of the Food and Agriculture Organization, states that the response of nature, when a species is threatened, is to increase the reproduction rate.[12] Fertility, he asserts, is inversely related to protein consumption—a thesis propounded by Thomas Doubleday in 1853. Chronic (but not acute) hunger leads not to depopulation but to overpopulation. He offers a correlation (page 72) which shows the highest birth rates connected with the lowest rates of daily consumption of animal protein measured in grams.[13] Figures 15.4 and 15.5 show the strong correla-

[12] See *The Geography of Hunger,* Little, Brown, Boston, 1952.
[13] Protein deficiency inhibits the functioning of the liver. The liver accordingly is unable to inactivate estrogens, and an excess of estrogens increases fertility (*ibid.,* p. 164).

tions between income per capita and calorie consumption per day on the one hand and percentage of daily calorie consumption from animal protein on the other. As far as they go, they bear out De Castro. But protein consumption and the birth rate may be unrelated to each other except for their mutual dependence on poverty.

One aspect of the De Castro thesis which must be borne in mind is that diet frequently declines with the early stages of development, which would account for an increase in birth rate. Under the plantation system or collectivization of agriculture, obstacles are put in the way of growing food for local consumption, and reliance is necessarily put on imported cereals. With this change, dietary balance is undone, which may stimulate fertility.

While crude death rates have declined from 25 to 10, crude birth rates have followed a somewhat different pattern, declining less and more slowly. In a number of countries an early upward movement in the birth rate as economic growth makes a start has been followed by a decline which proceeds more slowly than the decline in deaths. The position is illustrated in Figure 15.6 for India, and the following table of averages:

Table 15.1 | *Indian Vital Statistics**

Years	Crude birth rate (per 1,000)	Crude death rate (per 1,000)	Population increase (per cent)
1905–1909	37.7	35.4	0.2
1911–1913	32.7	29.9	0.3
1921–1925	33.3	25.0	0.8
1926–1930	33.2	24.3	0.9
1931–1935	34.3	23.4	1.1
1936–1940	33.3	22.1	1.1
1941–1945	28.3	22.8	0.6
1946–1950	26.3	17.4	0.7
1951–1955	25.3	13.4	1.2
1956–1960	21.7	10.5	1.1

* Data to 1940 for British India; 1930–1946 for British Provinces; beginning 1947, Republic of India.
SOURCE: *Demographic Yearbook, 1951,* United Nations, New York, pp. 146, 160, 161, 188, 200, 201; *Demographic Yearbook, 1954,* pp. 256, 257, 521; *Demographic Yearbook, 1961,* pp. 171, 273.

These data are grossly underreported, but the degree of under-estimation is likely to have been constant or declining, and roughly the same in both, so that the changes give an appropriate picture.[14]

One important point on the side of the pessimists is that the birth rates in underdeveloped countries have started down from levels far higher than any experienced in Western Europe and the United States when family limitation by means of contraception began there about 1880. Birth rates higher than 60 per thousand are virtually impossible, and 50 per thousand cannot long be sustained. A birth rate which stays in the 40s is very high, e.g., Guatemala at 49.9, the Dominican Republic at 47.0, El Salvador at 46.1, Mexico at 44.9, Tunisia and Costa Rica at 43.2, Panama at 41.5, Jamaica at 41.0, British Guiana and Malaya at 40.0, Mauritius at 39.8 are the only ones right at 40 or higher for which both income and birth-rate data are available for 1961 in the United Nations source. More of the underdeveloped countries are in the 30s or high 20s. But the 30s were high for Western Europe in the eighteenth century.[15] For the most part, these countries now have rates in the high teens or the low 20s.

RATES OF POPULATION INCREASE

Birth rates and death rates are given per thousand. When the resultant rate of population increase is calculated, the decimal point is moved over one place, and the result expressed per hundred, or in per cent. A birth rate of 40 per 1,000, which is high, and a death rate of 10 per 1,000, which is low, will lead to a rate of increase of 3 per cent, which is about as high as a country is likely to go. Three per cent is the figure reached by Ceylon, Venezuela, Mexico, and Nicaragua.[16] Costa Rica has indeed reached 3.7 per cent;[17] but the figures for Pakistan and India have been hovering at about 1.5 per cent, and for Japan at 1 per cent.

The Malthusian model can be illustrated by comparing curves repre-

[14] See K. Davis, *The Population of India and Pakistan,* Princeton, Princeton, N.J., 1951, and S. Chadrasekhar, *India's Population: Fact and Policy,* rev. ed., Chidambaram, 1950.

[15] Kingsley Davis, *American Economic Review,* May, 1956, p. 315.

[16] See *Processes and Problems of Industrialization in Underdeveloped Countries,* United Nations, New York, 1955, p. 15. In Venezuela economic development between 1945–1949 and 1960 brought the death rate down from 13.5 to 8, while the birth rate was rising from 38.5 to 49.6. This would give a rate of increase close to 4.2 per cent. See *Demographic Yearbook,* 1961, United Nations, New York, 1962, pp. 169, 271.

[17] Davis, *op. cit.,* p. 316. This table assembles statistics for the eighteen fastest growing countries for which the data are reliable, which condition excludes the Philippines, Egypt, and Thailand.

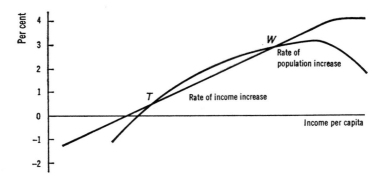

Figure 15.7 | The low-level equilibrium population trap.

senting population growth and income growth, plotted as rates of change, each against levels of per capita income. The higher the rate of income per capita, the higher the rate of increase of income. This is because savings vary positively with income per capita and serve as a basis for capital formation and increments in output. At some level of income per capita, gross savings are just enough to keep the economy stable. At lower rates, capital would be used up and the rate of growth of income would be negative. For convenience, the curve representing the rate of growth of income in per cent (dY/Y) is shown in Figure 15.7 largely as a straight line. In fact, however, above a certain income it will tend to level out to give a constant percentage rate of increase as a limit is reached to increases in savings.[18]

The rate of population increase can also be plotted in terms of income per capita. At some low level the rate of population change will be nil. Population is then stagnant. But higher incomes will bring about an increase in population under the pressure of falling death rates.[19] This increase may well be faster than the rate of income change at the relevant income per capita. Beyond a certain rate of population increase, however, given in Figure 15.7 as 3 per cent, the rate levels

---

[18] See pp. 55–56.

[19] Note that in the British case, the death rates were maintained while the birth rate increased, which still gives a rapid increase in population growth. The death rates failed to drop since crowding in the cities and the resulting spread of disease offset the gains in nutrition and medical care until about the 1880s. Birth rates increased, lacking the means of family limitation, because the marriage age dropped with the move from the farm to the city. Note also Irene Taueber, *The Population of Japan,* Princeton, Princeton, N.J., 1958, who says that the death rate is correlated not with small increases in income but with public health measures.

off. With still higher incomes it may be expected to decline as the birth rate falls.

In Figure 15.7, the curves are drawn so that they intersect one another twice, at T and at W; T, which happens to be drawn at a positive rate of population increase and income increase, is a stable equilibrium. A small impetus, such as a foreign loan which increased income, would bring about a faster increase in population so that income per capita would decline again to the equilibrium level. At W, however, the equilibrium is unstable. A decrease in income will be cumulative as far as T; an increase will perpetuate itself. T is what has been called a low-level equilibrium trap, which illustrates the Malthusian thesis.[20] If the rate-of-income increase and the rate-of-population increase represent functions of per capita income which intersect in this fashion, population and income can grow at the same rate, but income per capita will be fixed.

Whether a country will be caught in the Malthusian trap depends, of course, on the absolute and relative positions of the income and population growth schedules. A change in the sociopolitical outlook can shift the population schedule which, of course, can move only horizontally, i.e., to the right or to the left. Such a shift in either direction may occur from a reevaluation of the desirability of having children; or a technological change in public health may displace the schedule to the left. A technological change or a crash investment program could produce a shift of the income-growth schedule, either horizontally or vertically.[21] There is no need, indeed, for the two schedules to intersect at all, if the income schedule lies originally left and up and the population schedule lies far to the right. In this case, the trap is not escaped but avoided.

This model is based on Harrod-Domar growth, with constant returns to capital despite a rising capital/labor ratio. But the applicability of this model in underdeveloped countries over long periods of time may be questioned. There may be diminishing returns to capital as the

[20] See H. Leibenstein, *A Theory of Economic-Demographic Development,* Princeton, Princeton, N.J., 1954; R. N. Nelson, "The Low-Level Equilibrium Population Trap," *American Economic Review,* December, 1956, pp. 894–908.

[21] Richard Nelson finds that Japan escaped from the low-level equilibrium trap between 1867 and 1890, not by an increased level of investment, but rather as a consequence of increased farm productivity as a result of the improvement of quality of rice seed, fertilizer, irrigation, and double cropping. Farm productivity doubled in the thirty years after 1870, with only a small capital investment in dirt roads, rickshas, carts, etc. After 1900 the rate of growth of capital exceeded that of the population. See his "Growth Models and the Escape from the Low-Level Equilibrium Trap: The Case of Japan," *Economic Development and Cultural Change,* April, 1960, pp. 378–388.

capital/labor ratio increases, but there is a much more serious problem in the falling land/labor ratio before technical change gets built into the system on a regular basis at a sufficiently high rate.[22] The Harrod-Domar model may be useful in the short run, but does not apply over longer periods. It is dangerous to apply geometric growth to long periods, in economic growth as in demography. Trees grow for a while at geometric rates, but as Churchill has pointed out, they never reach the sky. It may be true that, if the world continues to increase in population at 1.5 per cent a year, the weight of the population would equal the weight of the earth by A.D. 4250.[23] But this is small cause for present alarm, since rates of growth do not hold constant. Apart from some inherent tendency for growth to conform to a Gompertz or S curve, the changes which come with a rise in income per capita—urbanization, education, change of occupation, and frequently the weakening of religious ties—are associated with lower fertility.[24] The significant question is not whether population growth will come to a stop, but at what level of population will the decline of birth rates catch up with the leveling out of death rates. It seems clear that the increase will be sizable in all countries, including those now densely populated. There is little means of determining how much.

AGE DISTRIBUTION

The initial spurt in population encountered by a country in the early stage of development increases total numbers, but not the number of workers. Both a rapidly growing population and one which has stabilized in numbers suffer from the same disability—a high proportion of dependents to actively engaged population. In a rapidly growing population, this is the result of large numbers of youth. In a stabilized population, the dependents are to a much greater extent old people.

The age pyramids of populations at different stages in the demographic revolution (and counterrevolution) are illustrated in Figure 15.8, which gives the population distribution by age for the United States, West Germany, Thailand, and Paraguay. If the proportion of the population between the ages of fifteen and sixty-four is regarded

[22] H. H. Villard, "Some Notes on Population and Living Levels," *Review of Economics and Statistics,* May, 1955, p. 189.
[23] *Ibid.*
[24] See J. J. Spengler, "Population Theory," in B. F. Haley (ed.), *A Survey of Contemporary Economics,* Irwin, Homewood, Ill., 1952, vol. II, p. 103.

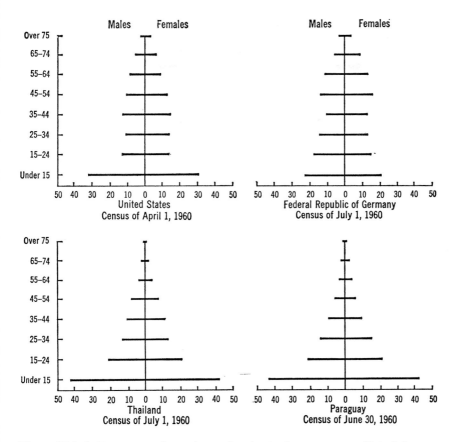

Figure 15.8 | Percentage of population distribution by age groups, United States, West Germany, Thailand, and Paraguay, 1960. SOURCE: *Demographic Yearbook, 1961,* United Nations, New York, 1962, pp. 146–155.

as economically productive, this varies between something like 55 per cent for underdeveloped countries and 65 per cent for developed. By itself, and apart from differences in average income per gainfully occupied worker, this fact reduces the capacity of underdeveloped countries to save and form capital. The major effect of improved public health methods is to increase the number of children who survive to adulthood. This does not change the proportion of economically active to total population, however, unless the birth rate changes, since the initial increase in number of adults is followed by a further increase in number of children.

Improved public health is not therefore an unalloyed blessing for underdeveloped countries. One of its major effects is to increase the dependent population. But it is equally not a curse. The control or elimination of malaria, smallpox, plague, cholera, syphilis, yaws, and trachoma does improve the quality of living, reducing debility as well as mortality and increasing vitality and productivity.

MIGRATION

External migration is no longer a cure for overpopulation of underdeveloped areas. There are some countries whose development would be furthered by immigration. Australia, Rhodesia, and Surinam, where land/labor ratios are very high, fall in this group. But these countries are unwilling to accept immigrants from most densely populated areas, owing to the difficulty of social integration, on the one hand, and lack of appropriate skills, on the other. In Brazil, where relatively indiscriminate immigration has been encouraged to maintain a cheap supply of labor for plantations, a change has been recommended to selective policies designed to settle independent proprietors engaged in mixed farming around the major industrial centers to assist in bringing down the price of food and thus to speed industrialization.[25]

Until recently emigration was sought as an outlet by some overpopulated countries, such as Italy, and welcomed within the British Commonwealth by Britain. Both attitudes have changed. In Italy, rapid economic growth has proceeded over a sufficiently long period to make the country conscious of the social cost of emigration of workers to the rest of Europe, leaving villages of women, children, and old people, bereft of men—today's concentration camps, as one Italian rural economist has put it. In Britain, on the other hand, the social difficulties created by the immigration of impoverished colored subjects of the Queen have led to roundabout restriction, whilst maintaining the freedom to migrate in principle. Inward migration is limited to those already holding jobs, which cuts down on the flow. The 1963 proposals for changes of immigration laws in the United States are designed with a view to ending discriminatory restrictions against southern Europeans and Asians, on political rather than economic grounds. The overall limitations remain. Emigration therefore appears to offer little prospect for alleviating the population surpluses of Asia and the Caribbean (except for Puerto Rican migration to New York).

[25] F. Bastos de Avila, *Economic Impacts of Immigration: The Brazilian Immigration Problem,* Martinus Nijhoff, The Hague, 1954.

Emigration from a poor country to a well-to-do one, like capital export in the same direction, is inappropriate from a welfare point of view. The poor country raises and educates a young man and then ships him off. It knows him only as a dependent, whereas the country of immigration receives him as a member of the labor force. The problem is similar to that of England, which complains that too many of its trained engineers emigrate to the United States. It is true that the country of immigration may be obliged to undertake some complementary capital formation as it receives new arrivals, in order to house, transport, educate, and govern them. If immigrants in all cases sent back remittances to the country of their origin, the capital export of a type which the country was well fitted to undertake might pay a high return. More and more, however, in the pressure of today's conformist age, the immigrant quickly shifts his level of living from that of his country of origin to that of his new homeland, with the result that the benefit accrues to him. Seasonal migration, between Mexico and the United States or between some African countries, has been one short-term means of getting around these problems.

Internal migration offers fewer social barriers and some considerable opportunities not unassociated with capital requirements of the sort just mentioned. Indonesia's population problem is limited to Java. Sumatra, Borneo, and Celebes have substantial room for settlement. Indonesia has proposed "transmigration" from Java to the islands. Unfortunately, the expense of building roads, clearing land, and constructing houses and villages means that the scale of migration makes little or no dent in the problem. Similar expenses, as well as the extent of the required change in living conditions, have limited the movement of people from the crowded Andean highlands to the lowlands of Bolivia, Ecuador, and Peru, but these countries, as well as Mexico and Guatemala, continue to see such colonization programs as useful. In India nearly half the people live in one-seventh of the area.[26] It is true that the densely settled eastern district is the most fertile because of the monsoon, but as technological change is introduced into agriculture and as village ties weaken, some resettlement may be possible.

One form of migration which has occurred everywhere is from the village to the city, as already discussed in Chapter 10. In India the percentage of urban population was 9.3 in 1881, grew slowly until 1921, and then began to accelerate. By 1941 the figure reached 12.8 per cent and by 1961, 18. Similar movements appear to have taken place everywhere in the world.

[26] K. Davis, *The Population of India and Pakistan*, Princeton, Princeton, N.J., 1951, p. 19.

In Brazil the rate of population increase is much higher in the cities than in the country as a whole, despite a much lower birth rate, because of inward migration from the rural areas. This migration is only one of four in the country. The others include a general movement from north to south, i.e., from the slower- to the faster-growing section of the country, a movement into certain frontier districts, and a churning around in rather tragic fashion of a number of seminomads.[27]

The distinction between positive migration, which is attracted by opportunities for economic improvement, and negative migration, which is driven away from a village by lack of opportunity, is an important one. The former requires a feeling of social cohesion which extends beyond the village and a certain amount of capital, enterprise, and interest in improving one's social and economic condition. The latter is a product of economic distress and is likely to lead to social and political unrest.

POPULATION POLICY

In the 1930s in Western Europe, population policy was directed to the maintenance of birth rates, which were sliding downward. Part of the interest in higher fertility had its origin in eugenics: the quality of population was believed to be deteriorating as reproduction rates were higher among lower-income and less educated groups than among the middle- and upper-income and educated groups. Part was a function of the depression: a slower rate of population growth reduced the demand for housing and overhead capital and intensified what was regarded as a dearth of investment opportunities.

Population does have supply, as well as demand, effects; but these are slower to be realized except in the event of migration. As already noted, there are a number of countries which want to increase immigration as a matter of national policy to improve the land/labor ratio. A more densely populated area would make for more economical construction and use of "railroads, roads, water supplies and electric power, not to speak of schools, hospitals and social services."[28] But for the most part the population problem consists today of limiting the rise and bringing it to a halt as rapidly as possible.

The only country in the world which has officially adopted family

---

[27] T. Lynn Smith, "Demographic Factors Related to Economic Growth in Brazil," in S. Kuznets, W. Moore, and J. J. Spengler (eds.), *Economic Growth: Brazil, India, Japan,* Duke, Durham, N.C., 1955, pp. 241–262.

[28] W. A. Lewis, *The Theory of Economic Growth,* Irwin, Homewood, Ill., 1955, p. 211.

limitation as a national policy is India. Unofficial groups elsewhere have urged dissemination of knowledge of and devices for reducing fertility. These are frequently opposed by the teachings of religion and by the cultural pattern in certain countries and are impeded, to be sure, by difficulty of communication.

Until recent efforts in India, there had been some doubt whether failure to practice family limitation had its origin in nonacceptance of the goal, ignorance or unavailability of the means, or the fact that the means are complex, difficult of operation, expensive, and uncertain. Recent Indian experience, and the widespread practice of abortion in postwar Japan, even in rural districts, has shifted opinion away from the first of these possibilities. There is still great desire for children in most societies, and opposition to birth control in many quarters. But a growing awareness of the possibilities of increasing the level of living has heightened interest in limiting the number of children. While the majority of people in many parts of the world are probably still some distance from recognizing a desire to limit their families to some relatively small number of children (such as four), elsewhere the problem is shifting from one of stimulating the desire for family limitation to providing a cheap, convenient, effective means. One promising avenue is the oral contraceptive in the form of a pill with temporary effect, still in the experimental stage. The suggestion has been made,[29] and even acted upon in the state of Madras in India,[30] that the state should pay parents of an adequate-sized family to undergo a vasectomy operation for sterilization. Research into other methods is going forward with wide support.

Apart from birth control, there seems to be little of a positive nature that can be done. Suggestions have been numerous that expenditures for public health be limited, or postponed, or that economic development programs should focus on social overhead capital and secondary industry, leaving the food supply untouched as long as possible so as not to support higher numbers of people. Still another suggestion is that public health programs emphasize quality, not quantity, and be

[29] See Stephen Enke, "Government Bonus for Smaller Families," *Population Review,* July, 1960; "The Economics of Government Payments to Limit Population," *Economic Development and Cultural Change,* July, 1960, pp. 339–348; and *Economics for Development,* Prentice-Hall, Englewood Cliffs, N.J., 1963, chap. 20.

[30] "Madras Limits Payments in Sterilization Program," *New York Times,* Mar. 26, 1963. It was reported that 38,000 men and 6,000 women had been sterilized in the state, which paid a fee of $16 to the person undergoing the operation and a $2 fee to "middlemen" who induced the patient to undertake it. The action of Madras in March, 1963, was to eliminate the $2 middleman fee because of protest. The news account noted that 330,000 persons throughout the country had been sterilized.

applied very narrowly in great depth. But none of these suggestions is of any great practicality. Humanitarian considerations suggest that no democratic society can ignore opportunities for inexpensive improvements in public health on a wide scale. A policy of restricting improvements in health to a narrow group for educative purposes is almost certain to run afoul of public opinion. Finally, there is the practical argument that increased output requires improved public health, which is difficult or impossible to dissociate from reduced mortality. In breeding livestock, perhaps, it would be possible to leave high mortality rates unchanged for the mass of the herd, while investing in complementary resources and reserving an investment in general health for the final stage. The clinical detachment necessary to achieve this and the passivity of the experimental group are probably unattainable in people.

Where positive steps are not taken to reduce fertility, and development programs are effective in raising income per capita despite population growth, the concomitants of increased income—city life, higher education, increasing rationality, higher status for women, and interest in material advance—will all ultimately reduce the level of fertility. The big questions are how soon and how much. In their answers optimists and pessimists differ.

SUMMARY

In many underdeveloped parts of the world, but not all, high population density and high rates of population increase have touched off a race between economic growth and population increase in which the latter threatens to win. Death rates have been reduced by cheap public health measures; they have also fallen with increased income per capita. Birth rates rise with more income, or decrease more slowly than death rates. The result is a large increase in population with growth until a new equilibrium is reached, with birth and death rates equal at lower levels. In the Malthusian low-level equilibrium trap, in fact, it is impossible to raise income per capita since any short-term increase touches off a faster gain in population than income which restores the initial position. Sharp changes in population rates bring about changes in the average age of a country and alter the ratio of workers to total numbers. Migration is not a very hopeful escape from the problem. Interest in family limitation has increased in underdeveloped countries, especially India. Abortion, oral contraception, surgical sterilization are among the means being studied.

BIBLIOGRAPHY

The most complete single source on population is *The Determinants and Consequences of Population Trends,* United Nations, New York, 1953, which is summarized in a paper entitled "Population Growth and the Standard of Living in Underdeveloped Countries," reprinted in Okun and Richardson (eds.), selection 21. H. Leibenstein's *A Theory of Economic Demographic Development,* Princeton, Princeton, N.J., 1954, emphasizes the need for a critical minimum effort to escape the low-level equilibrium trap. See also the Hagen and Villard papers mentioned in footnote 1, in the debate whether the issue is of prime importance. For a useful historical and theoretical discussion, see the papers by H. J. Habakkuk and G. Ranis and the comment upon them, *American Economic Review,* May, 1963, pp. 607–633.

PART THREE | *International Issues*

THE CASE FOR COMPARATIVE ADVANTAGE

The classic case for specialization and trade, based on comparative advantage, is a static one: with two countries, two commodities, two factors (fixed in quantity and mobile within but not between the two countries), identical production functions in both countries, full employment, perfect competition, and a few other assumptions, it has been easy to demonstrate that both countries will be better off with free trade than with restrictions on trade, or at least that one country can be better off and the other no worse off. Comparative advantage will generally arise from differences in factor endowments in the two countries, and each country will export the commodity which is produced with a high proportion of the factor which it possesses in abundance.

The static nature of comparative advantage does not make it inapplicable to countries engaged in economic development, in the view of many economists. If a country is pulled into world trade for the first time by the opening up of transport, or if new opportunities for trade are created by reductions in transport cost, the country can and should maximize its real income by specialization along lines of comparative advantage. If factors should be changed by discovery or population growth, a new basis of comparative advantage is reached, but the same reasoning applies. Resources should be readjusted so as to give a new maximum.

The law of comparative advantage establishes a presumption that an incremental balanced unit of resources should be invested in the export industry rather than in the import-competing industry, to stick to two commodities. The country is more efficient in the production of the export good. Even where demand is strongly biased in favor of the import good, the presumption holds. More of the import good is acquired by producing the export item and exchanging it for the desired one. This is the presumption in favor of comparative advantage which its opponents must overcome.

While land and labor remain relatively unchanged in the short and intermediate run, capital accumulation proceeds at a steady pace. The theory is readily adjusted to accommodate this change.[1] As capital accumulation proceeds faster in one country than another, the factor endowments underlying comparative advantage, and comparative advantage itself, change. The basis for trade is altered. But a new basis exists.

THE OPPOSITION TO COMPARATIVE ADVANTAGE

Exception is taken to this view along a wide front. The earliest argument invoked increasing returns. A long line of economists, from the German and early American protectionists to Allyn Young and John H. Williams, have insisted on leaving room for the possibility that static free trade will give less than an optimum position for the world because of increasing returns to scale available in an industry but unrealizable at the low prices maintained under free trade. With protection and higher prices, an increase in scale will make possible an ultimately lower price than that which prevailed with free imports.

For a long time the infant-industry argument was the only exception to the free-trade case which commanded respectable support. Recently, however, a host of new arguments has been put forth, at a variety of different levels. Dynamic counterweights to static comparative advantage have been found in short-run instability, in long-run behavior in the terms of trade, in disparity between social and private costs, and, more fundamental, in the relevance of the two-country, two-factor, two-commodity world to the world of factor movements, capital accumulation, changing technology, and intermediate goods. There are other arguments, but these are the principal ones.

Short-run instability in export markets is an argument against specialization, insofar as, in the short run, investments are lumpy, resources are immobile, and wants are incompressible. A country might do well to specialize in a food item, an agricultural raw material, or a mineral at the long-run average price, if this were steady; but wide short-run fluctuations in price around the average slow down development. In the first place, it is not possible to vary domestic consumption or investment over the range required by large annual changes in export proceeds. The average year-to-year fluctuation in the prices of

[1] D. M. Bensusan-Butt, "A Model of Trade and Accumulation," *American Economic Review,* September, 1954, pp. 511–529.

fifty commodities studied by the United Nations Secretariat was 14 per cent per annum over the period from 1900 to 1950.[2] As the value of exports fluctuates widely, a specialized country lacks control over national income, money supply, and hence over its rate of development.[3] It may be desirable, in these terms, to accept a somewhat lower degree of specialization and lower level of real income at the outset of a development program in order more surely to be in control of it.

The instability argument rests partly on the proposition that demand is inelastic. It is possible to make a static case on this point. It is sometimes maintained that comparative advantage is well and good as far as a country has gone, but that additional investment in the export industry will depress prices. If demand is inelastic, calculation of marginal revenue for a given incremental unit must take into account not only the return on that unit but the impact on profits on inframarginal sales. It may then happen that a country will do well to leave resources currently engaged in exports where they are, but to invest additional available resources elsewhere. The average revenue in this case could be higher in exports than in an import-competing good, but marginal revenue lower. Average comparative advantage would dictate expanding exports, but marginal comparative advantage would lie with the import-competing good.

Or the difficulty may lie not so much in the price elasticity of demand abroad as in the income-inelasticity or uncertainty about the income-elasticity of alternative investments in the home market, as claimed by Nurkse. It was argued in Chapter 11 that balance in demand could be achieved by displacing existing producers; among the producers whom it is easiest to supersede are the foreigners. If foreign producers have built a market for shoes in a country, the country knows that it can invest safely in shoe production, provided it excludes the foreign product.

Another argument runs to the effect that specialization is an undesirable policy in the long run, since it condemns underdeveloped countries specializing in raw materials to ever-declining terms of trade, as contrasted with developed countries which produce manufactures. It was originally thought that the terms of trade would favor primary production, which obeyed the law of diminishing returns, and respond adversely to manufactures, which followed the law of diminishing

---

[2] *Instability in Export Markets of Underdeveloped Countries,* United Nations, New York, 1952, reprinted in Morgan, Betz, and Choudhry (eds.), selection 23.
[3] See H. C. Wallich, *Monetary Problems of an Export Economy,* Harvard, Cambridge, Mass., 1950.

cost. But observation has made clear that there is no real evidence to support the view that the different sectors followed different laws of production, and some to suggest that, in fact, the terms of trade have run the other way. The major evidence cited is decidedly weak: primarily the inverse of the British terms of trade from 1870 to 1938. More generally, the theorem rests on generalizations such as Engel's law, which requires a progressive shift of resources out of foodstuffs into secondary and tertiary industry as world income per capita grows, but failing which, foodstuffs will be overproduced and hence decline in price relative to manufactures; or the increased efficiency in the consumption of raw materials used in manufacturing, which enables a given amount of raw-material production to support a higher and higher value of manufactured output. This means, of course, that if the physical outputs of raw materials and manufactures grow at equal rates, the terms of trade will shift against raw materials. Or the argument runs in terms of comparative monopoly power: increased efficiency in developed countries takes the form of higher prices for factors of production and constant prices for goods, whereas in underdeveloped countries, factor returns hold steady in spite of increased productivity and the benefit goes abroad to lower prices.

As it happens, there is evidence from Europe's terms of trade to suggest that, while there is no necessary trend in the terms of trade between manufactures and raw materials, the terms of trade seem to favor developed and run against underdeveloped countries.[4] The statements become reconciled when it is realized that many countries, such as Britain (coal), Germany (coal), and the United States (wheat and cotton), export primary products, and a number of underdeveloped countries export manufactures (Japan and India, textiles). The basis for the tendency of the terms of trade to deteriorate for underdeveloped countries, however, is found in their immobility of supply. They may be lucky and find themselves producing a commodity in which profitability is high and imitators are kept at bay by natural advantages. But typically, the underdeveloped country finds that competitors swarm in when it does well, which limits the improvement possible in terms of trade, while it is unable readily to

---

[4] See C. P. Kindleberger, *The Terms of Trade*, The Technology Press of Massachusetts Institute of Technology and Wiley, New York, 1956, esp. chaps. 10, 11; see also Theodore Morgan, "The Long-run Terms of Trade between Agriculture and Manufacturing," *Economic Development and Cultural Change*, October, 1959, pp. 1–23, reprinted in Morgan, Betz, and Choudhry (eds.), selection 25; and Gottfried Haberler, "The Terms of Trade and Economic Development," in H. S. Ellis and H. C. Wallich (eds.), *Economic Development for Latin America*, St Martin's, New York, 1961, pp. 275–307.

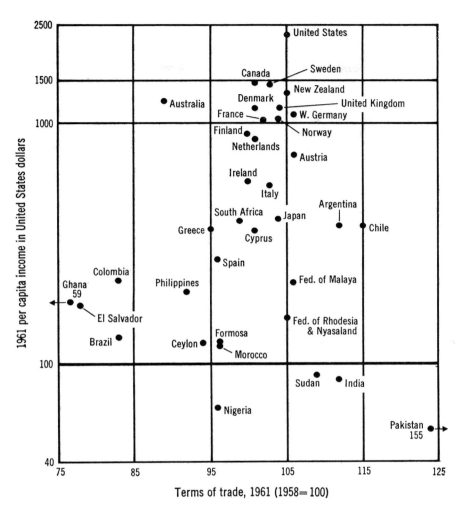

Figure 16.1 | Terms of trade in 1961 (1958 = 100) compared with income per capita, about 1961. SOURCES: Terms of trade (unit values of exports divided by unit values of imports) derived from *Monthly Bulletin of Statistics,* United Nations, New York, May, 1963, pp. 88–108; income per capita, table 1.1, Average Income per Capita in Selected Countries, 1949 and 1961.

reallocate resources when demand shifts away from its products, which leads prices to fall. Supply is elastic for price increases and inelastic for price declines.

Interest in the Prebisch thesis of declining terms of trade will naturally fluctuate with primary product prices. In the early 1960s the concern of underdeveloped countries with it was excited by the decline of many such prices. Figure 16.1 shows the terms of trade in 1961, based on 1958 as 100, compared with national income, and indicates that some poor countries, notably Brazil, Colombia, El Salvador (coffee), and Ghana (cocoa), had experienced a sharp decline. But not all had. The terms of trade for the developed countries improved, except for the primary producer, Australia, but not by so much as those for Pakistan and India. Nonetheless, the deterioration of the terms of trade of underdeveloped countries as a whole in the 1950s led to pressure in the United Nations for a world trade conference to "do something about it," even though there was little clear idea what of a practical nature that something might be.

A possible tendency of the terms of trade to turn against underdeveloped countries, however, is not an argument against specialization in foreign trade. It supports, rather, greater flexibility in the allocation of resources so as to take advantage of the benefits in working for the foreign market and to limit losses when demand shrinks or a competitor outdoes the country. This shifts the argument, but it does not rob the contention of the underdeveloped countries of all force. The difficulty may be less that the terms of trade behave in a certain way, but that whatever way the terms of trade of underdeveloped countries behave, they respond to them differently than a developed country would. If the resources of underdeveloped countries are relatively fixed, for example, the terms of trade can turn in favor of them or against, but they cannot do anything about it. The position is unfavorable especially if supply elasticities are asymmetrical; i.e., if entry is easy into existing lines, so that supply will respond to a higher price, but exit is difficult because resources are unable to shift into new lines. In these circumstances, the terms of trade will decline in the long run, because underdeveloped countries will respond to an improvement but be unable to respond to a decline.

Opposition to foreign trade based on the disparity between private and social costs is represented particularly by Manoilescu's *Theory of Protection*,[5] to which previous reference has been made. This holds that the existence of underemployment or disguised unemployment in the agricultural sector brings about a condition in which private cost, on which comparative advantage calls for exports of agricultural products and imports of manufactures, is unrepresentative of social costs. In the agricultural sector, private cost is too low, because wages are depressed; in industry, private cost is too high, because manufac-

---

[5] King, London, 1931. See also E. E. Hagen, "An Economic Justification for Protection," *Quarterly Journal of Economics*, November, 1958, pp. 456–574.

turers pay unduly high wages which would be lowered if the disguised unemployed freely competed in the labor market. Accordingly, Manoilescu recommended tariffs on imports to assist in the transfer of labor from unemployment in agriculture to employment in industry. This argument rests essentially on differing sets of factor proportions in different sectors, a dual economy. It fails to take account, however, of the possibility that the exact opposite condition exists in the capital market, that its private cost is below social cost in manufacturing and above in the agricultural sector. To the extent that this is true, part of the qualification of the theory of comparative advantage is offset. But a more general solution is to merge factor markets and equalize factor prices, rather than to interfere with specialization based on incorrect factor prices which are allowed to continue.

A somewhat different argument, equally based on imperfections in factor markets, is that made by Hla Myint.[6] In his view, foreign enterprise which gives rise to international trade produces an initial productive change in technology and specialization, but tends to freeze the domestic factors at their initial productivity and rate of return. This may well be true of plantation agriculture, but there is no necessary reason for all exports of primary production to produce technological "fossilization." This is a question of forward and backward linkages on the one hand, and on the other, of the capacity to respond to stimuli, already discussed in Chapter 10. In Canada and the United States, not to mention Australia, New Zealand, Denmark, Sweden, and Norway, primary-product exports stimulated technological change. Some commodities have more linkages than others— dairy products, for example, more than cattle raising or sheep, and wheat more than furs or fish. Moreover, some methods of organizing production for export may be stimulating when others are not, such as peasant farming of cocoa versus plantation culture. These differences in commodities and in industrial organization apply not only to primary products, however, but to manufactures as well, as suggested by the earlier discussion of growing points.

The view that imports have more and better linkages than exports may be related to the classic exception to comparative advantage based on increasing returns, relying on the presumption that external economies—largely in training—are much more substantial in import substitution than in export expansion.[7] That this is so is not proven,

---

[6] Hla Myint, "The Gains from International Trade and the Backward Countries," *Review of Economic Studies,* 1954–1955, pp. 129–142.

[7] The best statement of this point is by H. W. Singer in "The Distribution of Gains between Investing and Borrowing Countries," *American Economic Review,* May, 1950 (reprinted in Okun and Richardson (eds.), selection 15), p. 473.

of course, and a number of economists such as Viner and Haberler would vigorously deny it.[8] Moreover, where export industries are primary goods produced with scientific technology and using substantial amounts of capital—as in Middle Western, Antipodean, and Danish agriculture—the training effect in the export industry may be large and cumulative. There is nonetheless considerable evidence to suggest that in labor-intensive economies, which imitate rather than initiate technological change, there may be a larger developmental gain in training from import substitution than export expansion. Japan is perhaps the classic example. The textile, electrical equipment, steel, machinery, and shipbuilding industries all had their start in protection. Where trade is based on differences in factor endowments, as mentioned presently, limiting imports and encouraging the acquisition of new techniques may be the path of more rapid development.

A more fundamental attack on comparative advantage, however, has been made by Romney Robinson, who suggests that the doctrine is more useful in explaining where a country has been than in indicating where it might go.[9] Factor endowments are not fixed. They change with technology, as we have noticed above. They can also be altered by international factor movements—at least of labor and capital. And where trade opens up opportunities for capital formation or labor training and where imports of intermediate goods (which are hard to distinguish from factors) bulk large in relation to gross national product, trade explains factor endowments rather than factor endowments trade.[10] This is the most telling blow to the theory of comparative advantage, but there are lesser ones. Since diffusion of technology

---

[8] *International Trade and Economic Development,* Free Press of Glencoe, New York, 1952, esp. pp. 60ff; Gottfried Haberler, *International Trade and Economic Development,* National Bank of Egypt, Fiftieth Anniversary Commemorative Lectures, Cairo, 1959 (reprinted in Morgan, Betz, and Choudhry (eds.), selection 22).

[9] R. Robinson, "Factor Endowments and Comparative Advantage," *Quarterly Journal of Economics,* May, 1956, part I, pp. 169–192; *ibid.,* August, 1956, part II, pp. 346–363.

[10] Japan has abundant labor and capital but lacks raw materials. Where these can be imported cheaply, and where markets are located not too far away, Japan finds itself with a comparative advantage in textiles, steel products, chemicals, etc., although it lacks their basic ingredients. One could perhaps net out the import content of exports, and calculate comparative advantages on the basis of values added, but the question of whether it is profitable to import raw materials for manufacture into particular exports depends partly on costs of transport and the location of the factory site (Japan's is appallingly bad) and partly on the prices of complementary labor and capital, which may be sufficiently low to overcome high transport costs in one case but not in another. These reflections are based on discussions with Prof. R. Komiya.

takes place slowly, trade may be explained at a given time not by differences in factor proportions but by differences in technology. Just because airplane manufacture is labor-intensive, this does not mean that India is able to export airplanes.[11] More than this, if a production function permits a very considerable amount of substitution along it, of land for capital and capital for land, the theory of comparative advantage has nothing to communicate: the United States with cheap capital can export rubber to Indonesia, or possibly Indonesia with cheap rubber-producing land can export rubber to the United States.

When technology is subject to change in ways which will sharply alter the proportions of factor inputs, specialization involves a risk. Technological change may undermine the basis for specialization as the history of synthetic nitrates, rayon, nylon, rubber, detergents, atabrine, and similar products proves. It is all very well to put all one's rocks into one sturdy basket, for they do not get hurt when they spill. With fragile eggs, it's different.

Finally, exception can be taken to the assumption of the classic model about tastes. For convenience, tastes are frequently assumed to be identical before trade and unaffected by commodity exchanges. But where an early result of new transport and communication is the demonstration effect, the gain from trade is offset, in some degree, by the change in tastes which trade brings about. Few would argue that isolation is possible or that taste changes are reversible in the event of a reduction in trade. But the classic economist should qualify his identification of more trade with more welfare to take account of the fact that economic intercourse may bring with it a shift of demand away from the abundant native product in the underdeveloped country toward the scarce imported commodity.

These, then, are the major bones of contention which have been picked with the theory of comparative advantage. It is not denied that the theory is correct, given its assumptions. But if, instead of perfect competition, demand curves slope downward; if factors within countries can change in quantity and have limited mobility, and immobility of factors between countries is not universally respected; if the state of the arts is permitted to change, and not all at once but continuously; if imperfect factor markets permit unemployment and

[11] See Staffan Burenstam Linder, *An Essay in Trade and Transformation*, Wiley, New York, 1961, who argues that trade in manufactures is explained not by factor endowments, but by the possession of domestic demand for a product, which must be produced and sold domestically before it is available for export. See also Irving Kravis, " 'Availability' and Other Influences on the Commodity Composition of Trade," *Journal of Political Economy*, April, 1956, pp. 143–155.

disparities between social and private cost, the theory of comparative advantage may not be relevant to development.

Nonetheless, foreign trade is capable of assisting a developing country out of the impasse created by the need for sectoral and vertical balance of investment; and a historical review suggests that there have been occasions when foreign trade has been in fact a stimulus to economic growth. The fact of the matter is that there are at least three foreign-trade models of a developing country which ought to be examined, not one; instances of development where export industry represents a leading (or primary) sector, a lagging sector, or a balancing sector. After discussion of each, it will be time to indicate how a country engaged in development decides which model is applicable.

FOREIGN TRADE AS A LEADING SECTOR

The classic example in which foreign trade has played a leading role is that of Britain. Up to 1913 its major exports were coal and textiles. The expansion in textiles proceeded at a rate which averaged 6.75 per cent per annum from 1819 to 1840.[12] Thereafter it slowed down to 4.3 per cent for the next twenty years, and to 1.5 per cent from 1870 to 1913. Coal exports increased from 12.7 million tons in 1872 to 44.1 million in 1900 and to 73.4 million in 1913. W. A. Lewis, who on the whole does not give much attention to the possibility of exports leading economic development, ascribes a considerable portion of the slowdown in development after 1870 to the fact that the rate of increase in exports fell from 6 per cent per annum to 2 per cent.[13] But this causation would hold only if exports as a leading sector were the only possible foreign-trade model. An equally effective explanation would be that of Svennilson: running into competition in textiles, coal, steel, and engineering products, Britain's rate of growth had to slow down unless it succeeded in transforming the economy so as to develop in other sectors on the basis of new or imitated technology.[14] Germany provides a case where economic development occurred at a rapid rate, based largely on the home market and with limited dependence on

---

[12] P. Rousseaux, *Les Mouvements de fond de l'économie anglaise, 1800–1913,* Institut de Recherches Économiques et Sociales, Louvain, 1938, pp. 173ff.

[13] W. A. Lewis, *The Theory of Economic Growth,* Irwin, Homewood, Ill., 1955, pp. 279, 345ff. For a contrary view see W. G. Hoffmann, *British Industry, 1700–1950* (trans. by W. O. Henderson and W. H. Chaloner), Blackwell, Oxford, 1955, where the decline in the rate of growth after 1860 is ascribed, among other things, to the reallocation of resources caused by the adoption of free trade.

[14] I. Svennilson, *Growth and Stagnation in the European Economy,* United Nations, Geneva, 1954, pp. 22ff.

foreign trade. But E. A. G. Robinson exaggerates when he implies that one method is surer than the other or that Britain would have been better off if it had tried to develop along lines which limited foreign trade.[15] The model which has foreign trade as a leading sector makes the economy more dependent upon the events of the outside world, but it also makes it less dependent on internal balance.

Other examples than Britain are by no means lacking. Sweden after 1880, Denmark for the same period, Switzerland, the Low Countries, and Canada from 1900 to 1913 and again after World War II come to mind. D. C. North, in fact, has written the economic history of the United States from 1790 to 1860 in terms of this model of export-led growth.[16] More significant for many underdeveloped countries today is the experience of Asia after 1950, when the Korean conflict touched off a scramble for raw materials. Export values more than doubled between the first half of 1950 and the first half of 1951. This expansion coincided with an increase of public investment undertaken under development programs initiated prior to the outbreak of the conflict. The expansion in real income from exports provided the financial resources both internal and external to launch the development program. Even the decline in exports after the first half of 1951 did not completely reverse the development impetus. Or a still more up-to-date example is that of Peru, which expanded its exports of fish meal for poultry and cattle feed from 29,000 tons average in 1953–1957 to more than 1 million tons, worth $100 million, in 1962.[17]

It remains true that a country with a large proportion of national income generated by exports is dependent on the rate of growth and the state of economic fluctuations in the world market. Much depends on the income-elasticity, the technological prospects, and the short-run instability of the commodities concerned. Oil, rubber, watches, chemicals, aluminum, and high-grade steels are better bets than cotton textiles, grain, or coffee. But dependence on foreign markets is not complete. Improved techniques and research in demand for export products are frequently the most productive investment in an underdeveloped country, since they improve the competitive position vis-à-vis other underdeveloped countries and broaden the market. To the extent that steps can be taken along these lines, the underdeveloped country is not completely dependent.

[15] E. A. G. Robinson, "The Changing Structure of the British Economy," *Economic Journal,* September, 1954, esp. pp. 454–455.
[16] Douglass C. North, *The Economic Growth of the United States,* Prentice-Hall, Englewood Cliffs, N.J., 1961.
[17] See "Fish Meal Spurs Peru Economy," *New York Times,* June 18, 1963.

FOREIGN TRADE AS A LAGGING SECTOR

The Economic Commission for Latin America is persuaded that the foregoing models do not apply to modern development, at least in Latin America. In its view, foreign trade is doomed to lag behind domestic growth, partly because of the failure of developed countries to buy raw materials as their development proceeds and partly because of the necessity of underdeveloped countries to buy capital goods from developed countries.

The factors limiting the demand of the developed countries have already been mentioned—Engel's law and the continuous increase in efficiency in the consumption of raw materials. Prebisch, the former Executive Director of the Commission, has put the income-elasticity of the United States demand for primary goods at 0.66, while that for Latin America for industrial products is 1.58.[18] If the volume Q_x is fixed, and the developing country has no control over the prices of exports P_x or of imports P_m, the country's total capacity to import is fixed. This, of course, leaves out the possibility of foreign loans discussed in the next chapter.

It is not altogether clear that it is appropriate to quote the income-elasticity of the United States for primary-products imports in connection with Latin American exports. A significant number of United States imports of primary products come from Southeast Asia. In addition, the foreign trade of a number of Latin American countries is closely tied with Europe and has grown substantially. In the period 1895 to 1899, for example, imports from Latin America accounted for

[18] See R. Prebisch, comment on G. Myrdal, "Towards a More Closely Integrated Free-world Economy," in R. Lekachman (ed.), *National Policy for Economic Welfare at Home and Abroad*, Doubleday, Garden City, N.Y., 1955, p. 278. In this passage Dr. Prebisch refers to the estimate of 0.66 per cent, representing the percentage change in imports of primary products associated with a given percentage change in income, as based on data of the Paley Commission. In the *Analyses and Projections of Economic Development, part I, Introduction to the Technique of Programming*, United Nations Economic Commission for Latin America, New York, 1955, p. 14, it is observed that according to a report of the Council of Economic Advisers, an increase of 1 per cent in domestic industrial production in the United States resulted in an increase in imports of 0.66 per cent. While the figure is identical, the concepts are different.

It should also be noted that, with equal percentage increases in income in the United States and Latin America, and lower income-elasticity in the former than the latter, it is still possible for the Latin American balance of payments to improve if, as is the case, national income is larger in the United States than in Latin America.

5 per cent, by value, of total British imports, whereas during the five years before World War I, they provided 10 per cent of a much enlarged import bill. During the fifteen years before World War I, moreover, production in Europe as a whole rose by 45 per cent, whereas imports from Latin America doubled.[19]

In stating that the capacity of underdeveloped countries to import is fixed, the Prebisch model omits the competitive effect. Total consumption of foodstuffs and raw materials may grow more slowly than consumption of services, for example; but it is by no means clear that total consumption determines the capacity of any country or even of presently underdeveloped countries as a whole to produce. An underdeveloped country can expand its sales if it can outproduce its fellow underdeveloped countries or, except where tariff policy intervenes too strenuously, if it can outproduce the primary-goods sector of developed countries. An example of the competitive effect is furnished by the success of the African countries—Ethiopia and Kenya—in invading the coffee markets of the world at the expense of Latin America. Other possible competition for Latin America from Africa is expected in bananas, hard fibers (like sisal), and hardwoods. This will be accelerated if the European Economic Community discriminates in favor of former African colonies against the rest of the world, including Latin America. Depletion is a major factor assisting the substitution of imports for domestic production in developed countries. As the example of oil shows, even where coal is abundant as in the United States and Western Europe, the competition of oil against coal opens ever-wider markets for exports of underdeveloped countries. Europe used to produce all its own wheat, wool, flax, meat, dairy products, etc. For some of these income-elasticity is substantial. But for others, Engel's law and the increasing efficiency of raw-materials consumption in manufacturing notwithstanding, competition has enabled overseas areas to expand their sales at a much more rapid rate than total consumption.[20]

The other element in the Prebisch model is that imports necessarily rise with economic development. In some instances, this is a consequence of the entry of workers into the market economy, with an

---

[19] *A Study of Trade between Latin America and Europe,* United Nations, Geneva, 1953, p. 1.

[20] But note that primary-producing countries may also suffer competition from developed countries, and not only through the development of synthetics. Technological innovation has enabled United States farmers to produce efficiently linseed previously grown in Argentina, rice, and Turkish-type tobacco, the first two in sufficient quantity to export.

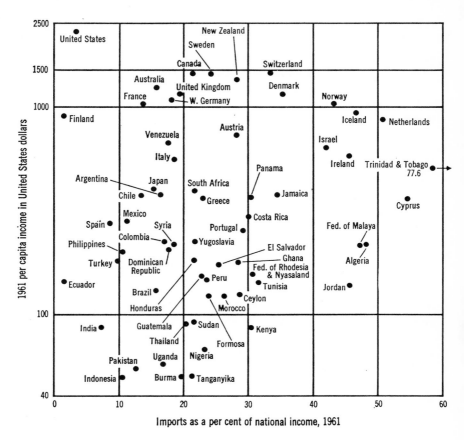

Figure 16.2 | Imports as a proportion of national income compared with income per capita, about 1961. SOURCES: Imports as a percentage of national income derived from imports in U.S. dollars (pp. 84–87), national income in national currency units (pp. 154–155) and exchange rates (pp. 158–163), all in *Monthly Bulletin of Statistics*, United Nations, New York, May, 1963; income per capita, table 1.1, Average Income per Capita in Selected Countries, 1949 and 1961.

increasing part of their consumption imported,[21] in response to demonstration effect or competitive forces.[22] In addition, however, the necessity to import arises from the import content of the investment program or the need for particular raw materials, especially fuel, for

[21] See *Processes and Problems of Industrialization in Underdeveloped Countries*, United Nations, New York, 1955, p. 59, which cites the budgets of Indonesian workers.

[22] Such as the displacement of the Indian handicraft textile industry by the English machine product in the nineteenth century.

which no convenient substitutes are available. A development program will produce a shift in the import schedule. Even where the development program is financed in a noninflationary way, by increased savings, there is likely to be a considerable shift of the import schedule, since the import content of investment, which rises, is likely to be greater than that of consumption, which declines.

The relationship between trade and growth is more complex than this, however. Not only is there the Prebisch view that imports rise in the development process. There is also the "law of declining foreign trade," which holds that the percentage of foreign trade declines as countries get richer.[23] Cross-section data in Figure 16.2 show no clear relationship between the proportion of imports to income and income per capita. Low percentages can be found at all levels of income—the United States, Finland, Spain, Ecuador, and India—as well as high ones—Norway, Trinidad, Cyprus, Algeria, and Jordan. More than income per capita is involved. The openness of an economy is also a function of its resource skewness, which in turn is related to size.

If any generalization is valid, it is probably that the relationship between trade and national income rises in the early stages of growth, particularly demand-led growth, and then begins to decline because of import substitution. In a well-known article, Hollis Chenery has concluded that import substitution is one of the major factors responsible for the changing pattern of industrial production.[24] Averaging the experience of a large number of countries, he found that while the final demand for investment products rose more than that for intermediate goods and consumers' goods, the income-elasticities being 1.59, 1.37, and 1.27, respectively, import substitution was much higher in investment goods than in intermediate goods. There was very little substitution in consumers' goods. The consequence of these trends was that imports of investment goods rose slightly less than income, intermediate goods still less, and consumers' goods, somewhat more.[25] But

[23] K. W. Deutsch and A. Eckstein, "National Industrialization and the Declining Share of the International Economic Sector, 1890–1959," *World Politics,* January, 1961, pp. 267–299. See also the skeptical view of R. R. Piekars, "Proportion of Foreign Trade and National Product and Economic Growth," unpublished doctoral dissertation, Johns Hopkins University, Baltimore, 1959, cited by Simon Kuznets, *Six Lectures on Economic Growth,* Free Press of Glencoe, New York, 1959, pp. 101–103. Historical data for ten developed countries from both sources are presented in tabular and chart form in my *Foreign Trade and the National Economy,* Yale, New Haven, Conn., 1962, pp. 180–181.

[24] Hollis B. Chenery, "Patterns of Industrial Growth," *American Economic Review,* September, 1960, pp. 624–654.

[25] *Ibid.* p. 642. The data can be put in tabular form, leaving out the details of

these are averages, and there is wide variability about them. In consequence, there is not much room for applying the general pattern in a particular case.

Moreover, it is vital to observe that this is the result of both conscious and unconscious growth, in changing proportions, and that to the extent that it is unconscious, it offers no guide to policy. Just as in industrialization, it is true that developed countries have industry, but it is not true that the way to achieve development is always to start with industry, so deliberate import substitution may not be the way to achieve the import substitution which comes with growth. Argentina is a country with relatively high rates of investment, a sharply declining proportion of imports—from roughly 25 per cent of gross national product from 1900 to 1929 to 15 per cent in the 1930s and 7.5 per cent in the 1950s—and a slow rate of growth. Import substitution seems to have run wild, with Argentina attempting to produce all kinds of products, with inadequate specialization and scale in many of them. Where growth leads and import substitution follows as a consequence of demand elasticities, locational advantages, changing factor proportions, and improved technology, the decline in imports relative to national income is normal and appropriate. To start with import substitution, however, is to begin at the wrong end.

The outstanding example of growth with declining ratio of foreign trade is perhaps the Netherlands, where the ratio of foreign trade to national income declined after World War I from 51 per cent in 1900–1908 to 26 per cent in 1919–1928 and 21 in the depression years 1929–1938. This was a spontaneous decline, not a contrived one. In the period of planning in the Netherlands, the ratio rose again as high as 45 per cent (in 1959), which underlines the lesson that while growth can produce import substitution, there are other ways than import substitution to growth, including the model in which exports lead.

each class, which are available in the original:

Growth Elasticities of Demand and Supply

Sector	Production (1)	Imports (2)	Total supply (3)	Import substitution (4) = (1) − (3)	Final demand (5)
Investment products	2.24	.97	1.64	.60	1.59
Other intermediate goods	1.72	.83	1.38	.34	1.34
Consumers' goods	1.32	1.07	1.29	.03	1.27
Total	1.55	.94	1.40	.15	1.36

E. A. G. Robinson has argued that Great Britain's high degree of specialization, compared with Germany's, made its economy very fragile.[26] It is true that more specialization means more risk and requires a greater transformation when other countries produce their own textiles and coal is displaced as a world fuel by oil. There was a decline in the rate of expansion in export markets.[27] But this view seems to assume that capacity to transform is low and that a country should fix its degree of specialization for long periods of time. When the market for textiles becomes saturated, investment should shift to new products of high income-elasticity, at home or abroad. If capacity to produce these goods had been readily developed, the decline in the rate of increase in exports need not have been important for Britain in view of its low income-elasticity of demand for food. But where the rate of increase in exports sags after a country's capacity to transform has declined, it is not certain whether the slowdown in growth should be blamed on export markets or on resource inflexibility.

The growth model in which exports are the lagging sector may not apply to every country in Latin America today, as the Economic Commission for Latin America seems to imply; nor is it relevant.to much of Africa, with highly skewed resources, nor to each Asian economy. It does appear, however, to represent the experience of Australia and the Union of South Africa, which have been growing rapidly in recent years but with the major emphasis on investment for the domestic market rather than for export. In Australia the deleterious effects on the balance of payments were offset for a time by improvement in the demand for wool and later by an increase in efficiency of wool production. Over the longer period, however, import restrictions appear to be called for by buoyant domestic investment, the lag of capacity to import behind demand for imports, and the unavailability of capital imports on a large scale.

BALANCE THROUGH FOREIGN TRADE

It has been indicated in Chapter 11 that the foreign market relieves a developing country from the necessity to seek balance, whether as an outlet in demand balance or as a source of production in balance for supply. W. A. Lewis puts it that a country must either improve its productivity in agriculture or export manufactures (thereby enabling

---

[26] *Op. cit.*, pp. 450ff.
[27] See also J. R. Meyer, "An Input-Output Approach to Evaluating the Influence of Exports on British Industrial Production in the Late Nineteenth Century," *Explorations in Entrepreneurial History*, October, 1955, pp. 12–34.

it to import food).[28] This seems to leave little room for the country which wants to specialize in exporting foodstuffs, such as Australia, New Zealand, and Burma, or to export raw materials and import food, such as Pakistan, Indonesia, etc. Nor is it necessary for food, raw materials, or manufactures to predominate in either exports or imports more than the other. The United States exports and imports food, raw materials, and manufactures, and so do many countries for one or more of these categories.

Japan is cited by Lewis as the classic example of a country which undertook exports of manufactures in order to balance its output. It is also mentioned as a country which balanced its output by expanding productivity in agriculture. Further, there is evidence that Japan falls in the category of Britain, with foreign trade as a leading sector, at least in the early period when silk was the major export.[29]

In economic terms, the question of whether to achieve balance internally or through exporting manufactures turns, of course, on the long-run slopes of the demand and supply curves of manufactures and foodstuffs. If the demand for manufactures in the foreign market is elastic, and the domestic supply of food is inelastic with respect to price increases, a prima facie case for exports of manufactures and imports of food is made, unless the supply schedule for food abroad is even more steeply vertical than that at home. On the other hand, if foreign markets for manufactures are inelastic and the supply of food at home is elastic, the presumption runs the other way.

Foreign trade always balances domestic demand and supply, and it may therefore be inappropriate to distinguish a special model of foreign trade which emphasizes this function.[30] And yet a separate model is useful to suggest a policy of foreign-trade expansion which differs from that in which expansion is demand-led (the leading model) or the policy of trade contraction (import substitution in the lagging model). Food may be imported to hold down agricultural prices and balance the demand for consumption, with supply-led expansion of exports in other lines. Or imports of capital goods or technicians' services may be undertaken to balance the supply of goods

---

[28] *Op. cit.*, pp. 324ff.

[29] Lakdawala puts it strongly in *International Aspects of Indian Economic Development,* Oxford, Fair Lawn, N.J., 1951, p. 11: "It is believed that Japan's decision to industrialize . . . mainly succeeded because at the time there was a very keen American demand for silk, owing to the outbreak of the silkworm disease in Europe."

[30] This point was put to me by H. Kitamura. It may also be noted, as pointed out above, that the requirements of balance of the Nurkse kind—in demand—may call for displacing imports to gain an assured market.

and services needed for development and paid for with supply-led expansion of exports. In the leading model, the autonomous variable is foreign demand (coupled with technological change in the developing country); in the lagging model, the impetus comes from domestic investment, which raises imports faster than exports grow. In the balancing model, the emphasis is on autonomous increases in exports brought about by supply pushes.

WHICH MODEL?

It seems evident that economic development is attainable by any of the three suggested routes—where foreign trade leads, where it lags, and where it balances.[31] Indeed, development is possible in a closed economy, as the Soviet Union example shows. Which is the appropriate model to follow, therefore, depends on circumstances. The question is, which circumstances.

The answer clearly must be the skewness of resources, both human and natural. Where these resources are highly specialized, the potential gain from trade is large and justifies instability and risk. Where, on the other hand, natural resources are abundant and varied, and human mobility and skills permit labor to be productive over a range of tasks, the significance of the contribution of foreign trade is reduced. In the long run, the natural resources are the more significant, since workers can be trained to new tasks. In the short run, the quality of the labor force is a significant consideration.

A country such as Australia, with a variety of resources and an adaptable working force, can contemplate a long-run development with less and less attention to trade. Australia possesses rich coal and iron resources, which give it capacity for cheap steelmaking once capital has been built up; oil has been discovered within the continental limits; density of population is such that food can be exported along with raw materials and ultimately manufactured products.

Whether India is similarly favored is difficult to judge. The first Five-Year Plan put its emphasis on food production, partly perhaps with the implicit view of a balanced program of investment in which increased food output was needed to stabilize the price of the wage good before one could expand industrial output. This is a closed-

---

[31] For a historical demonstration that economic growth can be helped or hurt by more exports, more imports and less imports, see my "Foreign Trade and Growth: Lessons from Britain and France, 1850 to 1913," *Economic History Review,* December, 1961, pp. 289–305.

economy model. In part, however, India appears to have operated on the assumption that the long-run terms of trade would favor food over industrial products—a Colin Clark rather than a Prebisch position. There was, however, also a strong element of mercantilism involved. India did not want to depend on outsiders for its essential food. It was not clear whether considerations of foreign exchange or defense dominated. To the extent that foreign exchange played a part, it was simple import substitution, regardless of price. Growing food is something we can do at home. We will therefore do it, irrespective of the relative prices of food and other things. In this period, with high income-elasticity for food and investment attention given to the agricultural sector, the marginal propensity to import operated negatively. Income rose because food production increased (with investment and a good monsoon); and as income rose, the demand for imports shifted downward, since home production was a substitute for imports.

In subsequent five-year plans emphasis has been given to heavy industry and conscious import substitution in steel, railway equipment, chemicals, and so on, partly on the ground that traditional Indian exports—jute, burlap, tea, and cotton textiles—are hopeless because of markets abroad which are inelastic with respect to price decreases and income increases. Foreign economists who visit India accept this view virtually without argument.[32] Occasionally when the matter is debated, the ground is shifted to the proposition that India needs steel and could not get it at any price during the Korean shortage, or still further, that India has great natural resources in coal, iron ore, and limestone, suitably located, and should have a comparative advantage in steel exports. But there are dissenting voices. Anne Krueger and Peter Bauer have suggested that Indian planners have neglected the possibilities of expanding exports,[33] and Jagdish Bhagwati has advocated serious consideration of devaluating the overvalued rupee—together with taxes on exports where the terms of trade would decline because of inelastic demands—for the purpose of stimulating marginal exports and import substitutions.[34] An overvalued rate, re-

[32] See, for example, W. B. Reddaway, *The Development of the Indian Economy,* Irwin, Homewood, Ill., 1962, pp. 27ff.; John P. Lewis, *Quiet Crisis in India,* Brookings, Washington, D.C., 1962, pp. 38ff. and chap. 9; Wilfred Malenbaum, *Prospects for Indian Development,* Free Press of Glencoe, New York, 1962, pp. 97ff.

[33] See her comment on S. J. Patel, "Exports, Prospects and Economic Growth: India," *Economic Journal,* September, 1959, pp. 490–506, in "The Capacity to Import and Economic Development: India," *Economic Journal,* June, 1961, pp. 436–446, with a rejoinder by S. J. Patel (pp. 446–449).

[34] Jagdish Bhagwati, "The Case for Devaluation," *The Economic Weekly* (India), Aug. 4, 1962, pp. 1263ff.; and "More on Devaluation," *ibid.,* Oct. 6, 1962, pp. 1581ff.

quiring a disequilibrium system of import controls and export subsidies, not only uses up scarce administrative talent; it favors imported
capital equipment over domestic labor, prefers existing and large
companies for import licenses to small and new, and discourages incremental exports. A shadow rate of foreign exchange may be sufficient for calculating costs and benefits on governmental projects, but
to get resource reallocation right requires converting the shadow rate
into an actual rate, with taxes on imports and subsidies on exports.
There is much to be said for short-cutting this labyrinthian system
and seeking the equilibrium exchange rate. It is significant that after
years of managing a disequilibrium system of controls, taxes, and
subsidies in Israel, a country with an abundant supply of administrative talent, finding the system baffling,[35] the Israeli government finally
devalued in 1962.

It may be thought that a country which has decided on a program
of economic development has no choice about what happens to its
foreign trade. If demand for its products increases, well and good.
But it cannot choose to follow the leading model. Otherwise, it is
obliged to follow the lagging model, unless it wants to neglect agriculture and push some form of manufactured exports to balance its
accounts. But this is hardly the case. Technology is not fixed, nor are
the technological limits likely to be fully exploited by investment in
the export sector. If increased investment can make exports cheaper,
whether through widening the application of existing processes or devising and installing new, there is room to push exports for balance
and even to the point where exports lead the development process. In
uncontrived development the stimulus sometimes came from demand
(cotton in the United States), sometimes from supply (cotton textiles
in England, watches in Switzerland), and sometimes both (Swedish
pulp and paper, Danish and New Zealand butter, bacon, eggs).

It is said that a distinguished economist, when he visits an underdeveloped country, first asks for a list of imports and considers which
of the leading items can be manufactured domestically. An equally
important question, which should not be neglected, is what exports
can be produced more efficiently. In Malaya, for example, the replanting of rubber trees with higher-yielding, disease-resisting strains may
be the most effective investment for development. The comparison
runs with Indonesia where production fell by 10 per cent between

---

[35] Cf. "The price mechanism is seriously inadequate as a basis for judging the
most economic allocation of the country's resources. This inadequacy stems from
the manipulation of prices by a complicated web of subsidies, different exchange
rates, the import licensing system, tariffs, and other indirect taxes." Falk Project
for Economic Research in Israel, *First Annual Report, 1954,* Jerusalem, 1955,
p. 36.

1950 and 1960, but replanting has been neglected, and output and exports must continue to decline.[36] Increased investment should not be pursued in an export area where marginal comparative advantage is lacking, i.e., where marginal revenue is lower than in import substitution. But where a country sells its exports in competition with other countries, including the import-competing sector of the importing countries, marginal revenue is unlikely to be much below average revenue, and the possibilities of cost reduction in the export sector are worth careful examination.

COMMERCIAL POLICY

Space does not permit a detailed discussion of the problems of commercial policy in countries embarked on economic development. An enormous amount of attention has been devoted to this problem. Perhaps it will suffice here to say a few words by way of summary. This discussion is organized not around the devices of commercial policy— tariffs, quotas, exchange-rate change, including multiple-exchange rates—but about the objectives. The most important of these may be said to be revenue, protection (or resource reallocation), defense of the balance of payments, stability, and maximization of income. It is assumed that the foreign-trade model is one where demand for exports lags in development and that the primary sector in development is internal, say, social overhead capital.

We have already indicated that the revenue aspects of commercial policy for underdeveloped countries are important and that the need for revenue modifies the normal case for free trade.[37] While import tariffs on luxuries may not give rise to resource shifts because of inelasticity of supply, it may be well to ensure that such tariffs afford no protection by imposing a parallel domestic excise. Unfortunately, this cannot be paralleled in export taxes. Here, if the incidence is on the domestic producer, the allocation effect is inescapable, since foreign producers lie outside the reach of the local tax collector.

The protective effect is frequently invoked in tariffs to stimulate an infant industry. The economist always prefers a subsidy, but is obliged to recognize that he differs in this respect from domestic producers, who somehow believe that a subsidy is degrading while a tariff is businesslike. Multiple-exchange rates and exchange depreciation have

---

[36] See Don D. Humphrey, "Indonesia's National Plan for Economic Development," *Asian Survey*, December, 1962, p. 13.
[37] See pp. 243–245.

their protective effects, along with ordinary tariffs and quota restrictions. When protection is given to an industry, there must be resources to move into it, available or readily released from other occupations. These resources include capital and land as well as labor, and labor of the appropriate skills and training. If this is not the situation, the extra demand for resources in the absence of supply is inflationary.

The primary object of commercial policy in underdeveloped countries is likely to be defense of the balance of payments. This arises from the desires to limit borrowing and to avoid the necessity to cut domestic investment. Domestic investment may be excessive in relation to total resources, so that demand spills over into imports all along the line; or an equilibrium position is adversely affected by a shift from consumption to investment which maintains national income at the old level but increases the propensity to import as the import content of added investment exceeds the savings in imports from the subtracted consumption. Investment may be excessive not in periods of boom but only on the average over the cycle, which originates abroad.

Multiple-exchange rates, exchange depreciation, quota restrictions, and, to a lesser extent, tariffs, are mainly directed to the balance of payments. Depreciation is not likely to be effective in expanding the foreign-exchange value of exports, where there is either inelasticity of demand abroad or full employment at home. Nor is it likely to be of assistance in reducing imports, where the level of living and real wages are not readily compressible. The result is likely to be the most temporary relief. Accordingly, many countries have turned to multiple-exchange rates, or the disequilibrium system. This, as we have noted earlier, requires for its effective functioning the spur of incentives which will outweigh the opportunity to make a profit by operating illegally. If such incentive is absent, the disequilibrium system is likely to work with low efficiency, with antisocial incidence, despite the efforts of the authorities to favor necessities and penalize luxuries, through the gradual distortion of investment and consumption.

In short, not commercial policy but monetary and fiscal restraint, or borrowing abroad, is the most effective means of coping with the balance-of-payments problem of developing countries in the long run. There are exceptions. Where resources are balanced and not fully employed, so that elasticities are high, import protection is likely to have considerable balance-of-payments effects, especially if the objects of protection—food and textiles in German development—have low income-elasticity, and the products with high income-elasticity—capital goods, housing services—are domestically produced. But this situation is rare in the underdeveloped parts of the world today.

Underdeveloped countries have talked much about the desirability of achieving stability through stabilization of the prices of primary products. A United Nations resolution called for the establishment of "fair and equitable" prices or terms of trade.[38] A majority opinion of an international group of five experts concluded that "fair and equitable" meant "long-run equilibrium"[39] but that it was desirable to reduce the amplitude of fluctuations about this level, if it could be determined. These experts, unfortunately, were unable to agree on any means for achieving this result; while opposing export restriction, they were disposed to favor neither international agreements with maximum and minimum prices and minimum quantities of exports and imports, on the one hand, nor buffer-stock arrangements, on the other. A particularly difficult problem faced in the last-named device is that of deciding whether the buffer stock is to be financed by producers or consumers, or some combination of the two. The balance-of-payments position of underdeveloped countries is much more stable in the cycle, assuming prices and production unchanged, if buffer-stock purchases are financed abroad rather than at home.

Various measures have been proposed for compensating underdeveloped countries for adverse changes in their terms of trade, for ensuring the terms of trade, or for enabling them to borrow more or less automatically from the International Monetary Fund when export prices fall. There is one serious problem hidden in most of these proposals for financing cyclical fluctuations of the balance of payments of primary producers. Most of them are interested basically in secular support, not cyclical stability. The "fair price" in their view is that which will sustain income and in fact provide for its growth, regardless of what such a price might do to unbalance supply and demand.

Underdeveloped countries are most anxious to pursue commodity price stabilization policies on a world basis, and involving all commodities at once. These countries insist that much of the financial help they received as aid from the developed countries is taken away again in worsened terms of trade. For a long time, the United States opposed major programs of commodity price stabilization, largely on doctrinal grounds, which became less effective in dealing with particular commodities in which United States interests were heavily involved: wheat, sugar, and to a lesser degree, tin. The doctrinal grounds were simple and sound: there is no basis for forecasting the long-run price. Producer interests usually outweigh consumer inter-

[38] Resolution 86 of the General Assembly of the United Nations, adopted Dec. 21, 1952.
[39] *Commodity Trade and Economic Development,* United Nations, New York, 1952, chap. 1.

ests; the stabilized price is fixed too high, supply expands, and the agreement ultimately collapses. Bauer and Paish have proposed a long-run moving average as the basis for making payments to producers, in contrast with the West African Cocoa Marketing Board, which has stabilized the price to producers at a low level and permitted the world price to fluctuate (as the Board claims).[40] The method used by the Cocoa Marketing Board, or a similar device of sliding-scale export taxes on commodities, where the tax is borne by the producer and passed neither forward to foreigners nor backward on labor, will stabilize the incomes of producers in the export sector, not necessarily at the appropriate level, but will render the balance of payments and governmental revenue unstable. Finally the United States was worn down by the pressures of the underdeveloped countries and assented to separate commodity-by-commodity agreements, beginning with coffee, which call for the disequilibrium system organized on a worldwide basis by export and import controls. Study groups, commodity committees, informal understandings and a few formal agreements have been worked out in a number of primary products with a view to price supports in those commodities where sharp declines would be politically dangerous. Balance of supply and demand has not been achieved: in most cases, the problem has been merely swept under the rug.

Open economies are bound to be unstable in some particular—in balance of payments or income. If governments want to achieve internal stability of income and growth, they can choose among a variety of alternatives—stabilization of the price of exports, countercyclical export taxes, built-in stabilizers in tax and expenditure—but they must make sure that operations balance around the long-run level. The temptation is to set the export price too high on the average or to spend the revenue and foreign exchange in prosperity which should be going into reserves for depression. The attempt to produce internal stability then results in inflation: exchange reserves and domestic sinking funds are unavailable when needed, and the balance of payments must be defended by quantitative or exchange restrictions.

Income stability in underdeveloped countries is attainable, but only with an impressive degree of discipline and self-control. In a few countries, such as India, where income and imports are negatively correlated, at least for a period, stability is more readily obtained.

Finally, commercial and fiscal policy are used to maximize the resources available for economic development, to improve the terms

---

[40] See P. T. Bauer and F. W. Paish, "The Reduction of Fluctuations in the Incomes of Primary Producers," *Economic Journal,* December, 1952, pp. 750–780; and P. T. Bauer, *A Survey of West African Trade,* Cambridge, New York, 1955.

of trade in merchandise, to redivide the gain from trade deriving from investments by foreigners, to convert marginal resources into foreign exchange without reducing the monopoly prices paid by prime exports. The capacity of underdeveloped countries to affect the prices of their imports is certainly limited. Here they are price takers, not price makers. But in exports the position may be otherwise. A high degree of specialization means that demand is inelastic, at least in the short run; and where foreign investors have a large commitment, their capacity to escape the incidence of taxes—or the revenue effects on them of multiple-exchange systems—is low.

It is vital, however, to distinguish between the short-run and the long-run elasticity. Export taxes may be passed forward in a sellers' market, but sellers' markets do not last. Export restriction will raise prices briefly, but hold up an umbrella under which foreign competitors can gain a foothold. Expansion of output among rival producers and rival products lies one or two years off to limit the extent to which prices can be raised.

Commercial policy can hardly make much of a positive contribution to economic development. The next chapter will discuss the taxation of foreign investors, which is perhaps somewhat more useful and has produced substantial revenues for development over the last twenty or so years. Tariffs have their purposes, for revenue and for protection. But commercial policy still falls short of refinement to the point where short-run instability of prices of primary products exported by underdeveloped countries can be overcome or where its effects on development in underdeveloped countries can be smoothly offset.[41]

The United Nations has observed the paradox that economic development needs favorable terms of trade to follow the road to balanced economic development so that it will not have to depend on its terms of trade any longer. But the more competing countries balance their resources and withdraw resources from exports, the higher the gains from trade for those countries that continue to specialize.

SUMMARY

The case for comparative advantage is largely a static one, which must be modified for risk, instability, and growth trends in demand, and must be set aside if there are external economies and economies of scale in import-competing but not in export goods. One concern of

---

[41] A rather more optimistic note is struck by G. Myrdal in his *An International Economy*, Harper, New York, 1956, chap. XIII.

underdeveloped countries is that the long-run terms of trade turn secularly against the primary commodities. Other arguments for protection are based upon imperfections in factor markets in underdeveloped countries or the possibility that development linkages are stronger in import-competing industry than in exports.

Three models relating trade and growth are examined: trade can lead growth, lag behind it and require import substitution, or neatly balance. Which model fits the particular circumstance of a developing country depends upon a variety of circumstances, including its resource skewness; the nature of the commodities in which it has a comparative advantage, their demand characteristics, and the strength of their linkages to other sectors; and finally the country's capacity to respond to stimulus. The question whether exports are being neglected and imports favored is particularly debated in India. The implications for commercial policy of underdeveloped countries are reviewed, along with the demands of such countries for support for primary-product prices.

BIBLIOGRAPHY

A first-class treatment of the problem and a full bibliography are given in Gerald M. Meier, *International Trade and Economic Development,* Harper & Row, New York, 1963. The Meier position is fairly close to that of Haberler and Viner cited in footnote 8. The contrary position is put in its sharpest form by Raul Prebisch in Economic Commission for Latin America, *The Economic Development of Latin America and Its Principal Problems,* United Nations, Lake Success, 1950, and in Gunnar Myrdal's book, *An International Economy* (footnote 41), chap. XIII. The theory is rigorously put by H. B. Chenery, "Comparative Advantage and Development Policy," *American Economic Review,* March, 1961, pp. 18–51, reprinted in Morgan, Betz, and Choudhry (eds.), selection 17. For a useful running debate, see the papers by Nurkse, Haberler, Schultz, Wallich, and Marshall and the subsequent discussion of them in Ellis and Wallich (eds.), *Economic Development for Latin America,* St Martin's, New York, 1961.

Addendum: the issues and proposals for the United Nations Conference on Trade and Development are thoroughly discussed in *Towards a New Trade Policy for Development,* a Report by the Secretary-General of the Conference (United Nations, New York, 1964) and in the Royal Institute for International Affairs, *New Directions for World Trade,* Oxford, Fair Lawn, N.J., 1964.

17 | *Borrowing Abroad*

THE NEED FOR FOREIGN CAPITAL

It is sometimes urged that foreign borrowing is necessary in economic development because the need for investment goods from abroad grows at a faster rate than the "capacity to import."[1] The latter variable, it will be recalled, is derived from the volume of exports and the terms of trade, both of which, it is claimed, lie outside the control of the developing country. If capacity to import grows at the rate of 2 per cent a year, while the need for investment goods requires an increase in the volume of imports at 3 per cent, capital imports at 1 per cent of the value of exports would be needed, on this showing, to preserve balance-of-payments equilibrium. This assumes no policy of consumers' goods import substitution.

Emphasis on the behavior of specific variables such as investment goods is appropriate only under certain limiting circumstances and in the short run. The general case for borrowing abroad is to add to resources overall, not to acquire particular resources. Foreign borrowing would be needed to obtain certain types of foreign equipment only if the economy had no capacity to redirect its efforts from one sector to another or no time to effect such transformation. Since economic development absolutely requires such redirection and is a time-consuming process, the view that it is necessary to borrow to get command of foreign investment equipment for developmental purposes can be said to be wrong, except in the short run.

One alternative to borrowing to finance capital-goods imports is increased domestic savings. Reduced consumption operates, in some part, directly on imports, which frees foreign exchange. In part, it liberates domestic resources which must then be reallocated to export

---

[1] See *Analyses and Projections of Economic Development, Part I, Introduction to the Technique of Planning*, United Nations, Economic Commission for Latin America, New York, 1955, p. 5; also H. J. Bruton, "Growth Models and Underdeveloped Countries," *Journal of Political Economy*, August, 1955, pp. 330ff., reprinted in Agarwala and Singh (eds.), selection 3.

or import-competing production to permit expansion in exports or a further reduction in imports.

Or foreign borrowing may be used to finance domestic capital formation without the necessity to purchase foreign capital equipment. As is well known, loans can be transferred in consumption goods. If capital formation requires mainly domestic resources, such as construction, the foreign loan may be used to import food which permits the transfer of workers from agriculture to construction without reducing current consumption.

The need for foreign borrowing is nonetheless identified with the need for foreign capital equipment, despite the restricted nature of the underlying reasoning. The identification can be said to be wrong, or it can be said merely to suppress assumptions of a critical nature: for example, that the balance of payments is in equilibrium at the start of the borrowing and is unaffected by raising the domestic portion of the capital investment or by the reallocation of domestic resources used to form the capital. Or it may assume that no increase in exports can be obtained from a reallocation of resources, owing to inelastic demands; or that a new comparative advantage cannot be achieved by a decrease in imports because of incapacity to transform into import-competing lines; or that transformation is possible only over a longer period than is allowed for foreign lending to result in capital formation. Whether in error, or suppressing assumptions, in its early loans and in most current negotiations, the International Bank for Reconstruction and Development usually lends only the foreign-exchange content of a project. Thus, for example, most of the funds for improvement of railroads, $777 millions lent by the Bank to fourteen different countries to the end of 1959, were used to buy locomotives or rolling stock.[2] Similarly, in the planning of the High Dam at Aswan, it was contemplated that the United States and British governments and the International Bank would cover the $400 million of foreign-exchange expenditure required over the fifteen-year building period, whereas the remaining estimated $900 million of domestic expenditure would be furnished by Egypt. It was the difficulty of Egypt's fulfilling this part of its bargain which was used by the United States and Britain as the basis or pretext for withdrawing their offer of aid.

Domestic capital expenditure can, of course, be provided locally in a noninflationary manner if it is matched by new savings and if the appropriate shifts in the economy occur. Income remains as before,

[2] International Bank for Reconstruction and Development, *The World Bank: Policies and Operations*, Washington, D.C., June, 1960, p. 62. The project basis for loans and limiting lending normally to the foreign-exchange content are defended in Chap. 5.

but consumption declines and capital expenditure takes its place. Double resource shifts may be required, if, for example, resources most readily transferred into capital construction come out of production for the export market. In this circumstance, the other resources released by saving must shift into new exports or into import-competing production.

The notion that foreign loans are needed for foreign capital goods is based on partial-equilibrium analysis, with all other things equal, or *ceteris paribus*. This is an inappropriate line of reasoning, since the problem is of the general-equilibrium, or *mutatis mutandis*, variety.

There is one important qualification to the foregoing, however. Internal investment can lead a development program without foreign loans and despite the need for foreign capital goods, if it is kept within the limits of total resources, but timing may produce a transitional balance-of-payments deficit to be covered by borrowing. After the initial shift of spending toward foreign goods, resources will have to be diverted into export or import-competing lines by depreciation or deflation to pay for incremental imports. If the process is export-led, the same rate of investment can be achieved without a transitional deficit. Whether development is export- or internal-investment led does not determine the need for foreign borrowing in general, which is a function of total expenditure in relation to total domestic production. Where expenditure is limited to the amount of resources, however, the way the process is initiated makes a difference for transitional borrowing.

The need for foreign capital over time is then determined by the rate of investment in relation to domestic savings. The equilibrium condition for national income is that domestic investment plus exports must equal imports plus domestic savings. If the balance of payments is to be in equilibrium, with no borrowing, exports are equal to imports, and domestic investment is limited to domestic savings. An increase in investment unaccompanied by an equal shift in the savings schedule must be financed in part by borrowing from abroad, since part of the increased income will spill over into imports (assuming a positive marginal propensity to import). Investment can increase without harm to the balance of payments only if exports expand simultaneously in the correct proportion or if the savings schedule shifts upward or the import schedule downward.

It is important to emphasize that foreign lending can make only a marginal contribution to the development process, and that where a country can transform its resources in international trade, that marginal contribution is merely additive. If 75 to 90 per cent of the capital formation must come from domestic savings, the 10 to 25 per cent from abroad can contribute only *pro tanto,* unless one adopts a theory calling for a Big Push, minimum critical effort, Big Spurt, or some such. Given capacity to transform, domestic savings are as good as foreign capital. It is just as well they are, as there is not nearly enough foreign capital to go around if it were the case that its contribution were somehow special and critical.

CAPACITY TO ABSORB CAPITAL

The International Bank for Reconstruction and Development has said that the problem in development is not, or perhaps has not been, the supply of loans so much as the limited capacity to absorb capital.[3] Millikan and Rostow have proposed that the developed countries of the world should make available to underdeveloped countries as much capital as they can absorb, by which they mean as much as can, with reasonable assurance, be productively used.[4]

The general-equilibrium view of the need for foreign capital leads to the conclusion that capacity to absorb capital is unlimited. And so it is if capital consumption is allowed, and plenty of time. With the requirement that loans must be productive the question that arises immediately is, "How productive?" Any positive productivity for capital is sufficient to define the capacity to absorb capital if the marginal value product schedule is sharply kinked, as in Figure 17.1*a*, so that even a small addition of capital after the kink at *W* will yield zero return. But if the schedule declines more gradually, as in Figure 17.1*b*, the capacity to absorb capital must be defined in terms of a rate of return. This may be zero, but it may also be something higher, such as 8, 12, or 16 per cent per annum. If there is no kink, the concept of a finite and calculable capacity to absorb capital is ambiguous without an explicit rate of return.

The general view is that there is a kink. The International Bank's criterion is the existence of well-engineered designs for a given project which must make sense in the context of a development program. The

[3] See the early IBRD *Annual Reports,* esp. the *Fourth Annual Report* for 1948–1949, pp. 8–9: "Perhaps the most striking single lesson which the Bank has learned in the course of its operations is how limited is the capacity of the underdeveloped countries to absorb capital quickly for really productive purposes. . . . In point of fact . . . the principal limitation upon Bank financing in the development field has not been lack of money but lack of well-prepared and well-planned projects ready for immediate execution."
[4] See M. F. Millikan and W. W. Rostow, *A Proposal: Key to an Effective Foreign Policy,* Harper, New York, 1957, pp. 56ff.

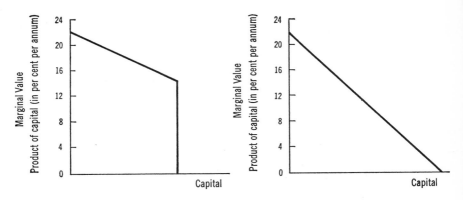

Figure 17.1a and Figure 17.1b | Capacity to absorb capital.

Bank limits its lending to projects, as a rule, because it believes this necessary to control the use of its funds and to inspire confidence in its obligations by capital markets in developed countries. With limited economic, engineering, and administrative talent, a developing country can prepare so many projects and no more. That establishes the kink.

But Millikan and Rostow, and other economists with field experience who believe in the existence of a kink and a limited capacity to absorb capital, base their view on more than project-design capacity. They have in mind all the resources complementary with imported capital equipment, and especially the administrative capacity or organization to put such imported capital equipment to work effectively. In Indonesia, for example, more capital equipment brought to the country would merely intensify the chaos at the major ports which now precludes any increase in capacity to absorb capital.

This illustration makes clear that the concept rests on certain assumptions which, however reasonable, are not always explicit. In Indonesia it might be possible to absorb more capital not in the form of equipment but in the services of foreign manpower to clear the ports and get goods moving through them. If administrative capacity is lacking, it too can be obtained from abroad with borrowed funds, along with equipment, and it may be efficient to do so. In normal circumstances, it is unlikely that an underdeveloped country will want to import skilled workers, organization, and other complementary resources whose absence inhibits capital formation. But it could. As an intellectual experiment to test the concept of a finite and fixed capacity to absorb capital, it is worth contemplating an estimated "capacity"—say, the $7.3 million for Libya calculated by Rosenstein-

Rodan,[5] and seeing if by dint of turning the job over to an outfit like Morrison-Knudson of Boise, Idaho, which specializes in enormous construction projects, or to Krupp, or the Seabees, or one of the big oil companies, one could not double this capacity. Time would be required, of course, underlining the fact that capacity to absorb capital may be more limited over six months or a year than three years hence. Over the intermediate run, the capacity to absorb capital is susceptible to enlargement by appropriate policies, even within the constraints of relying only on native administration and so on.

The "capital needs" of underdeveloped countries have been estimated along with the "capacity to absorb capital." The first have been derived from projections of trade data: if import requirements rise in this fashion, and exports only amount to so much, capital imports of so-and-so much are needed to fill the gap. The other method is to start with a desired level of growth, such as 3 per cent, and a capital/output ratio (perhaps 4) to get an overall savings requirement. From this, one subtracts domestic savings, which change as the economy grows because the marginal propensity to save differs from the average. In the early years, however, if total investment is 12 per cent of national income, and domestic savings are only 8, capital imports of 4 per cent of national income are required.

These two methods of estimation for a given country should give the same results, for not only is foreign borrowing (negative investment or $-I_f$) the difference between domestic investment I_d and savings S. It is also the difference between exports on current account X and imports M.

$$-I_f = I_d - S$$

and

$$-I_f = M - X$$

It should make no difference in a general-equilibrium system whether one estimated borrowing requirements from projections of trade or from projections of domestic investment and savings. In fact, however, the differences can be wide. Rosenstein-Rodan's estimates for world capacity to absorb capital in the middle of the 1970s, based on a capital/output ratio of 3 and fairly high internal marginal propensities to save, runs between $3 billion and $4 billion.[6] The annual report for 1961 of the General Agreement on Tariffs and Trade (GATT), calculating capital needs from foreign-trade data and using rather pes-

---

[5] See his "International Aid for Underdeveloped Countries," *Review of Economics and Statistics*, May, 1961, p. 132.
[6] *Ibid.*, p. 137.

simistic assumptions about the capacity of developing countries to produce their own requirements and to sell exports, gets a gap of $14.4 billion. If the terms of trade deteriorate from the base year, the GATT report adds, the need for borrowing will increase.[7] But in a general-equilibrium model, the projections of exports, imports, capital/output ratios, marginal propensities to save, and the like must all be related. To project high levels of imports, for example, implies high capital/output ratios and low marginal propensities to save, whereas to project a low ICOR and a high MPS implies that the economy will be effective in producing for export and in replacing imports. The assumptions used by GATT and Rosenstein-Rodan evidently do not converge.

CAPACITY TO REPAY

The capacity to repay foreign loans also differs in the long run and in the short, like the capacity to absorb foreign loans. In the short run, capacity to repay is dictated by the foreign-exchange impact of the investment undertaken, whether it be export-increasing or import-decreasing. Over time, the only determinant of the capacity to repay is the loan's contribution to productivity of the economy as a whole and the capacity of the system to skim away the necessary portion of that productivity in taxes or pricing and to reallocate resources so as to transfer debt service abroad. An increase in productivity brought about by foreign loans in purely domestic overhead, such as public utilities in an internal city, carries its own capacity to repay if the loan is productive. The requirement for repayment is that the fiscal system raise the necessary funds and that transformation occur to shift resources into export-increasing or import-decreasing lines.

This is not to suggest that repayment is easy. It may seem so when the initial investment is made in an export industry, and so it is in the short run. In the long run, however, developing countries have a tendency for investment to exceed domestic savings, i.e., to borrow abroad. Any requirement for repayment is a requirement that savings exceed investment and calls for an "uphill" movement of capital. It is appropriate for an individual loan, perhaps, to require amortization and for an individual project to pay amortization out of its gross earn-

---

[7] *International Trade, 1961*, GATT, Geneva, 1962, pp. 15–17. The use of the partial-equilibrium analysis to calculate the additional requirements if the terms of trade change is wrong too. If the terms of trade change, a great many other variables will change as well, especially the quantities exported and imported and amounts produced. Accordingly, the calculations cannot be extended but must be reworked from the beginning.

ings. But a country as a whole typically borrows net in its developing stages. Amortization places a burden upon it since in the event that loans were suddenly unavailable, it would have to transfer capital outward instead of inward. The banking requirement of amortization gives underdeveloped economies the opposite problem from that of the International Bank and the Export-Import Bank, which are receiving so much capital repayment in recent years that they have to lend very considerable amounts annually to prevent the capital movement from changing direction.

Similar considerations apply to capacity to pay interest on foreign loans. In the short run, the closer the project is to increasing exports or reducing imports, the more readily the interest on the debt can be paid. In the long run, the test is productivity in general, plus fiscal and transforming capacities. The notion that foreign resources made available to government for social overhead capital must be made on the basis of grants, rather than loans, is therefore based on short-run considerations.

A series of well-known articles on the repayment problem tends to ignore various of these considerations. W. S. Salant[8] and E. D. Domar[9] discuss mainly the effect on the lending country, and focus on the question of when the lender's balance of trade turns adverse. This occurs, they assert, when the rate of interest on outstanding loans, plus the rate of amortization, exceeds the rate of growth of lending plus the rate of amortization. Conversely, underdeveloped countries must borrow at a rate higher than the rate of interest on outstanding issues (leaving amortization out of it) if they want to prevent the balance of trade from turning positive. But surely it is the current account and not the balance of trade which ought to be the criterion. If the current account is negative, and balanced by capital inflow, it is not appropriate to say that the country is borrowing abroad to pay interest on old debts. The positive capital formation pays interest on old debts, and new capital is being formed with the new capital inflow.[10]

---

[8] "The Domestic Effects of Capital Export under the Point Four Program," *American Economic Review, Papers and Proceedings*, May, 1950, pp. 504ff.
[9] "The Effect of Foreign Investment on the Balance of Payments," *American Economic Review*, December, 1950, pp. 805–826.
[10] J. J. Polak in "Balance of Payments of Countries Reconstructing with the Help of Foreign Loans," *Quarterly Journal of Economics*, February, 1943, pp. 208–240 (reproduced in *Readings in the Theory of International Trade*, American Economic Association, Blakiston-Irwin, Philadelphia, 1949, pp. 459–493) emphasizes the difference made by investment in the export sector on the one hand or the domestic sector on the other, but neglects, in his interest in an income model, all possibility of transformation.

The Salant-Domar analysis is thus applicable to income transfers rather than to capital movements. It fails to give attention to the increase in consumption in the lending country, which spills over in part into imports and assists the balance of payments, or to the growth of capacity in the borrowing country, which, either directly or indirectly with the aid of transformation, makes possible the necessary expansion in exports. Income transfers, where the transfer is consumed in the receiving country and (possibly) comes out of new savings but produces no income in the remitting, require an entirely different analysis than capital movements.

The fact is that geometric growth can be made to do almost anything. If it is assumed that transformation will take place and that growth will occur with a very high marginal propensity to save and a low capital/output ratio, a country can cease borrowing in short order despite payment of a relatively high rate of interest. Using "arbitrary" assumptions, Millikan and Rostow state:[11]

> . . . if the initial rate of domestic investment is 5 per cent of national income, if foreign capital is supplied at a constant rate equal to one-third the initial level of domestic investment, if 25 per cent of all additions to income are saved and reinvested, if the capital output ratio is 3, and if interest and dividend service on foreign loans and private investments are paid at the rate of 6 per cent a year, the country will be able to discontinue net foreign borrowing after fourteen years and sustain a 3 per cent growth of income out of its own resources.

A general measure of capacity of a country to accept and service foreign borrowing has been devised in the investment/service ratio.[12] This is the relation of outgoing interest and amortization (which are debits in the balance of payments) to total exports of goods and services (a credit). Figure 17.2 shows the debt-service ratios for a number of countries in 1958, compared with income per capita in 1961. In Iraq and Iran the ratios are very high—in the high 30s. Most of the others are lower than they were during the 1930s. Moreover, between 1955 and 1958, for which Avramovic and Gulhati studied the ratio,[13] out of 41 countries, 16 showed declines in the debt-service ratio as compared with 24 increases (1 unchanged).

[11] *Op. cit.*, pp. 157–158.
[12] See D. Finch, "Investment Service of Underdeveloped Countries," *Staff Papers,* September, 1951, pp. 60–85.
[13] D. Avramovic and R. Gulhati, *Debt Servicing Problems of Low Income Countries,* 1956–58, Johns Hopkins, Baltimore, 1960.

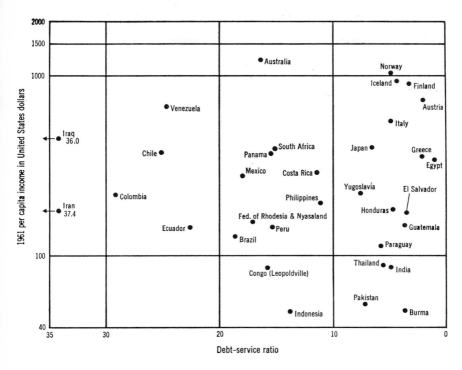

Figure 17.2 | Debt-service ratio in 1958 compared with income per capita, about 1961. sources: Debt-service ratio (ratio of service payments on public and private debt to total external receipts on current account), D. Avramovic and R. Gulhati, *Debt Servicing Problems of Low-Income Countries, 1956–58,* Johns Hopkins, Baltimore, 1960; income per capita, table 1.1, Average Income per Capita in Selected Countries for 1949 and 1961, except for Iraq, Iran, and the United Arab Republic from P. N. Rosenstein-Rodan, "International Aid for Underdeveloped Countries," *Review of Economics and Statistics,* May, 1961, p. 126 (GNP reduced by 10 per cent).

But the debt-service ratio does not tell one a great deal. Assume that there are two countries, A and B, and that both start out with national incomes of 500, exports and imports of 100 each, and then borrow 100 on a continuous basis at 10 per cent interest annually. Suppose that A spends the foreign borrowings on consumption in the first instance, and thereafter spends as much on consumption as is left after interest payments. B, on the other hand, invests its foreign loans at a capital/output ratio of 4 and increases exports to the extent of 10 out of the 25 of increased production. The paths of the two economies will be as follows:

Year	Domestic output	Increase in C	Increase in I	X	M	I_f	ΣI_f	Interest	Debt/Service ratio
Before Borrowing									
	500			100	100	...	...	...	...
With Annual Loans of 100									
Country A									
1	500	+100	...	100	200	100	100	10	10
2	500	+ 80	...	100	200	100	200	20	20
5	500	+ 50	...	100	200	100	500	50	50
Country B									
1	525	+ 15	+100	110	200	100	100	10	21
2	550	+ 30	+100	120	200	100	200	20	16⅔
5	625	+ 75	+100	150	200	100	500	50	33

C = consumption, I = investment, X = exports of goods and services, M = imports of goods and services, including interest; I_f = foreign borrowing. In the second year, the debt-service ratios will not be far apart, at 20 and 16⅔ per cent, and even in the fifth year, the difference between them—50 and 33—will not be striking. The debt-service ratios are rising in both countries, and fairly rapidly. But country A, which is consuming its foreign loans and borrowing to pay interest so that its total available for consumption is shrinking, is doing very badly, while country B is getting better off all the time. The debt-service ratios throw little, if any, light on the important issues whether or not a borrowing country is investing productively and transferring its interest by means of effective transformation.

FORMS OF FOREIGN BORROWING—DIRECT INVESTMENT

Direct investment has traditionally been viewed as a desirable form of international capital movement. The traditions on which this view is based, however, are largely those of the developed countries. The reasons given have been that this investment is accompanied by technical assistance and training possibilities for the country where the investment is made; the investor may, in the case of very large companies dealing in very underdeveloped areas, provide its own social and economic overhead capital, and the transfer of profits imposes a supportable burden on the economy, since these investments have been typically in the export sector, and the increased profits have been associated with increased exports which automatically transfer them. The training impact has been mentioned in an earlier chapter, and is intensively discussed in a number of studies of *United States Business Performance Abroad* undertaken by the National Planning Association (along with other aspects of that performance).[14] In several instances, such as Venezuela, the governments of countries in which large and profitable investments have taken place express themselves as thoroughly satisfied and levy taxes on the profits of foreign enterprises which are used to finance development investment.

There is, nonetheless, a substantial controversy over the role of direct investment in developing countries. Part of this is simple xenophobia which leads frustrated politicians to divert attention from difficult tasks by attacking foreigners. We set this problem aside until Chapter 20. In addition, however, there are some questions about the value of the training that comes with direct investment, and whether the underdeveloped countries are exploited by the foreign capitalist. These issues were real enough in the colonial period. In newly independent countries, there is the tendency to identify foreign direct investment with "neocolonialism."

Hla Myint objected to foreign investment in plantations because it produced a once-and-for-all change in technology which then became fossilized or frozen.[15] Another view expressed by Simon Hanson, based on experience in Latin America, is that the foreign investor joins hands with the local capitalist to maintain the gap between the mass of the workers and the small industrialist and landowning class.[16] A third opinion is that the gap in technology between developed countries and underdeveloped is so wide, in the majority of cases, that the foreign investment functions in an enclave, linked to the country from which it emanated, but not stimulating the local economy. In some instances, there will be dual economy, in which labor-saving techniques are em-

[14] See the National Planning Association studies of Creole in Venezuela, Casa Grace in Peru, Sears Roebuck de Mexico, the Philippine American Life Insurance Company, Firestone in Liberia, The United Fruit Company in Latin America, etc.
[15] Hla Myint, "The Gains from International Trade and the Backward Countries," *Review of Economics and Statistics*, 1954–1955, pp. 129–142.
[16] S. G. Hanson, *Economic Development in Latin America*, Washington, D.C., Inter-American Affairs Press, 1951, pp. 9, 15ff.

ployed in foreign investment alongside great numbers of unemployed and underemployed in the subsistence economy. Where this occurs, and Singer has pointed out the possibilities,[17] it may well be a result of failure of the local economy to respond rather than failure of the foreign investor to stimulate. The linkages, to use Hirschman's phrase, are felt by developed countries abroad, because the economy where the investment takes place is unable to supply inputs of factors and intermediate products or to respond to the opportunities arising from new low-priced outputs.

The possibility that foreign investors exploit the host country is discussed in economic terms by E. T. Penrose.[18] In connection with the Iraq Petroleum Company, she concludes that the company did in fact exploit the country because it received a higher return than the minimum it would have been willing to receive and still stay in business. But this is a peculiar way to define exploitation, which is a highly pejorative word. If there is a wide gap between the minimum the company would accept and the maximum the country would pay, and the country would exploit the company if it paid it less than it would be willing to and maintain the arrangement, then the possibility exists that company and country exploit each other simultaneously. This is in fact initially a certainty. Direct investment frequently represents bilateral monopoly with a wide gap between the maximum and minimum prices of the two parties to the bargain. When this is the case, the gain may accrue all to one party or the other, or may be divided on some basis. If one party tries to increase its gain to the point where the other gets less than its minimum, the arrangement breaks down in withdrawal by the company or nationalization by the country. It is possible, though unlikely, that one party gets all the gain, the other none. When this occurs it can be called exploitation. But where both parties are better off than their minimum-gain position, this word is hardly useful.

Typically, bargaining strengths of the country and the company change through time. At the outset, the underdeveloped country is likely to have few alternatives, and the company, taking on most of the risks, can drive a profitable bargain. As time goes on, and the company's commitment grows and the country becomes more sophisticated, the weight of bargaining strength shifts. The country can now increase taxes on foreign investors and redistribute the gains. It can

[17] H. W. Singer, "The Distribution of Gains between Investing and Borrowing Countries," *American Economic Review*, May, 1950, p. 473.
[18] E. T. Penrose, "Profit Sharing between Producing Countries and Oil Companies in the Middle East," *Economic Journal*, June, 1959, pp. 238–254.

use not only its taxing power, but also foreign-exchange regulations, labor legislation, laws requiring foreign companies to buy their materials and components locally, and so on, to reshape the arrangement entirely. If it goes too far, the company can withhold further investment, as the copper companies did in Chile, or withdraw, as the automobile companies have done in India.

These considerations of training effect, political influence, and exploitation have produced a remarkable ambivalence in underdeveloped countries about foreign investment. They want the output that foreign investors can generate and the capital they bring or form, but they worry that they may be bilked, both paying too much and getting too little. This ambivalence is perhaps best illustrated in India where a socialist state has been proclaimed, but private foreign investment is said to be given national treatment. In fact, the treatment of foreign investment in India is highly selective, as evidenced by the fact that one large United States motor company withdrew its investment in the country at a time when two oil companies were reaching agreements to construct refineries. Officially, the Indian government welcomes foreign investments which:

1. Have a genuine program for manufacturing, not trade or distribution
2. Are located in a field where domestic investment is inadequate or domestic technology below the level abroad
3. Help the foreign-exchange position by being export-increasing or import-decreasing
4. Increase productivity
5. Make provision for training Indian personnel for higher technical administrative posts
6. Admit Indian capital at all stages of the venture

The provisions about training and productivity have already been discussed. The third requirement, that the investment must help expand exports or save imports, is the analogue of that in project analysis more generally: it assumes no transformation so that a productive project in the domestic sector cannot bring about reallocation of resources to exports or import-competing uses. Insistence on manufacturing is, of course, a classic example of the widespread fallacy of identifying secondary production with development and ignoring the contribution of distribution. Part of its roots are no doubt traceable to fear of foreign monopolists. The Indian stipulation that domestic capital be admitted at all stages is one which is increasingly adopted in underdeveloped countries but is often meaningless in the absence of sufficient savings or readiness to invest in industrial equities. The Hanson point about strengthening domestic monopolists is also relevant.

In the present form, it furnishes a contrast to other views on the same subject. Frequent objection is made to the foreign entrepreneur who puts in the smallest possible amount of equity capital and borrows debt capital locally to increase his leverage. At one time it was explicitly stated by the Australian Prime Minister that his country was not prepared to encourage companies which put in only a small equity in dollars and borrowed the rest locally, since they would be earning dollars on sterling investments.[19]

The position in foreign direct investment today is something of a standoff, such as frequently occurs in bilateral monopoly. Both parties would benefit from getting together and working out mutually advantageous arrangements. But the investor wants a high return to compensate him for the risks of confiscation, and the country where the investment takes place is inclined to confiscate because of the high return earned by the investor. The result is stalemate. Exceptions abound: even in the developed countries of Canada and France there is some nervousness that, compared with domestic entrepreneurship, foreign capital is somehow more grasping, and at a great advantage. It is understandable that the underdeveloped countries with less reason for confidence should welcome the positive contribution of foreign investment but fret about possible disadvantageous side effects and about the missed opportunities for domestic enterprise.

FORMS OF FOREIGN BORROWING — GOVERNMENT BONDS

The traditional form of borrowing up to 1914 was government bonds. Government was the borrower, but the lender was the private investor. After World War I, the market revived and shifted from Europe, and especially from London, to New York. During the depression it collapsed, in part because of its overinflation during the late 1920s. It was slowly reviving in the 1960s when the United States government proposed a tax on foreign borrowing in an effort to defend the U.S. balance of payments.

In the period from 1945 to 1960, investors wanted no part of foreign government bonds, leaving aside the special cases of Canada, which was tied closely to the New York capital market, and Israel, where ties of sentiment mixed with business considerations. Slowly the position improved, and European borrowers, and then Australia and Japan, sold dollar bonds in New York. A number of underdeveloped

[19] See "Australia Welcomes Dollar Investments," *New York Times*, Sept. 10, 1949.

countries made settlements of their old obligations from the 1930s with the Council of Foreign Bondholders. In 1961, a $100 million bond issue for a Mexican governmental enterprise in electricity was privately placed with a United States insurance company.

Equity financing of international development is important, but debt financing is needed, too. Where productive investment opportunities exist, a country, like a private company, is warranted in borrowing at fixed rates of interest. Where productive assets are of considerable durability, long-term debt borrowing is entirely appropriate. Governments, as it happens, sell neither equities nor mortgages. Since much of the investment is for government account, especially in social and economic overhead capital, the lack of a foreign bond market is a handicap to development.

FORMS OF FOREIGN BORROWING— LENDING BY INTERNATIONAL AGENCIES

In the vacuum created by the need for borrowing on government account and the absence of a private bond market, the Bretton Woods conference established the International Bank for Reconstruction and Development (IBRD) to serve as a link between borrowing governments, on the one hand, and lending governments and private capital, on the other. The complex arrangements of the Bank, which have been described too frequently elsewhere, amounts to a sort of domestic government guarantee of some private lending in the country where the Bank's obligations are sold. The Bank then furnishes some government capital to underdeveloped countries and provides a channel whereby timid private capital can move with governmental help.

The initial flow of loans by the Bank was fairly small. Currently it has reached more than $600 million to $700 million gross annually, and outstanding loans amount to more than $6 billion. In addition to its lending, the Bank has conducted economic surveys of various countries' prospects for development, furnished experts to study development problems, helped to negotiate agreements, recruited technical personnel, and operated an Economic Development Institute.

The Bank's loans, as mentioned, are mainly on a project basis and made on banking terms, i.e., at the cost to the Bank of its borrowed funds plus a 1 per cent charge for administration and a fractional charge for reserves. The total comes close to 6 per cent, and loans are rarely for more than twenty years. Various organizations have been proposed and some have been acted upon to make funds available on less rigid terms or for special purposes. The Latin American countries after years of lobbying finally established an Inter-American Development Bank for the purpose of making loans to Latin America, especially for social overhead projects, such as town water systems. These loans are made for periods of fifty years, with frequently a period of grace of ten years before interest payments must be made. The International Development Agency (IDA) and the International Finance Corporation (IFC) were both created as agents of the International Bank to make different types of loans, the first for social overhead projects and long periods of time, repayable in local currency, with low interest rates and frequently a grace period, the second for investment in equities with a view to stimulating private enterprise. The amounts were far smaller than those of the International Bank, $1 billion and $100 million, respectively. IDA loans are often packaged with an IBRD "banker's-type loan" to lower the average interest rate and lengthen the average maturity on the package as a whole.

The United Nations General Assembly pushed hard for a Special United Nations Fund for Economic Development, or SUNFED, which would raise money from countries on the basis of their ability to contribute, and distribute it on a grant basis, presumably according to need.[20] The United States, which would be the largest contributor, consistently voted against the project in the Economic and Social Council, and finally succeeded in reducing the proposal to that for a United Nations Special Fund of only $100 million which is used to finance special projects of technical assistance, such as resource surveys.

Whether foreign assistance should take the form of loans or grants does not, of course, turn on whether it is to be used for social and economic overhead capital or for primary or secondary production. This follows from the section above on capacity to repay. If the economy lacks capacity to transform because of zero supply elasticity in exports and in import-competing industries, or if demand abroad has price elasticity of unity or less, which prevents expansion in exports, and if imports are of great importance to the economy—either necessities, such as food, materials and fuel, or capital equipment already slated for investment projects—a grant may be needed for overhead projects or a disequilibrium system on the international front cannot be avoided. On the whole, however, it is appropriate to say that capacity to repay foreign assistance is primarily a function of the productivity of the investment, and grants are needed for projects of low or uncertain productivity. It is not clear that these should be undertaken on any basis, given the existence of certainly productive investments.

---

[20] See United Nations experts' report, *Special United Nations Fund for Economic Development,* New York, 1954.

It is true that grants raise income more than loans, typically by 5½ or 6 per cent annually, if the contrast is between IDA loans during a ten-year interest-free grace period and IBRD loans. If this can be re-invested, or used in "productive consumption," there is reason to favor grants over loans, insofar as the borrower or grantee is concerned. But that the grantee would prefer not to pay in order to get more benefit from the capital transfer is different from saying that it cannot pay.

FORMS OF FOREIGN BORROWING— GOVERNMENTAL LOANS AND GRANTS

Where governmental assistance to economic development abroad is part of general foreign policy, and the country does not, because of the terms of its participation in an international lending agency, exercise some measure of control over the latter's actions, there is a strong argument for unilateral rather than international action. Particularly where each country has one vote, and a few countries contribute while numerous countries benefit, it becomes difficult to use international assistance as a tool of foreign policy except in a very long-run sense. The international organization may assist unfriendly countries unduly or fail to be sufficiently heedful of the needs of friends.

A variety of unilateral forms of assistance has come into being. The Export-Import Bank in the United States was begun as a depression measure to assist United States exporters in selling abroad, and is still frequently used to bail these exporters out of situations in which credits extended to foreign importers have been blocked. This in fact is a frequently sought type of development loan—now wanted by countries such as Brazil to clear up the arrears of past indebtedness, now a block to growth.

Major direct assistance to underdeveloped countries is furnished by the Agency for International Development (AID) in the Department of State. This and its predecessor agency, the International Cooperation Administration (ICA), started giving primarily grants, but shifted gradually to a preponderance of loans, made available from the Development Loan Fund (DLF). When the balance of payments of the United States weakened after 1960, aid from the DLF was almost entirely "tied," i.e., restricted to purchases from the United States. Some of the recipient countries complained that tied aid was 20 to 30 per cent more expensive than funds which could be used to buy supplies anywhere in the world that they were cheaper. The United States administration argument conceded that there was less real aid per dollar of DLF loan, but made the rebuttal that tying made possible more real aid per dollar of balance-of-payments deficit, which was the binding constraint.

Economic aid and military aid are hard to distinguish, since much depends upon what is taking place in the assisted countries. If nothing is changed, or on a partial-equilibrium basis, a dollar of military aid would help the military position of a country by one dollar, and a dollar of economic aid would help the economic position by a like amount. But it cannot be taken for granted that other things will be equal. A dollar of economic aid may enable a country which needs military help to transfer its own economic resources from development to military expenditure, or military aid can be transmuted in converse fashion into economic. It is naïve to insist on a sharp distinction between aid for various purposes unless one can be certain at the same time that the assisted country is not reallocating its own resources to offset the effects of the added resources from outside.

Considerable amounts of direct assistance are made available by the United Kingdom to the Commonwealth, and by France in Africa. The release of blocked sterling balances owned by countries or colonies which furnished supplies to England during World War II in advance of agreed schedules is a paradoxical form of "aid," and does increase unrequited exports in the short run. Soviet assistance to underdeveloped countries appears to take the form primarily of agreements in which the Soviet Union delivers capital goods and is later repaid in primary products. These carry a nominal 2 per cent rate of interest—well below that of the International Bank for Reconstruction and Development—for the credit advanced.

FORMS OF FOREIGN BORROWING— AGRICULTURAL SURPLUSES

The Agricultural Trade Development and Assistance Act of 1954 in the United States—so-called Public Law or P.L. 480—provides for the use of agricultural surpluses for economic development. The idea is attractive to those concerned with getting rid of surpluses. In addition, as we have seen, it is not necessary for foreign borrowing to take the form of imports of capital goods. Agricultural commodities can do as well if resources previously engaged in producing, say, food, are shifted out of agriculture into the export sector—to the extent that imported capital goods are needed, and into capital formation—to the extent that the demand is for domestic capital such as construction.

It would be possible, indeed, for agricultural surpluses to be used for capital formation without transformation if they replaced existing purchased imports and released foreign exchange for capital purchases or purchases of other consumption goods. The difficulty, however, is that the Act of 1954 requires that exports be incremental to cash sales. It also stipulates that they must not impair the competitive position of friendly countries.

But the foremost assistance which agricultural surpluses can provide in economic development is to prevent capital formation from being choked off, or the balance of payments turned adverse, through a lack of consumer goods arising from inability of agriculture to respond to the stimulus of increased demand. As stated previously, the rate of capital formation turns on the capacity of the economy to provide consumer goods for the resources engaged in producing capital. It would be economic to borrow and spend exchange for this purpose, even though most economic planners are insufficiently sophisticated to appreciate the fact that capital imports can take the form of imported foodstuffs. Where imported foodstuffs are surplus in the exporting country, and hence unwanted there, total resources are increased by imported food and increased capital formation made possible. Where the rate of capital formation has already been raised to overly ambitious levels, the agricultural surpluses may justify them.

The mechanism works in ways already described in Chapter 12, in the discussion of balance, and again in Chapter 16, on foreign trade as a balancing sector. As manpower is transferred out of agriculture into social overhead or industrial capital formation, the demand for food rises, both on the part of the workers left on the farm and those in nonagricultural areas. If domestic supply is inelastic, and if agriculture is protected by prohibitive tariffs or quotas, the terms of trade shift against industrial products and in favor of farmers. Or the demand may spill over into imports and turn the balance of trade adversely. The difficulty may originate in a short crop which encourages speculators to hoard grain, raise the price of foodstuffs, and threaten the program of capital formation by raising the price of the wage good. In either circumstance, agricultural surpluses, on hand or available from abroad, can steady the terms of trade between foodstuffs and industrial products and sustain or enlarge the rate of capital formation. Wheat loans to India and Pakistan in the 1950s saved the programs of those countries from setback when they were threatened by a bad monsoon. The Pakistan episode illustrates the need for food stockpiles. The mere arrival of the shipment was sufficient to induce wheat sales by speculators, with the consequence of a sharp drop in price and the inability of the government to sell at appropriate prices all the wheat made available.

FOREIGN RESOURCES AND PLANNING

A number of countries, particularly India and Pakistan, have embarked on investment programs without the necessary resources in hand and relying on foreign assistance. If nothing goes wrong, such a country may still find its commitments uncovered. If there is bad luck—a poor monsoon. a sudden demand for defense equipment to repel an attack from the Chinese, a miscalculation about the demand for imports from the private sector—the balance-of-payments deficit will become intolerable. What happens? Does the country cut back on its development program, or does it take its hat in hand and seek more assistance? The sudden calls for meetings of the Aid-to-India, Aid-to-Pakistan, Aid-to-Turkey, and Aid-to-Argentina clubs, to mention only a few of the exclusive organizations to which the United States and Western Europe belong, suggest that more aid, rather than less program, is the usual answer.

In the long run, of course, this answer is unsupportable, because it erodes incentive to get the balance of payments under control. By planning for deficits above the long-term loans a country is entitled to, it can increase its share of loans.

Some margin for safety is, of course, needed, and it is important to calculate the margin of error in the original calculation of import requirements. In India this is large. With a good monsoon, imports decline and foreign exchange is available for capital goods imports. In Pakistan, the difference between good and bad harvests is again critical, but operates through exports: good harvests provide, rather than save, foreign exchange. In both cases the investment plans presuppose average harvests, but reality can bring good, bad, or indifferent. There is a chance, then, that foreign sources of loans are not needed to the extent that the plan calls for external financing or, if the planners are overly optimistic, a greater chance that more borrowing will be needed than indicated.

In short, calculation of the foreign-exchange content of an investment plan on a project basis, presupposing that exports and imports go on as before except as directly reduced and increased, respectively, is a risky business. *Ceteris* have a way of not being *paribus*. If planning were flexible, with investment projects capable of being advanced, postponed, speeded up in the time taken to accomplish them, or dragged out, it might be possible and desirable to take account of harvest-to-harvest changes in the need for and availability of foreign resources and to adjust investment undertakings as the program went along. This would involve fitting the requirements to resources, rather than the other way round. Since underdeveloped countries lack control over the monsoon and over the availability of foreign loans, there is some logic to looking at it this way. But to encourage loans, it may be best to put the other face on it to the world. This is what we must do; this is what we need from abroad, suppressing the qualification *plus* or *minus,* and this is what we need from developed countries in loans, or preferably grants.

SUMMARY

Borrowing abroad is needed to add to total resources available for economic development, not to make development possible by providing a limited range of resources which the country does not possess. Without loans, but with capacity to transform, a country could develop, though the rate would be slowed down by overall lack of resources. With virtually unlimited loans, but without capacity to transform, economic development would be impossible. Foreign loans could be used to add to consumption, and possibly to increase productivity in existing lines to some degree. But development as a process would be impossible.

Capacity to absorb capital is another partial-equilibrium concept which makes certain assumptions about the desired rate of return (assuming no sharp kink) or about a kink in the marginal value product of capital as a consequence of a sudden cutoff of complementary resources such as organization. The need of developing countries for foreign capital can be calculated by various partial means. Ideally, they should converge, since the separate answers are linked into the same general system.

Capacity to repay loans does not raise problems of the necessity to borrow forever, to pay interest, and to pay interest on the interest. Most loans are not used for consumption, but produce a yield which can be used, with transformation, to transfer interest abroad. Debt-service ratios tell something but not a great deal about the repaying capacity of borrowing countries.

The pros and cons of foreign investment in the developing process are discussed, including the contribution in technology and the likelihood of political interference and "exploitation." Other forms of lending on a national and international basis are listed.

BIBLIOGRAPHY

R. F. Mikesell has edited a major survey of United States private and government lending, *United States Private and Government Invest-*

ment Abroad, University of Oregon Press, Eugene, Ore., 1962, which treats most of these issues in detail. For a historical comparison, see Ragnar Nurkse, "International Investment Today in the Light of Nineteenth Century Experience," *Economic Journal,* December, 1954, reprinted in Supple (ed.), selection 5. An interesting case study is L. Gordon and E. L. Grommers, *United States Manufacturing Investment in Brazil: The Impact of Brazilian Government Policies, 1946–60,* Harvard Business School, Cambridge, Mass., 1962. See also the excellent paper by G. M. Alter, "The Servicing of Foreign Capital Inflows by Underdeveloped Countries," in H. S. Ellis and H. C. Wallich (eds.), *Economic Development for Latin America,* St Martin's, New York, 1961, and in the same source, Felipe Pazos, "Private vs Public Foreign Investment in Underdeveloped Areas," which argues that debt and equity investment in underdeveloped countries should stand in a ratio of 7:3.

WHAT IS A REGION?

In some economic contexts, the region is a unit smaller than a nation. In the present discussion, it is larger. The type of regional cooperation, collaboration, or integration frequently invoked for purposes of development is on an international scale.

In the draft charter of the International Trade Organization—an inoperative document but one of some significance in the history of ideas—a region was defined in terms of geographical propinquity. Neighboring countries together make a geographical unit which for some economic (and political) purposes may be said to form an entity. The British delegation argued long and hard against this restriction. In its view, the essence was that a region was a unit with political cohesion. Geography was secondary. The British Commonwealth was thus claimed to be a "region" for the purpose of collaboration for economic development, and entitled to any exemptions from general rules granted for this purpose.

Something must be granted to the British point, if not everything. Proximity between countries is not a sufficient condition of a basis for regional cooperation, as India and Pakistan, Egypt and Israel illustrate. There must be a basis of common interest, such as usually arises between neighbors, and a common if frequently limited purpose. On the other hand, geography cannot be abandoned altogether. Israel and Burma do not constitute a region, despite the friendship which has sprung up between the two countries; nor can the British claim be admitted that political bonds are sufficient. But it is the contention of this chapter that the basic obstacle to regional cooperation for economic development is political, not economic. This applies in the various types of economic cooperation to be discussed: trade preferences, commodity stabilization, river-valley development, banking and payments arrangements, and regional development planning. Only in regional technical cooperation is the economic benefit so substantial and the competitive element so small that regional cooperative arrangements find little obstacle in political indifference, although enmity may constitute a block.

TRADE PREFERENCES

The General Agreement on Tariffs and Trade, which succeeded the stillborn International Trade Organization, provided two exceptions to the general rule of conduct which required most-favored nation treatment and prohibited discrimination in trade. One was a customs union (or a free-trade area). Countries forming a customs union could eliminate tariffs between them and adopt a common tariff against the outside world no higher than the average of the previous national duties. (In a free-trade area, the countries involved remove tariffs among themselves but keep the old national tariffs against outside countries.) The other was the granting of 100 per cent mutual preferences in specified commodities by developing countries. The first exception applied to developed and underdeveloped countries alike. The second was adopted at the insistence of the underdeveloped countries for their benefit. In fact, however, the major moves by developing countries in trade preferences have all been customs unions or free-trade areas.

Superficially, customs unions, free-trade areas, and 100 per cent preferences in specified commodities seem a useful means of cooperation among underdeveloped countries. Their markets are too narrow to enable new industries to get a flourishing start. By merging these markets they can achieve the scale necessary for efficient production. If the underdeveloped countries as a whole experience foreign-exchange gaps, moreover, mutual exchanges even of high-cost products are a means of getting goods which they might otherwise have to do without.

In fact, there are few success stories in preferential trade arrangements among developing countries. The Latin American Free Trade Association (LAFTA) exists but is experiencing difficulty. In Central America one organization after another has failed and been succeeded by a new arrangement, without finding the key to something which works. Gran Colombia, the specific cooperative arrangement among Colombia, Venezuela, and Ecuador, has failed both in general and in its attempt to run a common steamship company. The Arab League, which was the most active in getting the developing-country exception into the ITO charter and GATT, has tried time and again to work out cooperative arrangements, but with no success. A West Indies Federation broke down, started again on a new basis, and broke down once more. The Common Services Organization among Kenya, Tanganyika, and Uganda by which these countries merge their customs arrangements and much of their civil service seems to proceed smoothly, and a customs union among the newly independent members of the French Communauté, former French colonies in Africa, may come into being. But the difficulties are many.

In the first place, developing countries typically trade very little with one another and mostly with developed countries outside. In Latin America only 10 per cent of total foreign trade is intra-American. The chances of major cost reductions in existing trade of commodities are therefore limited. Trade creation, or the opening up of new trade channels in goods which one or another participating country produces cheaply and efficiently, is not a bright prospect, as compared with trade diversion, or the production of high-cost goods in the area after the exclusion of lower-cost goods from outside.

Second, in new goods which might be produced in the area, it is difficult to arrange who produces what. The original Central American undertaking for economic integration worked out between 1953 and 1958 proposals for a free-trade area and an industrial agreement, only to have them break down when Costa Rica refused ratification. LAFTA's arrangements for tariff reduction are complex and by no means assured. In currently traded items, tariffs will be reduced at conferences which meet annually and are committed to reduce mutual tariffs by 25 per cent in three years, 50 per cent in six, 75 per cent in nine, and virtually all in twelve. The average annual rate of reduction is to be 8 per cent. It is easy to foresee that, after all the easy reductions have been accomplished, the later stages of this process will prove difficult. But mutual tariff elimination in goods that are currently not traded will take place in special conferences called "from time to time." This provision raises even stickier questions of bargaining, as countries with a slight head start in an industry will want to push ahead rapidly with tariff reduction, but those behind will seek delays until their chances of competing effectively improve. The exception to the most-favored-nation clause for customs unions and free-trade areas states that these can be undertaken gradually only if the contracting parties are committed to the goal of 100 per cent elimination. GATT accepted the Montevideo Treaty as meeting this requirement, but from a practical viewpoint considerable doubt must remain that the mutual tariffs among Argentina, Brazil, Chile, Colombia, Ecuador, Mexico, Peru, and Uruguay will in fact be eliminated by 1972.

Third, tariff reductions are difficult for countries with a weak balance of payments. It is frequently not tariffs which restrict trade, but quotas and foreign-exchange control. Without special payments arrangements, to be discussed presently, the choice is between withholding prefer-ences or a worsening balance of payments. In the spring of 1963 Uruguay devalued the peso from 9 to 6¼ cents, and imposed a sur-charge of 20 per cent on imports to correct the drain on its balance of payments. The measures not only applied to the other members of LAFTA: they were taken without notifying them. And a new exchange rate evidently alters the original calculations made by the contracting parties and thus puts strain on the underlying agreement.

Fourth is the problem of the gains and losses among the various countries. A country which is less advanced than others may be set back in its development, rather than helped, by opening its market to the industries of its neighbors. The most famous case is southern Italy. The political unification of 1860 involved in effect a customs union between southern and northern Italy. The north was helped by uni-fication but the south was relatively hurt. It is apparently not true that southern Italy was as rich per capita as the north prior to unification, but the gap was not nearly so wide as it later became with integration. The problem of less advanced regions is recognized in the provisions of the European Economic Community (EEC) for associate mem-bership—sought by Greece and Turkey—where access to the Common Market is granted, but reciprocal tariff reduction by the less advanced country proceeds at a slower pace. It is also implied in the provision of investment funds for lagging regions. Chapter VIII of the Monte-video Treaty also sets out a series of similar measures favoring the relatively less advanced countries—a status explicitly accorded to Bolivia and Paraguay in a separate protocol. But after signing the treaty Bolivia failed to ratify it, largely on the ground that it was too weak to compete with the more advanced members.

Despite the economic points against trade preferences, and espe-cially the cosmopolitan argument that trade diversion worsens the optimal allocation of world resources, the real problems are political. Trade diversion may well help the underdeveloped countries as a whole at the expense of the developed if the terms of trade improve the gains from trade more than losses from misallocation of resources hurt. But it would aid some more than others. It is all very well for a Latin American economist to say that "the problem of replacement of imports should not be considered by each country in terms of its purely national interests but should be visualized within the broader and more flexible framework of the common interests of all the Latin American countries."[1] In fact, it is impossible for these countries politically to merge their interests when they are competitive in so

[1] Victor L. Urquidi, *Free Trade and Economic Integration in Latin America,* University of California Press, Berkeley, Calif., 1962, p. 11.

many respects. The separate countries believe that they cannot afford to make sacrifices for the general welfare, and especially the poorer countries for the slightly more advanced. In consequence, one country after another pulls back at the last moment.

No underdeveloped country wants to give up its trade preferences in developed areas: those that the Philippines had in the United States, the British former colonial empire in the United Kingdom, or the former French colonies in France. The United States objects to the extension of these last preferences to the rest of the European Common Market, as the former colonies of France and Belgium obtain preferences in Germany, the Netherlands, and Italy, to the disadvantage of the rest of Africa and Latin America. The Trade Expansion Act of 1962 provided the possibility of mutual tariff reductions between the EEC and the United States in tropical products to the point of complete elimination, which would be extended by most-favored-nation treatment to the whole underdeveloped world. French interest in securing a favored position for its former colonies in Africa south of the Sahara makes the prospect of establishing free trade in these products unlikely. Nor is the solidarity between British and French former colonies in Africa such that the latter would be desirous of sharing such preferences.

Preferences for developing countries of the sort allowed by GATT are a controversial issue and nowhere more so than in Latin America. Free-trade economists believe they involve more trade diversion than trade creation, and are therefore harmful. Latin American economists, on the whole, and many enthusiastic developers in advanced countries recognize the problems involved but believe that economic development requires broader markets, protection from the competitive power of the United States and Western Europe, and hence support tariff discrimination for the underdeveloped. But the better way to regard the problem is to look at the limited amount of administrative and negotiating talent available in developing countries and to ask whether these countries can afford to use as much of it as is required by economic integration for that purpose. If it be granted that the benefit is positive, is it sufficient to cover the cost, and does economic integration provide the most effective use of this scarce resource? On this showing, there may be less of a clear-cut verdict in favor of trade preferences.

STABILIZATION SCHEMES

Commodity stabilization schemes have already been touched upon in Chapter 16. Here we need only refer to the difficulties of negotiating and administering such arrangements exclusively among underdeveloped countries, and where they have to provide the finance to buy up surpluses. No such agreement exists today. The stabilization measures in effect in wheat, sugar, coffee, and tin all involve developed countries. Although the tin buffer-stock scheme is financed by the exporters, it is British and Dutch producer interests in Southeast Asia which provide the necessary leadership. It is worth observing that within the overall coffee agreement the Central American countries undertake to restrict production of their high-quality grades even more than called for by their assigned quota, and so do the African producers. This regional cooperation is assisted by the assurances that action is being taken on similar lines elsewhere in the world.

There is no economic reason why underdeveloped countries cannot work out arrangements to stabilize prices—although there is the general danger that the price will be set too high and encourage new entry outside the contracting countries. The most conspicuous example is that of the Organization of Petroleum Exporting Countries (OPEC), which was formed shortly after the price reduction in Middle East oil in August, 1960, with a view to restoring the cut. OPEC consists of Middle East producers and Venezuela. But note the problem of all cartels. The established producers want higher prices and constant market shares. The new entrant wants price control, too, but his main concern is a larger percentage of the market, and he is often willing to cut prices to get it. The long-run interest in price conflicts with the short-run interest in quantity. And there is considerable question whether developing countries can take a sufficiently dispassionate view of their joint interests to set price at a level which will maximize returns over the long run, i.e., not serve to attract new entrants, and be content to adjust market shares from time to time without sacrificing the long-run interest to the short.

TECHNICAL COOPERATION

The most substantial success achieved by regional cooperation has been in the field of technical cooperation. It remains true that the major source of technical assistance is the developed countries. But Colombo Plan experience in Asia and a limited amount of United Nations experience elsewhere have shown that there are real benefits to be gained from narrowing the technological gap between countries and having an underdeveloped country assisted by another which is not far in advance of it. This question has already been referred to in Chapter 14. The outstanding illustration is furnished by the technical assistance arrangements of the Colombo Plan, which undertakes training of individuals for development tasks in neighboring countries and uses experts from Asian as well as non-Asian membership of the Consultative Committee.

Of special interest is the possibility that Japan may be in a better position to furnish technical assistance for other parts of Asia than the United States and Western Europe because of the narrower cultural as well as technical gap. Israel's quest for friends in the underdeveloped world to offset the enemies with which it is surrounded has led it to offer technical assistance to a number of countries, notably Ghana. In Asia, too, Indian experience with community development projects has been made available to visitors from other Asian countries and particularly through visits of Indian experts to Indonesia, where the program has been adopted.

Substantial technical assistance is furnished through regional meetings of experts. The United Nations regional commissions in Europe, Latin America, Asia, and the Far East, and the newest for Africa at Addis Ababa in Ethiopia serve less as planners of development projects or programs, discussed below, than as clearinghouses for ideas. The same is true of the Colombo Plan. Conferences are held on planning techniques, the process of development, and the analysis of developmental blocks. Experience is exchanged. It is evident that intellectual and technical cooperation is much the easiest to organize and carry out. Advice is cheap and can always be ignored. One can learn from strangers or even enemies—the latter is not only possible but advisable —and where the process is mutual, among countries at not too different stages of growth, the highly structured relationship of teacher and pupil, with its inevitable appearance of patronization, is avoided. Not only does intellectual collaboration not require a solid political basis; it can help to build one. The process of intellectual communication and exchange may serve as the basis for ultimate collaboration of a more substantial and expensive sort.

REGIONAL PAYMENTS ARRANGEMENTS

One of the moot questions in LAFTA is whether special payments arrangements should accompany those in trade. Initially the countries with exchange control—Argentina, Brazil, Chile, and Uruguay— wanted to organize a payments agreement along the lines of the highly successful European Payments Union (EPU) under the Marshall Plan. EPU, it will be recalled, replaced a network of bilateral clearing agreements with a multilateral one, and reversed the constricting pattern of intra-European trade by making exports to European currencies earn largely convertible currencies or widely acceptable ones.

In Latin America, however, the difficulties began when Mexico and Peru joined the negotiations for LAFTA. These countries had convertible currencies, and saw no gain in acquiring blocked exchange on the southern members if they experienced export surpluses within the area. Moreover, the prospect for multilateral balancing of bilateral balances is small in Latin America, as compared with Europe. The EPU countries on the average had about 60 per cent of their trade with one another. In addition, the convertibility of sterling within the sterling area made it possible for them to balance off even more of their trade through Britain. In Latin America only 10 per cent of trade is regional. The basis for effective cancellation of multilateral balances on a significant scale does not exist.

Where multilateral clearing and compensation are needed is not in trade within Latin America, but in the trade of separate Latin American countries with European countries. The so-called Hague Club was organized in 1955 by Western Germany, the Netherlands, and the United Kingdom to clear net balances of opposite sign in their trade with Brazil. Austria, Belgium, France, and Italy later joined the Hague Club. A similar arrangement with the same European countries plus Switzerland and the Scandinavian countries was later organized for Argentina as the Paris Club. But the two clubs never merged, and it is evident that clearing of separate countries of Latin America with Europe is more significant than clearing with each other.

For a while there was some interest in establishing an Asian Payments Union, comparable to the European Payments Union. In 1955 the United States, which had contributed $565 million as capital to the EPU, offered $200 million to the Simla conference of Asian countries for regional cooperation, presumably along similar lines. The Simla conference, however, failed to produce any useful suggestions how the money might be used, and the offer was finally withdrawn. The Japanese and the Indians were interested in using the $200 million to finance Indian purchases of capital equipment in Japan. But this was a long way from the original proposal of a revolving fund, presumably one which would revolve more than once.

It is argued that one reason the $200 million offer of the United States at Simla was not accepted was that the sum was too small to make it worthwhile for the countries participating either to overcome their mutual suspicions or to use their imaginations to productive effect. If so, this was the remote cause. The proximate causes of failure were inability of the countries present to agree on a basis for sharing and lack of any proposals which would enable the funds to be used more than twice.

Capacity to share requires a very high degree of social and political cohesion, as the European Recovery Program made clear. In Asia, a number of small countries have said that they wanted to deal bilaterally with outside benefactors and not to be told that their own plans had to be cut back in the interest of greater Asia. Such planning in the "common interest" was too reminiscent of the Greater East Asia Co-Prosperity Sphere. But even if the countries had been able to divide the amount, the United States proposal appeared to call for more than splitting a melon.

RIVER–VALLEY DEVELOPMENT

Much is hoped for from international river-valley development by underdeveloped countries. A number of rivers lend themselves to, or rather require, international treatment—the Nile, rising in Ethiopia, Kenya, and Tanganyika, flowing through the Sudan before reaching Egypt; the Jordan, with its source in Lebanon, serving as a border between Syria and Israel before flowing into Jordan; the Indus (Pakistan, Kashmir, and India); the Mekong (Tibet, Burma, Laos, Thailand, Cambodia, Vietnam); the Helmand, Salween, Zambezi, Congo, Amazon, Orinoco, etc., to name but a few. Some of these present few problems because of abundance of water, remoteness of the source, limited extent of the flow, or other reasons. But the international character of these leading rivers presents a great problem. The basic difficulty is in the division of the water—either its diversion to irrigation, as in the Jordan and the Indus, or the amount of evaporation as a result of dams, which is the difficulty in the Nile and the Helmand. Whether power should be generated and floods controlled by one large dam downstream or many small ones upstream is a debated issue in the United States. Where upstream and downstream lie in different countries, and small dams upstream may so regulate the flow and increase evaporation as to make it impossible to generate power and irrigate on the desired scale downstream, there is evidently room for disagreement. Mexico complains of pollution of the waters of the Colorado River before it crosses the border. While the international regulation of navigation and power on the Rhine is well established and runs smoothly, the Danube has presented difficulties since the split of Europe, and even Canada and the United States have had disagreements on whether and how to develop rivers which run between or in both countries. When the countries are ancient rivals, competitors, or enemies, as in the Pakistan-India dispute, that between Israel and Lebanon-Syria-Jordan, or the Bolivia-Chile Lauca River controversy, the prospects for cooperation are dim.

These difficulties may not be unmixed curses. River-valley development involves high costs and an uncertain and long-delayed return. Even the long-debated St. Lawrence Seaway built by Canada and the United States seems to have been a disappointment in terms of navigation, with overestimate of benefits. Transport as a major object of investment may have a substantial payout, but irrigation and power suffer from high capital/output ratios and are dubious items of expenditure early in the development process. The multipurpose project too readily embarked on, following the TVA analogy, frequently results in monumental waste.

Where it is clear that the payout is high and near in time and the cost modest, river-valley development has much to recommend it. All that is then needed is the political cohesion sufficient to agree on the division of the water, the division of expenses of joint projects, and the sharing of the joint benefits. This is a tall order among friends; impossible between enemies.

REGIONAL PROJECTS

Aside from rivers, it is difficult to find regional development projects. This is not for want of trying. The Inter-American political system, under its various forms, worked for many years before it hit upon the Inter-American Highway, the value of which is largely national and mainly symbolic on the international front, although it may ultimately lead some United States tourists beyond Mexico. In Europe various international bodies such as the European Economic Community and its subsidiary banks and funds, the associated European Coal and Steel Community (ECSC), and so on, do most of their actual investing within the borders of a single country. The canalization of the Moselle has been completed—another river—and the Alps tunnel of France and Italy, the projected Channel tunnel or bridge, and that is about all. Some improvement in the railroad and highway systems may take place. But the main cooperation of developed countries on single jobs is in research: in the fields of atomic energy, defense, and recently supersonic aircraft. After long study, the Economic Commission for Europe (ECE), searching hard for an international project involving southern Europe, has been able to offer only another highway for the purpose of attracting tourists—this time from Trieste to Belgrade, Istanbul, Athens, Patras, (ferry to) Brindisi, Rome, and back to Trieste.[2] There may be merit in exploring whether underdeveloped countries might do more to team up on research problems. Many of

[2] "Southern European Bank," *The Times,* Mar. 31, 1956.

these, to be sure, are undertaken on a worldwide basis by United Nations specialized agencies in health, meteorology, agriculture, and so on. Where developing countries have a common problem in research too large for any one to tackle separately, however, international cooperation might make advance possible.

REGIONAL PLANNING

Numerous writers have urged the creation of organs of regional planning or regional integration of national plans.[3] The Colombo Plan is sometimes cited as an example of what is intended, or reference is made to the European Recovery Program, which was thought to be a "coordinated" or "integrated" plan.

There is merit in expert and ministerial meetings to compare national development plans. This is the nature of the Colombo Plan, which is neither a plan nor an organization but a three-week annual meeting, which disappears for forty-nine weeks of the year, and at which the main task is an editorial one. There is no sharing of external contributions, since developmental aid, except for technical assistance, is furnished on a bilateral basis.[4]

The European Recovery Program went further. There were the recommendations for the amount and sharing of aid. In the single field of oil refining, there was integrated planning, assisted by the fact that the industry involved large units and a small number of companies which were able to lend their personnel to the respective governments for the purpose. A few absurd national projects were frowned upon by the group and abandoned. The Organization for European Economic Cooperation (OEEC) and the European Payments Union provided a means whereby pressure could be brought to bear by the group against the inflationary or other unwise internal policies of a given country, and in favor of trade liberalization, on a discriminatory and

---

[3] See, e.g., W. Y. Elliott (ed.), *Foreign Economic Policy for the United States,* Holt, New York, 1955, esp. chap. 7.

[4] CF. F. Benham, *The Colombo Plan and Other Essays,* Royal Institute of International Affairs, London, 1956, p. 2: "There is no general Colombo Plan Fund, from which loans or grants are allocated to the various Asian members. Each country has its own development programme, which, of course, it draws up and revises from time to time exactly as it pleases. Every offer of assistance, whether financial or technical, is the subject of bilateral negotiation between the two countries concerned, who settle all the details entirely between themselves. Nor does the Consultative Committee, or any other body, exercise any control over either the general planning of a country or its administration of its various projects."

ultimately on a nondiscriminatory basis. But primarily integration was accomplished on a limited basis through the removal of trade barriers and the broad and rough harmonization of monetary and fiscal policies. During the period of acute shortages, the OEEC and the ECE allocated short supplies. Statistics of foreign trade and national income were made comparable and aggregated for the group. But planning in the sense that national programs were laid aside and a single international investment plan was agreed upon was not even remotely approached in the earlier period. International planning by the ECSC may be regarded as an indecisive experiment. In the privately operated field of steel, the removal of tariff barriers, equalization of freight charges, and adjustment of taxes provide for much greater rationalization of production and distribution in Europe. But in coal, where various countries owned and operated mines, less was accomplished. An attempt was initially made to expand production: ultimately the solution of a large surplus arising from underestimation of the inroads of oil led to a breakdown of international adjustment and the resolution of surplus problems on a national and even nationalistic basis.

Foreign-trade planning in the Soviet bloc Committee on Mutual Economic Assistance (CEMA, or COMECON) has no greater successes to its credit. No principles have been evolved for unifying the plans of the separate countries following "planned proportionate development" (whatever that may be). In the spring of 1963, Rumania made it clear that it was not content with the role of producer of raw materials which had been assigned to it, but adjustment of these conflicts appears to be made on a purely pragmatic and *ad hoc* basis.

There has in fact been considerable disintegration and duplication in developmental investment since World War II. The finely articulated jute and burlap industry of British India was divided by partition with jute production in East Pakistan and jute manufacture in the vicinity of Calcutta. Since partition, jute production had been started in India and jute manufacture in Pakistan. The oil refinery at Haifa in Israel has been isolated by blockade and duplicated by new installations at Sidon. The Anglo-Iranian Oil Company has built a large new refinery at Aden to replace the confiscated Abadan installation. The growth of textile industries in virtually every underdeveloped country has brought about world excess and overproduction.

How much regional development boards may succeed in arresting this trend toward duplication and autarchy within regions is an open question. The Alliance for Progress with its "Nine Wise Men" mostly reviews individual country plans to ensure that development programs are reasonably consistent, to see that proper use is being made of external assistance, and to apply pressure for land and tax reforms where these can release energy and resources for development.

Whether the Alliance can go beyond this and plan in the negative sense of removing duplication, or in the positive direction of assigning new industries to countries, is much more doubtful.

One important planning effort falls in the division of aid. In the European Recovery Program this proved so difficult after the first year, and so perverse were the incentives, that the European countries hit on the device of extending the percentages of one year to the unknown amount of aid of the next. But it is not at all clear whether this process should be carried on on a regional basis, since there is a worldwide task of division to be performed. This is the job, for example, of the International Bank for Reconstruction and Development with its regional loan departments for Europe and Africa, Latin America, and Asia and the Middle East. The French and the Soviet Union like the idea of spheres of influence in which one country produces all the aid and assists in its division. This runs counter to American doctrine under which the developed countries have an interest in promoting development everywhere, and no country should benefit or lose from the particular wealth and generosity of its "protector." If regional development boards like the Alliance for Progress were established everywhere, the division of economic aid on a world basis would have to be made once and for all between the various regions; and any attempt to modify the original division would be strongly resisted by the regions which were cut. In a global organization, on the other hand, there is always the possibility of correcting and amending tentative regional breakdowns, by subtracting resources from, say, the Europe-Africa area and making them available to Latin America. The International Bank operates on the working level on a regional basis, as any politico-economic organization must do. Objective criteria governing assistance must be modified to make sure that every country in good standing gets something and that prizes are passed out for economically good behavior. But there is no known continental division. If each region were given a quota, it would be much clearer that a loan for A means less for its neighbor, B, which would be divisive rather than unifying. And where the countries are themselves asked to divide the aid, instead of enlisting the services of presumably objective and disinterested expert groups such as the International Bank, the opportunities for friction are magnified.

THE POLITICAL BASIS OF REGIONAL COOPERATION

It is easy to exaggerate the political solidarity running among underdeveloped countries. United against "colonialism" and capitalistic exploitation and joined as a bloc in the United Nations to vote more projects which aid economic development in general, their interests are often opposed when it comes to development in particular. Some countries have ties which bind them particularly to one developed country or another—the Philippines to the United States, or Morocco and Tunisia to France. In Latin America there is a basic cleavage between the countries belonging to the dollar bloc and those producing commodities which compete with United States exports and maintaining close trade ties to Europe. The jealousy of Latin America over United States concern for European recovery has not been concealed. It would be easy to open up similar divergences of interest between the Middle East and the Far East, or Asia and Latin America. The growth of Ethiopian and Kenyan production in coffee threatens Brazilian long-run interests. The Egyptian assumption of leadership in the Arab world arouses antithetical feelings of pride in Nasser's defiance of the West and fear of his ascendancy over the other members of the Moslem world.

Where the political basis for federation or union exists, larger units are better than smaller. But the test is an exacting one, as the formation and collapse (sometimes more than once) of the United Arab Republic, the Central African Federation, the Federation of the British West Indies demonstrate. Whether the French Communauté or the 1963 formation of the Federation of Malaysia will pass the test remains problematic.[5] The resolve to share at whatever cost has preceded the actual necessity to do so. The political compact does not so much eliminate regional differences as it arranges for their settlement in organized fashion, along with the agreement to face the outside world as a unit.

Where political cohesion falls short of this pitch, however, as is largely the position in the underdeveloped world, limited interests will coincide from time to time and present opportunities for occasional cooperation. To attempt to force more substantial tasks of cooperation on these countries, regionally or otherwise, however, is to jeopardize whatever cohesion they may have achieved.

It has already been noted that the way to political cohesion may lie through efforts at economic cooperation. This is true. But before one can go far in economic joint effort, the political underpinning must be built into place.

The relations between economic and political action are full of

---

[5] It is illustrative of the political difficulties of sharing that the oil-rich Sultanate of Brunei withdrew its adherence to the Federation of Malaysia in July, 1963, at the last minute in a dispute over its financial contribution.

paradox. The economic theorem that trade and factor movements can equalize factor prices has it exactly backward. If free trade and large-scale factor movements be not imposed by the power of the sovereign, they are tolerated in a democratic society only so long as a measure of political cohesion exists, and this cohesion requires an original rough degree of factor-price equalization. Factor-price equalization (or its original underlying social unity) produces free trade and free immigration rather than the reverse.[6]

The underdeveloped countries have this bond in common: they are poor. But there is a great difference in the solidarity of the poor when all know that they are likely to remain so and the stresses and strains which arise among the poor as they compete to climb out of poverty. It may be true that all can make economic progress more effectively together than apart. But there is always the chance that one can move faster and farther alone. This possibility serves as a great inhibitor of regional economic cooperation.

SUMMARY

Regional cooperation in economic development takes many forms, but few of them have contributed greatly. Customs unions and free-trade areas offer the possibility of wider specialization and exchange. There are difficulties in making progress in this field, and the record in Central and Latin America is not a hopeful one. Commodity price stabilization and the division of economic assistance are best done, if at all, on a world basis. Technical cooperation among developing countries offers some hope for success. Payments arrangements and regional planning—except in the difficult river-development field—offer limited prospects at best. Successful economic cooperation on a continuous basis, or integration, requires a degree of political consensus and identity of view which is unusual in developing countries.

BIBLIOGRAPHY

See especially the optimistic and authoritative Victor L. Urquidi, *Free Trade and Economic Integration in Latin America,* University of California Press, Berkeley, Calif., 1962. Raymond F. Mikesell has written a great deal on Latin American integration, knows all the dif-

[6] See G. Myrdal, *An International Economy,* Harper, New York, 1956, chaps. I, II, and III.

ficulties, but remains hopeful. See, for example, his "The Movement toward Regional Trading Groups in Latin America," in Albert O. Hirschman (ed.), *Latin American Issues*, Twentieth Century Fund, New York, 1961, with a comment by Urquidi. See also Robert L. Allen, "Integration in Less Developed Areas," *Kyklos*, vol. 14, no. 3, pp. 315–336, 1961; and Elizabeth Wallace, "West Indies: Improbable Federation," *Canadian Journal of Economics and Political Science*, November, 1961, pp. 444–459, and the first five appendices on development and cooperation in Africa, the Middle East, Southeast Asia, Latin America, and between mother countries and colonies in Jan Tinbergen, *Shaping the World Economy*, Twentieth Century Fund, New York, 1962, pp. 195–261.

THE ECONOMIC INTEREST

Among the numerous and varied interests of developed nations in countries engaged on programs of economic growth, the material ones include direct markets for exports, competition of new industries in third markets and in the home market, sources of supply for imports, and outlets for profitable investment. Growth brings changes in these relationships.

The impact of development on markets for exports of developed countries is a dual one. On the one hand is the market-destroying effect of the establishment of new industries, generally of an import-competing character, frequently designed specifically to substitute for imports. On the other, development raises income in general, which spills over into imports in general, and increases the demand, in particular, for imported capital equipment.

Which of these effects will predominate in any particular instance will depend upon the foreign-trade structure of the developed country and its capacity to transform. If a country is highly specialized in consumer-goods exports, such as textiles, and fairly inflexible, as was Britain in the 1920s, development abroad may be adverse to its exporting interests. By and large, however, there is almost no doubt that the market-creating effects overwhelm the market-destroying. For United States goods, imports of developed countries were $5.80 per capita in 1948, compared with $1.25 for a group of countries only moderately developed, and $0.70 for underdeveloped countries.[1] The correlation between the stage of growth and imports from the United States is not very high, however, as Figure 19.1 shows. Proximity plays a large role for countries in the Western Hemisphere, and special cases like Israel and Japan produce a level of imports higher than the norm. Statistical investigation indicates that more of world trade consists in machinery and vehicles, and less in food, drink, tobacco, raw materials,

---

[1] *Point 4,* Department of State, 1949, p. 10.

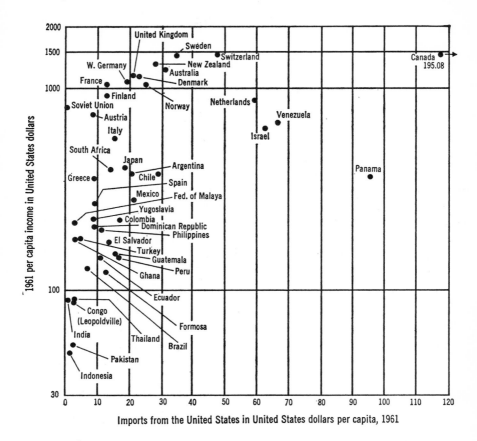

Figure 19.1 | Imports from the United States compared with income per capita, about 1961. SOURCES: Imports from the United States (excluding special category shipments consisting mostly of military supplies) in U.S. dollars, *Yearbook of International Trade Statistics,* 1961, United Nations, New York, p. 680; population, *Monthly Bulletin of Statistics,* United Nations, New York, May, 1963, pp. 1–4; income per capita, table 1.1, Average Income per Capita in Selected Countries, 1949 and 1961.

and textiles, while metals, chemicals, and miscellaneous products hold their own.[2]

Within these broad groups have been changes involving loss of old markets and the creation of new. If developed countries have capacity to develop new products and new ways of producing old commodities and are able to shift resources from old lines of production into new,

[2] See *Industrialization and Foreign Trade,* League of Nations, Geneva, 1945; E. Staley, *World Economic Development,* International Labour Office, Montreal, 1945; H. Tyszynski, "World Trade in Manufactured Commodities, 1899–1950,"

growth in poor countries is on balance stimulating. The old view that the export of machinery is "economic suicide"[3] is virtually dead, although traces of it are occasionally found.

Growth of competition in third markets and even in the home market is a wider extension of the market-destroying effect. The classic case used to be the expansion of Japanese textile trade which pressed Britain everywhere in her colonial empire until Empire preference was invoked to help. Today's classic case is India, inside the imperial preference system, long since a serious competitor for her own market and now shipping cotton gray goods to Britain or Hong Kong. Market destruction in third markets and in developed countries must therefore be added to market destruction in the developing country itself. It is important in particular cases, but still insignificant compared with market creation.

The view that the United States should foster the development of underdeveloped areas in order to expand supplies of imported raw materials was expressed in the Paley Report,[4] and supported by subsequent official studies of the foreign economic policy of the United States.[5] This justification of aid to underdeveloped countries seems contrived. Neither the general necessity for expanded supplies of imported materials nor the likelihood that economic development abroad is needed to achieve them is clear. Where additional imports of iron or petroleum would be useful in keeping down raw-material costs, direct investment, frequently in such developed countries as Canada, may be capable of providing them without general plans of economic development. And such general plans, as a rule, leave little room for domestic investments in raw-materials production. Indeed, the (unfulfilled) prediction that the terms of trade would favor raw materials over manufactures by 1960[6] was based on the assumption that developing countries would allocate incremental or even in-

---

Manchester School, September, 1951, pp. 272–304; A. K. Cairncross and J. Faaland, "Long Term Trends in Europe's Trade," *Economic Journal,* March, 1952, pp. 25–34; and A. Maizels, *Industrial Growth and World Trade, World Trends in Production, Consumption and Trade in Manufactures,* Cambridge, New York, 1963.
[3] See A. O. Hirschman, "Effects of Industrialization on the Markets of Industrial Countries," in B. Hoselitz (ed.), *The Progress of Underdeveloped Areas,* The University of Chicago Press, Chicago, 1952, p. 276, quoting the title of a German tract of 1907.
[4] *Resources for Freedom,* President's Materials Policy Commission, 1952, vol. I, chap. 11 *et seq.*
[5] *Report to the President on Foreign Economic Policies* (Gray Report), 1950, pp. 59–60; Commission on Foreign Economic Policy (Randall Commission), *Report to the President and the Congress,* 1954, pp. 39ff.
[6] C. Clark, *The Economics of 1960,* St Martin's, New York, 1942.

framarginal resources to manufactures as opposed to raw materials in a measure which exceeded the demand requirements for manufactures. It can therefore be argued either way without much confidence in either outcome: development will enlarge or shrink the supply of imports available to developed countries. A policy of assisting development on any impressive scale, however, could hardly be based upon the view chosen.

Finally, it seems likely that economic development will hurt the investment interest of developed countries before it improves them. It is true that developed countries undertake investments in one another, particularly in import-competing, differentiated, and frequently patent-protected products. Canada and the United States both have investments across their mutual border. The United States invests in Europe and Europe in the United States. Before this stage is reached, however, a more painful and difficult period will probably have to be undergone. In this period, political independence and increasing self-confidence on the part of the underdeveloped country and its component sectors are likely to lead to higher wage costs, higher taxes, and increased regulation, if not nationalization or confiscation. The sovereignty of the underdeveloped country is likely to increase along parallel political and economic paths with reduced direction, increased complication, and a reduced share of profit for the owners in the developed country. That conditions will get better after they have gotten worse is some consolation—unless, to be sure, they have gone completely bad during the intermediate stage and cannot recover. But it can hardly be maintained that economic development should be sought by developed countries so as to increase the profitability of their investments in countries now underdeveloped.

On this showing, it is hard to make a case that the development of presently undeveloped areas carries economic benefits for the developed countries which justify their assistance. The export-creating effect, coupled with the long-run favorable impact on direct investment, probably justifies the conclusion that growth is on balance favorable. But in any particular instance, the effect is uncertain, and may run the other way. Moreover, the receipt of benefits from development abroad depends on transformation, including innovation and reallocation of resources, and a country which is capable of these adjustments may be said to produce its own prosperity. It makes little sense as a precept for the conduct of business to subsidize one's customers, or even to teach one's competitors to run their businesses more successfully. There will be occasions, however, when it pays off handsomely.

We conclude, therefore, that economic interests are not sufficient to induce developed countries to assist underdeveloped. Development abroad may redound favorably, and need not hurt. But the argument that no country can be prosperous in a world where there are countries which are not prosperous is rhetorical nonsense. Parts of a country can wax rich, despite poverty elsewhere in the nation and elsewhere in the world. A country needs only enough customers, at home or abroad, and not that every potential customer be as rich as it is. A country can become rich in a world of poverty even without exploiting the poor, as the example of the United States proves—though Marxists will not agree with this statement. To attempt to sustain prosperity through improving the economic condition of all underdeveloped countries runs the risk of neglecting capacity to transform, which is the critical condition of prosperity.

NONECONOMIC INTERESTS

The major noneconomic interests used to justify assistance to economic development today are defense and humanitarianism, to counter the designs of the Soviet Union and to prevent unrest or revolution, which might spread so as to involve other countries and lead to war.

The defense argument is often put in a short-run context, sometimes in more long-run terms. In the former, development is needed to strengthen existing allies, to increase their allocation of resources to defense needs currently and their capacity to produce defense goods over time. In the latter, the underdeveloped country is regarded as committed to a program of development. To give assistance is to win its friendship so that it will become a defensive ally, or "neutral for" the West rather than neutral or active against.

To assist a country's economic development program for the sake of winning friends is not very different from assistance given to counter or match economic assistance given by the Soviet Union. The theory is identical. It assumes that if the West does not give aid, aid given by the Soviet Union will win allies, friendship, or benevolent neutrality for it to the detriment of others. This, then, is a simple variant of the long-run defense interest.

Humanitarian or ethical considerations have been used on the part of mature nations to justify interest in the development of underdeveloped countries—in the Atlantic Charter, the United Nations Charter, the Articles of Agreement of the International Bank for Reconstruction and Development, and in many similar international documents. It is difficult, however, to distinguish selflessness from long-run enlightened self-interest. Even where the motives are clearly separable, the conduct may not be: witness the medical missionary, such as

Albert Schweitzer, and the oil company, each of which establishes clinics and ministers to the health of native peoples. The missionary is unaware, the oil company conscious, of the feedback. Assistance to development on a humanitarian basis can be undertaken because of the existence of the need: or the same action may be forthcoming under enlightened self-interest in the realization that the need, left unfilled, may give rise to trouble. This may not be a specific kind of trouble —the spread of communism, an alliance with the Soviet Union, a fascist movement, or a similar disturbance. It is not necessary to foresee the nature of the untoward result; the more profound insights into social behavior, indeed, suggest that it is impossible to forecast clearly the nature of the outcome of economic, political, and social disintegration.

It is equally impossible to forecast the social and political consequences of economic development. If development gets under way, and the growth of appetite outruns the capacity for satisfying it, or if development brings with it a marked increase in skewness of the distribution of economic wealth and political power, development itself may lead to anomie. All that can be said as justification of programs of assistance to economic development is that the chances of avoiding political and social disintegration, such as results from a sharp dichotomy between social needs and their fulfillment, is likely to be greater when economic development is assisted from abroad than when it is not. Such is the increase in communication and transport, and such the narrowing of intellectual distance, that economic aspirations of most countries have increased. In some cases, this increase has not yet penetrated deeply into the peasant, the fellah, the Latin American Indian, or the untouchable. But it is under way. National leaders, the middle class, the urban proletarian—all are conscious of the gap in levels of living and economic power between developed and underdeveloped nations and are determined to close it by one means or another. A program of assistance to underdeveloped countries by developed ones will assuredly raise aspirations, along with capacity. It is likely, however, to raise capacity more than short-run aspiration, and hence to assist in closing the gap. So long as economic progress is being made with help from abroad, the chances of social breakdown with the creation of power vacuum into which new power is violently sucked may be reduced.

This is by no means assured. Dankwart Rustow, a political scientist, has called political stability as a consequence of economic development "a vanishing dream," and his plea for direct assistance to political growth to parallel assistance to economic growth emphasizes the new uncertainty over the exact nature of the relationships running between increases in income and growing political unity and widening participation in the political process.[7] A great deal of research is going forward in this field, and theories of political development, or modernization, complete with stages, and substitution of one ingredient for another, or for differences in initial conditions, are in process of formation. At the moment, therefore, one cannot be certain whether economic development will promote peace or disturb it.

This, then is not a solid argument or rationale for assistance from abroad to underdeveloped countries; it is nonetheless the primary argument. And it has an important corollary. The underdeveloped countries are bound and determined to make progress in economic development. If they receive assistance from the developed countries, they may or may not succeed in achieving that development while maintaining political freedom and benevolent neutrality internationally. If, on the other hand, they do not receive aid, their chances of failing to develop, and therefore undergoing internal convulsions, or of adopting totalitarian methods to make progress toward development, and succeeding or failing, are increased. The gamble involved in assisting development may not be very appealing, but it may be more attractive than the gamble of standing idly by.

In a cynical view, foreign aid is nothing more than the traditional bribery which those countries that have arrived pay to the barbarians to stay their advance. Hans Morgenthau, the political scientist, divides United States foreign aid into six types: humanitarian (to help in periods of disaster), subsistence (especially in impoverished countries such as Jordan), military, bribery (supporting particular regimes in Korea, Vietnam, Taiwan, etc.), prestige (for the construction of objects of conspicuous industrialization), and aid for economic development. All but the first, in his view, are political, in that their purpose is to advance the foreign interests of the United States. And all should be, he thinks, since "foreign economic aid is too important to be left to the economists."[8]

To the purist, of course, aid should involve cost to the donor but not benefit; and benefit to the recipient, but no cost. When the donor gets a benefit, the transaction becomes a purchase rather than assistance. It is difficult to include as aid British foreign lending at commercial terms or German short-term loans at substantial interest rates tied to export transactions. Or the benefit may not be economic, as in the

[7] Dankwart Rustow, "The Vanishing Dream of Stability," *AID Digest,* U.S. Department of State, August, 1962, pp. 13–16.
[8] Hans J. Morgenthau, "A Political Theory of Foreign Aid," *Political Science Review,* June, 1962, pp. 301–309.

French support of budget deficits in those of its former colonies which maintain their foreign policies allied to France. Where the cost is negligible, moreover, as in United States grants of surplus agricultural commodities, the transaction may be regarded as aid to the recipient (benefit without cost), but not for the donor. The point has importance when it comes time to assign shares of the burden of foreign aid among contributing countries.

Of course, aid for one purpose can often be diverted to another if the recipient country has some capacity to transform. Assistance received for military use can be diverted to economic through reducing the domestic allocation for defense and raising that for development. Or vice versa. Aid for specific purposes assumes partial-equilibrium analysis, with other things equal. If other things can be changed, the assistance can be diverted. This is the principal objection to restricting foreign assistance to particular projects of an approved sort, rather than programs which cover a country's full range of resources. The assisting country can be handed a collection of projects which would have been undertaken in any event, and the resources freed by the transfer used for quite other purposes.

LOANS OR GRANTS

The writer sees little merit in grants. Whether or not charity begins at home, it has nothing to do with development. The sharing of treasure is appropriate to defense, war, and reconstruction from war, and to alleviate human suffering from disaster. Defense, reconstruction, and relief grants are therefore appropriate. Grants may also assist in raising consumption, for which charity is appropriate. But development is a business matter. Since loans are not available privately on a business basis, governments which have awakened or heightened expectations as to rates of development can appropriately make loans for economic development.

There are a number of arguments in favor of grants which are invalid or, more politely, which involve a number of implicit assumptions not necessarily appropriate. The aid may be for some project which neither expands exports nor substitutes for imports. This does not mean, however, that it must be financed by grant because it cannot produce the foreign exchange to meet debt service. Other things need not be equal. If the project is really productive, it will free other resources for export expansion or import reduction, to enable the debt to be serviced. Nor do public goods, such as roads, mean that foreign help must take the form of grants. If they are really productive, some part of the productivity should be capturable through the fiscal mechanism and provide resources for incremental exports or import-saving. A long delay between investment and output is again no basis for insisting on grants rather than loans. The cost of the investment is its initial cost plus the compound interest on that and other costs until its product is forthcoming. The yield of the project should be measured against this cumulated amount, not the original cost. It is legitimate to borrow the initial cost plus the interest until the flow of output reaches its long-run level, and for this amount, foreign debt service should be available through export expansion, import substitution, or the transformation process.

When a good is both public and of a long payout, with the addition of uncertainty as to yield, as in foreign expenditures for health and education, there may be some warrant for grants rather than loans.

But the major reason for grants rather than loans is to raise the level of living. Consumption loans provide no base for debt service, as loan sharks have demonstrated in many countries of the world. Aid for disaster or aid to raise the level of subsistence cannot provide its own repayment and should be on a grant basis. But in development aid, where projects are truly productive and the economy aided has enough capacity to transform to suggest that it is a good development bet, the presumption should be that aid would take the form of loans. The significant questions are how much and on what basis.

THE AMOUNT OF LOANS

Reference has been made in Chapter 17 to scientific attempts to establish the appropriate amount of international loans. Most of these are rather unscientific. The balance-of-payments criterion applied in the European Recovery Program (for the first year) is backward—it is not the program which determines the balance-of-payments deficit so much as the balance-of-payments deficit that can be financed which determines the program.[9] Moreover, its incentives are perverse. The worse a country performs in terms of limiting consumption and raising the

[9] See F. Machlup, "Three Concepts of the Balance of Payments and the So-called Dollar Shortage," *Economic Journal,* March, 1950, pp. 46–68. This dictum applies less completely to the ERP where the program was partly determined by the requirements of reconstruction, having in mind some historical and politically required levels of living, than it does to economic development. There may, however, be a touch of a politically necessary level of living in development, because of aroused expectations, which makes some of the causation run from the program to the deficit.

marginal propensity to save, the worse its balance of payments and the greater its need.

The concept of capacity to absorb capital developed by Millikan and Rostow and discussed above[10] is not entirely free from these ambiguities. Capacity to absorb capital is partly a balance-of-payments notion, with the proviso that consumption is held down and all the complementary resources for capital formation are available. But suppose that there are two countries which differ in no respect except the marginal propensity to save. Is their capacity to absorb capital equal or different? If they attempt to form the same amount of capital, and the one with the lower marginal propensity to save runs a higher balance-of-payments deficit, should it get greater foreign loans or not? What if the government made every effort to raise the marginal propensity to save, but failed because the country had previously always lived within its means and therefore lacked the heavy burden of agricultural debt which soaks up savings so rapidly when income rises?

Millikan and Rostow, moreover, tend to toss aside their criterion of loans on the basis of capacity to absorb. In estimating how much capital their program would absorb, they divide the underdeveloped countries into two classes: those whose development is already under way, and those not.[11] The latter are estimated to absorb something like 30 to 50 per cent above existing levels of capital formation, and so are the former, even though their capacity to absorb capital is certainly higher.

One objective criterion would be strictly economic bidding, with a fixed amount of loans allocated among underdeveloped countries according to the rate of interest offered. But this sets an inappropriate standard. It is assumed that loans would be contracted at rates of interest approaching the marginal productivity of capital in the United States, or the rate at which asset holders are willing to part with their liquidity to hold United States bonds and the equivalent. This should be well below the marginal productivity of capital in underdeveloped areas after complementary resources have been found or provided for. The demand for capital should thus exceed the likely supply at the going price. Some basis for rationing should therefore be found.

There is no scientific basis for rationing. The process is clearly a political one. So is the international division of the costs of a war, or the agreement on contributions to the costs of the United Nations, or

[10] See pp. 325ff.
[11] See M. F. Millikan and W. W. Rostow, *A Proposal: Key to an Effective Foreign Policy*, Harper, New York, 1957, pp. 98ff.

the quotas in the International Monetary Fund. Economic criteria can help approach the stage where the bargaining gets intense. In the League of Nations formula there was an amalgam of percentages of world income, world trade, etc., which gave the basis for final negotiation. In the final analysis there must be a consensus that the division of aid is somehow right. The more that appeals to economic formulae are convincing the more they assist in the political process. But it remains political.

There is also an important question of how to share the burden of aid among the donors. Here, again, a balance-of-payments criterion is wrong. A country should not cut its donations to economic assistance of developing countries because its balance of payments is in deficit any more than a rich man should cut his contributions to charity because his bank balance is unseasonably low. In charity, as in taxation, the widespread equitable standard is income, not liquidity. Most observers, moreover, would agree on a progressive basis for economic assistance rather than a proportional one, i.e., a system under which countries with higher per capita incomes give higher rather than equal percentage contributions of national income, compared to lower. In a significant article, Rosenstein-Rodan has attempted to estimate the aid needs of all the countries of the world and share the burden of assisting them on the basis of the United States income tax schedule. Only countries with more than $600 per capita income per year—the standard United States exemption—would contribute at all, and the contributions would be progressive. On the basis of real GNP per capita, with the U.S.S.R. not contributing, the United States would be expected, on the basis of its internal schedule of personal income tax, to pay some 65 per cent or approximately $3 billion of annual aid estimated at $4.5 billion.[12]

The nature of the sharing process raises the question whether future allocations out of a possible second provision of loan assistance should be geared closely to performance on the first. The difficulty is that need and incentives may be perversely related: the better a country has used its initial aid, the less it needs and the more it deserves, and the converse. The point should be familiar to economists in public finance who worry about the effects of taxes on incentives. They conclude that all taxes on sales or on income have adverse effects on incentives, and welfare considerations require a most impractical system of lump-sum progressive taxes, i.e., taxes levied on capital, which leave

[12] See P. N. Rosenstein-Rodan, "International Aid for Underdeveloped Countries," *Review of Economics and Statistics*, May, 1961, pp. 107–138, esp. p. 137.

people with the incentive to earn all they can, and progressive in that they take more revenue from the people with higher incomes (or capital).[13] The same holds true for subsidies or partial subsidies, which is what loans at less than the marginal productivity of capital come to: these should be lump-sum progressive subsidies so as not to distort incentives. This means that the loans should be decided on without reference to performance so that no country would have any incentive to waste its resources. But only those countries which have some capacity to form capital with foreign assistance should receive loans.

If foreign loans are not to be granted to the point where they equate the marginal efficiency of capital in the United States (and Western Europe), on the one hand, and the underdeveloped countries, on the other, the amount of such loans on an annual basis is also a political question. How much should the United States spend on schools each year? There is no scientific answer because there is no necessary amount of training that a young man or woman should have, nor any necessary ratio of expenditure to students.[14] We should spend on schools what we feel is needed to bring them up (or down) to the standard we have in mind, given the various other objectives of common expenditure and the rate at which we are prepared to tax ourselves. The same is true of loans for foreign assistance.

The question of the amount to be spent for schools is somewhat easier than foreign aid because we have a long history of educating our children, and we are dealing not with a new objective of expenditure but with changes in an existing one. The same might be said of foreign loans except that most people are conscious of the fact that we are not doing nearly enough to meet the expectations that have been aroused, so that the change in the rate of expenditure should be substantial rather than of the normal order of magnitude of such changes.

[13] See J. E. Meade, *Trade and Welfare*, Oxford, Fair Lawn, N.J., 1955, p. 49.
[14] The scientific answer is, of course, that we should equalize the marginal utility of the tax dollar spent on schooling with that of every other dollar spent for given purposes. In the absence of capacity to measure this marginal value, it is possible to say only that we should spend a little more on this, and less on that, with a fixed government revenue or, if all objects of government expenditure have a higher marginal utility than objects of private expenditure, that we ought to increase taxes to meet new governmental needs. Senator Taft's frequently repeated warning that foreign aid would make the United States bankrupt meant primarily that he did not value foreign aid as much as he did objects of private expenditure, and so was unwilling to tax for the purpose. In part, however, it might have meant that the United States was prepared to spend on foreign aid without raising the necessary revenues in taxes for the purpose, which leads to inflation.

CONDITIONS OF AID

There is a considerable and persistent temptation on the part of various groups, represented in the Congress, to use the fact of international aid, as in the European Recovery Program, to gain short-run ends for the United States. Various special interests urge the restriction of aid to goods shipped in American bottoms or goods covered by American insurance policies. Aid is sometimes tied to general United States interests, such as the provision of raw materials for the defense stockpile. Certain branches of government, including the legislative, are interested in acquiring local currencies for expenditure by the United States government, generally for purposes which would not have merited as much attention if it had been necessary to appropriate the monies directly for them, e.g., congressional travel and the construction of handsome embassy offices and residences.

Apart from these mundane interests, there is a temptation to use the bargaining power inherent in capacity to give or withhold aid to secure other United States interests, both political and ideological. In the political realm, aid may be offered as a reward for taking part in defense pacts or to gain bases. Ideologically, there is the urge to advance United States positions on other fronts, particularly when this country is convinced that the United States position would benefit the other country as well. The abandonment of neutralism would be one such requirement, closely allied with defense pacts. Less politically touchy, the British loan was made to win British adherence to the doctrine of multilateral trade and convertible exchanges. Many voices were raised in the European Recovery Program to insist on agreement to an enlargement of the European economy through some sort of customs or economic union: others wanted to obtain renunciation of socialism as a *quid pro quo* of aid.

In 1963 the Congress of the United States became thoroughly worked up over the issue of an AID loan for a government steel plant at Bokaro in India on the ground that it was aiding socialism. The suggestion that the United States assist this large and expensive project costing more than $1.5 billion was American in origin and arose from the feeling that United States aid had been used in ways which did not strike the imagination of the Indian people. A special committee headed by Lucius D. Clay appointed by President Kennedy to make recommendations on foreign aid opposed the plant on the ground that it was state-operated. Private Indian steel interests indicated their unwillingness to tackle a project of the contemplated size. American steel companies expressed certain technical reservations without speaking to the socialism-capitalism issue. But the congressional reaction was highly ideological, rather than pragmatic.

Most ideologues, of course, regard themselves as pragmatists. Professor Friedman of the University of Chicago opposes all foreign aid on the ground that it extends the influence of government in the development process, which he regards as deleterious to development. In a widely cited article he urges the United States to stop all foreign aid and to compensate underdeveloped countries by eliminating tariffs on imports from these countries into the United States.[15] The pragmatists, on the other hand, incline to regard each government project on its own merits and to judge whether the government concerned has the capacity to administer aided projects, or a program as a whole, as enlarged by aid. In this connection it is worth recalling that the Burmese government recently found itself dealing with sixty-nine separate governmental and nongovernmental aid agencies and sent home all but ten, including among the ejected AID and the Ford Foundation, because of the impossibility of treating with so many (and to emphasize its political neutrality).

A particularly tricky question is posed by aid to a country which confiscates property belonging to the donor's nationals. The United States cut off aid to Ceylon, where American oil properties were nationalized, and faced similar decisions in Latin America when similar action was taken against utilities by a Brazilian state, but not the national government, and against oil production by Argentina. Where the action is based on pure xenophobia arising from incapacity to handle domestic development problems, there may be a case for stopping aid because of the poor development prospects. But actual cases are never pure. And where growth and nationalization (with compensation) are possible, aid based on the strict objective of economic development may be obliged to overlook a disagreeable attitude on foreign property.

Opposed to these positions of conditioning aid on ideological grounds is one that assistance should be given with no strings attached. In defense of this position it is asserted that to lay down conditions is to compromise the sovereignty of the country receiving aid or to interfere in its internal politics. This is too simple and idealistic by

---

[15] Milton Friedman, "Foreign Economic Aid: Means and Objectives," *Yale Review*, June, 1958, pp. 500–516. P. T. Bauer attacks United States aid to India as promoting too much government control, but stops short of recommending the termination of aid. See his *United States Aid and Economic Development*, American Enterprise Association, Washington, D.C., November, 1959, esp. pp. 104ff.

half. Sovereignty is not inviolable, nor are internal politics sacrosanct where they stand in the way of development. Development by itself changes the balance of political forces, as the next chapter will indicate. And if the borrowing or assisted country chooses to reject aid which imposes conditions that will ensure its effective use, it protects its "sovereignty" at the expense of its long-run sovereign interest.

Another position, and the one advocated in these pages, is to require as a condition of aid that every possible effort be made to proceed expeditiously toward economic development, wasting neither domestic nor foreign resources, insofar as possible. This requires careful analysis of the development program of the country to ensure that its premises are realistic and its objectives within reach. It also generally entails some machinery for analysis of future plans and evaluation of current progress.

If the sole condition of foreign aid is that it be used effectively, the abridgment of sovereignty which comes from consultation with foreign missions, with the International Bank, or a United Nations agency is supportable. If such outside forces are to be effective, moreover, they must take positions on issues which are subjects of internal struggles, and thereby find themselves interfering in internal politics. Where very weak governments exist, it may even be helpful to establish a system of counterpart funds, under which the local-currency proceeds of goods procured with foreign aid and sold in the domestic economy are sequestered and spent only with the agreement of the granting agency or country. The deflationary effect of the foreign aid is more readily maintained when these proceeds cannot be spent without regard to their monetary impact. The forces in the government standing for monetary sobriety are strengthened. But counterpart funds are not the means to impose budgetary restraint on a country which lacks any semblance of it: central-bank loans to the government can inflate as rapidly as or more rapidly than any increase in counterpart funds can bring about contraction.

In Latin America, as already indicated, the Alliance for Progress has made land reform and tax reform the touchstones of a domestic resolve to tackle internal development difficulties and especially the domination of politics by a landed oligarchy. But weak governments find difficulty in pushing through major reforms. They want the aid first, whereas the donor wants the returns first. Like Gaston and Alphonse going through a door, there is danger of stalemate.

The administration of conditions of foreign aid is full of pitfalls. If a country is committed to manifestly uneconomic projects of development, it may be impossible to persuade it to modify its development program and undesirable for political reasons to withhold assistance altogether. United States–Egyptian experience over the High Dam at Aswan does not provide the appropriate illustration. This project was first supported and then rejected on political grounds, although the excuse given for rejection—that the project was too large and involved too long a commitment of too much Egyptian savings before any increment in output would be realized—should have been the basis for an initial refusal to give support. But when the Egyptian government or any other acquires an *idée fixe* in developmental programming, it is difficult to say yes or no.

Interference in domestic affairs is inevitable, as has been suggested, since all developmental change involves a shift in the strength of opposing political forces. Where the primary condition of assistance is its productive use, this may require foreigners to approve action which will harm the class in the society which is most friendly to them politically. This is hard. But where long-run and short-run interests are thus opposed, the former should prevail. Since underdeveloped countries are too poor and frequently too politically ineffective adequately to safeguard their long-run interests at the expense of the short-run, it is necessary to administer development loans in such a way as to promote the future when it is under attack from the present.

ADMINISTRATION

The major issue in the administration of loan assistance is whether it should be done by a political body or by experts, and whether in the former case the lending should be on an international or a bilateral basis. The issue is political rather than economic. But it is sufficiently important to warrant some attention.

The case against bilateral arrangements is that they provide opportunity for exploitation and political interference. The major argument in their favor is that international bodies have their own particular form of political behavior not free from logrolling, deals, or bloc voting. The suggestion that multilateral administration is somehow more likely to operate on the basis of principle instead of *ad hoc* expediency or power politics is frequently put forward but has little basis in fact. Where principles are well established to the point of being cut and dried, international administration is desirable but gains very little. Where objective criteria are elusive and principles of administration must be developed by accretion, it is safer to have programs prepared by experts, adopted by international bodies, but subject to the veto of the contributing nations—or roughly the formula of the Marshall Plan. The Alliance for Progress officially follows this formula, with national programs approved by the Nine Wise Men, representing both expertise and political interests, before an approach is made to national and international funds. Latin American demands for a more direct voice in allocation led to the decision late in 1963 to name an individual coordinator, but it was not clear that this new official could have much power.

In a democratic country it is possible to have the many, through their representatives, tax the few for objects of common expenditure, since there is a fundamental political compact, whether written or understood, under which expenditures and taxes are voted. In international matters, such understanding is still lacking. The underdeveloped countries lack the power to tax the developed and must therefore win their consent for the amount of subsidy contained in loans below the marginal product of capital in underdeveloped countries. It makes sense that this consent should be explicit in the continuous administration of intergovernmental developmental loans rather than implicit in the discontinuous replenishment of funds when the pool runs out. To give a contributor of 72 per cent of the funds only one vote in seventeen, where no objective principles of distribution have been devised, as was true of UNRRA, is to run the risk that the recipients and minor contributors will use the aid for purposes for which it was not created. And in these circumstances the project is likely to be wound up by the major donor when the fund runs out.

OTHER EFFECTS

Loans and grants are by no means the only way in which developed countries affect the rate of growth in underdeveloped countries. Direct aid is also provided through technical assistance, discussed in Chapter 14. But the indirect effects are also of great importance. In some of these the developed country may not even be conscious of the impact it has.

The most obvious, the most frequently cited, and the most important indirect means of assistance to underdeveloped countries is the stabilization of the economies of the developed countries at high levels of employment. This contributes to the steadiness of the prices and volume of exports of primary products in developing countries and to the stability of the availability of private capital, much of which is dependent for its investment in underdeveloped areas on the expansion of markets in developed.

With high, stable, or expanding levels of output in developed countries, it would still be possible to have considerable fluctuations in the demand for the exports of primary-producing countries if there are inventory cycles, generated by speculators or by business consumers. There is perhaps little that governments can do to counteract this source of instability for developing countries, except not to add to it. It was inexcusable during the Korean conflict for the United States government, through its defense stockpile, first to join the private market in bidding up the prices of tin, rubber, wool, etc., and then at the top of the market actively to undertake to drive these prices down. Governments are expected to get less panicky than private dealers and to lean into the wind.

Whether it is possible for the developed countries to go further than abstaining from destabilizing speculation is a troubled question. Underdeveloped countries are naturally eager for schemes of commodity stabilization, financed by international contributions, which would come largely from developed countries. Until there is agreement on methods of such stabilization, there is little to be done. Proposals abound for stabilizing all commodity prices, individual commodity prices, export proceeds of underdeveloped countries, to ensure terms of trade, to provide automatic access to the International Monetary Fund when terms of trade or export proceeds fall by a stipulated percentage, and so on. At the time of writing these and other proposals were scheduled to be debated by the United Nations Conference on World Trade, called for the spring of 1964 at the insistence of the underdeveloped countries which believe that the present system of trade somehow provides an ineffective setting in which they can develop. It seemed unlikely that positive conclusions could emerge from that conference for lack of consensus in the field. The cry of "Trade Not Aid" originally heard from Europe has been adopted by the developing countries, with, however, the strong implication that the trade to be substituted for aid is to be stabilized on an expanding basis, unlike any other trade previously known. There is much that the developed countries can do to admit simple manufactures among imports, to reduce tariffs on coffee, tea, cocoa, and bananas, and to stabilize their own economies. But innovations in trade beyond these analytically simple and politically difficult measures are unlikely. "Trade and Aid" is perhaps a better slogan.

The major negative requirement, perhaps, is to make aid to development through grants, technical assistance, and loans at less than the demand price for capital available to underdeveloped areas without insisting on short-run concessions in the area of defense and political commitments. There will be countries which will need defense aid, and will ask for it. Here it can be granted, along with but separately from developmental assistance. As other countries make developmental headway, moreover, their neutralism may be threatened from other directions, which in turn may lead them into closer understanding of the defense problem. But an unwilling ally is of little help in crisis, and bought friendships are no bargain, however cheap.

We conclude that the developed Western nations have a long-run political interest in helping the rest of the world to catch up with their economic development or at least to make a rapid start in raising their national income. There are many negative aspects to this interest: it is not economic, nor defense, nor diplomatic in the short run. It involves, moreover, a gamble; for there is a chance that economic development as a slogan creates larger appetites than it can satisfy and is politically disruptive. Nonetheless, it seems clear that the continuous shrinkage in the size of the world and the heightened mutual awareness among continents and peoples which that shrinkage brings call for greater political and social cohesion to preserve stability and the very survival of the earth. Toward the goal of this cohesion some equalization of incomes among nations is needed. Developed-country support for developing nations with no strings other than its efficient use is enlightened self-interest.

SUMMARY

The arguments for developed countries aiding the development of the underdeveloped rest less on economic and short-run political grounds than on long-run political. Rising national expectations must see some prospect of satisfaction, or low-income countries are likely to be prey to economic, political, and social breakdown, with convulsive results. In its pure form, aid involves a cost but no benefit to the developed country, and a benefit but no cost to the aided. Aid for restricted purposes can be diverted to others if the country aided can transform its own resources.

There are difficult problems in devising an optimum method of dividing a given amount of aid among developing countries and assigning the costs among the donors—although the tax system of some country can be used for the latter. In economic terms, the most appealing condition of aid is that the aid be used with optimum efficiency. In practice, particular acts like land and tax reform are likely to become touchstones of such head-on tackling of development problems. Opponents of foreign aid question whether it does not promote socialism, or government domination of the economy. There is much sentiment for international administration of aid, but some political difficulty in using it until there are accepted principles for its distribution among donors and recipients.

BIBLIOGRAPHY

A useful little book is F. Benham, *Economic Aid to Underdeveloped Countries,* Oxford, Fair Lawn, N.J., 1961. For a wide-ranging debate, see *Why Foreign Aid?* Rand McNally, Chicago, 1963, in which Max F. Millikan defends foreign aid, and Morgenthau and Banfield attack it. The Rosenstein-Rodan article cited in footnote 12 is indispensable as an illustration of the view that amounts of aid can be worked out objectively and divided among recipients, with the burdens assigned to donors. See also Irving Kravis and M. W. S. Davenport, "The Political Arithmetic of International Burden Sharing," *Journal of Political Economy,* August, 1963, pp. 309–330. The Clay report mentioned in the text is the *Report of the Committee to Strengthen the Free World,* released by the White House, Mar. 22, 1963. A somewhat outdated case study is Charles Wolf, *Foreign Aid: Theory and Practice in Southeast Asia,* Princeton, Princeton, N.J., 1960.

VICIOUS CIRCLES

One can conclude from the foregoing that economic development is a difficult and complicated business. There is the difficulty of charting a course and steering the developmental process after a start has been made. There is also the difficulty of getting development under way.

Poverty abounds in what the cliché expert calls vicious circles. The Malthusian circle keeps countries poor by expanding their numbers when increases in output occur. "The rich get richer and the poor get children." The capital circle is also familiar. At low incomes it is impossible to save enough to form new capital.[1] "It takes money to make money." But there are other circles and paradoxes.

It has been noted, for example, that industrialization needed to relieve population pressure tends at an early stage to introduce improved health. This increases the rural population, causes excessive fragmentation of landholdings, and becomes one of the chief sources of rural migration to the cities to increase population pressure there.[2]

How does a developing country escape the paradox of income distribution? To accumulate savings on a nationwide basis requires austerity, which in turn demands equality of sacrifice and more equal income distribution which reduces savings; but to promote high profits as a source of savings for capital formation may lead to unrest, on the one hand, and may fail to produce socially desirable investment, on the other, since the profit-making classes are not necessarily interested in the common good.[3]

---

[1] See "Extension Is Voted for Colombo Plan," *New York Times*, Oct. 2, 1955: "A vicious circle has developed. . . . Development is checked for lack of financial resources; resources remain low for lack of development."

[2] *Processes and Problems of Industrialization in Underdeveloped Countries*, United Nations, New York, 1955, p. 121.

[3] D. R. Gadgil, *Economic Policy and Development*, Gokhale Institute, Poona, 1955, p. 181.

Poor countries, which need strong government more than rich, have less chance of having it.[4]

Underdeveloped countries have difficulty with their terms of trade: when they are adverse, they lack the resources needed for economic development; when they are favorable, they lack the incentive.[5]

And yet, despite the barriers presented to economic development by this amount of negative feedback, economic development *has* occurred as part of an unconscious process, generally in not very densely populated areas. It has also occurred as a consciously willed objective, as in Japan and the Soviet Union, the former fairly densely populated. How does a country break out of the stable equilibrium or vicious circle of poverty into an area where the process of development becomes interacting and cumulative?

DEVELOPMENTAL STARTS

The answer to the foregoing question is that we don't know. Theories abound; opportunities for rigorous testing are limited.

In unplanned development, as in Western Europe, the most important dynamic force seems to have been the evolving character of the people, and particularly of the "new men," the merchants and bankers, who gradually worked themselves free from the confining embrace of feudalism. Where, in Southern and Eastern Europe, the middle class was weak and ineffective, dependent upon the landed classes and subservient to them, it was because it had failed to reach the size and strength to enable it to challenge the old order. Up to a certain critical level of the middle class, the vicious circle perpetuates itself; beyond it, change becomes the established order—self-perpetuating and interacting change in capital formation and technology.

The process has been historically slow. In Britain the Reformation of the sixteenth century led to political revolution in the seventeenth century and the Industrial Revolution in the eighteenth, before the rapid period of development in the nineteenth. In France, Germany, northern Italy, western Austria, Bohemia, and Scandinavia, the pace was faster after a slow start. And in many areas—southern France, Spain, parts of Italy—commercial revolution failed to be followed by industrial revolution for reasons which are not clear.

One cannot quickly dismiss the role of climate in giving rise to the

[4] W. A. Lewis, *The Theory of Economic Growth*, Irwin, Homewood, Ill., 1955, p. 382.
[5] *Repercussions of Changes in the Terms of Trade on the Economies of Countries in the Process of Development*, United Nations, E/2456, June 11, 1953 (mimeographed).

initial breakthrough from the vicious circles of underdevelopment. In the period of unconscious development, international communication was limited, cultures were isolated and independent, and culture change occurred primarily as a consequence of internal stimuli.[6] Where economic energy was required to produce an adequate level of living in temperate climates, it was relatively easy to develop more energy and for it to push on in other directions and break out of the restraints of tradition. Where the climate was benign, on the other hand, the output of economic energy was initially low and lacked the internal stimulus to reach the cumulative, self-reinforcing stage. When the external stimulus was provided, however, as in Japan in the nineteenth century and in Asia and Africa in the twentieth, climate was not such a barrier. Some such line of reasoning is needed to explain, with Huntington, why high levels of economic development have not been reached in the tropics in modern times and still to leave room for the possibility of tropical development in future. As A. J. Brown, M. Bates, and T. S. Simey have emphasized, the inhabitants of the tropics today are undernourished, not lazy, while the enervation experienced by the white man under tropical conditions is cultural, not physiological. When the external stimulus has been provided, there is sufficient energy to meet the requirements of growth.

With planned development, it is not clear how the vicious circle is broken. There may be no unique way. Japanese experience differs substantially from that of the Soviet Union. In the former, the economy was kept open, imitation of Western technology took place on a wide front, an entrepreneurial class was grafted onto the old class society with the adoption of the institution of private enterprise and the use of the price system to allocate resources and distribute income. In the Soviet Union, on the other hand, the emphasis was on industrial capital formation, first and foremost, with the application of enough compulsion to achieve the necessary resource allocation and restriction of consumption. The Soviet capital-cumulation pattern may or may not be capable of transformation into one where a desired degree of consumer choice and pattern of income distribution are achieved.

CUMULATIVE GROWTH

Once growth has started, the questions become what does it consist in, what keeps it going, what slows it down and brings it to a halt. Our

---

[6] This is subject to wide qualification, as, for example, the forcible impact of some cultures on others—Moorish and Christian, Spanish and Aztec and Incan, French and British and North American Indian, etc. In addition there was economic stimulus, such as that received by the Crusaders from the Moslem world.

discussion was divided into five ingredients and two aspects of change —resources, capital formation, labor, technology, and organization in the first category, and scale and transformation in the second. But these convenient labels, it will be recalled, are not necessarily conceptually distinct, either from one another or from the noneconomic factors. Resources must be defined in terms of technology; technological change springs from the social structure, as does the capacity to transform or the desire to resist transformation. Physical capital equipment is difficult to distinguish analytically from improved land or from investment in human capital, i.e., education. Once growth has started, the question is mainly whether it is further changes in people which speed the process, or primarily the accumulation of capital which feeds on itself.

It may be well to recur to the human analogy used in Chapter 1 to describe growth in relation to income per capita. What is the nature of the growth process in people? As a person grows, is the basic change physiological, or does it lie in the metamorphosis of his social, emotional, or technical capacity? Is a grown person more effective at producing income than a child because of his larger size, his wider technical education, his possession of more tools and implements, or his greater interest in economic well-being? The questions answer themselves. There is no unique way to describe the growth process, and it is foolish to insist on one. Growth involves a dynamic interacting system of linked changes. The *causa causans* lies deep in some control mechanism—possibly the endocrine glands insofar as physiology is concerned; but it has a variety of social and cultural dimensions which are linked to the physiological in ways unique for separate cultures. The economic equivalent of the endocrine glands remains perhaps to be discovered, but even if it is isolated it is not clear how much matters will have been advanced.

We have suggested in Chapter 4 that resources above a certain minimum volume are not critical, since changes in technology and increases in capital can be substituted for them. This is acceptable as a very general statement. Yet it is troublesome that Japan, which we regard as having been through the developmental process, has such a low income per capita. Is Japan developed or not? With $400 per capita of income in 1961, it ranked with Malta, Argentina, and Jamaica as an underdeveloped country; and yet it has achieved scale, undergone transformation, and formed capital in cumulative fashion, which is the essence of the developmental process. For a considerable time it appeared that Japan could be regarded as developed in terms of the process, but underdeveloped insofar as levels were concerned. More recently, the acceleration of the process with a number of years of growth at 10 per cent per annum or better has suggested that Japan has freed itself from the confines of its narrow resource base and is likely to achieve a high level of living too.

STRATEGIC FACTORS IN GROWTH

The interrelations among resources, capital formation, social structure, technology, scale, and transformation are, as has been said, many and complex. The random elements in the growth process are innumerable and important. The contingencies, as the historians say, overwhelm the invariable relationships. And yet it appears that the social factor is in many ways the strategic element. This is true in a positive sense in unconscious or private-enterprise development, and negatively true where development is imposed from the top. Where private forces bear the brunt of the responsibility, capital formation and technical change are both functions of the social position. The open society, with social mobility, opportunities for workers with energy to rise to the middle class, and for the upper classes to achieve distinction in ways which are socially productive, provides incentives for saving and for innovation. In those societies where government assumes the leadership in efforts at economic betterment, development can be blocked by unwillingness or inability of the masses to respond to work incentives, to assume burdens of austerity, and to turn their backs on traditional ways without becoming rootless and restive.

Emphasis on the social element leads to priorities in investment in transport and communication, on the one hand, and in education, on the other. The distinction between producers' and consumers' goods is important here. Transport and communication are designed to link markets and promote personal contacts but not necessarily to provide for pilgrimages to religious places or for family visits. Education equally should be biased in practical ways and limited in its attention to the higher reaches of cultivation, beyond those important to social cohesion.

Transport links markets as well as people. As such it increases elasticities, improves the efficiency of the price system, and permits the achievement of economies of scale in production and distribution. Education also sends out its effects in many directions. The spread of calculation is basic to income maximization. Capacity to communicate is needed for organized markets with formal prices. A minimum of rationality and understanding of cause and effect are prerequisites for changes in techniques. And universal education through grade school (preferably high school) must underlie the effective recruitment of the foremen, supervisors, straw bosses, and shop stewards on whom effective organization of production and distribution at basis rests.

Transport, communications, and education are therefore general investment priorities. Some observers add electric power. Decisions must be made in separate cases on the basis of the facts. But to admit electric power into the select circle of priority investments in principle is difficult. Its introduction has a large element of demonstration effect in it; it requires the use of capital in proportions frequently inappropriate to the factor endowments existing and in short-run prospect in underdeveloped countries. Many of the multipurpose hydroelectric projects, as contrasted with thermal, yield a very low rate of return. It is true that the International Bank has made many loans on power projects, and there may be an irreversibility about technology, which means that it is impossible to produce today with methods which were in vogue at the turn of the century when there was little electric power centrally distributed. Moreover, there is something to be said for the attraction of technological assistance from developed countries, and from the young men and women of underdeveloped countries who have been educated abroad and "corrupted" by Western levels of living, which would come from the provision of electric power in houses—making possible air conditioning, food refrigeration, efficient lighting, etc. Charles Issawi at the Harris Foundation lectures in Chicago in 1951 mentioned " 'lectricity" as one of the "four L's" of development. But it is possible to have reservations.

Are there strategic factors beyond investment priorities for transport and education? What about balance, the secret of all development problems, as Lewis says? Or cheap foodstuffs, which make capital formation possible? To emphasize transport and education is simply to assert the view that there are external economies to be had in investment in these areas. There may be other external economies. In particular situations, indeed, the economies in transport and education have been fully exploited. But the demand for balance implies the view that the price system does not function at all, in contrast to external economies which claim that it does not function in all particulars. If the price system is made to work, increased investment in agriculture will be indicated when the price of foodstuffs has risen relative to other goods. One of the secrets of development, recommended here instead of balance, is the use of the price system to the fullest extent possible, taking into account economies of scale and without too many shortcuts in anticipation of changes in demand and supply of factors.

There is a temptation in developing countries to interfere in the price system in a variety of ways—overvaluing the exchange rate, buying up farm produce below the urban market price less transport, establishing controls over price, allocation, or distribution. Where governments interfere in the price system and then make investment decisions because the price system does not work effectively, there may be an opportunity to economize by eliminating two offsetting sets of actions.

Admittedly, the price system does not work perfectly, as the discussion of economies of scale makes clear. The question is whether to ignore it or work with it, whether to plan investment and to a considerable extent output, because elasticities of demand and supply are low—demand does not turn away from items in short supply, nor do resources rush in to produce them—or whether to encourage more responsiveness to price, and to change prices where external economies, or internal economies blocked by monopoly behavior, make price ineffective. Again circumstances will alter cases, but the general predilection of the writer is to salvage the most that .can be saved of the price system. It is more economical of administrative talent to rely on private incentives. There is less chance of the enormous errors which freewheeling outside the price system can bring in monumental and wrong investments. An effective price system encourages those social responses which are the strategic basis of development—rationality in perception, specificity in interpersonal relations, and universalism in choice of roles. The market is a school as well as an engine of distribution.

RELATIVE VERSUS ABSOLUTE GROWTH

This book has focused on the problems of getting development started in underdeveloped countries and of keeping it going. Very little attention has been paid to the *rate* of development, so long as it is positive, or to the question whether development can be revived after it slows down. Many of these problems belong to the economies of middle and old age rather than early youth. It makes little sense to worry whether a baby will end up five or six feet tall when the question is whether the growth process can be stimulated at all and brought safely through the problems of infancy, childhood, and adolescence.

For some purposes, however, growth is seen as a closing of the gap in the level of living between developed and underdeveloped countries. So long as the rate of growth in the rich nations is as high as anywhere in the world, growth is not taking place elsewhere on this showing, because the gap is widening rather than narrowing. This attention to relative rates of growth makes sense for some problems, particularly in fields of defense or long-run politics. But for the most part what counts is whether the underdeveloped country is growing at all. Differences between positive rates of change are less significant than the difference between a positive rate of change and static equilibrium. The slower rate of growth once under way can pick up speed —and of course can slow down too. And the higher rate of growth has the prospect of slowing down. The Gompertz or S curve of growth applies more or less roughly to growth problems. On only a small portion of it can geometric rates of growth be extrapolated, and then not for long. New technological change, or spurts of investment, or even deep-seated social resolves can stimulate new growth processes at the flattening part of the curve as rates of change die down. Institutionalized research and competitive innovational investment may even carry the secret of eternal economic youth. If so, they may be open for all countries when a higher level of income has been achieved. But I doubt it.

There is no reason, then, for a developing country to lose courage because of the gap between its level of living and that of developed countries, a gap which is growing wider in absolute and possibly even in relative terms. It is sufficient at the early stages to get the growth process started. Too little is known about it, much less about how the rates can be sustained and how rejuvenated when they slow down. It is a sufficient achievement to get economic development under way.

Richard S. Eckaus | *Appendix on Development Planning*

The calculated and purposeful direction of economic policy toward development has an obvious appeal in those poor countries where ambitions far exceed reality. Since these economies have not produced satisfactory levels of living for their populations, there is an obvious although not necessarily warranted intimation that they may do better with economic planning. Aside from the understandable passion for new policy instruments, there are good reasons to believe that there are special justifications for planning in the less developed areas. These reasons arise mainly from the relative lack of effectiveness of conventional market processes in bringing about drastic changes in economic processes. Yet such changes are necessary if economic growth is to begin from the low levels of activity which now characterize the less developed areas. The inadequacies of the price system in overcoming the obstacles to economic growth are discussed in Chapter 11 above.

Planning can be conceived and carried out in widely different degrees and detail and with a variety of instruments. Moreover, as pointed out previously, any type of economic policy involves some commitment to planning to the extent that projections are made and direct and indirect methods are used to guide the economy.

THE APPEARANCE AND THE REALITY

The emphasis in the less developed areas now is on conscious and explicit planning. A substantial amount of attention is being given to the subject at all levels. Professional economists are producing a steady stream of alternative planning "models," or analytical schemes, of increasing intricacy. Committees, commissions, and councils are

widespread; and private, national, and international planning conferences abound on the "Why," "What," and "How" of economic
planning. Yet in spite of all this apparent activity, the reality of economic planning is relatively uncomplicated and straightforward. In
most of the less developed countries, even among those most committed to a "planned" development, the type of plans made is relatively simple and addressed to specific and obvious problems rather
than being complex and overall.

A recent conference of United Nations experts provides an example
of the difference between the appearance and the reality of economic
planning. This conference was called with the intention of developing
practical methods useful to "practicing" planners. The product was a
pamphlet embodying some of the more sophisticated frameworks of
mathematical economics.[1] However interesting the analytical schemes,
it could not possibly be claimed that they will be applied in the near
future anywhere. First of all, the authors were not successful in making their proposals intelligible to the intelligent, but nonspecialized,
civil servant. Second, while the data requirements of the planning
models are not insuperable, they cannot, with few exceptions, be met
anywhere in the near future.

Yet, though there is now a vast distance between the scholarly proposals and the practical procedures used in planning, the gap is diminishing. Thus, both the simple techniques currently employed and
the more complex procedures of the future should be appreciated.

THE LANGUAGE OF PLANNING[2]

"Static" is used in some circumstances as a synonym for "bad," and
"dynamic" as if it meant "good." In the language of planning, however, these words usefully distinguish conditions existing at a point of
time, which sometimes may be defined as a year or even five years,
and the pattern of conditions changing over time, respectively. Dynamic plans are, therefore, more ambitions than static plans in that
they attempt to specify a time path of change, while static plans are
content with describing the situation of a particular hour, day, month,
year, or plan period. The components of economic plans are the

[1] *Programming Techniques for Economic Development,* report by a group of
experts, United Nations, 1960.
[2] For a useful discussion of language and methodology see J. Tinbergen, *Economic
Policy: Principles and Design,* North Holland Pub. Co., Amsterdam, 1956, and
Centralization and Decentralization in Economic Policy, North Holland Pub. Co.,
Amsterdam, 1954.

"variables." The *data*, which are known or "given" and are not within the range of influence of the planner, include the economy's endowment of natural resources, its inheritance of capital equipment from previous generations, and the technical parameters of production processes. The *target variables* are those whose behavior is the ultimate concern of the planner and the object of the plan, e.g., the consumption of individuals or the growth rate of the economy. The *instrument variables* are those subject to the control of the planner and may include tax rates, monetary policies, or industrial licenses, depending on the type of control. No matter how comprehensive the scope of the planning model, there will always be some variables which are irrelevant for policy, such as the number of traffic tickets or perhaps immigration or emigration where they are relatively small. Of course, which variables are *data* or *irrelevant*, *targets* or *instruments*, depends on such factors as the comprehensiveness of the plan, the types of economic tools available, the time horizon, and also the certainty with which behavioral relations are known. The rate of growth of population, for example, is generally believed to be related to the level and rate of change of economic activity. Yet, since the nature of the relationship is unknown, population growth is usually treated as a datum in economic planning even when policies for changing it are part of the plan.

THE PROCESS OF PLANNING

Making economic plans requires specification of the *choice elements* or target variables, the tracing of their implications, and the determination of the instrument variables by means of an analytical planning framework. One of the choice elements is the set of output targets fixed for some future date. These may be specified in terms of per capita levels or total output levels and will in either case include provision for continuing growth after the target year if, of course, that is not also the millennium. The *terminal year* of the plan or what amounts to the same thing, the *planning period*, is also a choice element and a part of the decision about how the benefits of growth are to be shared. *Intermediate consumption* levels are choice elements, as is the *initial level of consumption*. The initial endowment of productive resources is a datum. The initial subsequent allocation of productive resources to growth-producing purposes or to current consumption depends on all these choices.

The structure of an economy and of a realistic planning process does not permit any complete set of choice elements to be specified in advance. Economic planning is intended to direct development along predetermined lines to predetermined goals. Yet no amount of planning will be capable of bringing India or Indonesia to the current per capita income level of the United States in the next ten, twenty, or thirty years, or even to the current Japanese level. The rates of growth implied are just too high in comparison to previous growth records. Plans with such targets are just not feasible. On the other hand, there is no single path which a country must follow; there are many alternatives. When all but one of the set of choice elements has been chosen, the fourth set can be worked out along with the other implications of the plan.

However conscientious economic policy makers may be, it would be unrealistic to suppose that they are aware of all the feasible and *consistent* choices open to them and that they can in advance specify a set of choices so that the economy will optimize, i.e., do as well as it possibly can. This exceeds the capabilities of the most nearly omniscient politician or civil servant. The analytical planning process should itself be used to generate alternative plans from which the policy makers may then choose. Alternative sets of choice elements should be clearly specified and their implications then traced out. The planning process working in this way would provide a set of "menus" of alternative feasible programs, each doing as well as possible, given its respective specifications. The policy maker could then see clearly the implications of one or another choice and, hopefully, make his choices more rationally.

This is the ideal procedure whatever the level of detail or scope of economic planning. Unfortunately, it is seldom, if ever, achieved. More typically, the making of one plan absorbs all the energies of the available technicians and is the focus of attention of the entire political process. It is subjected to partial revision and compromises, the implications of which are not fully explored. This concentration on preparing a single plan without alternatives is partly the result of misunderstanding the planning process and partly the result of devoting inadequate resources to the planning effort. Finally, the economic analysis necessary for rational planning is itself still at an early stage of development and has not yet been fully understood.

PLANNING MODELS

The forms which planning models take depend on their intended scope and the tools available for implementation. A highly disaggregated plan framework tracing the evolution of many separate productive sectors and the consumption of a number of different income groups is hardly suitable for a country whose politics and/or administrative capabilities restrict it to a rather general and overall set of policies. A highly aggregated static model is inadequate for the task which many countries set of detailed supervision of their economies. There is, therefore, no single best planning theory or model. Each country and each set of circumstances requires a "tailor-made" procedure. Nonetheless, the different approaches fall into a few broad categories which can be described.

PROJECT PLANNING

Economic planning of individual projects and sectors is like speaking prose. Every country does it whether or not it is aware that it is "planning." Roads have to be built, ports constructed, schools put up, and these projects preferably done in a time and a manner which avoid the wastage of bottlenecks, on the one hand, or of excess capacity, on the other. In many of the less developed areas governments exercise direction or control or ownership in particular industries and for these may exercise detailed supervision of current operations and capital formation. The procedures in these cases are not so different from those followed by individuals or private businesses in the normal course of affairs. As in the projects of individuals and businesses, there are, of course, enormous differences in the foresight and effectiveness with which such projects are executed. In the least advanced countries where economic change is embryonic, overall planning of any sophistication would often be quite pointless; the basic facts of population size, growth rate, occupational distribution, agricultural output, and so on are not known with any degree of confidence. In such areas, which include some of the newer African and southeast Asian countries, government planning for economic development at best means planning to resolve some of the most obvious problems for a few sectors.[3]

Planning in these areas often starts with education. Since too often there has been little education of any kind, it is easy to make a survey of the existing resources. These will nearly always turn out to be desperately limited. At this point, if not before, it will become obvious that some painful choices must be made. General literacy is a promise of most new constitutions; yet the available teachers and most other

---

[3] See the forthcoming book, *Planning without Facts* by Wolfgang Stolper, Department of Economics, University of Michigan.

educational resources will be inadequate to fulfill this promise in a short time and there will also be other important educational goals. Doctors and engineers will be wanted; college graduates for the civil service; high school graduates as technicians, supervisors, and nurses. Not all desirable goals can be simultaneously achieved. Choices must be made among future targets and the intermediate use of teachers to create the kind of general education or special skills which are like physical capital in that they contribute directly to economic growth.

The next stage is a step into the unknown: educational "planning" is in its infancy in spite of the fact that, at least in implicit form, it is done everywhere. There are no simple and easy criteria for education. Little is known about the contribution of various types of education to economic growth in spite of the fact that recent studies have demonstrated, if anyone had doubted, that education does make a contribution. Educational planning is in practice done as a kind of manpower planning.[4] Projections are made, usually on the basis of tenuous comparisons with other countries, of future requirements for persons with various levels of skills and education. On this basis and with whatever allocation of resources to general literacy is politically and economically feasible, educational plans are made.

Frequently, where overall planning is not feasible or considered necessary, it will be clear that a special project or set of projects will dominate the economic future and should, therefore, be the subject of programming. Such projects will often be apparently straightforward: producing more coffee or cocoa in some African countries or setting up a steel mill in Turkey or a papermaking plant in Nepal. In projects of the latter type, technology and technicians can be imported, although there are many local problems. In the former type, the nature of incentives and of producers' response to them, which will affect the costs and benefits of the project, are difficult to determine. Likewise, in a project such as that intended for the Volta River in Ghana, which encompasses aluminum and irrigation, the projection of costs and benefits will be quite difficult.[5] For example, regional roads might legitimately be considered a cost, but it is not clear that new housing should be. Increased agricultural productivity from irrigation is a benefit, but so is the gain from flood control and the latter cannot be so easily measured. Of course it is important for the purposes of a

---

[4] E. g., Frederick Harbison, "High Level Manpower for Nigeria's Future," in *Investment in Education, the Report of the Commission on Post School Certificate on Higher Education in Nigeria,* Federal Ministry of Education, Lagos, 1960, pp. 50–72.

[5] *The Volta River Project,* statement by the Government of Ghana, Government Printing Department, Accra, 1962.

persuasive loan request that the proper costs and benefits be taken into account.[6]

MACRO PLANNING

The first step, and in some cases the only step taken, toward overall economic planning is the projection for the future of a consistent set of national income accounts.[7] This is essential in order to know what amount of resources or output the economy will command. In this exercise also alternative sets of *choice elements* can be subjected to initial tests of feasibility and general goals of development can be expressed.

Suppose the current national income or gross or net national product is symbolized by $Y(0)$, current population as $P(0)$ and the population growth rate by g. Then national income must also grow at the rate g in order that per capita national income in any future period t, $Y(t)/P(t)$, may maintain itself; that is

$$(1) \qquad Y(t)/P(t) = Y(0)(1+g)^t/P(0)(1+g)^t$$

If the overall objective is a different higher growth rate for per capita national income, say r, then $Y(t)/P(t)$ should be $[Y(0)/P(0)]$ $(1+r)^t$. Since $P(t) = P(0)(1+g)^t$, then national income must be

$$(2) \qquad Y(t) = Y(0)(1+g)^t(1+r)^t$$

National income by final use is not easily computed by estimating and adding up the value added in each sector. Nonetheless in a macro-planning exercise the breakdown by use is a natural step. A goal may be formulated for per capita consumption $C(t)/P(t)$, for some future period, or equivalently by aiming for some growth rate from initial levels. The consumption sector will usually be subdivided between *private* and *government* consumption; the latter being most directly under central control. Exports may be projected on the basis of past behavior and, with a little bit of imagination, imports and foreign aid as well. This leaves investment as a residual: $I(t) = Y(t) - C(t) - G(t) - E(t) + M(t)$, where in period t, $I(t)$ is aggregate invest-

---

[6] For a sophisticated approach to sectoral planning, see T. Vietorisz, "Sector Studies in Economic Development Planning," in A. S. Manne and H. M. Markowitz (eds.), *Studies in Process Analysis*, Wiley, New York, 1963.
[7] As an example see the *Schema di Sviluppo dell'Occupazione e del Reddito in Italia nel Decennio 1955–1964*, popularly known as the "Vanoni Plan" for Italy.

ment: $C(t)$ is aggregate private consumption; $G(t)$ is aggregate government consumption; $E(t)$, exports; and $M(t)$, imports. Such a set of accounts will often be made for each year of the conveniently or conventionally chosen plan period of five years, or ten or fifteen years if "long-term" planning is the goal.

It will be at this point, if it has not previously occurred to someone to do so, that the following calculation will be performed

$$(3) \qquad \frac{\sum_{t=1}^{n} I(t)}{Y(t+n) - Y(t)} = \text{capital/output ratio of the plan}$$

(Note that $\sum_{t=1}^{n} I(t)$ is the sum of all investment undertaken during the plan period of n years.) In many instances a causal interpretation is read into the relation: so much investment times the inverse of the capital/output ratio will create so much additional income. The assumption that investment is the only thing necessary to achieve this implies that it is the only "scarce factor," and that skilled labor, natural resources, managerial talent, government organization are all available and waiting for the additional investment.

More sensibly, the capital/output ratio is treated as an observed or observable relation which has been found to take on a certain range of values, depending on the initial economic conditions and the pattern of development. There has been a good deal of experience in calculating capital/output ratios based on observed experience as well as on projected intentions. Still it has not been possible to establish a one-for-one relation among any set of these variables. Even so, it is often possible on the basis of this experience to form a judgment as to the plausibility of a capital/output ratio implicit in a macroeconomic plan projection and, therefore, on the plan itself.[8]

Further deductions from macroeconomic projections are often made by use of a labor force/productivity ratio, $Y(t)/L(t)$, where L is employment and separate information can be developed for the ratio. Multiplying national income by the inverse of this ratio produces an employment estimate.

The macroeconomic information also serves to compute a domestic savings rate since total domestic investment must be based on domestic savings plus foreign investment in the country which is $M(t) - E(t)$. Again, previous experience in the particular country

---

[8] For an example of the critical use of capital/output ratios see, W. B. Reddaway, the *Development of the Indian Economy*, Irwin, Homewood, Ill., 1962.

studied and in other countries makes possible an informed judgment as to the plausibility of the savings ratio.[9]

Rather than allowing the savings rate and capital/output ratio to remain implicit, these ratios are now more frequently used to prepare the plan projections. Implicit ratios will in any case be exposed eventually by the criticism of the economists who have not participated in the plan preparation or by the impersonal study of some United Nations expert or Ph.D. candidate.

With a capital/output ratio B, and assuming a one-year lag between investment and the resulting output, the following system can be constructed with the income accounts simplified by ignoring the government and foreign sectors and putting all investment on a net basis

$$(4.1) \quad Y(1) = Y(0) + 1/B\,I(0)$$
$$(4.2) \quad Y(2) = Y(1) + 1/B\,I(1) = Y(0) + 1/B\,I(0) + 1/B\,I(1)$$
$$(4.3) \quad Y(3) = Y(2) + 1/B\,I(2) = Y(0) + 1/B\,I(0) + 1/B\,I(1) \\ + 1/B\,I(2)$$
$$(4.4) \quad Y(4) = Y(3) + 1/B\,I(3) = Y(0) + 1/B\,I(0) + 1/B\,I(1) \\ + 1/B\,I(2) + 1/B\,I(3)$$
$$(4.5) \quad Y(5) = Y(4) + 1/B\,I(4) = Y(0) + 1/B\,I(0) + 1/B\,I(1) \\ + 1/B\,I(2) + 1/B\,I(3) + 1/B\,I(4)$$

This outline of a five-year plan can highlight many of its most important aggregate aspects, though it remains highly simplified in focusing only on capital and investment and their overall relationships.

The productivity of capital $1/B$, and the lag of output behind investment are important in the plan. These are taken as technological parameters in the macroeconomic exercise and unfortunately are often considered not susceptible to incentives and organization. Yet they are only partly determined by technology and depend very much on the efficiency with which men and equipment work. The effects of the initial level of output and, therefore, of the initial endowment of resources are revealed in this outline as is the importance of the preplan investment activity, $I(0)$. By making saving, and therefore investment, a linear function of income, the plan is converted into a Harrod-Domar-like model in which the capital/output ratio and the savings rate determine the rate of growth. The plan framework has now become explicitly dynamic.

In the Harrod-Domar type of planning model the initial conditions are part of the data. If the plan period is set and the savings/con-

[9] See P. N. Rosenstein-Rodan, "International Aid for Underdeveloped Countries," *Review of Economics and Statistics*, vol. 43, no. 2, pp. 107–138, May, 1961.

sumption ratio and the capital/output ratio are fixed by technological and behavioral relationships outside the model, everything else is determined: the target incomes for the end of the plan and the intermediate levels and rate of growth of consumption.

The analytical framework above can also be used to illustrate other approaches to planning. Suppose that the plan period and plan target are specified as well as the initial level of income, consumption, and investment. The question then posed is: what uniform rate of growth of consumption in the intervening years would be consistent with these choices? The analytical framework in equations (4) could be rewritten with investment in each period the residual after consumption and consumption growing at a constant rate g. In the resulting system of equations only g would remain as an unknown and could, therefore, be determined. This would be the rate of growth of consumption *consistent* with the other, specified choice elements. By making different specifications of $Y(5)$, $Y(0)$, and $C(0)$, values of g consistent with them can be mapped out. Alternatively, the three other choice elements could be specified and the consistent values of the remaining fourth choice element would be determined.

While the approach described above emphasizes consistency, there is in the literature of planning a good deal of discussion of *optimizing*. In order to define an optimization procedure a *criterion* must be specified. "The best of everything" is not in this world. Since the results of an optimization procedure are quite sensitive to the choice of criterion, it has to be made with care. Maximizing consumption in the target year, for example, would require using up all available capital for that purpose and making no provision for future growth. Thus, although the choice of criterion may be a matter of political taste, it cannot be made rationally until its full implications are recognized, and these are not always obvious. Maximizing the level of employment, for example, might force the use of the most labor-intensive procedures whether or not they were the most efficient.

Constraints must be added to an optimizing criterion to ensure that when achieving the optimum certain minimum conditions are also satisfied. Maximizing the rate of growth with no constraints would force consumption and other "nonproductive" uses of inputs to the lowest possible subsistence levels to enable as much output as possible to be plowed back into producing more output. Therefore, if it is the growth rate which is to be optimized, constraints will ordinarily be added in order to ensure certain desired minima of consumption.

A simple, aggregate optimizing planning framework which extends the previous model would optimize with respect to total consumption over the plan period: $C(1)$, $C(2)$, $C(3)$, $C(4)$, $C(5)$. This would require the definition of a criterion or *objective function*. It could be just the weighted sum of the consumption items in the different periods

$$(5) \qquad W_1C(1) + W_2C(2) + W_3C(3) + W_4C(4) + W_5C(5)$$

Or it could be a more complex utility function

$$(6) \qquad U[C(1),\ C(2),\ C(3),\ C(4),\ C(5)]$$

which has the property that equation (5) does not have of declining marginal utility of consumption in any period. One of the problems in making optimizing models operational is the inherent difficulty in specifying a utility function.

Production conditions also have to be specified for consumption and investment goods, if these are to be distinguished

$$(7) \qquad C(t) = F_c[L_c(t),\ K_c(t)], \text{ for } t = 1, 2, 3, 4, 5$$

and

$$(8) \qquad I(t) = F_I[L_I(t),\ K_I(t)], \text{ also for } t = 1, 2, 3, 4, 5$$

F_c and F_I indicate the production relationships which determine output when the inputs of labor and capital used in consumption-goods production, $L_c(t)$ and $K_c(t)$, and the inputs into investment-goods production, $L_I(t)$ and $K_I(t)$, are specified.

The amount of labor used in each period can be no greater than the amount available, $L(t)$, which is assumed to be determined exogenously, or

$$(9) \qquad L_c(t) + L_I(t) \leq L(t), \text{ for } t = 1, 2, 3, 4, 5$$

Likewise, the amount of capital used can be no greater than the total available in any period. This is

$$(10) \qquad K_c(t) + K_I(t) \leq K(t), \text{ for } t = 1, 2, 3, 4, 5$$

Capital is produced by the system and, except for the initial period, is not determined outside the model, as is labor supply. The initial availability of capital is determined by pre-plan conditions; that is

$$(11) \qquad K(1) = K(0), \text{ where } K(0) \text{ is given}$$

For subsequent periods the availability of capital can be no greater than the initial endowment and previous production of investment goods, neglecting depreciation for the purpose of this exercise

$$(12) \qquad K(2) \leq K(0) + I(1)$$
$$(13) \qquad K(3) \leq K(0) + I(1) + I(2)$$
$$(14) \qquad K(4) \leq K(0) + I(1) + I(2) + I(3)$$
$$(15) \qquad K(5) \leq K(0) + I(1) + I(2) + I(3) + I(4)$$

Objectives for the terminal year must also be specified; in this case this can be done by stipulating the capital stocks desired for that year. That is

$$(16) \qquad K(5) = \text{stipulated amount}$$

Now (5) or (6) can be optimized subject to conditions (7) through (16). By varying (16) a range of "best alternatives" could be mapped out. This menu would be more interesting and useful than any single solution of the optimizing model, as it would demonstrate to the planner the consequences of alternative strategies.

MULTISECTORAL PLANNING MODELS

Although planning in aggregate terms is most common, the economic issues which present themselves to planners arise most frequently at the level of the industry sector or even of the firm. This is clearly the case where planning is associated with exchange controls or investment licensing. In these circumstances decisions must be made on an industry and firm-by-firm basis. Even overall controls have differential effects on various sectors, and if the planner has overlooked these, they will be brought to his attention by industry and other interest groups. On the other hand, review of sectoral progress comes naturally to the most aloof of planners, in large part because his data come to him in that form. The national-income estimates most easily available are built up from information on value added by sectors; only at a later and more difficult stage can one estimate the uses of national output. Thus, the progress of agriculture, and more specifically, the production of different crops, and of industry and its separate sectors, naturally present themselves for consideration.

Where there is no attempt to exercise direct controls, sectoral forecasts may be desired in order to help formulate goals and general policies and to estimate needs for related government programs in, say, road building or education. In those countries where detailed controls are exercised, methods must be found to provide guidance.

Even in its simplest form the multisectoral planning problem is quite complex: to project sectoral output levels, investment requirements, and the allocation of resources by sectors for production, consumption, investment, and other purposes. Since controls are often exercised at the most disaggregated level, the objective of multisectoral planning models should be to provide detail. In other cases, in which general controls are used, more aggregate approaches may be adequate.

When planning is carried on for a number of sectors of the economy, the problem immediately arises of coordinating the sectors. This emerges, if in no other way, when the attempt is made to set consistent targets. Suppose, for example, that a breakdown of national income by producing sectors is followed by establishment of future targets for development. This exercise may be carried out for such major sectors as agriculture, mining, manufacturing, and services or in many-sector detail which distinguishes, perhaps, several different types of agricultural production and mining, twenty or more manufacturing sectors, and so on. Because of the interrelationships among sectors, their target output levels cannot be set independently of one another. If there is to be some amount of railway cars produced, there must also be some steel. Steel is required in other engineering industries as well. On the other hand, there is no point in producing more steel than is necessary for current maintenance purposes and other final uses, including exports, and as an input into other industries. Thus, the target outputs of the steel industry must be consistent with those for railway cars, machinery, and so on; the output of machinery must be consistent with the targets for petroleum production, and the latter consistent with chemicals and transport and, in turn, with steel targets.

How can the consistencies required by the interdependences of sectors be maintained in planning? One approach is to estimate statistical relations among the sectoral outputs. For example, steel output X_s might be found to have a statistically significant relationship with the production of transport equipment X_t, nonelectrical machinery X_m, electrical machinery X_{em}, and construction X_c, in the form

(17) $$X_s = aX_t + bX_m + cX_{em} + dX_c + e$$

where a, b, c, d, and e may be estimated by multiple-correlation techniques. Such an approach presupposes that time series or cross-section data exist for industry outputs in sufficient detail to make the estimation procedure reasonable. It also presupposes the maintenance into the future of the previous relationships with no way of taking into account prospective changes in structure-of-industry interdependences. For advanced countries in which changes in interindustry relations are marginal rather than fundamental, this method can give reasonably good results. When these conditions are not satisfied, another approach is necessary which explicitly takes interindustry relationships into account. The "input-output" accounting system can do this.[10]

The output of steel, denoted now by the symbol X_i, must include all of its uses as an intermediate product in all industries X_{ij}, where J is a subscript which indicates every industry and deliveries to final uses. These final uses are for private and government consumption, X_{iC} and X_{iG}, respectively, investment X_{iI}, and exports X_{iE}. However, since the uses of steel include imports, in order to keep X_i equal to domestic production imports, X_{iM} must be subtracted. Thus

$$(18) \quad X_i = \sum_{j=1}^{n} X_{ij} + X_{iC} + X_{iG} + X_{iI} + X_{iE} - X_{iM},$$

for sectors 1 through n

$\sum_{j=1}^{n} X_{ij}$ indicates the sum of deliveries of steel to the sectors 1 through n being considered. Of course, what is true for the steel industry is true for every other industry, so i runs from 1 through n as well. Such relationships can be shown in a tabular or matrix form in Table A.

Summing across a row from columns 1 to n gives the total intermediate uses of the product of any sector. Adding up the next five items in a row, imports with a minus sign, gives the total of final uses or *bill of goods* for the sector. The sum of all items in a row is equal to the total output of a sector. Adding all items in any column also gives the gross output of any sector. The sum of the first n items when subtracted from the column total is equal to the sum of wages, rent, interest, and profits or value added.

Table B presents a condensed input-output table for India for 1953–1954 where all measurements are in crores (ten million) of rupees.[11]

The next step is to transform this accounting scheme into an analytical tool for planning. Establishment of static consistency among sectors in a target year might be the objective. Suppose that the deliveries of one sector to another could be related in the target year in the following way

$$(19) \qquad\qquad X_{ij} = a_{ij}X_j$$

[10] An excellent description of input-output accounting methods and analysis is given in H. B. Chenery and P. Clark, *Interindustry Economics*, Wiley, New York, 1959.
[11] From Jan Sandee, *A Demonstration Planning Model for India*, Asia Publishing House, New York, 1960, p. 8.

Table A

Column					n+1	n+2	n+3	n+4	n+5	n+6
	1 2 ..j ..n				Consumption		Investment	Exports	Imports (−)	Total output
Purchasing sector / Row producing sector	Intermediate uses				Private	Govern-ment				
	1	2 ..j ..n								
1	X_{11}	$X_{12}..X_{1j}..X_{1n}$			X_{1C}	X_{1G}	X_{1I}	X_{1E}	X_{1M}	X_1
2	X_{21}	$X_{22}..X_{2j}..X_{2n}$			X_{2C}	X_{2G}	X_{2I}	X_{2E}	X_{2M}	X_2
3	..	..								
i	X_{i1}	$X_{i2}..X_{ij}..X_{in}$			X_{iC}	X_{iG}	X_{iI}	X_{iE}	X_{iM}	X_i
..	..	..								
n	X_{n1}	$X_{n2}..X_{nj}..X_{nn}$			X_{nC}	X_{nG}	X_{nI}	X_{nE}	X_{nM}	X_n
n+1 wages	W_1	$W_2..W_j..W_n$			W_C	W_G				W
n+2 rent	R_1	$R_2..R_j..R_n$			R_C	R_G				R
n+3 interest	D_1	$D_2..D_j..D_n$			D_C	D_G				D
n+4 profits	P_1	$P_2..P_j..P_n$			P_C	P_G				P
n+5 total output	X_1	$X_2..X_j..X_n$			C	G	I	E	M	X

Produced inputs

Primary inputs

Table B | Condensed Input-output Table for India, 1953–54

(Rs. crores)

	Agriculture	Large-scale food manufacturing	Iron and steel	Electricity	Coal	Transport	Engineering	Other large-scale industry	Construction	Other small-scale industry	Services	Total inter-industry flows	House-hold and govt. consumption	Other final bill of goods	Total output
Agriculture including small-scale food manufacturing	2268	296	...	...	...	104	3	192	12	29	93	2997	5111	–1	8107
Large-scale food manufacturing	70	43	...	...	...	2	...	11	...	1	39	160	449	51	666
Iron and steel	...	...	22	...	...	8	27	5	61	8	6	137	...	–28	109
Electricity	...	2	1	3	1	3	1	12	1	...	12	36	16	...	52
Coal	...	2	6	7	3	19	1	9	4	2	2	56	13	1	70
Transport	1	17	3	...	...	12	4	32	37	16	45	167	510	24	701
Engineering	5	3	...	4	2	53	5	3	30	3	26	133	23	–1	155
Other large-scale industry	18	21	13	2	3	61	16	280	68	164	83	709	644	–103	1250
Construction	25	...	...	...	...	2	...	1	84	...	10	122	76	716	914
Other small-scale industry	56	...	...	...	...	1	...	...	58	26	29	170	414	49	633
Services	96	53	6	1	2	53	9	138	122	67	178	715	3465	110	4200
Total input	2549	437	51	17	11	319	66	652	467	316	523	5408	10721	818	16947
Value added	5558	229	58	35	59	382	89	598	447	317	3767	11539			
Output	8107	666	109	52	70	701	155	1250	914	633	4290	16947			

404

where the a_{ij} are determined from separate investigation outside the model. Then, equation (18) could be rewritten as

$$(20) \quad X_i = \sum_{j=1}^{n} a_{ij}X_j + X_{iC} + X_{iG} + X_{iI} + X_{iE} - X_{iM},$$

where i runs from 1 to n

If the future targets for the bill of goods, X_{iC}, X_{iG}, X_{iI}, X_{iE}, and X_{iM} are specified for each sector, then the total outputs required from each sector X_i and each of the interindustry deliveries X_{ij} can also be determined. Equations (20) become a system of n simultaneous equations in n unknown variables which can be solved if it satisfies certain economic requirements which imply that every sector requires at least one input from another sector and that no two sectors require inputs in identical proportions.

This is a type of static planning model; it establishes consistency as of a particular date in the future. It requires a good deal of information which is only infrequently available about the a_{ij}'s, that is, about the structure of interindustry relations. Where data permit its use, it has a number of virtues. It forces planners to make their future sectoral goals explicit. Or to put the point in another way which is closer to actual practice, it provides planners with a method by which they can explore the consequences of alternative goals in considerable detail. Rather than using mathematical techniques which permit "jumping" to an immediate solution, a step-by-step method can be used which allows flexibility in the assignment of availability to domestic production or to foreign sources via imports. Some of the best examples of flexibility in use are in the work of Hollis Chenery and his associates.[12] Although experiments have been made with the method for a number of countries, there are few indeed in which it has yet had a major impact on planning procedures.

Starting from input-output accounting even more ambitious planning models are now being prepared which may play an increasing role in the future development schemes. In equation (20) nothing was said there about how the "bill-of-goods" items for future years would be determined. These had to be set outside the formal model itself. The

[12] See, for example, H. B. Chenery and K. S. Kretchmer, "Resource Allocation for Economic Development" *Econometrica*, vol. 24, no. 4, pp. 365–399, October, 1956, and H. B. Chenery and T. Matanabe, "International Comparisons of the Structure of Production" *Econometrica*, vol. 26, no. 4, pp. 487–521, October, 1958.

method used for the projection of final demands depends to a considerable extent on the policy framework within which planning is done. At one unlikely extreme, if all consumption is controlled by government, then the sectoral consumption targets can be set by government fiat and fed into the model. At the other pole, consumers may be allowed to buy anything that they want from domestic producers or from foreign sources. This is an extreme position also since most of the less developed countries impose some restrictions on imports, for example, by regulating the number and type of private automobiles or air conditioners which can be bought abroad. To the extent that consumption decisions are privately made, forecasts must be made of sectoral consumption patterns. This can be done by more or less conventional econometric techniques based on independent statistical projections or by means of estimates of demand elasticities.

Since they depend mainly on conditions abroad, exports must also be based on independent statistical projections. Imports, on the other hand, depend on internal conditions and to a considerable extent on the level of output itself. One approach is to estimate what the future relationship of imports and output will be. These may be simple extensions of past relationships or may take future considerations into account. Such projections can take the form

$$(21) \qquad\qquad M_{ij} = m_{ij}X_j$$

Government consumption will depend on plans for the government budget. Some parts of the government budget, such as transport expenditures, may also be projected by statistical estimates of economic relationships. Other parts of the government budget will be set arbitrarily; that is, they will depend on general and political considerations, such as the size of government clerical staffs in various ministries and the extent of government service programs in various areas.

The investment component in the target "bill of goods" involves rather different considerations. The amount and composition of investment in the terminal plan year will determine the rate and pattern of future growth, and these, in turn, are, in part, a matter of policy choice. In some of the recently developed approaches to planning there are techniques for embodying these policy decisions.

Suppose, as a special example, that a common rate of growth r were projected for consumption in each sector for the postterminal year: that is, in the context of a five-year plan the ratio of consumption of sector i goods in the sixth period to consumption in the fifth period were $1 + r$. In order to produce additional output there must be additional investment. The output of an investment-goods-producing sector *i*, required for the expansion of capacity in any sector *j*, will be assumed to be determined by the relationship

(22) Output in period *t* of investment goods by sector *i* in order to expand output in sector *j* in period *t* + 1 $\left.\right\} = b_{ij}[X_j(t+1) - X_j(t)]$

This is a simplified version of an investment relationship in which b_{ij} is a type of capital/output ratio. Since each sector will have its own requirements for expansion, there will be a matrix of b_{ij}'s relating such expansion to deliveries from capital-supplying sectors.

If all the equations like (22) are substituted in (20) and all exogenous sectors except consumption are put aside for the moment, we would have for *T*, the last year of the plan

$$(23) \quad X_i(T) = \sum_{j=1}^{n} a_{ij}X_j(T) + \sum_{j=1}^{n} b_{ij}[X_j(T+1) - X_j(T)] + C_i e^T,$$

for *i* running from 1 to *n*

The immediate problem now becomes one of finding a solution to (23) which is an *n* equation system of difference equations. Since the *a*'s and *b*'s as well as *r* are assumed to be known, this can be done in a straightforward manner to give the levels of output in the terminal year consistent with the desired postterminal growth rate of *r*. The assumption of a postterminal growth rate *r* common to every sector, or equiproportional growth, is, of course, quite arbitrary. In any practical application it would have to be relaxed, and this could be done so as to embody nonproportional postterminal growth objectives in the terminal-year targets.[13] The multisectoral planning techniques described above are static; they are methods of achieving consistency in a particular period which may be a target year or a period of years. There is a further and more complicated planning problem of achieving the phasing of output and investment within the plan periods consistent with plan targets and other production, export, import, and consumption constraints. One approach to this problem is the consistency model. This has as its objective the achievement of a set of sectoral inputs, outputs, investments, and deliveries to other sectors which will exactly match the targets and constraints. This analytical framework, as others, should properly be viewed as a device to ex-

[13] A somewhat different approach to the same problem is embodied in Richard Stone and Alan Brown, *A Computable Model of Economic Growth*, Chapman & Hall, London, July, 1962.

plore the consequences of alternative choices of targets, consumption patterns, and so on.[14]

If the production relations are those described in equations (20), (22), and (23) above, the following system can be written

$$(24) \quad X_i(5) = \sum_{j=1}^{n} a_{ij}X_j(5) + \sum_{j=1}^{n} b_{ij}[X_j(6) - X_j(5)] + C_i(5) + E_i(5)$$
$$+ G_i(5) - \sum_{j=1}^{n} m_{ij}X_j(5) \text{ for } i = 1, \ldots, n$$

$$(25) \quad X_i(4) = \sum_{j=1}^{n} a_{ij}X_j(4) + \sum_{j=1}^{n} b_{ij}[X_j(5) - X_j(4)] + C_i(4) + E_i(4)$$
$$+ G_i(4) - \sum_{j=1}^{n} m_{ij}X_j(4) \text{ for } i = 1, \ldots, n$$

$$(26) \quad X_i(3) = \sum_{j=1}^{n} a_{ij}X_j(3) + \sum_{j=1}^{n} b_{ij}[X_j(4) - X_j(3)] + C_i(3) + E_i(3)$$
$$+ G_i(3) - \sum_{j=1}^{n} m_{ij}X_j(3) \text{ for } i = 1, \ldots, n$$

$$(27) \quad X_i(2) = \sum_{j=1}^{n} a_{ij}X_j(2) + \sum_{j=1}^{n} b_{ij}[X_j(3) - X_j(2)] + C_i(2) + E_i(2)$$
$$+ G_i(2) - \sum_{j=1}^{n} m_{ij}X_j(2) \text{ for } i = 1, \ldots, n$$

$$(28) \quad X_i(1) = \sum_{j=1}^{n} a_{ij}X_j(1) + \sum_{j=1}^{n} b_{ij}[X_j(2) - X_j(1)] + C_i(1) + E_i(1)$$
$$+ G_i(1) - \sum_{j=1}^{n} m_{ij}X_j(1) \text{ for } i = 1, \ldots, n$$

Since there are n equations in each of five periods there are a total of $5n$ equations. All the a's and b's and m's are assumed to be known, but the significance of alternative estimates of these parameters can be investigated by solving the system with the specified alternatives. The E's and G's are usually determined by estimation procedures independent of the model. $X_j(6)$ may be specified by the method described above for determining the implications of postterminal year targets.

At this point several different procedures are open to the planner in specifying the knowns and the unknowns of the problem. All the consumption items may be set provisionally. Only the X's will then be

---

[14] See S. Chakravarty and R. S. Eckaus, "An Approach to a Multi-sectoral Intertemporal Planning Model," in P. N. Rosenstein–Rodan (ed.), *Capital Formation and Economic Development*, Allen and Unwin, London, 1964.

left as unknowns and there are n of these in each of the five periods or, again $5n$ in total. In principle, therefore, the problem can be solved. The answers for each period in this case will include the total sectoral outputs and their allocation among intermediate uses and to final demands. These will be consistent with the terminal year targets, with the intermediate requirements, and with the structural parameters.

The solution to any such planning model only demonstrates the implications of the goals, structure, and constraints ascribed to the economy. In order to explore the significance of different goals, different estimates of the parameters, and different constraints, there must be repeated solutions for various combinations of these conditions.

Dynamic, multisectoral planning models can also be constructed to embody optimization procedures. As in the case of aggregate models, a criterion or objective function must be defined and the various production and distribution constraints stipulated.[15] Such models are still at an early stage of experimentation. Their computational requirements are large even by the standards of modern, electronic computers, and this poses an especially difficult obstacle to their implementation.

Planning models can be extended in other directions as well. Regional planning is a field in which a comprehensive approach is particularly necessary. Location choices and transport decisions in one region clearly affect such choices and decisions in another region and often in a decisive manner. Some progress has been made in developing and implementing models addressed to these problems, mainly for particular industries or groups of interrelated industries.

Planning models require theoretical formulation, the filling in of empirical content and experimentation by means of computation for alternative conditions. All three of these stages are under active development, and though much remains to be done, much is now being learned. Certainly planning models cannot now tackle all or even most of the issues of economic development, nor will they ever be able to do so. They can be directed toward rather specific problems of forming and coordinating policy and making forecasts. For these purposes they may come to be extremely powerful tools. No one need ever fear, however, the advent of push-button development, or that the time will come when the next five-year plan will be run out of a computer. Development models cannot be used that way. At best they

[15] The work of Jan Sandee, *A Demonstration Planning Model for India, op. cit.*, and Alan Manne, "Key Sectors of the Mexican Economy, 1960–70," in A. S. Manne and H. M. Markowitz (eds.), *Studies in Process Analysis*, Wiley, New York, 1963, provides good examples of the most recent trends.

help explore the significance of alternative patterns of development. They imply no view in favor of (or against) the use of controls in the development process. Like national income, price, population, and resource data, development models are one but by no means the only method of knowing more about the detailed structure and workings of a developing economy.

SUMMARY

The search for methods of devising economic policies which will help underdeveloped countries to achieve the dramatic improvements they desire is understandable. Although there is no philosopher's stone, the methods of carefully analyzing and comparing the implications of alternative policies which are embodied in planning models can be of great help. The theoretical development of these models has become quite sophisticated. In actual practice most forecasting and planning is relatively simple and straightforward. Much of it is concerned with working out the implications of particular projects and comparing costs and benefits in the small. Aggregate economic models are also often used to map out on a grand scale the potential lines of development of an economy. Multisector, intertemporal models are the most ambitious. Their objective is to project the structure of developing economy in detail and in a manner consistent with future targets and the present and future constraints imposed by production conditions and consumption behavior.

BIBLIOGRAPHY

Michael Bruno, *Interdependence, Resource Use and Structural Change in Israel*, Bank of Israel, Jerusalem, 1963.

S. Chakravarty, *The Logic of Investment Planning*, North Holland Pub. Co., Amsterdam, 1959.

Hollis B. Chenery, "Development Policies and Programmes," *Economic Bulletin*, vol. 3, p. 51.

E. E. Hagen, *Economic Planning*, Irwin, Homewood, Ill., 1963.

Roy Radner, *Notes on the Theory of Economic Planning*, Center of Economic Research, Athens, 1963.

J. Tinbergen and H. C. Bos, *Mathematical Models of Economic Growth*, McGraw-Hill, New York, 1962.

NAME INDEX

Abegglen, J. C., 116
Abramovitz, M., 53, 83
Adelman, I., 19, 60
Advisory Committee on International Technical Assistance, 265n.
Ali, Mohammed, 128
Allen, R. L., 360
Alter, G. M., 344
Anderson, C. W., 220n.–221
Avramovic, D., 330–331

Ballot, C., 147n.
Banfield, E. C., 380
Baran, P. A., 16, 152n.
Barlow, W. J., 17
Barnett, H. J., 42, 79, 81
Bass, H., 30
Bastos de Avila, F., 286n.
Bates, M., 78, 383
Bator, F. M., 212
Bauer, P. T., 16–17, 152n., 177, 190, 314, 319, 374n.
Becker, G. S., 107–109, 116
Benedict, R., 36
Benham, F., 355n., 380
Bennett, M. K., 11
Bensusan-Butt, D. M., 296n.
Benviste, G., 17
Berg, E. J., 106n., 116
Bernstein, E. M., 237n., 247
Bhagwati, J., 314
Biesanz, J., 24–25, 142n., 275n.
Biesanz, M., 24–25, 142n., 275n.
Bishop, R. L., 151n.
Blank, D. M., 114n.
Blitz, R. C., 109
Bloomfield, A. I., 248
Boeke, J. H., 258n.

Bohr, K., 264n.
Bos, H. C., 61, 410
Boskey, S., 124n.
Brand, D. B., 25
Brimmer, A. F., 121n.
Brown, A., 407n.
Brown, A. J., 78, 383
Brownlee, O., 149
Brozen, Y., 139–140
Bruno, M., 410
Bruton, H. J., 251, 322n.
Buchanan, N. S., 83

Cairncross, A. K., 60, 84n., 363n.
Cameron, R. E., 81n., 147n.
Campos, R. de O., 228n., 247
Carroll, T. F., 221n., 225
Chadrasekhar, S., 281n.
Chakravarty, S., 408n., 410
Chaloner, W. H., 304n.
Chenery, H. B., 85, 93, 103, 309, 321, 402n., 405, 410
Clairmonte, F., 16
Clark, C., 58, 159, 171, 175, 178–179, 183, 314, 363n.
Clark, P., 402n.
Clay, L. D., 373
Cobb (Cobb-Douglas), 49, 51
Cole, A. H., 120n.
Cole, G. D. H., 24
Cole, H., 144n.
Cole, W. A., 58n.
Combined Mexican Working Party, 119n.
Commission on Foreign Economic Policy, 363n.
Connell, K. H., 65n.
Coutsoumaris, G., 225

411

SUBJECT INDEX

417